GLIMP
THE FALKLANDS WAR

by

British Modern Military History Society

Editors: Andy and Jerry Cockeram

Glimpses of the Falklands War
by British Modern Military History Society (BMMHS)

ISBN: 979-88-07560-23-0
First edition: June 2022

Cover art by David Rowlands
Cover production by Richard Macauley

Edited by:
Andy Cockeram and Jerry Cockeram

Blind Veterans UK is a registered charity in England and Wales (216227) and in Scotland (SC039411).

Dedication

'For all those who were touched by this war, those who fought and those who did not return in the name of freedom and self-determination'

Table of Contents

Introduction

2022 marks the 40th anniversary of the Falklands War. For much of the world it was and probably is still regarded as a minor spat between two countries whose governments were under great pressure at home. However, for the UK and Argentine governments and their peoples the dispute leading to war was a significant affair and a notable point in the history of both countries.

Prime Minister Margaret Thatcher and her Argentine counterpart, the head of the military Junta General Leopoldo Galtieri, both faced immense political pressure at home, and the small set of islands in the South Atlantic, the British Colony nearly 8,000 miles from the UK yet a mere 300 miles from the Argentine mainland became the full focus of their attention. For both, it became a matter of principle to prove to their people that their claim to the Falkland Islands was just and was worthy of war.

From the moment Argentine 'scrap metal dealers' landed without authority on South Georgia followed two weeks later by their soldiers landing near Stanley, the feisty British Prime Minister was never going to back down on this breach of international law. The Falklands were British and that principle was worth protecting by whatever means available.

As a twenty something year old, I along with the vast majority of the British population watched events unfold from thousands of miles away through the censored smokescreen of HM Government's Ministry of Defence front man Ian MacDonald and without the benefit of today's instant 24/7 news. The sight of British ships being sunk and lives lost on the grainy news footage of the day came as a shock to us all. Despite the national rejoicing at ultimate victory, many realise it was a much closer run thing than was admitted at the time.

This book however is not about the pure history or the politics surrounding the Falklands war although undoubtedly it is touched upon from time to time. It is about the men and women, whether British, Argentine, military personnel, civilians and Falkland Islanders who lived through those events of 40 years ago.

It tells of their stories and memories, and indeed their reflections looking back over four decades. The news of the time and the subsequent history books do not often tell of those 'anonymous' people who did their job for their country. The dockyard workers who laboured at short notice to prepare the ships for their long journey south. The 17 year-old radar operator or the cook on HMS *Hermes* who were below decks while war was raging above. The Lynx helicopter pilot who was fired upon by British warships, and those who fought to survive from stricken ships. The grit and professionalism of the ground forces which persevered in terrible weather conditions across the barren landscape. The doctors and nurses who treated British and Argentine casualties tirelessly with equal skill and endeavour, doing their best for even the hopeless cases. Many saw their friends and buddies wounded or killed in front of their eyes, memories of which still haunt them. There are others who carried out the less savoury roles such as the Military Police who had to escort the coffins of British servicemen back to UK, and the chaplains who had to comfort the wounded and dying.

A huge amount of thanks goes to those Falkland Islanders who told their tales of what it was like to be under occupation, albeit for a few weeks. Few of us can imagine how it felt.

The Falklands War, not conflict as I am constantly reminded, brought new words, names and vocabulary into our language and many remain with those of us of a certain age. Exocet, yomp, *General Belgrano*, Goose Green, Stanley, are but a few that still resonate.

This book is for every single person who was touched by the Falklands War. Spare a thought for those servicemen who suffered long term injuries, mental and physical, from this war, as well as those who did not make it home. In Argentina, the loss of *Las Malvinas* was regarded as a national disgrace and humiliation. Their young mainly conscripted soldiers were treated by their government and their countrymen as outcasts in much the same way as Vietnam veterans were treated in the USA. In stark contrast in Britain, the return of the service men and women, and the civilians who accompanied them brought scenes of great triumph and jubilation across the nation.

Nearly one thousand people lost their lives in those short weeks, with many more injured. They all deserve to be remembered and we hope this book goes some way to document what they all experienced and went through.

Andy Cockeram
Editor

Foreword

Alan Holderness, Trustee Blind Veterans UK

Alan Holderness, Trustee Blind Veterans UK

A 16 year-old boy goes along to the local Army and Navy Careers Office, not really to join up, but to give his best mate some much needed confidence for his interview to join the army. Having wandered aimlessly into the naval section, the large Royal Marine Colour Sergeant bawls out "*So you wanna be a Marine?*" "*Not really*" says I, and thirty minutes later I am heading back to my parents with the forms clutched eagerly in my hand awaiting a signature!

That is how my journey from boy to man began over 40 years ago. If I knew then that I was to lose my sight, lose my career and my Royal Marine family, over the next few years would I have done the same?? Damn Right I would!

I joined Blind Veterans UK in 2007, again by way of a chance meeting at a Royal Marine Association Reunion. I was armed with a white cane and was mistaken for one of the St Dunstan's group. Fortunately, I was regaled with all the amazing work they did for Visually Impaired Veterans, and to my amazement I was accepted as a member. I found out first-hand the work they did and the care the staff had for us, allowing us to live an independent life, fully trained on computers and up to date technology. Over time I needed to give something back, and in 2018 was successful in becoming a member Trustee of the Charity.

So back to the start of my service. After my initial training I was posted to 40 Commando RM, they had just returned from a very long stint in Northern Ireland, so fitting into a very close-knit team would be hard work. However, a few Exercises in Thetford, Salisbury, Dartmoor and Lundy Island and it was like I had always been part of this amazing family. Commando Sea Trials on HMS *Invincible* and *Intrepid* with the whole unit further cemented me as a fully Paid-up member of the Fighting Forty as the unit was known.

It was at the end of March/Beginning April 1982 that the unit was on Spearhead, ready to deploy anywhere in the world with 24-hours notice, that we had gone to Altcar Firing Ranges to brush up on our *live firing*. At the end I along with a few others who lived in the north-west managed to wangle the weekend away with our families, prior to Easter. On Saturday morning after a heavy session catching up with old schoolfriends, I was in the shower when my mum shouted up to me that my Colour Sergeant was on the phone for me. Obviously, I thought it was a bite, a prank, however it was not. My family found it highly amusing that I was stood, dripping wet, with a towel around my waste and stood to attention saying, "*Yes Colours*" over and over again until I put the phone down and said SH#t ! I need to get to Plymouth immediately as we could be heading to the Falklands. It was then we saw that Argentine scrap dealers had landed on South Georgia all over the national news. My parents thought that the Falklands were up in the Highlands, however I knew it was thousands of miles away as I considered a posting there on one of the naval parties.

Finally, after many days of waiting around for ships and supplies getting ready, we set off from Southampton in the setting sun. Cars and well-wishers lined the headland as we sailed silently by, hooting their horns and flashing headlights. We waved back as we lined the walkways of SS *Canberra*, the so-called *Great White Whale* as it later became known, not really knowing who we were saying farewell to, but revelling in the excitement that was slowly building. The journey south was slow, with ships joining our group at every point. Our sun-filled days consisted of exercise, training and sunbathing, and we were getting paid for it! The mood onboard was one of total disbelief, and that all the sabre rattling of the politicians would end and we would return to Blighty with our national show of force intact and respected.

As we moved further south into the rough and icy waters of the South Atlantic, the mood altered, the training and exercise became more serious and intense, we saw that we had a purpose and the reality of what was about to happen was palpable. Daily almost hourly reminders of the dangers we faced came by way of Air Raid Red warnings over the tannoy. Then on the eve of invasion we were transferred to the landing ship HMS *Fearless* due to a leaked report that troops were onboard the biggest whitest ship in the ocean. The transfer from the cargo bay of a civilian ship to a landing craft in South Atlantic waters was a daunting prospect, as one minute the landing craft was a few feet below, and seconds later was thirty feet below. Having to launch yourselves with kit weighing around 120kgs, in the darkness, in huge seas with only your mates trying to grab you was in itself a test of faith. A close friend of mine wasn't so lucky, and fell into the icy sea, narrowly missing being crushed between ship and landing craft, and luckily being hooked by the Craft Coxswain and dragged aboard, cold wet and very much alive.

Two very memorable moments during the conflict that will be forever imprinted on my mind, was standing aboard a landing craft, waiting to go ashore, whilst overhead a full naval barrage of big guns pounded the mountain lines that surrounded the beaches we were to land on. It took my breath away, and thoughts ran through my head that this is what the thousands of D-Day soldiers who landed in France must have heard and felt during the Second World War.

My other memory was on the 27th May when we were caught out by the Argentine aircraft. We had been cleaning kit after patrolling and standing to. Aircraft appeared in the sky over the mountain range, quite low. We at first were unconcerned thinking they were our Harrier jets, as we had not had the usual loud warnings from the ships and our own HQ crying 'Air Raid Warning

Red' as the aircraft approached, things started to move in slow motion as long silver tubes dropped from the sky with black and white parachutes attached. The ground erupted as Argentine Skyhawks dropped bombs and strafed cannon fire across our positions. We all dived for cover, some not lucky enough were caught out in open ground, myself being one of them. Thankfully I was dragged into a nearby trench after being thrown through the air by a blast. No real injuries sustained, thankfully, however we were later to find out that one of our friends had sadly lost his life firing on the enemy planes with his GPMG and one of the bombs had exploded on his trench.

14th June 1982 not only marked Liberation Day for the Falkland Islanders, and surrender for the Argentine forces, but also my 18th birthday, one I shall never ever forget as long as I live, but for totally different reasons for most 18-year-olds. A small can of Mackeson, a half bottle of Old Spice and a Falklands pound note given by one of the Islanders marked my celebrations, along with the cessation of hostilities.

The journey home was a blur, and nobody would have guessed the unbelievable welcome home we received at Southampton from family, friends and the people of the UK. Massive crowds waving flags and banners, military bands playing, and accompanied in by a flotilla of vessels. I remember feeling numb and confused by it all, and only a long time afterwards recognising the impact of what we had done and had on the general public.

Looking back 40 years ago, I remember my grandfather, who was a Ship's Marine manning the big ships guns during the Second World War and thinking what he had experienced 40 years prior to me, and my own experiences of warfare. He seldom spoke about his time during the war, and when he did and I was a child on his knee, he only gave me the funny stories he had experienced. I am now at that point in my life, with my eldest grandchild at an age to ask questions about my life, what am I able to pass down to him? I shall probably speak of the amusing anecdotes, and there were many to tell during my time, but I will probably skip the horrors that did occur that will accompany me to my grave.

My time and experiences I have had in the Royal Marines and in particular during the Falklands War have made me the person I am today. Having been medically discharged and losing my sight have also contributed to the person I am today. A steely determination to succeed even in challenging times, when you feel at your lowest, the will to endure is strong. My time with Blind Veterans UK enforces those qualities, giving me strength to carry on when you feel that you are unable to. I will always know that when I am at my lowest ebb my Royal Marine family will always be there to put a smile on my face, and a boot up my backside, and when I fall Blind Veterans will be there to pick me up, dust me down and point me in the right direction.

Time flows like a deep running river, all seems still and peaceful on top, yet underneath the waters, time runs fast. Forty years have gone by in what seems a blink of an eye, and memories fade even faster. Books such as this that encapsulate memories are vital for our future generations, as it's not always what is said, but what remains unsaid that is important.

Blind Veterans UK is a registered charity in England and Wales (216227) and in Scotland (SC039411)

Background to the Falklands War

Five Hundred Years of Controversy and Conflict

The Falkland Islands Story

At the time of the Falklands War, the Argentine writer Jorge Luis Borges said the conflict was "a fight between two bald men over a comb." That somewhat disparaging comment could equally be applied to the last five hundred years of the Falkland Islands. It is a tortuous history of territorial claim and counter claim, obscure conflicts and forgotten treaties

European explorers only became aware of the Falkland Islands archipelago in the 16th Century. Until 1592 all these sightings were made by either Spanish or Portuguese navigators.

It was left to Sir Richard Hawkins, adventurer, explorer and pirate to actually claim the Islands for the English Crown in 1593 in honour of himself and Queen Elizabeth I. However, the Spanish Crown disputed this claim.

In 1600, Sebald de Weert, Vice Admiral of the Dutch East India Fleet was the first explorer to accurately plot the Falkland Islands. For at least the next century, the archipelago would be known as the Sebald Islands.

The French established the first settlement on the Islands in 1764. It was named Port Louis after its founder Admiral Louis de Bouganville and was situated on East Falkland. He named the archipelago Les Malouines since most of the settlers were fishermen from the French port of St Malo. The modern Spanish name for the islands, *Los Malvinas*, derives from this.

Throughout the eighteenth century, the question of the Falkland Islands' ownership became more confused and disputed. In 1713 the Treaty of Utrecht was signed by Spain, France and Great Britain bringing to an end the long and bloody Wars of the Spanish Succession. The Falklands fell into the half owned by Spain.

In 1770, the Falkland Islands Crisis blew up after hostile encounters between British and Spanish ships. The two countries came to the brink of war when a Spanish military force expelled the British Garrison from Port Egmont. Spain, once French support was withdrawn, realised this was a conflict they were now unlikely to win. Both sides agreed to talks. Crucially, the question of the Falklands sovereignty was kicked into the long grass.

In 1775, economically crippled by the cost of fighting the American War of Independence Britain began abandoning many of its far-flung possessions. The Spanish burnt Port Egmont to the ground. With no British settlement on the Islands and Port Soledad in Spanish hands it seemed as if they now possessed the Falklands.

Under a treaty known as The Nootka Convention, Britain conceded to Spain sovereignty of all the latter's traditional territories in the Americas. However, the *actual* sovereignty of the Falklands was omitted either by design or accident

Throughout the early nineteenth century there was virtually no permanent habitation on the Falklands. The chaos of war on the South American mainland prevented the newly independent country of Argentina from any real action over claiming the Falkland Islands as part of its territory.

In 1820, a Captain Jewett made landfall on the Falklands in the Argentine frigate *Heroina* and lost no time in claiming the islands for the United Provinces of the River Plate (Argentina). Three years later, the United Provinces appointed their own commandant of Puerto Soleda (formerly Port Louis).

In 1824, Louis Vernet, a Hamburg born merchant based in Buenos Aires appeared on the scene. His wife Maria was related to the former Spanish Governor of Puerto Soledad on East Falkland. He set up a cattle and fishing venture in East Falkland with his business partner called Jorge Pacheco. However, it was doomed to failure. First the horses went lame, then the gauchos could not capture the feral cattle because of the boggy ground and ferocity of their bulls. To complicate matters, supplying the expedition was hampered by a Brazilian blockade.

In spite of all this, in 1828 Vernet managed to re-establish the settlement of Puerto Soledad and changed its name back to Port Louis to keep on side with the French. The Buenos Aires government granted him rights over all the East Falkland's resources and subsequently extended it to exclusive fishing and sealing rights. Nevertheless, that single act by the newly independent government in Buenos Aires would make Vernet a national hero of Argentina for all time. Subsequent disputes with American sealing and naval ships left most of the buildings of Port Louis in smouldering ruins. Vernet himself had already left the islands before the *Lexington* raid and would never return to the Falklands, dying in greatly reduced financial circumstances in Buenos Aires in 1871.

Disputes with claims and counterclaims continued for the following years and after an orgy of violence and murder the British decided to restore order and stamp their authority on the Falklands once and for all. Lt Henry Smith was despatched to the islands to reassert British sovereign control over them. Ironically the brutal perpetrator of the violence, Antonio Riveiro, has become celebrated in Argentine folklore as a heroic freedom fighter against the British Colonial oppressors.

Lt Smith was the first permanent British resident of the Falkland Islands. This marked the beginning of the Falklands' transformation from wild and lawless islands with sporadic attempts at habitation to a stable permanent community. The islands' population grew from 200 in 1849 to 3,398 in 2016.

Interestingly in 1841, the Argentine Government came close to giving up its claims of sovereignty over the Islands. At the time, the Government in Buenos Aires was deeply in debt to the City of London. President General Rosas thought relinquishing ownership claims to a few windy islands to avoid paying back many thousands of pounds was a good deal. The British Government refused the offer. How future events in the islands would have changed had they accepted is one of history's many ifs.

The years 1841 to 1845 saw the next important steps forward in the Falklands development. Firstly, it was officially declared a colony of the British Crown with its first Governor. Secondly, the newly built town of Port Stanley was proclaimed capital of the Falkland Islands in July 1845.

In the early years of the British re-colonisation of the islands, much of their early commercial and agricultural development was down to one company. In 1851 an energetic entrepreneur called JD Whittington was granted a Royal Charter becoming the Falklands Islands Company. It would continue to play an important role in the Falklands' development right up to the 1982 invasion and beyond.

With all this flurry of commercial and legislative activity, the Argentine claims to the Falklands had all been forgotten. However, they had not gone away. In 1884, Argentina officially requested Britain to allow the question of sovereignty to be taken before an independent tribunal. Once again, the request was refused and despite a further diplomatic protest from the Buenos Aires Government, the matter was not raised again until 1941.

With the outbreak of the First World War, even a remote location such as the Falklands would not escape the winds of war. On 8th December 1914, the major naval engagement known as the Battle of the Falkland Islands commenced in the seas around the islands. In the running battle that followed, the German fleet was driven out into the Atlantic where all but two of their warships were sunk. It was a major victory for the Royal Navy and a shattering blow for the Germans. They lost the battlecruiser *Scharnhorst*, one of the jewels of the Imperial German Navy, in the engagement. The wreck of the *Scharnhorst* was finally located by a marine expedition in 2019.

Between 1946 and 1953 Britain offered to take the sovereignty dispute for arbitration to the International Court of Justice at the Hague four times. Argentina refused each offer. In 1955, Britain unilaterally took the case of her sovereignty of the Falklands and their Dependencies to the ICJ. However, Argentina refused to recognise the Court's judgement.

Apart from these abortive legal attempts, the sovereignty issue between Britain and Argentina remained alive but largely dormant. It was raised by Argentina in its inaugural speech to the fledgling United Nations. Then in 1953 Argentine President Juan Peron made an unsuccessful offer to buy the islands.

The slow burning fuse to the 1982 Falklands War was probably lit by two Argentine incursions into the islands. In September 1964, an Argentine registered Cessna aircraft landed on the racecourse at Stanley. The pilot, an Argentine called Miguel Fitzgerald planted an Argentine flag on the racecourse. He then marched over to a bystander and handed them a letter claiming the islands for Argentina. He then promptly flew back to Argentina.

Fitzgerald's stunt was designed to coincide with an Argentine Government approach to the U.N. Decolonisation Committee with its claim for sovereignty of the Falklands. Two years later, there was a much more determined incursion called *Operativo Condor* by its perpetrators.

In September 1966, eighteen young Peronists and nationalists hijacked an Aerolinas Argentinas DC4 airliner en route to Patagonia. The pilot was forced to fly to the Falkland Islands. Since the islands had no runways at the time, the plane made a bumpy landing on Stanley Racecourse. The plotters failed in their aim to occupy Government House but they did take four Islanders hostage. Finally, after a freezing night aboard the plane, the hijackers surrendered. The passengers and hijackers were then transported back to Argentina by ship. The hijackers were eventually put on trial and given light prison sentences.

The whole incident was acutely embarrassing for the Argentine Government for two reasons. Firstly, Rear Admiral Jose Guzman, Governor of Tierra Del Fuego was one of the hijack hostages and secondly, the Duke of Edinburgh was on a state visit to Argentina at the time. The whole incident was wildly popular amongst the Argentine public prompting many demonstrations in support of the hijackers.

The Aerolinas Argentinas hijacking proved to be a classic case of the law of unintended consequences. At the same time the plane landed on Stanley Racecourse British Government minister Lord Chalfont was visiting The Falklands in an attempt to persuade the Islanders of the merits of becoming Argentine citizens. This was because in August of that year Britain and Argentina reached a

Memorandum of Agreement that transfer of sovereignty would be discussed but only with the acquiescence of the Falkland Islanders. Unsurprisingly, the hijack torpedoed this whole diplomatic initiative.

The attitude of successive British Governments to the Falkland Islands between the mid-1960s right up to the 1982 conflict is not one of which the UK can be particularly proud. It seems the politicians and the Foreign Office regarded the islands as a costly and anachronistic hangover of colonial times to be disposed of as quickly as possible. If this meant forcing the British citizens to become citizens of an Argentina that was a brutal military dictatorship at the time, well so be it.

In an attempt to make the transfer of sovereignty to Argentina a *fait accompli*, development of the islands in conjunction with Buenos Aires was increased throughout the 1970s. Direct air, sea, postal and telephony links were established between the Islands and Argentina. A regular air service between the Falklands and Argentina was inaugurated in 1972. To service it the Argentines built the islands' first runway and used an airline that was actually run by the Argentine Air Force. Improved medical services and the provision of fuel were provided by Argentina

It also seems that British Governments of all hues simply did not understand the Argentine mindset and deep-seated belief that the British were no more than colonial pirates who would soon get their just desserts and be forcibly evicted from the islands. There were warning signs of Argentina's intentions

In 1976, the new Argentine military government built a clandestine military base on South Thule in the British dependencies of the South Sandwich Islands. This was only discovered in the following year when a British research ship *RRS Bransfield* stumbled upon it.

To his credit, British Prime Minister James Callaghan responded very promptly to this intrusion by despatching a small Task Force consisting of both surface warships and a nuclear submarine to the

Falklands. Known as *Operation Journeyman* it was secret at the time but enough to deter the Argentines from invading the islands.

In 1978 The Falklands Islands Association became alarmed at the British Government's moves to dump the islands and its inhabitants in Argentina's unlovely lap. They set up an office in London to lobby MPs about the plight of The Falklands.

In 1979 Nicholas Ridley, a close ally of Margaret Thatcher, became Minister of State for the Foreign and Commonwealth Office. As such, the Falkland Islands became his responsibility. He was despatched to the Islands to canvass the opinions of the Islanders. His somewhat abrasive and offhand style put the Islanders' backs up. He seemed to be of the opinion that Britain was best shot of the Falkland Islands rather than defend them. This was also the attitude of the Foreign and Commonwealth Office.

His plan to "lease back" the islands in which they would be run by Britain for 99 years then handed over to Argentina went nowhere. Nor did the 1981 sovereignty talks between the two Governments. At this time, intelligence sources reported to the British Government that the Argentines would invade if they felt there was no chance of a peaceful transfer of sovereignty.

Meanwhile, the British Government announced that the Royal Navy ice patrol ship *HMS Endurance* would be withdrawn, the British Antarctic Base at Grytviken, South Georgia would close and the rebuilding of the Royal Marine barracks at Moody Brook would be put on permanent hold. To cap it all off, the Islanders were deprived of their British Citizenship under The British Citizenship and Nationality Act 1981. All this sent a clear message to the Argentine Junta that Britain would not defend the Falklands if they were invaded.

On 2nd April 1982 the Argentinian Government led by General Leopoldo Galtieri actioned the fateful decision to invade the Falkland Islands.

****

Timeline

<u>**1982**</u>

19th March

Argentine scrap metal dealers land on South Georgia

2nd April

Argentina invades Falkland Islands. The first Argentine troops land by helicopter at 0430 local time three miles from Stanley. The main force of 1000 troops land two hours later. The garrison of Royal Marines is vastly outnumbered and by 0930 hours the Argentines are firmly in control.

3rd April

UN Security Council demands immediate withdrawal of Argentine forces

4th April

The nuclear-powered submarine *Conqueror* sets sail from Faslane

5th April

First Task Force ships leave Portsmouth. Three nuclear submarines have already been dispatched but preparing a fleet of warships and support vessels takes longer to organise. The fleet of more than 120 ships will take nearly three weeks to sail the 8,000 miles to the South Atlantic. Lord Carrington resigns and is replaced by Francis Pym.

7th April

Britain announces its intention to impose 200-mile exclusion zone around Falklands with effect from 12th April.

19th April

Argentina rejects US Secretary of State Alexander Haig's peace proposals.

25th April

South Georgia retaken by Royal Marines. British destroyer HMS *Antrim* arrives off South Georgia on 21st April. British troops easily take control of the small Argentine garrison.

Prime Minister Margaret Thatcher tells the nation to "rejoice" at the news of South Georgia's recapture.

1st May

Operation Black Buck. First Vulcan bomber raid on Stanley airfield, with an 8,000 mile round trip from Ascension Island. There is only one direct hit on the runway.

Initial SAS and SBS units land on Falkland Islands.

2nd May

British submarine HMS *Conqueror* sinks Argentine cruiser *General Belgrano* with loss of 368 crew.

4th May

British destroyer HMS *Sheffield* is sunk by Exocet missiles with loss of 20 crew. It is the first British warship to be sunk in the conflict.

12th May

QE2 leaves Southampton with 5 Brigade on board

15th May

SAS launch attack against Argentine airfield on Pebble Island

18th May

Argentine Junta rejects British peace proposals.

20th May

UN peace talks fail ending any hope of a diplomatic solution to the crisis.

21st May
3000 British troops land on East Falkland at San Carlos Water. HMS *Ardent* is sunk. HMS *Argonaut* and HMS *Antrim* are hit by bombs which fail to explode.

23rd May
British frigate HMS *Antelope* hit and later sinks.

25th May
HMS *Coventry* sunk with 20 deaths. Container ship *Atlantic Conveyor* also sunk with loss of 12 crew and substantial quantities of supplies and equipment.

28th May
Battle for Darwin and Goose Green. British troops are vastly outnumbered but win the battle and take more than 1000 prisoners of war. Commanding Officer Lt Col H Jones is killed leading the assault and is posthumously awarded the VC.

31st May
British forces advance east towards Stanley. In poor weather conditions, progress is slow but they succeed in taking the Argentine positions of Mount Kent and Mount Challenger

8th June
RFA *Sir Galahad* and RFA *Sir Tristram* bombed as British troops are ferried from San Carlos to Bluff Cove and Fitzroy ready for the southern offensive on Stanley with heavy casualties.

11th June
Mount Longdon, Two Sisters and Mount Harriet taken.

12th June
British destroyer HMS *Glamorgan* hit by shore launched Exocet missile.

13th June
Final Argentine positions Mount William, Wireless Ridge and Mount Tumbledown taken.

14th June
British forces liberate Stanley. After taking the heavily defended high ground surrounding Stanley, British forces march into Stanley almost unopposed. The Argentines lay down their weapons and surrender.
The ceasefire is announced at 1530 hours local time

20th June
British forces declare end to hostilities.

22nd June
Two days later the head of the Argentine military Junta General Leopoldo Galtieri resigns to be replaced by retired army General Reynaldo Bignone.

11th July
Canberra arrives home at Southampton.

Maps

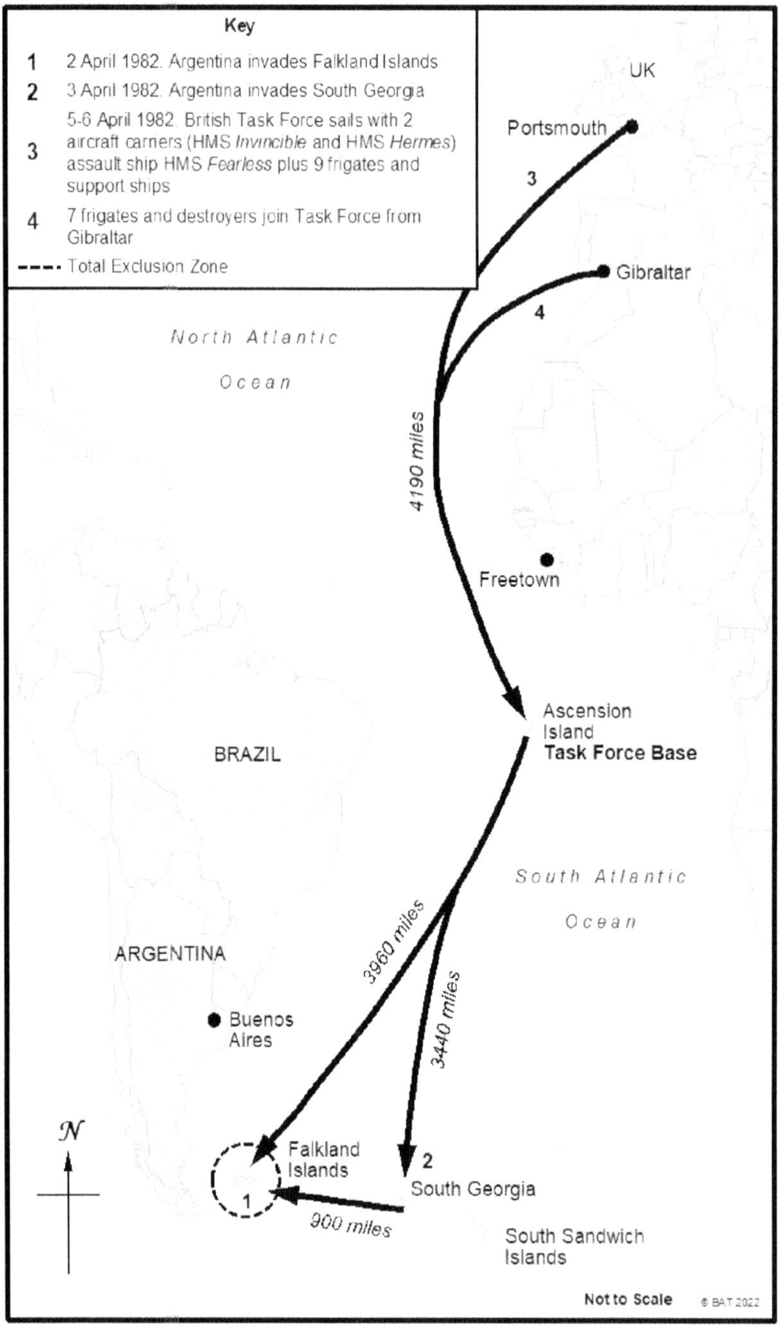

Key
1 2 April 1982. Argentina invades Falkland Islands
2 3 April 1982. Argentina invades South Georgia
3 5-6 April 1982. British Task Force sails with 2 aircraft carriers (HMS *Invincible* and HMS *Hermes*) assault ship HMS *Fearless* plus 9 frigates and support ships
4 7 frigates and destroyers join Task Force from Gibraltar
Total Exclusion Zone
UK
Portsmouth
3
Gibraltar
4
North Atlantic
Ocean
4190 miles
Freetown
Ascension
Island
Task Force Base
BRAZIL
South Atlantic
Ocean
3960 miles
3440 miles
ARGENTINA
Buenos
Aires
N
Falkland
Islands
1
2
South Georgia
900 miles
South Sandwich
Islands
Not to Scale
© BAT 2022

Falkland Islands War – Area of Operations

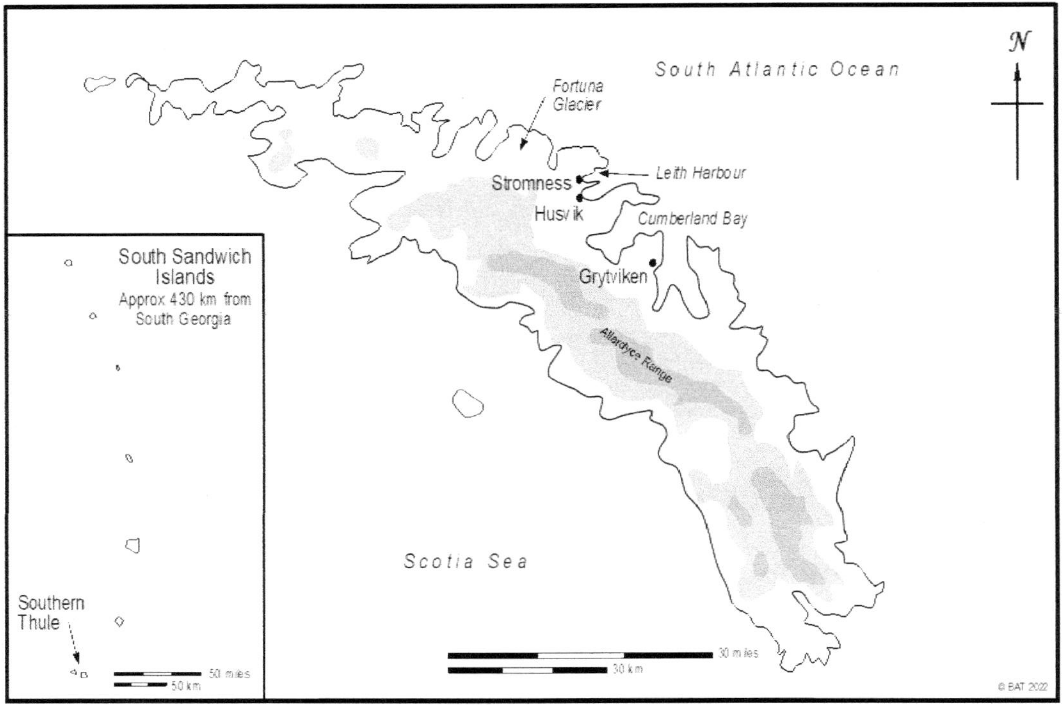

South Geogia Area of Operations
21-27 April 1982

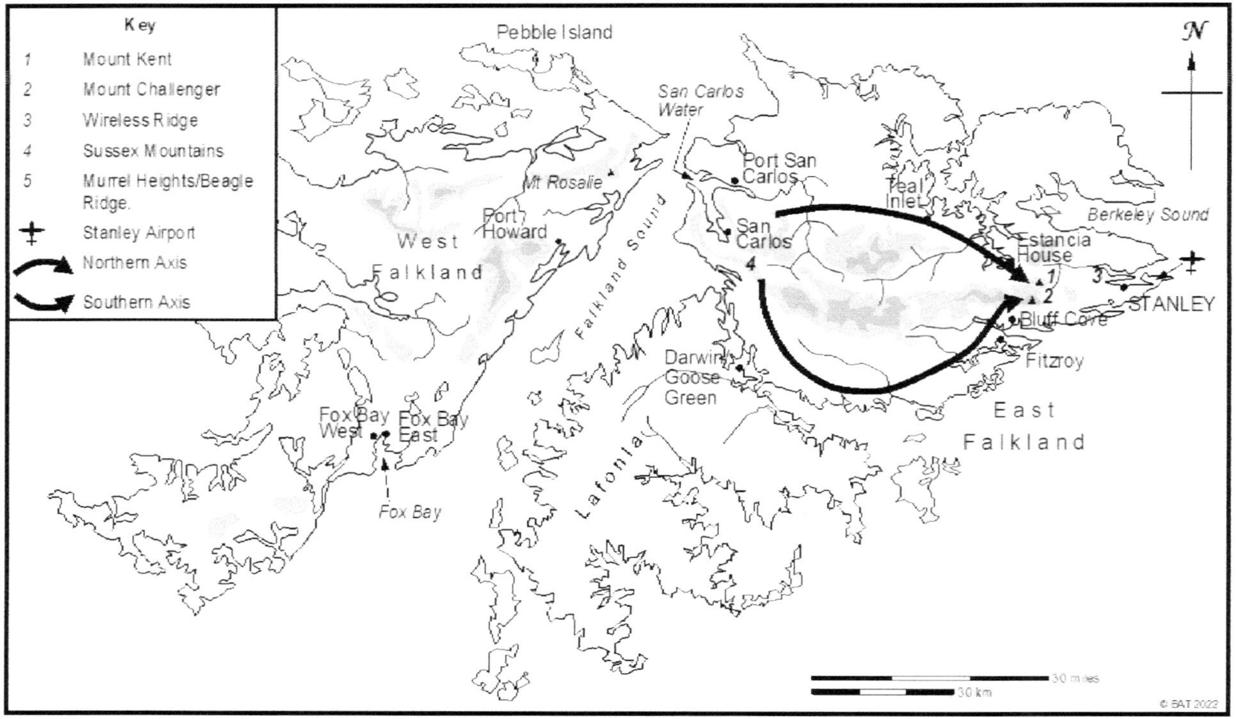

The Falklands Area of Operations
11 May – 15 June 1982

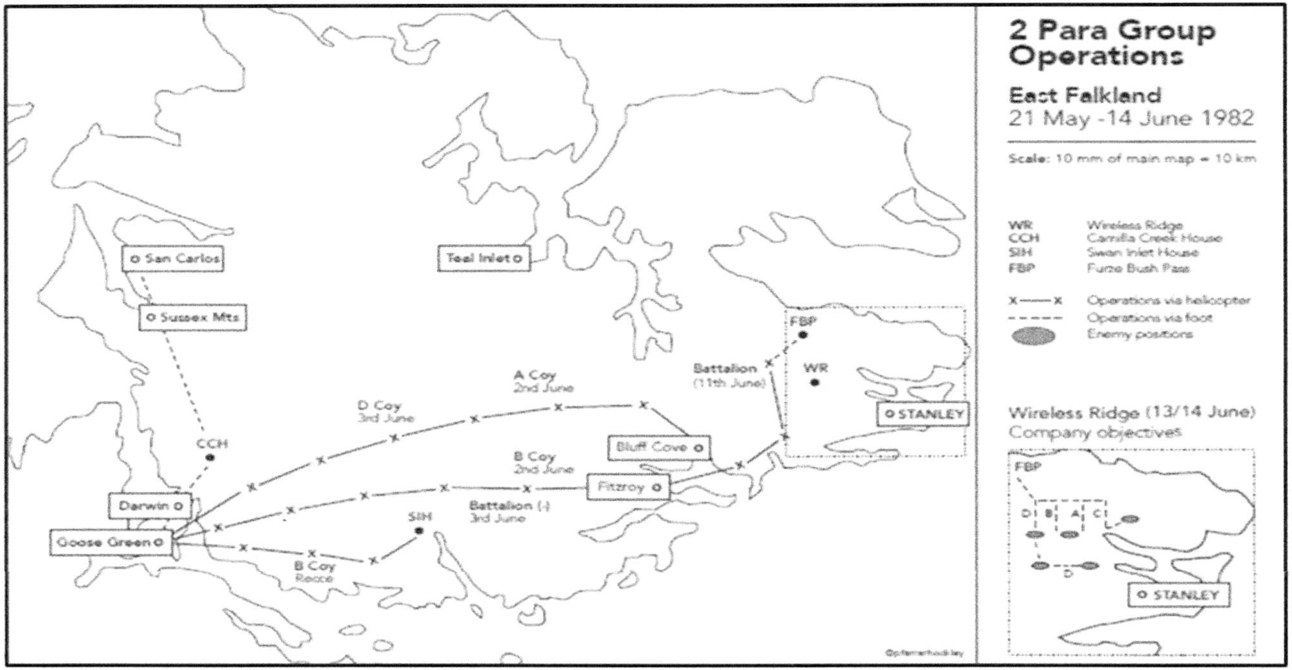

2 Para Group Operations Map on East Falkland.
Dair Farrar-Hockley archive

Chapter 1 - Invasion and First Response

Amidst internal discontent in Argentina with high inflation and a very weak economy, there was a growing clamour for 'repatriation of *Las Malvinas'*. This was fuelled by General Galtieri and his Junta to attempt to distract his people from their economic hardship at home. On 19th March 1982., a group of Argentine Marines, posing as scrap metal merchants, landed on the small island South Georgia, 800 miles to the east of the Falkland Islands hoisting the Argentine flag on this British territory, this act started a sequence of events and actions that lead to war between Argentina and the United Kingdom.

On 2nd April, a large force of Argentine troops landed on the Falkland Islands, significantly outnumbering the small Falkland Islands Defence Force (FIDF) and the detachment of Royal Marines. The Governor Rex Hunt ordered arms to be laid down the same day and the occupation of the Islands commenced.

Two days later, British Prime Minister Margaret Thatcher ordered the creation of a military Task Force to liberate the Islands, while at the same time the United Nations ordered the Argentinian Government to withdraw its troops. While the Task Force was being prepared for its journey 8,000 miles southwards, a period of intensive international diplomacy commenced led by UN Secretary General Perez de Cuellar and US Secretary of State Alexander Haig to try to prevent war. These attempts to avert potential war ultimately failed as the Argentine Government's pre-condition for any withdrawal by the Argentinian forces was an insistence that sovereignty would revert to Argentina.

The Falkland Islanders (approximately 2,000 men, women and children) were subject to military occupation with movement, communication and provisions all greatly restricted, and armed Argentine troops patrolling the key points – airfield, port, power station and Cable and Wireless radio station - and the various settlements across the islands.

On 7th April, the British Government announced the imposition of a 200-mile Total Exclusion Zone (TEZ) around the Falkland Islands, whereby any Argentine forces entered those waters at peril of being attacked by British forces.

With the naval Task Force taking at least three weeks to reach the TEZ, Prime Minister Thatcher was determined to demonstrate her resolve as quickly as possible. Initial military activity saw the Royal Marines re-take South Georgia (Operation Paraquet) and the bombing of Stanley airfield by RAF Vulcan bombers, (Operation Black Buck), having flown from Ascension with multiple refuelling operations en route on 1st May. The following day, the sinking of the Argentine battleship *General Belgrano* by nuclear submarine HMS *Conqueror* on the fringes of the TEZ with high loss of life caused international consternation as to its disputed legality.

The strategic impact of these actions had significant effect on how the military actions developed. The bombing of Stanley airfield showed the Argentine Junta that Buenos Aires may not be safe, while the sinking of the *General Belgrano* forced the Argentine Navy to stay in home ports for the duration. These actions proved a great boost to British morale whilst at the same time it made those service personnel in the Task Force realise that conflict was increasingly likely with all the incumbent risks and potential loss of life.

****

Olly Burton, Petty Officer UC1 (sound room)
HMS Valiant, British nuclear-powered Submarine

HMS *Valiant* - Somewhere in the Atlantic

February 1982 found me in various ports in Florida and South Carolina. Whilst on that side of the pond HMS *Valiant* made rendezvous with two of her sister-ships HMS *Conqueror* and HMS *Courageous*. The latter was returning from an eighteen-month deployment based in San Diego. I thought this was great as I was soon to experience this type of running.

Well, it wasn't long before we were on our way home. I was settling into my new boat reasonably well. Somewhere in the Atlantic on our way home the captain addressed the ships' company on the main broadcast system. He said "*Do you hear there, Captain speaking? I have just heard that a war has started somewhere. I don't know by whom, or who is involved or even if we are involved. Be on your toes." "Be on your toes."* I thought. How can we be on our toes? We do not have a single weapon on onboard.

Twelve hours later he addressed the ships' company again and informed us that Argentinian forces had invaded South Georgia and the Falkland Islands and that a British Task Force was being formed to retake the islands. Yep! Life was becoming more exciting.

The captain had the radio operator's tape-recorded BBC Radio Two News; they recorded one in the morning and again one in the evening, then filling in the gaps by writing out both recordings. What a way for a warship to learn that it is at war. Later the captain explained that the authorities in London knew we were on our way home and unarmed, also knowing we were nowhere near the enemy. Therefore, their priority was to muster a Task Force, and probably would be running around like chickens with their heads cut off.

It is interesting to note that by definition a submarine is considered to be an offensive weapon and therefore could be attacked by a foe. We were unarmed to boot.

Stuart Lawrence, Master of RRS Bransfield on location in the South Atlantic

RSS *Bransfield* - Listening to the Invasion

My memories of listening were first the Argentine Junta's invasion of Stanley and its immediate environs from Patrick Watts on the Falkland Islands Broadcasting Station up until the station was shut down. This allowed their Commander, Menendez, to make "Goodwill" broadcasts to the Islanders which with our on-board radio station we made every attempt to superimpose with recordings of the National Anthem, *Land of Hope and Glory* and *Jerusalem*. This was followed by the invasion of South Georgia the next day, where we were kept apprised of the events. The British Antarctic Survey base commander, Stephen Martin, who was in charge despite the presence of the Royal Marine detachment from HMS *Endurance* (The Red Plum) who took over at the moment of the invasion and used a High Frequency radio channel for all his communications knowing that we would be monitoring. These events will live with me forever.

Whilst the best that we could achieve through a *Ham* Operator on the west coast of America was to be "patched through" to our British Antarctic Survey Headquarters in Cambridge UK where I was able to advise our Deputy Director of the fact that The Falkland Islands had been invaded. The Governor Rex Hunt had destroyed all of his communication cyphers, but that, despite the sound of gunfire we had heard from the vicinity of Government House, all was well and at that point Patrick Watts was forced at gunpoint to hand over the Broadcasting Station, Mr Hunt had not surrendered the Islands. This information was passed to the Foreign Office who passed it to the Ministry of Defence who immediately informed Margaret Thatcher, the Prime Minister.

After making contact with our headquarters, despite the determination of my Falkland Islands crew members to take over the ship and take her to Stanley where their idea was to sink her in the entrance to Stanley harbour, we continued south on our passage to take vital stores to our Station "Faraday" on the Antarctic Peninsula and thence to "Signy", our scientific research station in the South Orkneys.

Then we proceeded to South Georgia where we were tasked to pick up the film team of the Honourable Lucinda Buxton and Annie Price from St Andrews Bay. We spent a tense few days in the vicinity of South Georgia, knowing full well that an Argentine submarine was in the area. In the end it was a MOD vessel, but we kept in contact with all the field stations still occupied by BAS and film personnel, of which there were four, until our communications failed crossing the Equator.

Given our very closeness to the Argentine Junta's fleet during the early hours of the morning of the invasion of Stanley, whilst we were on departure from the Straits of Magellan and having volunteered our support for Operation Paraquet, we were eventually tasked to return to Southampton directly but staying well clear of the Task Force and not to call at any interim ports, I strongly feel that my entire crew are well worthy of mention.

****

Andrew Lockett, HMS Endurance

HMS Endurance was the only Royal Navy vessel on location at the time of Argentina's invasion of South Georgia and the Falkland Islands.

HMS *Endurance* - Growing Tension

As a member of the Royal Naval Oceanographic and Meteorological Branch, I was appointed to HMS *Endurance* during early 1981 and set sail for the South Atlantic on the 13th October 1981. My role as the flight's weatherman was not the only duty; I soon found myself a bridge watch keeper, flight deck officer, crypto custodian, confidential bookkeeper, doing public relations, education, transition and the occasional inspection visits to Antarctic bases of varying nationality under the Antarctic Treaty.

Late 1981, the ship's company took part in the battle day commemoration in Stanley (8th December) and then set sail for South Georgia (800 miles to the east) with Governor Rex Hunt and his wife Mavis. South Georgia was then part of the Falkland Islands Dependencies. During the visit, in which the Governor and his wife crashed in the Wasp helicopter, due to sudden katabatic winds, there was much talk about the negotiated contract to allow Argentine Constantino Davidoff to recover the valuable scrap from Leith Whaling station. There had already been suspicions of Argentine ships visiting the island without securing port of entry clearance. Governor Hunt viewed these arrangements as allowing the Argentines a foot in the door enabling them to use minor conflicts with the British to escalate into bigger things.

Endurance visited the Argentine submarine base at Mar Del Plata as a mid-deployment rest and relaxation, in February 1982. The ship's company was well looked after and got to know many of the submariners – the significance of this erupts about ten weeks later.

By the 12th March, the Antarctic season had come to a close with a visit to the ships located furthest south at the Rothera British Antarctic Survey (BAS) base. We called in to South Georgia, once more, to collect a Joint Services expedition for onward travel back to the UK. By the 19th March, we had arrived in Stanley and were moored opposite the FIC jetty. Many people had gone ashore and I was left as the duty man. An encrypted message came in from the BAS base in South Georgia for Governor Hunt, which I sent ashore with a messenger.

Then I had a call from the Governor saying he had received the encrypted message but needed to know how to decode it. I explained the key technicalities. I was informed later that an Argentine ship had entered Leith Harbour on South Georgia, set up a base, hoisted the Argentine flag and military-looking Argentines had gone shooting reindeer for food.

The next morning there was a quickly arranged meeting on board *Endurance* to discuss the evolving situation and to ensure the

Foreign Office fully understood the situation. *Endurance* was then quietly sailed early morning of the 21st March for South Georgia with its company of 12 Royal Marines increased to 22 from the resident detachment in Stanley. Room was made for them by leaving the Hydrographic Department behind in Stanley to work on the surveys they had conducted during the deployment.

To give credibility to *Endurance's* passage north the captain asked me to provide plausible but fake six hourly coded weather observations for such a track. The ship continued on a course to the east south east. Weather synops were sent as '*immediates*' to the headquarters in Northwood and, where appropriate, distributed through the World Meteorological Organization network. It is well-known that interruptions or changes in the supply of synoptic met data often accompany civil strife or military aggression in the area of action.

It takes about three days to get to South Georgia and, by the time we got there, things had escalated, and political deals were being attempted to save a physical encounter between British and Argentine representatives. The role of *Endurance,* for the time being, was to carry out covert surveillance and work alongside the British Antarctic Survey scientists.

By late 30th March a clearer picture was beginning to emerge. International negotiations and third-party arbitration had all but failed and the prospect of an attack on the Falkland Islands became evermore likely. We sailed away from South Georgia with a darkened ship and no navigation lights; it was a dangerous departure but nonetheless successful. The party of 22 Royal Marines had been left at Grytviken under the command of my co-flight deck officer Keith Mills. Their role was to work with and protect the British Antarctic Survey scientists and then offer an effective defence if an attack came from Argentine Forces.

About halfway to the Falkland Islands the ship was directed to return to South Georgia and on arrival found that the Argentine attack had occurred, a bullet riddled Argentine corvette *Geurrico* was in Cumberland Bay and there was no sign of the Royal Marines or the BAS scientists. The ship was in the situation of being unwelcome in both the Falkland Islands and South Georgia. The ship was directed to continue to collect intelligence. Hiding at night amongst the tabular icebergs, and in daylight, in the coves and fjords of South Georgia, we listened in and made covert landings and observations. By this stage the ship had lost its 12 original Royal Marines at Grytviken and its Hydrographic Survey department in Stanley as prisoners of war.

During most of the time that *Endurance* was down south it was possible to receive the meteorological analysis charts from the Buenos Aires met office fax transmissions. As soon as the conflict got underway the Argentines continued to transmit the chart but covered both the Falkland Islands, South Georgia and surrounding ocean with a piece of paper. It was relatively easy to complete the isobars and finish the analysis and then focus more on the satellite cloud images.

After a couple of days, with fuel and food reaching low levels, the ship was directed north to just south of the tropics to replenish from RFA *Fort Austin*. That done, participants in Operation Paraquet gathered and began a voyage south to South Georgia. *Endurance* had been joined by HMS *Antrim*, HMS *Plymouth*, and RFA *Tidespring* and acquired some 70 SAS personnel including John Hamilton. When the vessels reached South Georgia, they went into intelligence gathering mode, formulating plans to overwhelm the Argentines and take back the islands. Many adventurous schemes were suggested. As the local met man, I was asked for advice about parachuting, crossing glaciers and the nature of the weather and sea state. The successive crashes of rescuing helicopters, on Fortuna Glacier, was the worst possible illustration of the dangerous nature of the weather on South Georgia. On the 23rd April, one of the ship's communicators came to the bridge during my watch to report that there was an approaching submarine some 100 miles north west heading in our direction. It had been heard communicating with its Mar Del Plata base.

This brought a new dimension to the plan. By morning of the 25th April, the submarine had been spotted and a Wessex from HMS *Brilliant* engaged it, followed by other helicopters and two Wasps from HMS *Endurance* with AS12 missiles which damaged the fin. One of the Wasp missiles failed to launch and the helicopter returned to the deck where an in-flight inspection was conducted. It was deemed too risky to land the aircraft so it was directed back to the open sea for it to dump the weapon.

The disabling of the submarine took one huge threat out of the balance and the changed momentum drove the British ships to a hasty attack on Grytviken, the main port of the island. Naval gun fire from *Antrim* and *Plymouth* presented a threatening message to the Argentine troops as the impact locations came ever closer to the Argentine defences. They surrendered quickly without loss of life. It was ironic that the prisoners from the Argentine submarine *Santa Fe* were now meeting their former guests in Mar Del Plata in entirely different circumstances.

The following day HMS *Endurance* and HMS *Plymouth* engaged with the small garrison of Leith not far up the coast from Grytviken. Leith was defended under the command of Captain Astiz, a notorious Argentine. Fortunately, all of the Argentines were required to muster in a prescribed location well away from the whaling station base where they surrendered. The whaling station was found to be set with many traps to cause fatalities and injury to those who entered without caution.

HMS *Endurance* remained in South Georgia until the Falkland Islands fell to the British on the 14th June 1982.

****

Brian Summers – Falkland Islander and member of the Falkland Islands Defence Force (FIDF)

Extracts from the audio transcript courtesy of the Falkland Islands Museum

FIDF - Lead up to Invasion

I was senior operations supervisor for Cable and Wireless and responsible for all external communications. We had HF radio links to the UK and telephone links to Buenos Aires. We operated 16 hours a day.

When the scrap metal dealers arrived on South Georgia with military support Governor Rex Hunt ordered the base commander to set up an observation post to watch what was happening. I would connect Rex Hunt with the base commander on South Georgia.

From 1st April we moved from 16 hours to 24 hours/day operations. As the most senior I got the night shift. That afternoon I went for a walk with Judy and I proposed to her! That same afternoon my very agitated father who was CO of the FIDF was told invasion was due at 6am next morning.

I changed into my FIDF uniform and waited for the announcement from Rex Hunt about the imminent invasion.

We were being regularly pestered by Simon Winchester and other journalists who wanted to know what was happening.

The FIDF – 40 people – only 32 reported for duty but was boosted by the Royal Marines arrival on *Endurance*. But we did not have enough weapons, so the Royal Marines helped themselves from the FIDF armoury.

The role of the FIDF was to guard the telephone exchange, the fuel depot, the power station, with also a group on the Racecourse guarding the Islander planes. Two men were posted on the rock by the airfield and their job was to shoot down any helicopters as it was felt the Argentines would arrive by helicopters and capture the Governor and take him to Argentina.

I was the C&W guard but had no magazine as it was taken by the Royal Marines, so I ended up with a Sten gun and 100 rounds of 9mm ammunition. Some of the guys had had no weapons training whatsoever.

I was on duty at 10pm on 1st April, and due to take over from Suzie Parker, but she decided to stay at C&W. We monitored radio traffic between London and Government House throughout the night.

In the early hours we detected another person on the radio. It was the Argentines trying to contact the Governor. This was how the surrender was arranged. I wanted the Governor to give authority to institute the emergency plan for communication with London, so the UK could hear us.

****

Adrian Martienssen, Technical Writer, Signaal BV

Working with the Argentines

From November 1980 to October 1982, I was employed under contract as a technical writer (English) in the factory of Signaal B.V. in Hengelo, Netherlands.

My role, together with several English colleagues, was to prepare maintenance documentation for electronic equipment manufactured by Signaal for the Argentinian Navy to modernise their frigates. The Argentinian Navy required these documents to be in English as this matched other documentation in their ships.

Argentina had also sent technicians from their ships and training organisation to Signaal to learn about this new equipment. My colleagues and I had met many of these Argentinians during the preceding months, making friends and being invited to parties. During this amicable period in our work environment the Argentine government decided to invade the Falkland Islands on 2nd April 1982. I don't think anyone in Signaal, from either side, had anticipated this event. Initially we were in shock.

One friend of mine told me he was out sailing with an Argentinian naval officer when they heard the news on the radio.

They sat on opposite sides of the cockpit taking in the news that they were now enemies!

"What are we supposed to do now? Throw the pepper-pot at each other?" one said.

For the first few days there was an uneasy tension in the air in the factory. Then we heard that Margaret Thatcher had ordered a Task Force to be assembled and dispatched to the Falkland Islands. In Hengelo we discovered one of our colleagues was a brilliant cartoonist and the first drawings of British lions in the UK peering over the edge of the world at these far away islands appeared on our noticeboards! As the Task Force set out so did these lions start paddling south through the Atlantic.

My colleagues, many of whom were retired RN or military personnel, became very uncomfortable working for the Argentinian Navy. The situation was exacerbated by the Argentine government deciding to indulge in some local propaganda by placing whole page advertisements/articles in local newspapers justifying their claims to the Falkland Islands. We had also been bringing ourselves up to date on the sovereignty issue and so this move was really waving a red flag at us.

I perceived the situation was getting serious and decided to use my personal contact with one of the directors to get to the management of Signaal. Initially the Dutchman took the view that the English team should just accept their contract and keep working, but I said it would not look good for the factory if there was blood spilled in the corridors of the factory. I think that comment was taken to heart as the next day the English team was asked to temporarily stop work on Argentinian projects until the matter was resolved at an international level.

After the cartoonist had drawn a lion sinking a ship close to the islands, the cartoons also stopped.

****

Marvin Clark, Falkland Islander and Member of Falkland Islands Defence Force

Imminent Invasion

In April 1982 I was working for the Falkland Islands Company Limited (FIC) as coxswain on the tug *Lively*, I was also a volunteer member of the Falkland Islands Defence Force (FIDF) as well as a volunteer fireman in the Fire Brigade.

Late afternoon of 1st April 1982, whilst loading the inter-island resupply vessel, *Monsunen*, I observed what appeared to be increased activity by the Royal Marines travelling through the streets of Stanley by vehicle in a manner of some urgency, clearly outwith the norm for a daily trip 'down-town'.

There was an air of increased activity and apprehension but nobody seemed to know just exactly what was going on. A short time later my father was tasked with providing heavy plant and vehicles and to position them on the runway at Stanley Airport as obstacles. As the evening progressed, an announcement was made on the broadcast system that the Governor, Rex Hunt, would be making an address to the nation, however, by the time the announcement was made, the diddle-dee telegraph had gone into overdrive. I like other members of the FIDF were already in uniform awaiting the broadcast, during which Rex Hunt informed the community that an Argentine Task Force was expected off Cape Pembroke by first light in the morning. He then called all active members of the FIDF to report for duty forthwith,

Members of the FIDF drew weapons, ammo etc and were briefed according to task. I was a GPMG gunner and along with my No 2 waited in the sidelines for orders. After all other patrols had been deployed, we received our orders, establish a gun position in the rocks above the football field, overlooking the rear of Government House and approaches from the north and east. The fact that we deployed without any form of communications was of concern, but, like many others, we thought that this was just more if somewhat escalated 'sabre rattling' and that we would be back home in the morning spinning a few 'war stories', how wrong were we.

Sitting in our position, watching the comings and goings, the night passed by without incident but a certain air of tension was present. And then, all hell broke loose, tracer flying in all directions, but it was impossible to determine who was who. A patrol of Marines had conducted a fighting withdrawal back through Stanley towards the football field and then across the football field to Government House. Having identified that these were from Moody Brook, we did not engage them as per our instructions, *"if anything moves on the football field or over the seawall, shoot it"*.

We were stuck in an impossible location compounded by no comms with anyone. A heavy firefight was ongoing down at the back of Government House and we were now cut-off, therefore, instructed to remain at the power station. The firefight in the area went on for some time and as daylight emerged, it was apparent that significant numbers of Argentine troops had landed with heavily armed amphibious troop carriers and were proceeding at speed to reinforce the ground troops that had carried out the initial assault on Moody Brook and Government House.

A brief moment of laughter, if somewhat strained, came when one of these troop carriers came towards the power station from the south, ploughed nose first into a swampy ditch, clouds of mud flew into the air, followed by some bemused looking heads appearing out through roof hatches, one can only guess at what was being said (possibly, *what the f*** was that*). The rear doors then opened and out ran a number of fairly irritated Argentine soldiers. By this time the main firefight had ceased, but tensions remained. I was in a total state of shock, because as the troops, who were clearly agitated, approached, they launched into a tirade of shouting, gesturing and pointing weapons in my direction, at which point I realised that I still had the GPMG strapped over my shoulder!

Needless to say we were taken prisoner and held for several hours. After negotiations, Rex Hunt ordered a laying down of arms, however, we were retained as POWs at the power station until later in the day. We were later released with very limited clothing and sent home, humiliated, defeated and very much feeling a complete and utter failure in the Islands' time of need.

Gerald Cheek, Falkland Islander and member of Falkland Islands Defence Force (FIDF)

The Argentines Invade - Troops in Stanley

I joined the FIDF in October 1966 together with around 20 other local volunteers. This came as a result of the hijacking of an Argentine DC4 airliner, which was on an internal flight when it was hijacked by a group who demanded the aircraft was flown to the Falklands. The captain elected to land on the racecourse and... after 36 hours negotiations the 18 hijackers surrendered and were shipped out.

When the Argentines invaded in 1982, I was a sergeant. (I finally retired from the FIDF in 1996 as a captain and second-in-command). I believe we were lucky having Royal Marines here as they were very professional and quite hard with the physical side of the training.

The first I heard of the invasion was when Government House rang me at Stanley airport at around 1630 hours on the 1st April, requesting my attendance at the Governor's office immediately. On arrival, all the other heads of the Government department were already there and Governor Rex Hunt informed us that he had received a signal from the Foreign Office in London advising that reliable sources advised an Argentine Task Force was at sea and was very likely to be invading the islands at dawn the next day. To say that this news was quite a shock would certainly be an understatement.

I agreed to block the runway at Stanley airport...with number of vehicles, but of course the Argentines quickly cleared them off with Armoured Personnel Carriers (APCs) shortly after they landed next morning.

Other decisions at the meeting included the schools were to remain closed, the hospital to be fully staffed in case of injuries, and the radio station to remain on air throughout the night (it normally closed down at 10pm). All active members of the FIDF should fall-in at the Drill Hall at 1930 hours.

When we all fell in – around 35 of us in total, the tasks we were to carry out included guarding of important government facilities including the radio transmitting station, the power station, broadcasting studio and the aircraft on the racecourse, and if any Argentine helicopters attempted to land, we were to shoot them down. Our weapons consisted of 7.62 SLR rifles and GPMG machine guns; the riflemen were issued with 100 rounds of ammunition and the machine gunners with 500 rounds.

At 0630 hours we heard one or two bursts of gunfire and what sounded like a grenade exploding... and realised the Argentines had landed and the invasion was definitely on.

At around 0830 hours we heard further bursts of gunfire in the Government House area, and this went on for 40 minutes or so. Two Argentines were killed, but no Royal Marines were killed or injured.

At 0930 hours, a number of Argentine troops approached from the racecourse ... and we surrendered to them (as earlier instructed by the Governor). We were told to take off our uniforms and the FIDF was disbanded ... and our weapons were taken from us when we surrendered.

****

Brian Summers, Falkland Islander and member of the Falkland Islands Defence Force (FIDF)
Extracts from the audio transcript courtesy of the Falkland Islands Museum

Laying Down Arms

We then started to receive calls that Armoured Personnel Carriers (APC) were on the road, and bullets started to hit the C&W building. I threw myself to the floor with lights off with the Morse keyboard trying to get through to London.

I could hear the Royal Marines shouting and returning fire on the Argentines on the ridge. Suzie and I were wedged on the floor between the equipment.

A message came through from the Governor to return to the Drill Hall and to lay down arms. I did as ordered, only in short sleeves. At the Drill Hall, the Argentine soldiers assembled the marines and FIDF members, now without weapons, and everyone was told to lie down in the road….

They went through our pockets and threw everything into the gorse, including all keys. As we lay there one of the most frightening things was the vibration of the APC. All the Argentine officers seemed to speak good English.

After a while various FIDF members were marched down the road and some told to go home, under escort. I was initially held in the Drill Hall once more but eventually allowed to go home.

****

Captain John Thain, Junior Ordinary Seaman on MV Monsunen. Story told by his son, Scott Thain (aged 14)
First published in The Falkland Islands Journal 2012 Vol 10

My Dad's Story of the Falklands War

1st April 1982. MV *Monsunen* was loaded and ready to sail on another voyage delivering fuel and stores to Falkland farms. My dad was working on the *Monsunen* as Junior Ordinary Seaman (10 years later he became captain). He was 16 years old. They were supposed to sail at 2000 hours but due to the imminent invasion by Argentine forces the vessel was ordered not to sail. Being the youngest crewman, he drew the short straw and was given the job as night watchman from midnight until 0600 hours on the 2nd April. The *Monsunen* was tied up alongside the FIC Jetty. During the early hours of the morning, dad recalls seeing tracers and hearing lots of gunfire both across the harbour and at both ends of it, with Moody Brook Barracks at the west end and the airport at the other.

After the Argentine forces had landed at Yorke Bay they made their way along the Airport Road towards Stanley in very large Armoured Personnel Carriers (APCs). The sheer size of them was fascinating to dad, so much so that when the APCs drove along Davis Street and down Philomel Street, dad decided to go to the bow of the *Monsunen* to see them, so he thought. Moving up Ross Road towards Government House and to his amazement there was one parked at the gates leading down to the jetty and the *Monsunen* with lots of Argentine troops running all over the place. This was a very frightening experience – one of several to come.

The Argentine troops ordered dad and the other three crew to march (walk really) up the jetty to the gates where the APC was waiting. There they made everyone stand face against the wall of the shed with their feet apart while one Argentine soldier held his gun at the back of their necks and another searched them. They were only wearing shirtsleeves and at about 7.30am on an April morning they were very cold. After the search they were made to sit on the concrete for about an hour until the rest of the crew (three others), who were all at home, could be found to move the ship because the Argentines wanted to bring in one of their ships, the *Cabo San Antonio*, which was a landing ship to which the amphibious APCs belonged.

All the while the Argentines were shouting at them but they did not know what was being said. Several days after the invasion the *Monsunen* was allowed to sail with the stores and fuel but not before changing the flag. This was really sickening for dad who had the job of changing it. Once he had put it up the mate wrapped it around the pole which was an insult to the Argentines but the wind soon blew it out.

****

The RT Station by Kerri Anne Ross (Age 11)
First published in the Falkland Islands Journal 1997 Vol 7

RT Station

The radio telephone service was installed in the Falkland Islands in the 1950s. It was set up after planes were brought to the Falklands. Sets were given to each farm manager and at that time there were about 40 farms. They were all connected to the main radio station on St Mary's Walk in Stanley. The sets on the farms were a radio and a microphone, powered by a 12 volt battery that was recharged by wind generators. Then in 1981 a telephone was put into the station so that people could talk to their families or the shops. The operator had a switch to control the conversation by switching it between the person on the phone and the person on the radio. At the end of every conversation the person talking had to say 'over' so that the operator could switch it back to the next person. Nothing was private and everyone would listen in to find out what was going on.

Invasion

On the 2nd April 1982 the Argentines invaded the Islands. On that day after all the fighting had finished and people were starting to go outside to find out what was going on, Eileen Vidal, known locally as *'the Voice of the Falklands'* went up to the RT station. The hostel children came up to the station wanting to talk to their parents. Some of the children were crying with fright, others were excited, but for their mums and dads it was a very worrying time.

After the children had gone, a call came through from HMS *Endurance, 'Stanley this is Endurance' - can you tell me the situation in Stanley please - over'.* Eileen told them all she knew, letting them know of troop numbers, aircraft and ships. The *Endurance* told her to 'stand by' then an officer came on and asked her to tell him what she had just said. By this time Eileen was getting a bit nervous as she didn't know if the Argentines were listening to her talking to HMS *Endurance* so she told the officer to keep *Endurance* away from the Islands. They passed this information onto London.

That night on the announcements on the radio Eileen put a message out that she would be in the station on Saturday from 9.00am for an hour. Next morning all the farms tried to get through at once so she told them that she would be there all day to take their messages and pass any more information over to them. She worked all day Sunday as well. During this time many Argentines came into the station, some quite nice, others quite nasty, but all the time she managed to keep operating. She worked for 10 days after the invasion before the Argentines closed the station down. The only people who were allowed to use the RT during the war were the doctors. They went in every morning with an Argentine doctor for half an hour and most farms called in every day to find out what was going on.

****

Neil Hewitt, 12 year old Falkland Islander in 1982

Invasion Day - Argentine Soldiers Arrive at our House

My story starts in earnest on the 1st April 1982, I noticed that there was a lot of activity with the Royal Marines that day. They were armed and looked nervous. I feared the worst as the Argentine activity was beginning to increase as well. I was at my mate Rikki Evan's place listening to Beatles records, yet in the back of my mind I knew I had to do my homework. There was a ring on the telephone and it was my mum asking me to come back home as there was an announcement on the radio.

When I got home we all crouched around the radio and we listened to the Governor's announcement, that it was very likely that we were going to be invaded the next morning. The strangest thing I remember him saying is that we should stay off the streets and not give the Argentines the excuse they needed to invade. I did not take a second telling to stay off the streets as I indeed did not want to get in the way of the Royal Marines! I was 12 years old at the time and would not have been any use to them whatsoever!

After the announcement was over my stepfather called and asked whether he should come to Stanley (he was working on building roads near Bluff Cove). My mum said she certainly did want him back in town and he obliged. My overpowering thought was that's good I don't have to do my homework as the schools were to be shut. I went to bed full of fear and I had a very restless night, I didn't know whether I was going to live or die and I was really worried about my mother who was very nervous and pregnant. She was not coping well with the ongoing situation. I decided my best course of action was to give her a long cuddle and I felt her physically shaking and there was a tear in her eye.

I was awoken at about 6.30 am by the sound of distant gunfire, which seemed to be coming from the east maybe towards an area of town called white city, which consisted of around five houses near the common gate which is the eastern entrance to the town. These buildings were of a slender structure and God knows how anyone survived it. The gunfire came nearer and nearer and louder and louder. The bangs were really loud and it felt like our roof was caving in. We were on Davis Street which was the front line. The radio droned on in the background and we moved from room to room when the firing got louder. Mum was terrified and we were calming her down (not very successfully). We all hugged the floor getting as low as possible. Bullets were pinging around the house and I am absolutely sure that the Royal Marines were shouting at one another, but I didn't see them, I did not dare lift my head. I thought any minute I would die and I prayed as hard as I could.

Then there were tremendous bangs on the back door of our house, the door seemed to be caving in. My stepfather shouted '*Ok, ok I am going to open the door'*. When he opened the door we were ordered out at gun point, there were about a dozen Argentine soldiers in our back garden and an Armoured Personnel Carrier at the end of our garden. We were sat in a horseshoe and my youngest brother Kevin was cold and my stepfather gave him a jumper. There was a large machine gun pointing at us with a young soldier on the end of it. My mum kept saying they are going to shoot us, so I hugged her tightly and said '*Mum, they won't I promise'*, (I had no idea whether they would or they wouldn't!) They searched our house. My biggest concern was that the Royal Marines would come back, but they were long gone. Our next-door neighbours refused to come out of the house and I remember thinking ''*God, they are brave*. Eventually we were let back in the house and the only thing I remember after that was a piece of shrapnel came through the wall, with a tremendous crack. Shortly after that the Governor surrendered and I remembered the relief of no more firing. We were not allowed out all that day and it was so boring.

The next day we went to Goose Green but that's another story!

****

Initial Response

Lt. Keith Mills, Royal Marines, Senior British Officer on South Georgia

The Battle of Grytviken

On 31st March 1982, HMS *Endurance's* Royal Marines detachment supported by 9 Marines from NP8901 and under the command of 22 year old Acting Lieutenant Keith Mills, landed at King Edward Point (KEP), South Georgia. He had been given three specific orders; to maintain a British presence on the island, to protect the resident British Antarctic Survey (BAS) personnel in the event of an emergency; to monitor the activities of the illegally landed Argentines at nearby Leith. As an Argentine invasion was still considered unlikely, even at this late stage, he was issued with no Rules of Engagement (ROE) other than the standard "Yellow Card" rules used in Northern Ireland at the time. Furthermore, he was to maintain radio silence between himself and *Endurance* and he was not allowed to inform the BAS personnel of *Endurance's* return to the Falklands or of the possible seriousness of the impending situation.

The following day, the Detachment commenced adventure training activities whilst the BAS personnel went about their normal business.

That evening, after dinner, one of the scientists decided to tune the radio to obtain Falkland Islands Radio hosted by local DJ, Patrick Watts. After listening to several records the mood changed abruptly when Watts suddenly interrupted his programme to announce a newsflash. The situation between the UK and Argentina had worsened considerably in the last few hours and an invasion was now likely. Mills and his Detachment Sergeant Major, Sgt Pete Leach, remained glued to the radio awaiting further information. Just after midnight the Governor, Rex Hunt declared a State of Emergency and just before daybreak the first reports of a full-scale invasion began to come through before, suddenly, all transmissions ceased. Mills immediately stood the Detachment to and all 22 of them lay outside in a Force 10 gale waiting for an invasion that was not to materialise that day.

At about 0800 hours, an Argentine naval ship, *Bahia Paraiso*, entered Cumberland East Bay. Fortunately, weather conditions were too extreme for her to be able to launch helicopters or boats so instead she made radio contact with the BAS personnel via maritime channel 16. She informed them that she would be returning the following day with a very important message for them and that they should continue to monitor channel 16. Having passed her message, she departed.

Mills then made a quick appreciation of the situation they were in. It was obvious to him that following their invasion of the Falklands, the Argentines would want to occupy South Georgia too. However, with limited resources he did not have capability to defend the entire island against an Argentine assault. He decided instead to try and defend KEP, the main British base on the island and the location where the Union Flag flew. Assault, he believed, would come from the landing craft on board the *Bahia Paraiso* either landing on the foreshore of KEP or the jetty at the end of KEP. To this end, he ordered that both be mined with improvised explosive devices (IED). He then set about preparing his defensive position and his Marines began to dig in.

Knowing that they did not have the resources to repel a prolonged or subsequent assaults, Mills ordered that all heavy and non-essential equipment be loaded on one of the BAS tractors and dumped some 2km to the rear of Grytviken towards Maiviken. This would aid a speedy withdrawal and be of use in future operations. At the same time, due to the extreme change in circumstances, Mills decided to break radio silence and send a coded message to *Endurance*. His message read, *"The Argentines have made radio contact with us and intend to do the same tomorrow. What are our instructions?"* The message was deliberately brief due to the complexities of the code being used.

Whilst awaiting a reply, Mills and Leach continued to supervise the defensive preparations. All BAS personnel were evacuated to the nearby disused old whalers church in Grytviken for their own safety.

Several hours later, Mills received his long-awaited reply. It read, *"When the Argentines attempt to make contact, you are not to co-operate"*. Mills was frustrated by the response as it did not give him the clear direction he now required. He rattled off a quick reply which read, *"Your last message is ambiguous. Please clarify"*. He informed Leach of his concerns, but together, in the absence of further information, they decided to continue with the original plan.

As the day went by, information was gleaned from the BBC World Service that Argentine occupation of the Falklands had become a reality. It was also stated that all British military and government personnel were in the process of being repatriated to UK as a matter of haste.

In the early hours of the next morning Mills received his response. It was to the point, "When asked to surrender, you are not to do so". Mills then briefed his men who were ecstatic at being given the opportunity to fight, as many had believed the politicians may have thought the time for fighting was over. Barely had Mills finished briefing his men when another message arrived. It read, "The OCRM is not, repeat not, to take any action which may endanger life". The last order appeared to contradict the previous but, again having consulted Leach, decided to pursue the original plan. Regardless, time was not now on Mills's side. The *Bahia Paraiso* appeared again and the Argentines made an announcement on channel 16, "Following our successful reoccupation of the Malvinas, the Governor, Rex Hunt, has surrendered the *Malvinas*, South Georgia and the British Antarctic Dependencies. A ceasefire is now in force and as part of this agreement we have come to occupy South Georgia. All British personnel are to gather on the beach for repatriation to the UK".

Mills pretended that the message was unclear due to interference and asked the Argentines to repeat their message on Long Wave which they duly did. The significance of this was that *Endurance* and the other BAS bases in Antarctica could now all be party to the conversation. A large part of the message appeared to be true as Mills had already heard via the BBC World Service that the Falklands had been lost and that British officials were in the process of being repatriated to UK. What he could not accept, however, was that the Governor would have surrendered South Georgia and the Dependencies as part of any deal. Furthermore, he had orders to "not surrender when asked to do so" but these orders appeared to be contradicted by later ones that stated he was not to take any action which may endanger life.

He was confused and decided to play for time in the hope that he would receive clarification from his superiors. He replied (on Long Wave again) that the Argentines' instructions appeared to contradict those received by him and asked for time to clarify his position with his superiors. The Argentines replied, "Yes, you can have 10 minutes". Mills knew that this would be inadequate and Argentine helicopters had already begun buzzing KEP.

In a further effort to stall for time Mills then announced to the Argentines that "there is a military force on the island and any attempt to land before clarification has been received will be met with force". The Argentines appeared to ignore this warning as almost immediately an Argentine corvette sailed into Cumberland Bay. She was the *Geurrico*, a corvette armed with a 100mm gun on her bow, a 40mm gun aft and four side mounted Exocet missiles. She appeared to be heading for the jetty at the end of KEP. Mills, accompanied by Marine Daniels (his Assault Engineer) decided to go to the jetty himself in the hope of deterring the Argentines from landing. If he failed to do so, Daniels had orders to detonate the explosives attached to the underside of the jetty. However, instead of attempting to come alongside, the *Geurrico* recce'd the harbour and once she had ascertained that *Endurance* was nowhere to be seen she turned about and slowly started heading back out to sea.

So distracted had Mills and Daniels been following the corvette's path, neither had seen the Alouette helicopter approaching until it was landing only yards from their position. Argentine marines immediately began to deplane. Even at this late stage, due the uncertainty of his orders, Mills was still keen to negotiate their peaceful withdrawal, if at all possible. He raised his right arm in attempt to gain their attention. The first two failed to see him but the third stood shell-shocked at the unexpected sight of a fully armed British soldier. He drew the attention of Mills to the marine following him, who immediately brought his rifle to bear in Mills's direction. At this point Mills decided that discretion was the better part of valour and both he and Daniels hard targeted their way back to their main defensive position some 250m away.

By the time they got back to their trenches, a second helicopter was approaching. It was a Puma and behind the air gunner in the door, Mills could clearly see that she was fully laden with Argentine marines. The Puma hovered as she prepared to land on the helicopter landing site, just 100m from his main position. Mills knew that he could not allow the helicopter to land and immediately gave the order to open fire. The noise was incredible as the entire Detachment began to unload on the helpless Puma. At such close range it was impossible to miss, but unfortunately, everyone aimed at the perceived threat, ie. the marines in the back. No one thought to shoot the pilots or the engine, which would have been more effective. Consequently, by some very skillful flying, the pilot managed to turn the aircraft around and, with thick black smoke bellowing from its engines, managed to fly the aircraft the thousand metres or so across the bay before crashing on the far side.

In response the *Geurrico*, which was by now some 2-3km away, turned about and immediately began slowly heading back towards KEP all guns blazing. The warship looked very impressive on her approach, but Mills quickly realised that, with her main gun in an almost horizontal position, her fire was almost ineffective against his dug in marines. Furthermore, as the seconds ticked by, she was getting closer and closer to their position. Mills gave the order to ceasefire and for his marines to prepare their anti-tank rockets. He was hoping that by not being under fire, the Argentines would be lulled into bringing the warship into a position at the narrowest point between KEP and a rock outcrop called Hobart Rocks at the mouth of the cove. If the *Geurrico* reached that point she would not have enough space to manoeuvre and she would be on the limit of the range of the Detachment's small arms.

Minutes ticked by as the *Geurrico* edged closer, all the time raining heavy but ineffective fire on the British position. Finally, she reached the critical point and Mills gave the order to fire. The noise was deafening as the Detachment's one and only 84mm Carl Gustav launcher roared. The missile flew towards the *Geurrico* but appeared to drop just short of its target. However, by a fluke of luck, it ricocheted from the calm waters of the bay and struck the *Geurrico* amidships just above the waterline blowing a gaping hole in her side.

Several 66mm rockets were also launched with most falling well short of their intended target due to the extreme range. Fortuitously, the one that did strike its target hit the 100mm gun housing on the foredeck causing it to cease firing. Concurrently, at a range of almost 1,800m, Mne Parsons managed to pick off the entire aft gun crew from behind their protective screen using his LMG. The *Geurrico's* guns fell silent as Mills's men unloaded as much ordnance into her starboard side as time would allow. Sgt Leach was keeping himself busy (and the ship's command) by firing his sniper's rifle into the ship's bridge! Suddenly, the firing stopped as the *Geurrico* left the Detachment's view and took temporary refuge behind the buildings at the end of KEP. When she reappeared a few moments later, heading back out to sea, she did so at great haste. Mills's men did not need a second invitation as they brought all weapons available to bear on the warship's port side.

Due to the ship's increased speed, the window of opportunity was much shorter on this occasion but long enough for another 84mm rocket to find its target, this time adjacent to one of the Exocet launchers.

Eventually, the *Geurrico* reached a point where she was beyond the range of the Detachment's small arms and began to take up a position some 3-4km offshore.

The Argentines from the Alouette that had originally been landed at the end of KEP now began to make their move. They had realised that the slightly elevated British position afforded them the opportunity to move, in what they thought was dead ground, to a position from which they could assault. However, Mills had foreseen this threat and had placed a GPMG position in a position at the end of the beach covering this dead ground. Once most of the Argentines were in his sights Mne "Brasso" Hare opened fire, sending the survivors scurrying back to the cover of the buildings at the end of KEP. Whilst all this was happening, the Argentines were using their remaining helicopters to ferry troops to the far side of Cumberland East Bay and these troops were moving slowly by foot towards Grytviken. Mills knew it would be only a matter of time before his escape route was cut off. To make things worse, the *Geurrico* had managed to get her main armament working again and 100mm shells began to rain down on their position, this time from a high angle making their fire much more effective.

Time was running out for Mills. Cpl Peters had been injured in the firefight and Mills knew it would only be a matter of time before he would be joined by others. His escape route was now blocked by Argentine troops in Grytviken and it would now be impossible for them to be reunited with their pre-dumped supplies. Also, there were no more Argentine troops within range of the Detachment's small arms whilst they, in turn, were still under fire from the enemy's longer-range weapons.

Finally, he knew there would be no cavalry riding over the horizon to save them on this occasion. There was only one decision to be made and that was the unpalatable choice to surrender before any more of his men were killed or injured. Mills took satisfaction from knowing that he and his men had inflicted heavy materiel and personnel damage on the enemy and that he had not "surrendered when asked to do so".

The Argentines treated the captive British marines in an exemplary manner and three weeks later the Detachment were repatriated to the UK.

Mills and Leach were later to receive the Distinguished Service Cross and Distinguished Service Medal respectively for their parts in the action with an additional four of his Detachment being given further awards for gallantry. It was the first time in history that shoulder launched anti-tank missiles had ever been used against a warship.

Note: In gratitude for Keith Mills' action during that time, a mountain 'Mills' Peak' was named ofter him on South Georgia.

****

Tony Shaw, SAS D Squadron, South Georgia

SAS on South Georgia

Friday 23rd April 1982

In the early hours of the morning on 23rd April, Boat Troop set off from HMS *Antrim* in five Geminis. The objective was to reach Grass Island in Stromness Bay to set up an LUP (Laying Up Position) overlooking Leith and Stromness Harbours. At first everything went well. The sea was remarkably calm as we were lowered over the starboard side of *Antrim*. The destroyer screened us from the wind as we grouped together on the starboard quarter. *Antrim* then sailed off into the night and almost immediately a squall was upon us and the wind dramatically increased in force. The wind pushed the boats apart from each other, waves started crashing over our heads and the outboard motors started failing one by one....

One of the outboard motors failed immediately after *Antrim* sailed and left us to our own devices. Then call sign 17 Alpha, the boat that I was in, had its engine cut out abruptly a minute or two later. One of the RIBs, 17 Echo, turned back and took two boats in tow, but then its engine failed too leaving 17 Alpha, 17 Bravo and 17 Echo in severe difficulties. Meanwhile 17 Delta took 17 Charlie in tow and succeeded in dropping the crew of three with their boat at Grass Island. 17 Delta then returned to look for the other three boats but saw nothing in the darkness.

Eventually Delta's engine also failed and with a supreme effort the crew managed to paddle ashore on a headland several miles distant from Grass Island where they remained until rescued after the enemy surrender. The three Geminis without functioning engines were initially tied together but this threatened to overturn the boats and we were forced to cast off from each other. This soon left us all over Stromness Bay and being forced out to the open sea in atrocious weather conditions.

The three of us on 17 Alpha had little choice but to take turns paddling with the two small paddles while the third crew member tried to start the outboard motor using a starter rope as there was no electronic ignition on our ageing engine. We were completely shattered by now, although the paddling kept us warm, too warm in fact as we were wearing waterproof immersion suits over our uniforms. When my turn came to have a go at getting the engine to start, I went through the motions like the others had already tried to no avail. In desperation, I sprayed gasoline directly into the carburettor and over the top of the engine. Finally, the engine sparked and there was a brief flash of flame as the gasoline caught alight and then the engine cut out. I thought this 'flare-out' may have helped to clear out the carb and also warm up the engine. I tried this highly dangerous procedure a second time with nothing to lose and this time the engine backfired a few times and finally started to run, albeit none too sweetly.

Wasting no time, we sped directly to Grass Island. The outboard motor cut out a couple of times on the way, but we managed to restart it by pulling the starter cord immediately before the engine had a chance to get cold. We didn't see the other two missing boats on the way to Grass Island. Only three Geminis had made it to Grass Island, meaning Boat Troop were now reduced to just nine men.

Two boats, 17 Bravo and 17 Delta with a total of six crew members, were missing.

By Kind Permission of Tony Shaw, Author of SAS South Georgia Boating Club

****

Lt. Chris Parry, Flight Observer, Wessex 3 aboard HMS Antrim
Having rescued the SAS from the Fortuna Glacier, Chris Parry tells of a second rescue of the SAS on South Georgia. By kind permission of Chris Parry an extract from his book Down South – A Falklands War Diary

Rescuing the SAS becomes a bit of a habit

It's St George's Day today and Shakespeare's birthday. I slept well for about four hours, but having heard about the SAS plan, I thought that I would get up and see what was going on, especially as I thought it involved some risk to the ship.

As I thought, the SAS were up to something. Last night, they talked the Captain into taking the ship into Stromness Bay – right in, opposite Leith – so they could insert five teams by Gemini. I felt that I had to stay up for this one, not only to witness the evolution, but also just in case we came under fire from the shore. I judged that it was a highly risky manoeuvre in a confined space and I could not help thinking about the fate of the *Geurrico* around Grytviken at the hands of Lt Keith Mills and his gallant team. If the Argies at Leith had 66mm rockets and recoilless rifles, as well as illuminants, we could be in for a rough ride. I kept on hinting to the Commander that the evolution might be dodgy, but he said the Argies would have their heads down and our gun teams would be fully briefed and ready to act in case.

We went to action stations at 0215 hours and entered the bay, silent and darkened, with our steam plant providing quiet propulsion and the ship closed down to the watertight condition, ZULU. The sea was flat calm, the night was pitch black and the wind still - apart from the inky darkness, not really what we wanted.

The Navigator was working really hard to keep us safe in very confined waters with only occasional single sweeps of 978 radar, in sector scan.

There was a ban, on pain of something worse than death, on the use of intercoms, broadcasts, radio or shouting on upper the deck. The MAA had patrols out looking for any chink of light – we were on red lighting anyway – and any 'Goofers' who were away from their Action stations. I suppose that I was 'goofing'. The gun crews were briefed and ready to fire if necessary.

From the starboard signal deck, I could see a couple of lights over by Leith and was sure that anyone worth their salt would have posted a guard. Surely, they know that we are here! They must be able to hear the noise of our main machinery and generators – another quick glance over at the lights.

We reached the selected drop-off point, but the Gemini engines weren't ready, so at 0245 hours we tiptoed away from navigational danger and out of possible range of gunfire. All of us, not least the Navigator, paused for breath, until the Gemini engines decided they would cooperate and start.

We went back to the bay at 0330 hours, but suddenly realised that we were still making a great deal of noise with our ventilation, which was immediately crash-stopped. We had to restart some ventilation almost immediately because the Ops Room displays and computer promptly crashed because of lack of cooling air.

The SAS were getting ready down aft, with their Geminis ranged on the starboard side of the quarterdeck, working in red lighting. You could discern the activity from where I was standing. I looked over to Leith through binoculars – just the two same lights. Then, from aft, I heard the faint sounds of Geminis being slipped over the side - on an improvised ramp that Chippy and his team had made – and saw in the dim light the personnel and kit being loaded.

There was a pause of about five minutes and then 'whirr – wump - wump - wump - wump - wump - wumpa - wumpa - wumpa - wumpa - wump - wump – whirr – whirr – clunk': the unmistakable sound of an outboard motor – or lawn mower – that does not want to run up. Then another one! And another! Each one seemed to be demonstrating its petulant displeasures at being put in the icy water in the middle of a freezing night.

Bloody Hell – you do not have to be a panel member on the Argie equivalent of *What's My Line?* To know what that noise is, I thought.

Also, why are they running up the engines on the side nearest to the Argies? They could have been launched and paddled round to the other side of the ship before starting!

This went on for about 10 minutes before at 0415 hours a couple of the engines decided that they wanted to play and the SAS went off into the night, with the two boats towing the other three.

Rather like ducklings, they seemed rather reluctant to go and within 10 minutes they were back alongside again, because they still had technical problems, had forgotten something or did not know where to go. By this stage, the Captain and the Navigator were ageing rapidly by the minute. However, by 0435 hours the Geminis were on their way and we were heading out of the bay. We were clear at 0445 hours. I turned, much relieved.

Of course, the engines, which had been carefully stowed and lovingly maintained in converted oil barrels, full of sea water (thought of that), in anticipation of such an occasion, had seriously objected to being taken out of the warmer atmosphere of the ship and to being invited to perform immediately in such extremely cold conditions (didn't think of that).

In the morning, I was just chatting with Ian and Carlos Edwards about what happened when Cedric Delves came bowling into the Wardroom, with a glum, but suggestive look on his face and headed straight for Ian and me. "We've got a problem; we've lost contact with two of the boats from last night. We don't know where they are' I remember thinking, this is becoming a bit of a habit!

So, I had a look at the charts and calculated the likely drift rates based on the elapsed time, the sea state, the wind speed and prevailing currents. We launched at 0840 hours to find them. Visibility was poor at about 100 metres and the cloud base at about

200 feet. After an hour's fruitless search, trying to locate the survivors in the vicinity of the mouth of Stromness and Cumberland Bays and evading any Argie activity ashore, I plotted and controlled a box search down-sea and downwind of where the Gemini should have been. The search legs were getting increasingly longer and we were reaching the limit of our endurance. I was thinking we don't like to come back empty handed; it's not our style.

On the last leg, I heard the faint tone of a beacon at extreme range and suddenly Fitz called that he could see something astern of us on the starboard side at about a mile. It was an orange flare. We closed quickly and found the boat, with three frozen yetis inside, looking very much the worse for wear. We winched the three survivors up, with their equipment, instructing the last man to sink the Gemini in case it was found by the Argies. They were not in a good way, with their dry suits brittle with ice and their faces grey with fatigue and cold.

I said, 'You were only supposed to have the boat for an hour. You'll lose your deposit!'

They were not amused and just kept themselves warm. We handed out blankets and gave them a flask of coffee. One man could hardly hold the mug, he was so cold.

They were lucky because they were well on their way to South Africa by the time we found them.

****

Brum Richards, 148 Commando Battery Naval Gunfire Support

<u>Heading to Gritviken, South Georgia, on HMS *Plymouth*</u>

Sunday 25th April

I am now on the bridge of the *Plymouth* witnessing a very rare sight, that of three British warships in line abreast crashing through the heavy swell at 25 knots. *Plymouth* has hoisted her battle ensign. It looks, after all that has passed, we now mean business.

Captain Brown lands and called me up on HF. We have good comms so I pass to him the fireplan targets. He begins to direct fire on to the reported enemy gun position and onto Brown Mountain. One ship on each target. We are pleased because we are the first to open fire therefore becoming the first warship in a long time to engage the enemy. We check that our battle ensign is still flying.

When we reach the western limit of the gunline there are anxious moments as we engage the southern shoreline of King Edward Cove. We engage a particular target which is due south opposite King Edward Point: the 40 salvoes land bang on target. The trajectory passes directly over the buildings where all the enemy are located. There are white flags to be seen.

The time is 1715 hours. Our own troops have not even come under fire yet. The enemy were simply frightened into surrendering after a devastating display of controlled accurate NGS (Naval Gunfire Support). It even surprised me and I have been doing this for 19 years. The speed and accuracy is unbelievable, perhaps it is all because there were no safety restrictions. The SAS troops begin to race towards the buildings with the hope of accepting the surrender but the O/C M Coy calls up a Lynx and beats them to it. When the SAS troops do arrive the enemy commander is amazed that they are all OK because they have just passed through a minefield he had recently laid. It is amazing that the whole action was bloodless.

Monday 26th April - South Georgia

At 0900 hours we cannot see any white flags but the enemy are calling us on channel 16. They assure us they are showing the white flag but we tell them we can't see it. Suddenly they put up some white flags which we can now see. We invite them to parade themselves at the main jetty but they decline this as it is mined so we tell them to move towards the hillside in the direction the civilians went. They agree but I suggest to our captain to tell them to do it in single file with the first man and last man holding a white flag. I also suggest each man put his hand on the man's shoulder in front of him so the SAS can see them easily and count them from a distance. They comply with this order. The enemy certainly look a sad sight as they file out and I cannot help but feel a sense of pity for them, even though yesterday I would quite willingly have blasted them away. They are very surprised when the SAS and SBS teams suddenly appear out of cover and surround them. As one, the Argies quickly and energetically raise their hands in the air.

In all there are 190 prisoners to be taken to Ascension when other things are sorted out.

Tuesday 27th April - South Georgia

The mammoth task of transferring men and stores begins as a storm hits us but we have to continue. *Conqueror* suddenly surfaces amongst all the mayhem. During these transfers two SBS men get blown off the casing of *Conqueror* by a Wessex. They are quickly rushed to *Antrim* to enjoy a few moments in the captain's hot bath. A Lynx helicopter lands on our flight deck and creates a first. It is a tight squeeze but it can be done. The pilot receives a bottle of champagne from our captain because it is the first time a Lynx has ever made a landing on the flight deck of a type 12 Frigate. Eventually the weather wins and all transfers have to be stopped.

****

Sqn Ldr Bob Tuxford, The Bombing of Stanley Airfield.

<u>Operation Black Buck 1</u>

30th April - 1st May 1982

On the 2nd April 1982 Argentina invaded the British Territory of the Falkland Islands. These islands are approximately 8,000nm from the UK and 400nm off the southernmost point of Argentina. In response, Prime Minister Margaret Thatcher announced that Britain would assemble an Amphibious Task Force to reclaim the islands and return them to British rule.

Chief of the Air Staff, Marshal of the RAF Sir Michael Beetham approached the Prime Minister and informed her that 'he had a plan that needed refining'. This plan was for a Vulcan bomber to attack the runway at Stanley, the enemy occupied airfield located on East Falkland Island. The British Protectorate of Ascension Island situated in the middle of the South Atlantic was identified as a potential Forward Operating Base (FOB). Located approximately 3500nm north of the Falkland Islands, a round trip for any bombing task would exceed 7000nm. Integral to this proposal would be the extensive use of Victor K2 tankers of Nos. 55 and 57 Squadrons, supported by the instructors and crews of No 232 Operational Conversion Unit, all based at RAF Marham.

From early April 1982, all squadron pilots were required to maintain currency in not only tanking (offloading fuel) but also receiving (uplifting fuel) during mutual Air-to-Air Refuelling (AAR) operations. In peacetime conditions, the practice of receiving fuel was normally restricted to daylight hours only. However, during the second week of April, a directive from Group HQ required that all pilots regain currency in receiving fuel at night. Engineering Wing was also tasked with bringing all hangared aircraft up to operational readiness as soon as possible.

As Flight Commander on No. 55 Sqn, I was called by the Station Commander and invited to fly the Victor at low-level (LL) and report back with my observations. Within 24 hours, two F.95 Cameras had been installed into the nose section of five aircraft. Along with two other selected crews, we embarked on the steep learning curve of Photo Reconnaissance (PR) training around the highlands and Islands of Scotland. The Victor's navigation suite was enhanced with the addition of a Carousel Inertial Navigation (IN) system and its associated H2S Radar equipment was also modified and improved to give it a Maritime Radar Reconnaissance (MRR) capability. By the third week in April, I had accumulated the additional disciplines of PR and MRR to add to my basic skill set in the AAR Role.

Similar hectic preparations were also underway at the Vulcan Medium Bomber base at RAF Waddington. The most pressing of these was the restoration of the dormant AAR capability of the Vulcan. Although refuelling probes had been retained on all aircraft, its associated fuel system components and galleries had not been serviced or modified since AAR trials some 25 years earlier. Moreover, none of the current Vulcan captains had qualified in the AAR role previously. A priority was placed on their immediate training and qualification as receiver pilots, a considerable task given the limited timeframe in the build-up to war.

On 18th April 1982 as the Carrier Battle Group set sail for the Falkland Islands, the first Victor K2 aircraft arrived on Ascension Island. Less than 48 hours later, the tanker detachment received its first tasking from the Commander of the Task Force. Radar reconnaissance sweeps were required over the oceanic area to the north of South Georgia and around the approaches to the Falkland Islands. 'Operation Paraquet', the retaking of South Georgia, would demand the services of the modified Victor K2s in their newly acquired MRR role. The aim was to gather any useful intelligence regarding the Argentinian surface fleet dispositions prior to any direct action. The missions would provide an invaluable opportunity for the deployed Tanker Task Force and Engineering Wing in generating long-range multi-aircraft formations engaged in AAR operations over expansive oceanic areas. After the initial frenzy of three demanding MRR tasks, there was a brief respite before the next phase of the air war in the South Atlantic.

In the meantime, the number of Victors on the Island had increased to thirteen. The nature of operations was about to change with the arrival of two Vulcan B2 aircraft on 29th April 1982. During the following evening on 30th April, all rested Victor crews, along with the two recently arrived Vulcan crews, sat side-by-side in the briefing tent of the combined operations complex located on the centre of Wideawake Auxiliary Airfield. A Vulcan bombing raid was outlined which seemed as audacious as it was ambitious. Every single island-based tanker would be needed to support the fuel thirsty mission, identified by the codeword 'Operation Black Buck 1'. Three elements comprising RED, WHITE and BLUE Sections would form the outbound wave including eleven tankers required to refuel and deliver the Vulcan to the target. A further seven Victors would make up the inbound wave tasked with recovering the bomber to Ascension Island after the attack.

At 2230 hours local time, the massed four jets started their engines simultaneously. Within minutes, one of the Victors suffered an inexplicable engine wind-down, its position within the taxi stream replaced without fuss by a manned ground reserve aircraft. In the pre-briefed sequence, thirteen aircraft assumed their positions within the carefully choreographed taxi plan: eleven Victors followed by the primary and reserve Vulcans. Under radio silence, the thirteen aircraft took to the runway in 1-minute intervals and staggered into the night sky. As each tanker made a brief after take-off check of its centre-line hose drum unit (HDU), WHITE-4 found to his horror that the hose would not trail – rendering him unserviceable for the mission. One of the Victors in BLUE Section flown by Flt Lt Steve Biglands (aka 'Biggles') was directed to take the place of the unserviceable Victor WHITE-4. Within minutes, the skipper of primary Vulcan BLUE-2 found that his aircraft would not pressurise during the initial climb. He too had to declare himself U/S and extricate himself from the snake-climb sequence. Flt Lt Martin Wither's crew operating the airborne reserve Vulcan as BLUE-4 was instructed to take over the primary bombing slot as BLUE-2.

After joining up at pre-planned stepped altitudes, RED, WHITE, and BLUE sections set course as a combined Balbo towards the first of four refuelling areas identified as Bracket One (BKT-1). Located 700nm down track after 1hr and 45mins into the mission, eight Victors from RED and WHITE sections separated into four pairs for the massive 50,000lb transfers of fuel. These demanding night refuellings would require the receiver aircraft to maintain contact for up to 30 minutes. Simultaneously, the remaining Vulcan BLUE-2 took the first of two fuel transfers from its dedicated tanker (the

Vulcan's fuel tanks having a smaller capacity than those in the Victor). Approximately 1600nm south of the Island, the five remaining aircraft began transferring fuel within the BKT-2 area. These transfers went well, although one of the returning tankers developed a serious fuel leak which dictated his issuing a MAYDAY call.

Approaching BKT-3 around 40 degrees South, I was leading the formation as WHITE-2, with Flt Lt Biglands' crew as WHITE-4 and Flt Lt Withers in the Vulcan, BLUE-2. At approximately 2,500 miles from Ascension, I transferred around 30,000lbs fuel to the Vulcan before planning to refuel the last remaining tanker. At that moment, we lost the clear horizon, and the aircraft encountered increasing degrees of turbulence. Flashes of lightning indicated the presence of thunderstorms and momentarily illuminated the dark silhouettes of the formating aircraft. Somewhat alarmingly, St Elmo's fire characterized by erratic sparks and jagged fingers of lightning appeared all over my cockpit transparencies.

With the radar equipment selected off to maintain radio silent procedures, we had flown inadvertently into the towering cloud activity of which the Met officer spoke at briefing almost eight hours before. I called the other tanker astern. With the three aircraft bucking like broncos, my centre-line hose and basket was flailing up and down over an arc of around 20 feet. After several aborted attempts, WHITE-4 valiantly made contact on my unstable hose and started to take on fuel. Shortly afterwards, radio silence was broken with a disconcerting call from Biggles; "I've broken my probe"! With little time to consider the options, I instinctively made the decision to reverse roles and swap positions with the other Victor. I slid astern his aircraft as soon as I could see that he was trailed and prepared to take back the fuel I'd just offloaded. We were facing a wildly unstable basket, just as Biglands had witnessed minutes earlier, I made severable unsuccessful lunges at the basket to make contact. After several minutes, I finally succeeded in making a latched contact with the basket and fuel started to flow into my tanks.

The prevailing turbulence was adversely affecting the stability of the hose in front of me as I desperately tried to stay in contact. Ripples travelling up to the serving carriage of the tanker's HDU were reflected down the length of the hose, threatening to swipe off my probe tip as Biggles had found to his disadvantage only minutes earlier. Moreover, I was acutely aware that my control inputs were becoming increasingly aggressive, and my flying bordering on the dangerous. I had to withdraw and break contact to regain my composure and take a brief respite. At that very moment, the turbulence started to abate, the hose in front of me began to stabilise and I was able to re-establish contact. Gradually, the horizon reappeared, and the stars began to show through the dispersing clouds. Taking fuel onboard once more, I was nevertheless aware of the fact that Biggles would not be able to receive fuel on his return to Ascension because of the broken probe. I broke radio silence to advise him to limit my transfer to ensure he would have sufficient fuel on board to make his recovery to the Island without the need for further refuelling. With the transfer complete, I cleared WHITE-4 to turn left without delay and pressed on towards the next refuelling area and the final bracket.

In the melee of the last half hour, there had been no opportunity for us to make an accurate check of our fuel on board. A brief check revealed that in fact we were some 20,000lbs short of the fuel required to complete the plan. Assuming we pressed on with the mission and gave the Vulcan the planned fuel at BKT-4, the remaining fuel on board would enable us only to fly to within 500nm of Ascension, at which point our tanks would be dry! At that moment, I could have turned the formation around and returned to Ascension whilst all aircraft had sufficient fuel on board. My gut feeling however was to put my trust in years of experience in the Tanker Force, or more precisely in the Air Commander and his ops team on Ascension Island. Without declaring my hand, I decided to address my crew and ask each one of them what they thought our course of action should be. One by one, each of my crewmembers stated that "having come this far, we might as well see it through".

Buoyed by that vote of confidence, I pressed on towards the last refuelling area which was barely 15 minutes away.

Approaching BKT-4, we prepared to transfer a further 13,000lbs to the bomber. We had calculated that this should be sufficient for the Vulcan to complete the task, whilst retaining sufficient fuel in my tanks to fly northbound to around 24 degrees south. At that Latitude, we could have expected to have around 1 hour's fuel remaining with which to locate a rescue tanker, complete a rendezvous, and take on fuel to get us home. This assumption was based on a tanker being made available and despatched to resolve our predicament. However, I was aware that all Victors on the Island, even those that had already flown on the short outbound slots, were designated to fly a second time in support of the inbound wave to meet with the returning Vulcan post-strike. As I cast off the bomber and turned my aircraft towards Ascension, the atmosphere amongst the crew was subdued to say the least. We calculated that our aircraft would run out of fuel 500 miles or so short of the Island. I took the opportunity to discuss with my crew the options that faced us. Because of the profile of the lower nose section, ditching the Victor was not advisable. We decided upon the better option of a controlled evacuation sequence prior to running out of fuel. Having gone through the drills and abandonment checklist a couple of times, we placed that option on the back burner.

Around 45 minutes later, the code word 'Superfuse' was received over the HF radio, signalling a successful bombing run. There was suddenly a great deal of euphoria in the cockpit. Having held off calling on the radio for a rescue tanker which might have prejudiced the Vulcan's approach to the target, my AEO was now able to make the HF call with impunity. The priority was to request a tanker to meet us on our return track to the Island at a provisional rendezvous position around 24°S. Three hours later around 1000nm south of Ascension, with barely one hour's fuel remaining in the tanks, we established radio contact with an approaching tanker. After a textbook RV, and in gin-clear conditions, I was able to make contact and take on the life-saving fuel that would enable the return to our safe haven.

A total of eighteen Victor K2s were launched during the night of 30th April/1st May 1982 in support of the outbound and inbound waves of Operation Black Buck 1. Twelve tanker crews accumulated over 109 flying hours, with five crews flying missions lasting over 10 hours in duration. Six tanker crews flew two sorties that night. Twenty-three individual air-to-air refuellings took place with a total of 635,000 lbs of fuel transferred between aircraft. The single Vulcan successfully bombed the runway at Stanley Airfield, achieving one direct hit on the runway surface. Damage to the runway from the attack ensured that the Stanley runway was effectively denied to the enemy fighter aircraft for the rest of the war. Forced to operate subsequently from Argentine mainland airfields, their time over target was severely restricted whilst mounting counter attacks against the Task Force. Use of the occupied airfield by Argentine resupply aircraft was also severely affected. Britain's military force on the remote Ascension Island had been able to demonstrate not only the capability, but also the will to attack the enemy on the Falkland Islands. Argentina feared the RAF might also attack airfields and other potential targets on the mainland. Facing the possibility of reprisal attacks, the Argentine Air Force relocated their Mirage Air Defence fighters to the north of the country. This contributed significantly to the air superiority that the Harriers enjoyed in the aftermath of the raid. The impact of Operation Black Buck 1 arguably influenced the outcome of Operation Corporate.

****

Tim McClement, 2 i/c HMS Conqueror, British nuclear submarine, and sinking of the cruiser General Belgrano

HMS *Conqueror* - South Atlantic Patrol

'*We Come Unseen*' is rightly the motto of the Submarine Service. Forty years later it is important to reiterate the important contribution of HM Submarines to the successful outcome of the Falklands Campaign. From the rumours of HMS *Superb's* deployment from Gibraltar, which seemed to initiate the invasion (she went north not south), submarines played a vital role. As was the norm, all submarines slipped unnoticed from their home ports and made covert passage to the Falkland Islands.

After a hectic time in our base in Faslane, storing HMS *Conqueror* with everything from torpedoes to toilet paper, we embarked 14 members of 6 Sqn Special Boat Service (SBS) and six tons of their equipment. HMS *Conqueror* sailed on 4th April and made a covert, high-speed passage to the South Atlantic, averaging 500 miles a day. The passage south was dominated by intensive training coupled with watching the diplomatic efforts to solve the crisis unfold. The overriding feeling on board was that we would not actually go to war.

HMS *Conqueror* arrived off South Georgia on 20th April. While there we experienced moments that were by turn exciting, frightening, and threatening; the experience as a whole corroborating the dictum that 'war is ninety-five per cent boredom and five per cent sheer terror'. After South Georgia had been recaptured we transferred 6 SBS and their equipment to the destroyer HMS *Antrim.*

We departed South Georgia heading to the southwest of the Falkland Islands, to locate the cruiser *General Belgrano* and her 2 escorting destroyers. The primary task of UK Boats was to counter the Argentinian Surface Forces up threat, particularly that of the Argentinian aircraft carrier, *ARA Veinticinco de Mayo*. On 1st May two events occurred that indicated something was afoot. First, we detected the *General Belgrano* group steaming eastwards, and began to trail; second, HMS *Splendid* sighted an Argentinian Type 42 destroyer escorting the three Type 69 frigates to the west of the Falkland Islands where the Type 42 left them, before transiting back to the north. Intelligence was then received that the *ARA Veinticinco de Mayo* and her Task Group were heading south-east, thus revealing a pincer movement against our own Carrier Task Group.

The aim was to sink the *ARA Veinticinco de Mayo* as it was believed this would have a devastating effect on Argentine public morale. The closest submarine was *Splendid*; but unfortunately she never made contact. Despite this disappointment there was still the opportunity to remove one arm of the pincer by ordering *Conqueror* to attack the *General Belgrano.*

When we detected the group on 1st May we could not attack them, because they were outside the 200-mile Total Exclusion Zone declared by the UK Government. On 2nd May we received a signal changing our Rules of Engagement (ROE) and ordering *Conqueror* to sink the *General Belgrano.* At 1400 hours we fired three torpedoes from a range of 1200 yards; two hit and the *General Belgrano* sank in less than an hour. Initially there was a cheer from the crew because we had successfully completed the task given us by our government; but within seconds you could hear a pin drop as each of us thought about the 1100 Argentinian sailors onboard the *General Belgrano*, who were also doing the task set them by their government, abandoning ship in a rough, cold sea far from land. We successfully evaded an hour's apparent depth-charging from the 2 destroyers.

The sinking of *General Belgrano* proved to be a decisive point because it forced the Argentinian surface navy back inside their territorial limits for the remainder of the conflict. However, this was obviously not known at the time, when we believed the Argentinian Navy still posed a substantial threat. To counter the surface and sub-surface threats *Conqueror* took up station to the north of the Falkland Islands, from where she could corner-flag in support of any of the UK Boats patrolling the Argentine twelve-mile limit.

The next task for *Conqueror* involved going into the gulf of San Matias, where the entrance channel is only 26 fathoms deep. Having penetrated the bay successfully *Conqueror* then proceeded due west to the 12-mile limit, a distance of 75 nautical miles, in search of one of the Argentinian Type 42 destroyers. The target never materialised and the submarine left the bay having remained inside for three days.

On day 56 of the patrol we went onto half rations, as we did not know how long the campaign would last and we could not restore. The plan was to go onto quarter rations on day 75 if required.

So, what was a typical day on patrol like? My two main memories are watch keeping and food! Some of us did six hours on, six hours off, others four hours on, eight off. This routine gave us the ability to conduct repairs on a 24-hour basis. Some of the lads were 'hot-bunking'; which is two sailors sharing one bunk. The person who got up would take his 'Oppo's' (friend's) sleeping bag out from under the mattress, put his own there and change over the family photos. He would then have something to eat before going on watch. The exact times were staggered from twenty minutes before the hour to thirty minutes after to ensure we did not have everyone changing over at the same time. The first question on going on watch was 'what has happened in the land battle?' The next was 'what has happened since I was last on watch?' *Conqueror* was invariably at periscope depth with her periscopes and radio masts raised and all sonars manned to collect as much information as possible. During the night the control room was in 'black-lighting' – just enough light to see the instruments, but not enough to spoil the night-vision of the periscope watch keepers. Working in black lighting was very tiring.

Throughout the boat, men went about their daily routine. In the galley the chefs prepared four meals a day. Mealtimes were the only social occasions each day and were very important; the quality of the meals had a huge impact on morale. Despite being on half rations for the second half of the patrol, the chefs performed magnificently. Meanwhile engineers were constantly going around the Boat checking the equipment was working correctly and carrying out routine maintenance or repairs where necessary.

Everyone went about their business as quietly as possible, aware of their sleeping Oppos and, more importantly, conscious that any noise they made might be heard by a patrolling Argentinian submarine. In the control room the sonar operators were listening intently to the noises in the sea and monitoring their equipment to see if our low frequency sonars had picked up anything that could pose a threat to us or our Task Group further to the east. If they got a 'sniff' of an enemy submarine everyone throughout our Boat was quietly alerted and all noisy activity would stop. Tools would be placed gently on mats, the galley would stop beating bread dough, those who were off-watch watching films would stop the projectors – and everyone would be thinking: 'Is this an Argentinian submarine?' Some were more frightened than others, and each of us dealt with it in our own way. Sometimes this period would last for five minutes and pass. Once it lasted for four hours and we came very close to firing a torpedo.

And then it would be time for another watch change, and life went on.

We remained on station, despite a number of defects, because a nuclear submarine has redundancy – some systems have four different, independent supplies. We also relied on the inventiveness of the engineers and their ability to repair from first principles and manufacture spare parts. Most importantly, we relied on the courage of the crew. For example: at one point in the patrol we got a wire wrapped around our propeller making a distinctive noise. We knew Argentinian submarines were in our area so we had to get rid of the wire. All the divers volunteered to do this very dangerous task. It was very rough – far too rough by peacetime rules to put people on top of the submarine, let alone put a diver in to the water - and we were close to Argentina. The captain surfaced the submarine and eight of us went onto the outside – we knew that if an Argentinian aircraft, ship or submarine was detected the captain would shut the hatch, dive the submarine and leave us to drown. Luckily we were successful and we all came home to tell the tale. The diver who successfully removed the wire was awarded the Distinguished Service Medal for his bravery.

Our final task was to act as an air early warning platform by sitting on the 12-mile limit just off one of the Argentinian air bases. As flights of hostile aircraft took off, their type and number were passed to the Commander of the Task Force by satellite communications, giving him 45 minutes warning, which allowed him to vector Harriers on combat air patrol to intercept. By shooting down one or two of them, the Harriers forced the remaining planes to turn back and return to base. These planes used to jettison their bombs before landing, and they did so around the 12-mile limit where we were stationed; it was a very rude awakening for us submariners. All the boats employed in this task experienced some random bombing, luckily without damage.

The Falklands Islands were recaptured on 14th June, and HMS *Conqueror* was ordered home two days later. We arrived back in Scotland on 3rd July after 90 days continuously at sea. We never saw the Falkland Islands.

****

Chapter 2 - Britain Prepares for War

When Prime Minister Thatcher announced the formation of a Task Force to re-take the Falkland Islands on 4th April 1982, the British armed forces were largely unready and ill-equipped for war, let alone one 8,000 miles away. The logistics of transporting thousands of soldiers, their equipment, aircraft and all the necessary support staff was the biggest military undertaking since the Second World War and was taking place after a period of economic recession which saw military spending reduced in all areas.

However, in the following days and weeks, a remarkable effort was put in by both military and civilian organisations to get ready for the task in hand. Royal Navy Dockyards across the UK and at Gibraltar saw 24/7 working to prepare both Royal Navy ships and to convert civilian ships (STUFT –Ships Taken Up From Trade) that had been 'commandeered' into troop transport ships, hospital ships and much more, with helicopter decks fitted, operating theatres and hospital wards constructed. The famous *QE2* became a massive troop transport ship while the schools' cruise ship SS *Uganda* became a fully-fledged and equipped hospital ship.

Meanwhile to assist the logistical effort, the British Army and Royal Navy developed a base at Ascension Island, a British territory in the mid-Atlantic 4,300 miles, from the UK and 3,800 miles from the Falkland Islands. Although it had an airfield with an excellent area, it had little hard standing and no port to handle large ships. Ascension became a major hub of activity and was a stopping off point for many Task Force ships, as well as for the RAF for resupply of materials and air-to-air refuelling for the Vulcan bombers that bombed Stanley airfield.

In total, the Task Force comprised 127 ships of which there were 43 Royal Navy vessels, 22 Royal Fleet Auxiliary ships, and 62 merchant ships.

Intelligence

Mark Norbury, Engineering Operations, MOD

Intelligence Gathering

I was seconded to the Royal Engineer Operations desk in the MOD during the Falklands conflict arriving a few days before the fleet sailed south.

Grid References

As the fleet sailed south the Engineer Operations desk realised that two lines of longitude joined in Falkland Sound necessitating the use of 2-letter prefixes on all ground grid references and the mapping of the islands did not really suit itself to ground operations let alone joint operations. The Royal Engineer Survey School at Hermitage was tasked with producing a map that was more user friendly to all three services and capable of accurate use by all units. Within 48 hours they came up with a product which was then tested using navigators from both the Royal Navy and RAF. With this done about a thousand copies of the map were printed and flown to Ascension Island to join the fleet.

Local Knowledge

At the start intelligence of any sort was strictly limited and largely hinged around a book written by Capt Ewen Southby-Tailyour who in 1978 commanded a Royal Marine detachment on the Falklands during which time he sailed the island waters and made extensive notes which proved invaluable during the conflict.

The lack of intelligence for the islands themselves however resulted in the Engineer Operations desk interviewing all returning island families to collect information. The returnees were spoken to by a military and civil engineer together with a draughtsman. The interview would go something like…

Which settlement did you live in? What was the layout of the settlement? How many buildings were there? What was the layout of the rooms in the buildings? Where were the doors and windows and did they hinge right or left opening in which direction? Where there locks on any buildings or doors? Where were the light switches and light fittings? How was power generated and by what? Where were the power cables and fuel lines? How long was the airstrip and its compass bearing? Was there any slope to the strip and if so how much and in which direction?

From these questions the draughtsman produced detailed drawings of the settlements duly annotated. These notes were compiled into folders one for each settlement and spread out on a huge table in the Old War Office building. The first people to recognise the value of these folders were Special Forces who appeared daily to update their knowledge.

Airstrips for Hercules

One day Special Forces posed a question asking where the Argentinians could be operating Hercules away from Stanley. We had the lengths of the airstrips but needed the length of airstrip to get aircraft off the ground. The RAF conducted a trial at RAF Lyneham using a Hercules empty apart from its crew and sufficient fuel to return to the 'mainland'. The Engineer Operations desk was only interested in the distance to lift-off ignoring any obstacles. The RAF provided a figure which was applied to our settlement folders and as Special Forces went ashore at…they saw a Hercules climbing into the cloud.

****

BBC Monitoring Service

In 1981 I joined the BBC Monitoring Service as an engineer and worked there until 1988. The Monitoring Service was then located at Caversham Park just outside Reading. There was a technical site a further 3 miles towards Henley, Crowsley Park, where the massive aerials and satellite dishes were located that enabled the radio signals from around the world to be detected. This period was a momentous time historically with the collapse of Communism in Eastern Europe, the assassination attempt on the Pope in 1981 and of course, the Falklands War in 1982. The BBC's Monitoring Service was then funded by a direct grant from the Foreign and Commonwealth Office (FCO) and, as such, had a quasi-governmental role. Each day they published a publication called Summary of World Broadcasts (SWB). SWB had been published since the run-up to the Second World War and ran until March 2001. One way to think of the BBC Monitoring Service at the time in question was that it performed a complementary role to GCHQ. Whereas GCHQ monitored private communications, the BBC Monitoring Service focused on broadcasts from around the world that were meant for the public. One of the key roles of the engineers at Crowsley was to select the appropriate antennas and frequencies for the clearest signals for the monitors (translators and journalists) to transcribe for inclusion in SWB.

As well as the above role, the engineers performed a wide range of technical tasks. This included measuring the frequencies of European broadcast stations for the European Broadcast Union (EBU) to check that they were precisely tuned so as not to cause interference with other broadcast stations. They acted as a relay for Radio Canada International (RCI) and Voice of America (VOA) programmes from North America to the transmitters located at strategic points about the UK for beaming into Eastern Europe. They also monitored the frequencies and broadcast times of pirate radio stations. So together, they had a lot of expertise in international and national radio broadcasting at all frequency bands from Long Wave, Medium Wave and Shortwave to the FM broadcast bands, right up to the TV broadcast frequencies and the satellite channels used to relay broadcasts around the world.

When the Falklands War started in April 1982, the BBC Monitoring Service was called upon to undertake various roles in support of the war effort. Firstly, the day-to-day business of monitoring the content of radio broadcasts from around the world became vital so that BBC News and the FCO could assess other countries' reactions to the war and gauge whether they were indeed supporting the UK's case for perpetrating the war. Then, perhaps little known by the public at the time, there was a propaganda war carried on, by both sides, alongside the military efforts. The Argentines broadcast, in English, on various frequencies to the British troops in the South Atlantic to try and convince them of the justice of the Argentinian cause in seeking to occupy the Falklands and generally demoralise them. The engineers at Crowsley Park were asked to try and detect these signals so that the FCO knew their content. The nature of these broadcasts seemed very strange to this young engineer. They were quite ethereal in style with oft-repeated statements such as *"I am Argentina, I am a spirit*". If they ever had an opportunity to hear these, what the average British soldier or sailor made of them was a point of speculation amongst us. We thought it was most likely to be mocking laughter.

However, the British also engaged in a propaganda war. The Government took over two BBC transmitters on Ascension Island to broadcast such to the Falklands and Argentina. This was controversial for BBC senior management, who treasured the BBC's independence of Government. Thus, we engineers were covertly asked, by BBC management, to daily record these broadcasts off-air so that they would be fully aware of what was being said on their transmitters. Technically this was a non-trivial task because the transmitters on Ascension were directed to the south-west towards the Falklands Islands and Argentina. So, we had to detect their broadcasts off the back of the aerials. Indeed, we could only get transcribable signals on days when the atmospheric conditions affecting shortwave propagation across the world were just right. Further, as an extension to our role making hourly checks on which BBC Russian and East European language broadcasts were being jammed by the eastern bloc, we also monitored the Argentinian jamming of the FCO's Radio Atlantica del Sur (as their propaganda station was called).

If the Falklands war had ever resulted in the Argentinians attacking the mainland United Kingdom, there would have been other roles for BBC engineers at Caversham and Crowsley. They were also responsible for maintaining emergency communication channels for Governmental broadcasts over the BBC during times of crisis. Fortunately, it never came to that.

Thanks to Ian Liston-Smith and Alistair Bolton, two former colleagues from BBC Monitoring Service, who checked my text for accuracy.

****

The Dockyards

Andrew Cave, HMS Hermes

A 17 year-old on board HMS Hermes in 1982, Andrew has campaigned to gain recognition for the 'dockies' who prepared the Royal Navy ships and other civilian/merchant ships for war.

Unsung Heroes

HM Naval Base Portland saw frenzied activity as the stores, equipment and personnel were assembled for the 8,000-mile journey to the South Atlantic in 1982. The dockyard performed miracles working around the clock to support both the Royal and Merchant Navies including RFAs and was soon crammed with trucks full of supplies with even more loads backed up outside the gates. It has been well documented that the dockyards did as much welding in a week as they normally do in four months. Portland was normally responsible for making sure that warships were ready to join the fleet by testing the crew's readiness through drills and exercises such as firefighting, damage control and simulated enemy attacks, and this process dramatically increased as more warships were sent to the South Atlantic.

Rosyth dockyard had converted five trawlers to be used as minesweepers for this conflict and once completed they sailed to Portland under the White Ensign where the dockyard workforce installed replenishment at sea equipment and deck fittings for the sweeping gear. They all sailed on the 25th April and once in the operational area spent a lot of time transporting troops, including Special Forces, and equipment in often appalling weather. After the Argentine surrender they were able to sweep a number of mines that had been laid in Stanley harbour.

Other vessels also went to Portland to have replenishment at sea equipment fitted such as the tanker *British Esk* which had been requisitioned from BP to keep the fleet refuelled. A fleet maintenance group was also in attendance at Portland and became heavily involved in the material preparation of warships, RFAs and ships taken up from trade.

The first ship to sail from the United Kingdom to the South Atlantic was the Royal Maritime Auxiliary Service Tug *Typhoon* which sailed from Portland on the 4th April 1982 after being made ready by the dockyard workforce. She was heavily involved in logistical duties during the conflict transferring fresh water to the Task Force and loading some of 17 Brigade onto MV *Norland* in preparation for the landings at San Carlos.

On the 8th June 1982 RFAs *Sir Galahad* and *Sir Tristram* were attacked by Argentinian Skyhawks whilst preparing to unload Welsh Guards at Fitzroy which resulted in RFA *Sir Galahad* being hit by a number of bombs which exploded causing fires and terrible damage. Sadly, this attack caused the deaths of 48 crew and soldiers. On the 21st June 1982, *Typhoon's* bosun performed the very sad duty of placing the Welsh flag onboard the *Sir Galahad* before she was towed out to sea by the tug and sunk by torpedoes from HMS *Onyx*.

****

Tony England, Chairman of the Chatham Dockyard Historical Society

Tony's father and grandfather worked at Chatham dockyard in the years prior to the Falklands War.

The Last Battle - Chatham Dockyard and the Falklands

The 1981 Defence White Paper tabled by the Defence Secretary John Nott in June 1981 included swingeing cuts to the Royal Navy with

- a general reduction in the surface fleet,
- the proposed sale of the new aircraft carrier HMS *Invincible* to Australia,
- the withdrawal of the ice patrol ship HMS *Endurance* ('The Red Plum') from the South Atlantic (enhancing the view of

the Argentine Junta that Britain was no longer interested in protecting the Falkland Islands)

- the phasing out of any large amphibious ability which would have seen the demise of the two amphibious assault ships HMS *Intrepid* and HMS *Fearless*.
- It also included, of course, the closure of Chatham Dockyard.

HMS *Endurance* had a close relationship with Chatham Dockyard and her Captain Nicholas Barker commented in his book "Beyond Endurance" that "*It was the kind of unity that comes from mutual pain that let our Chatham refit continue without any form of industrial disruption.*"

The ship sailed for sea trials on 7th September 1981 and was due to return in May 1982. In the event she made a triumphal return to the Medway in August 1982 and according to the captain "*It was the greatest day of our lives. HMS Endurance was the only HM ship to return from the Falklands to the Medway and the people of south-east England waited to welcome her in their tens of thousands.*"

Apart from the "Red Plum" other Royal Navy ships involved in the Falklands War that had undergone fairly recent refits at Chatham were HMS *Minerva* (Exocet conversion), the Rothesay class frigates HMS *Plymouth* and HMS *Yarmouth*, the Valiant class nuclear submarine HMS *Valiant* and later, almost straight from her refit and refuelling, her sister submarine HMS *Warspite.* (HMS *Conqueror* had her refit and refuelling in 1977).

Although the dockyard had in some respects begun running down, the workshops did join the prefabrication programme, sending metalwork to both Portsmouth and Devonport. In addition, there were also many ships collecting stores (the dockyard was still a major stores and equipment provider) during the period including RFA *Black Rover*, the landing ships RFA *Sir Percivale* and RFA *Sir Lancelot*, the landing craft HMAV *Ardennes*.

Chatham was home to the 'Stand-by Squadron', mainly Rothesay and Tribal class frigates on the proposed "disposals" list.

Some of these were now needed to replace the ships that had been allocated to the Falklands Task Force. HMS *Falmouth* was one of the first to be made ready for sea (using spares taken from HMS *Berwick*) and she was recommissioned in June 1982 to serve in home waters and NATO areas. HMS *Berwick* was in a poorer condition with serious corrosion problems because of lack of maintenance, but after a superb effort was able to be recommissioned in August and joined the 5th Frigate Squadron.

The Tribal class frigates had been laid up since 1979/80 but were now needed to replace the losses occurring in the Falklands. HMS *Zulu* was able to be recommissioned in August, and HMS *Tartar* was sent to Devonport and HMS *Gurkha* to Rosyth for eventual recommissioning. The remaining Tribal class were stripped for spares to allow the other three to return to sea. HMS *Zulu* had parts taken from her sister ship HMS *Nubian* - echoes of HMS *Zubian* from 1916!

****

Jack Bedbrook RCNC, Managing Director HM Dockyard Devonport 1979-1984

By courtesy of Jack's widow Sylvia Bedbrook

<u>The Devonport Dockyard's Contribution</u>

In 1982, Devonport Dockyard was the largest ship repair organisation in Western Europe. The workforce numbered 13,500 and there were nine blue collar and five white collar Trade nions, often working with internecine friction.

The Devonport programme included aircraft carriers, a triple stream of hunter killer nuclear submarines, diesel submarines, frigates, destroyers, survey ships and Royal Fleet Auxiliaries. In fact, 65% of the navy's ships were refitted and modernised at Devonport.

It is a trait of the British, that wars and conflicts bring out the best in people. This was dramatically demonstrated in the Second World War and the Falklands War was no exception.

The Task Force

A Fleet was quickly assembled, consisting of Aircraft Carriers, Types 12, 21 and 22 Frigates, Assault Ships, RFAs, Fishery Protection Vessels, Ocean Tugs, Survey Ships and a Hunter Killer Submarine.

However, it was quickly realised that the Task Force would require Merchant **S**hips **T**aken **U**p **F**rom **T**rade (STUFT), to transport the men and equipment to the war area, some 8,000 miles away.

Many of these ships were dotted around European ports, and steps were taken to commandeer these vessels and sail them to dockyards so that essential conversion work could be undertaken in the minimum of time to equip them for their war role.

Modus Operandi for STUFT Ships

Having located the vessels in their various ports, a cell in MOD(N) decided what was required in each vessel and to which yard they should be allocated. Each yard nominated a professional officer, in Devonport's case a Constructor who was a naval architect, who would visit the ships. By experience and thumbnail sketches he would then telephone back to the yard the material requirements. By this means, the bulk of the material would have been allocated and would be waiting on the dockside when the ship arrived in the yard.

Time was of the essence. There was no time for detailed drawings, approval and the usual peacetime procedures. Ordering and tendering procedures were set aside. Professionalism and experience were the order of the day.

Upon the ship's arrival, an acceptance meeting was held with officers to agree the work package and to settle the conversion details. On completion of the meeting, dockyard middle management and first-line supervisors briefed the workforce on board the ship. Everyone was encouraged to volunteer ideas and these were often used if it meant a saving in time or labour.

Middle management spent most of their time on board either in direct supervision or discussing additional requirements with the customers. This greatly aided the task and conveyed to the workforce the urgency and involvement of all concerned. The usual administrative procedures were abandoned for these projects although sufficient records were made to satisfy accounting needs.

Demarcation of work between trades and Trade Unions, as with demarcation between blue collar and white-collar personnel was completely set aside. For example, shipwrights did joiners' work, coppersmiths did plumbers' work, officers swept up dirt and did labourers' duty etc etc.

But this was a national emergency and war - there was only one trade union viz Great Britain. The workforce was carried forward on a wave of patriotism. The one aim was to get the job done as quickly as possible and get the ships ready to join the Task Force.

The Ships Involved and the Dockyard's Response

On 16th April, the first merchant ship, the ill-fated *Atlantic Conveyor*, arrived at Devonport for her conversion. During the next ten weeks, ten more ships arrived for conversion to their military role. They comprised four container ships, two roll on/roll off ferries, two tankers, a cable repair ship, a dry cargo vessel and an ocean tug. The average time taken for a conversion was of the order of eight days using two 12-hour shifts.

Whilst the merchant ships were being converted, the dockyard brought forward the refit completion dates of a number of warships already in hand, and where necessary fitted additional weapons and war equipment.

The Task in Conversion

The major task in converting the merchant ships lay in the manufacture and fitting of large structural units, such as aircraft landing platforms, aircraft hangars, and structural extensions for additional accommodation. Six hundred tons of steel were fabricated for this purpose, and 400,000 feet of welding was deposited.

Considerable work was also undertaken to cater for the six to seven-fold increase in the number of men who had to be supported on board in the new role. This included additional galleys, laundries, bathrooms, hospitals and lifesaving equipment. The long periods at sea that were expected meant that replenishment at sea arrangements together with additional fuel tanks, pumps and pipework had to be designed and installed. Guns, communications equipment and firefighting gear were also fitted to equip the ships for the new war role.

Round the Clock Working

There was a workforce of around 250 men per shift on board, with an additional 100 involved in shift working ashore, in support of these conversions.

The workforce was organised into twelve-hour shifts with management overlapping at each end of the shift to achieve continuity. Twice daily meetings were held at the start and end of the shifts and discussed the progress of work against the schedule. New ideas were discussed so that there was a common feeling of achievement. These plan-of-the-day meetings laid down objectives for each shift and very briefly itemised the rest of the programme, thus enabling everyone to feel in control of their own destinies and more involved with the project. A sense of competition was also achieved between the shifts at these meetings and this enabled some outstanding targets to be attained during the conversions.

Most of the management team and its workforce had been together for a number of years and were able to build on known strengths. The expertise, knowledge and trust that had been developed in the management team and within the industrial workforce enabled the entire team to work as a single unit. The whole exercise enabled the dockyard to achieve quite remarkable targets.

****

Mike Huitson, Portsmouth Dockyard

Falklands Memories - Portsmouth Dockyard

With a redundancy letter in my pocket and feeling very let down by the government's job slashing decision I left work and drove home along the M275. Suddenly six Sea Harrier jets appeared alongside me flying really slowly towards the dockyard. It was surreal as I could clearly see the pilots in their cockpits.

Upon arriving home, I received a telephone call from a friend asking me if I'd heard the news – that the Argentinians had hoisted their flag on the Falkland Islands 8,000 miles away.

As I reached for my atlas to check where the Falkland Islands were my boss called and asked me if I would return to work.

The next day was incredible – a sight I'd never seen before (or since). Lorries laden with stores and equipment stretched nose to tail through the entire length of the dockyard and beyond into the gridlocked Portsmouth streets, all bound for the ships of the Task Force.

Despite the staff feeling very aggrieved by the government's decision everyone rallied and gave 100%. I didn't hear "*it's not my job*" throughout the conflict. Jobs that would previously have taken weeks to complete were finished in days. Workers came up with innovative ideas and solutions to resolve problems rather than negativity.

I worked nightshift for months and frequently arrived home from my shift at 9am to then receive a request to return to work. My role was maintenance electrician of the dockside cranes and plant. Capital plant and machinery were all working 24/7 which was way beyond their design intent. Hence machinery was breaking down and required speedy repairs.

With a colossal amount of steel fabricating and modifications being carried out on most vessels the night sky over Portsmouth was continually lit up with all the arc welding flashes.

The atmosphere on site was electric; people you've never spoken to would approach you with updates or *"hot off the press"* news. There was a real sense of *"we can do this,"* and we did. We all watched the Task Force leave Portsmouth on April 5th. I remember being shown copies of a couple of ships' signals. HMS *Hermes* thanked the yard for "*their magnificent support*" and RFA *Stromness* signalled "*the dockyard is a worker of miracles*." Great for morale of course and "who knows" (we all quietly thought) our achievements could save our jobs.

****

Loading the Ships

Howard Ormerod, Civilian Crew, Atlantic Conveyor

Preparing *Atlantic Conveyor* for War

While serving on RFA *Fort Grange*, I met Liz, a nursing officer based at the Royal Naval Hospital in Stonehouse, Plymouth. I moved into a rented property with her in late 1981. I did ask her to marry me; an offer which was not readily accepted at the time.

On Friday 2nd April, we were first told to start stocking and resupplying ships with all haste. Some ships were already deployed. For us preparations meant round-the-clock working. Additional ships (STUFT) arrived for conversion and storing. When it arrived, on 16th April, one such ship attracted quite a lot of attention. This was the *Atlantic Conveyor*.

Another ship requisitioned and sent to Gibraltar to be converted into a floating hospital was the SS *Uganda*. When a call came from the hospital to Liz, telling her to cut short her time off from night duty and report immediately for possible deployment, we realised that there was going to be a hospital ship. She, along with many other members of the RN clinical and non-clinical staff, was flown to Gibraltar to join the ship, SS *Uganda* and which then departed Gibraltar on 19th April.

I constantly thought about Liz. We hadn't been together that long anyway and there was no end date for our separation, not to mention whatever might happen next.

What did happen next was that on or about 18th April, my boss in Plymouth called me in, explained that it had been decided that, in addition to its high priority cargo of aircraft and the multitude of army stores, *Atlantic Conveyor* would carry a range of stores to supply the Task Force – hardware, electronics and fresh and frozen foods etc. The ship needed someone with the right background and experience. *"Would I volunteer?"* he asked.

"Yes" I said. I had an idea that it might just be possible that *Atlantic Conveyor* and *Uganda* might meet, although hopefully in non-medical circumstances. I reported on board 20th April. The

ship was buzzing with activities of all kinds. Stuff was everywhere. A pile of NAAFI goods, including "nutty" was in an exposed position on one of the vehicle decks where it had been left. This was quickly moved.

Because of the number of personnel on *Atlantic Conveyor*, the ship's accommodation and ancillary areas were under strain. We shared a cabin with, I think, six Wessex helicopter pilots of 848 NAS. We had no working party to help with stowing and later offload and all we had by way of mechanical assistance was a diesel powered forklift truck and a hand pallet transporter. We would have to improvise.

What I had was: seven large refrigerated articulated vehicle trailers full of frozen food with one in reserve. Half a trailer load of fruit and vegetables. Containers of electrical and electronic spares, and NAAFI Stores, various items of general naval stores and finally several boxes of 'Chaff' and other "in transit" goods for nominated ships.

The plan was for the foodstuff, the electrical /electronic stores and the NAAFI stores to be passed over to RFA *Stromness*.

On 25th April, after testing the Sea Harriers' ability to land on *Atlantic Conveyor's* foredeck, we left Plymouth. The first stop was Freetown, Sierra Leone where we replenished the ship's fuel. The journey to Freetown was largely uneventful as far as I was concerned - checking, documenting and more checking. For example, the refrigerated trailers needed to be checked at least every six hours, to make sure that failure of the refrigeration system did not go undetected. After sailing and then transferring the Harriers to HMS *Hermes* and HMS *Invincible*, most of the rest of the stores I had were duly sent across, again by helicopter, to the escorts, and other ships.

****

Tony Babb, Weapons Action Repair Team (WART), HMS Southampton

Preparing for War

My time on HMS *Southampton* started in 1981. 1982 was momentous for the Royal Navy, but at this time of need we were still doing trials in the channel.

Of course, the Royal Navy, like all our military, learns from incidents, and it is incredible just how quickly they reacted. First, a two-week war workup with our first missile firing then into Portsmouth Dockyard for two weeks of modifications.

The 4.5" magazine suddenly held twice as many shells as normal, there was just enough room left to send shells up the hoists, but that was all. They also fitted 20 tons of pig iron in the engine room bilges to counteract the extra weight. Naval Gunfire Support was one of the main tasks of ships at this time, so it made sense.

As a defence against sea-skimming missiles, the safety firing arcs on the gun were readjusted to nothing so that we could try and fire at incoming missiles over the bow. Better to risk knocking a small hole in my ship seemed to be the lesser of two evils.

Most of our ordinary upper deck lockers, which would normally be full of seamanship items, buckets and brushes etc., now had extra 3" chaff rockets in them; these were our only real Exocet defence. Draped over them was heavy coir matting which we had to keep cool with water when in the tropics.

Two 20mm World War 2 vintage guns were mounted on the back end and we could at least throw some more lead at the enemy just like those in the thick of the war. When the Task Force had left in April, we gave them our General-Purpose Machine-Gun deck mounts and guns. Now it was our turn to go, and we could get the guns, but no deck mounts.

Emergency Life Saving Apparatus (ELSAs) was delivered and placed in all compartments that were manned. Consisting simply of a hood with a small bottle of compressed air, they gave six minutes' breathing duration and comforted those working inside the ship.

Personal survival was high on my priority list and our everyday clothing was polyester cotton, which melted in extreme heat when it caught fire. We were each issued two pairs of cotton overalls, and we were instructed to buy cotton underwear.

The last change was a new routine of State 2 Condition Z relaxed for Defence watches. This had the benefit of compartmentalising the ship in all war states. All the passageway doors had two stripes painted on them, and these would be closed using only 2 of the many clips that normally held them shut.

Just before we left Portsmouth to head south a young member of the crew asked me quietly the following question, *'will our weapons systems work?'* An answer immediately formed in my mind, *"they will, but will our operators use it properly?"*

I have always been far too truthful, well known for opening my mouth to "change feet", and I had my concerns, who didn't? Quickly I changed it to *'they will, and I will do everything I can to keep it working'*, keeping my reservations to myself for once in my life.

He needed reassurance, and my answer hopefully did that. I was 34 years old at the time and possibly twice his age, tact was never my strong suit, but maybe that's what the prospect of war does to you.

****

Stephen Potts, Military Police at Military Port Marchwood

<u>Military Port, Marchwood - Loading the Ships</u>

On 2nd April 1982, I was serving as a constable in the Ministry of Defence Police at Military Port Marchwood in Hampshire. MP Marchwood was the home port of the RFA LSL (Landing Ship Logistic) fleet, which included the ill-fated RFA *Sir Galahad* and RFA *Sir Tristram*.

The port became a hive of activity following the Argentine invasion on 2nd April. Soon after the invasion RFA *Sir Lancelot* and RFA *Sir Percivale* were in port and being loaded with munitions and the men of 45 Commando. The 52 Port and Maritime Regiment were rushing about in their Fiat-Allis forklifts, busy loading pallet loads of munitions into the belly of the ships. I watched in amazement as three Royal Marine Gazelle helicopters were landed onto the helipads of each ship and rotors tucked away. No mean feat especially when flown into such a small area.

The Port Regiment worked through the night loading the ships until the holds were stacked high with ammunition and Maritime Regiment ferried mexi-floats around the harbour and they too were craned onto the side of the ships. I'd never seen the ships' holds stacked so high with munitions. My sergeant visited me that evening to watch what was happening. He thought that a peace deal would be struck and the ships would return without a shot being fired. I disagreed with him believing that neither our Prime Minister Thatcher nor General Galtieri, head of the Argentine Junta, would back down and that there would be a conflict.

The ships sailed off on the 5th April. I heard one of the 52 Port Regiment mutter, *'I hope we don't have to unload that lot!'*

Note: a mexi-float is a landing raft normally used to off-load supplies from ships to land. They have a crew of 6 and range between 20 – 38 metres long.

****

Peter Galloway, Weapons Engineering Officer, HMS Glamorgan

Film Interrupted by the War

I joined HMS *Glamorgan* as Weapons Engineering Officer on the 1st March 1982 and a month later we were off Gibraltar conducting missile test firings, together with other destroyers. The Commander-in-Chief Fleet, Admiral Sir John Fieldhouse, was on board and had taken up residence in the Admiral's accommodation forward. One evening, the officers decided to watch a film in the wardroom and at a particularly tense moment in the film, a door from the wardroom into the captain's day-cabin was opened and bright lighting flooded the screen.

"*Shut that b.... y door*" grumbled someone from the rear of the stalls.

"*So sorry*", came a timid and squeaky reply, "*But do you have a copy of Jane's Fighting Ships?*"

We then realised that 'Squeaky' was the Admiral's Flag Lieutenant and we had better oblige. The film was stopped and on went the main lights. The book was quickly located in the wardroom library and we sent him on his way, mumbling his apologies and thanks. Ten minutes, the film had progressed to the point where the hero was, or at least we all hoped he was, about to make an advance towards the very pretty heroine, when the same door opened and light flooded the screen again.

"*Oh really! For goodness sake! Now what?*" came the same voice from the back.

"*Do you happen to have a copy of Jane's Fighting Aircraft?*" came Squeaky's next request.

However, we were not to enjoy the possible moment of passion on screen since a few moments later we heard the pipe "*Hands to Flying Stations*". Since it was now about 2130 hours and there had been no plans for night flying on the programme, we realised that something significant was up. It was the night of 1st to 2nd April and the Argentinians were on the move and invading the Falkland Islands.

We headed south and it was to be another 101 days before we were to put a foot ashore again.

****

Steve Walsh, Bombardier, Royal Artillery on board the QE2

Call Sign - Golf 33 - Getting Ready

I was a full bombardier within the regiment, 88 Battery Royal Artillery, and by now an experienced artillery forward observer.

Typically, the forward observation teams were made up of five team members, one officer with one full bombardier and three gunners. Our role was to be deployed with the infantry and provide the artillery support to the infantry by advising and delivering artillery fire for the infantry commanders.

In early May, having been placed on 12 hours' notice to deploy, we were working long hours to prepare for a potential deployment to the South Atlantic. I was immediately press ganged into helping with the preparations. 12 x L118 Artillery Light Guns and supporting equipment were being packed up in readiness.

I spent the next seven days taking lorry loads of stores to ships such as the MV *Norland* currently docked at Hull. 29 Battery had now been tasked to support 2nd Battalion of the Parachute Regiment (2 Para), as the deployment became a reality.

I was told that 97 Battery (Lawson's Company) were to be deployed on the second wave and would travel on the world's most luxurious cruise ship, the *QE2*. They required an additional Forward Observation team. We were to support the newly formed 5 Infantry Brigade. The Brigade consisted of Scots Guards, Welsh Guards and a battalion of Gurkhas. We had never worked with the Guards and I understood both battalions had spent much of their recent deployments on royal duties guarding Buckingham Palace and the like.

We had now been formed into our Forward Observation Team, call sign 'Golf 33'. As normal, our team would consist of a Forward Observation Officer (FOO), we had been allocated Captain Mike Johnson, myself as second-in-command and three gunner soldiers, Gunners Moctor DeVos, Mark Woodhouse (Woody) and Dean Jenkins (Jenks). I was quite happy with our team of experienced soldiers.

****

Tony Pitt, Commander RFA Sir Percivale
Extracts from his personal diary

An Inauspicious Start

RFA *Sir Percivale* was loading cargo at Zeebrugge when the orders were received to expedite the operation and proceed to Marchwood to prepare for Operation Corporate. At this time certain officers, including the Commanding Officer, were playing golf at Ostende and, although a driver was despatched, he did not carry out his instructions and the message was not passed until the round was completed.

Meanwhile, as the weather was becoming foggy, the Chief Officer decided, with the local pilot, that it would be prudent to sail the vessel and await the arrival of the errant officers clear of the harbour confines. A very worrying time for the CO to find his command had sailed. A short boat ride later and the two were reunited and the vessel proceeded to Marchwood Military Port (MMP).

The ship berthed, bows in on the north side of MMP jetty at 0445hrs 3rd April 1982 which was a Saturday. Because the ship was shortly due to commence refit she had to be completely re-stocked with fuel, lubricating oil, fresh water, provisions, bonded stores and medical stores. Signals were hastily compiled and sent. All that could be done then was to sit back and wait to see what happened.

Throughout Sunday and Monday the loading of cargo and stores continued as and when it became available. A lot was accomplished in a short time. The passengers commenced arriving late Monday morning and continued throughout the afternoon. Three Gazelle helicopters of Brigade Air Squadron were also embarked in the early afternoon.

The ship finally sailed from the jetty on Monday the 5th April at 1820 hours, 14 inches over-loaded and in possession of a quite lethal deck cargo. That night the ship anchored in Lyme Bay, well clear of prying eyes.

The period at anchor was spent conducting routine drills for the embarked force and generally settling down. The embarked forces including 45 Commando, Royal Artillery batteries and various other units totalling 310 Persons. It was also a period for taking stock to see what we might have missed. It was realised that food, water, beer and minerals would be a problem in the long term and, from day one, these were all rationed.

****

Clifford Ball, MOD Royal Naval Supply – HMS Hermes

Getting *Hermes* Ready for War

I was serving with the Ministry of Defence as the Officer in Charge at the Royal Naval Supply and Transport Service MT Depot, Northern Parade, Portsmouth. It was the largest of its kind in the country and supported Portsmouth Naval Base, the Royal Navy and Royal Fleet Auxiliary ships based there.

Late in the afternoon of Friday 2nd April, the very day of the Argentinian invasion, the phone rang. I was summoned to a secret meeting in the naval base where together with a group of others, I was made privy to the fact that the Prime Minister had decided to despatch a Royal Navy Task Force to retake the islands. It was further announced that the aircraft carrier HMS *Hermes* was to be the flagship.

After the initial euphoria, jaws dropped all around the room when it was further announced that the First Sea Lord, Sir Henry Leach, had decreed that HMS *Hermes* was under just 72 hours' notice to sail. She hadn't been scheduled to do anything for months ahead and was alongside, partially de-stored and in a state of some disrepair.

We at Northern Parade had the ship's vital All Wheel Drive aircraft towing tractors in a multitude of pieces and in various states of overhaul. Their role was twofold: as well as the obvious, moving aircraft to and from the hangar and around the flight deck, they also carried and supplied demineralised water. This was injected into the Sea Harriers' Pegasus engines to improve thermal efficiency and increase lift – essential during fully armed V/STOL operations and critical in Operation Corporate.

After their initial shock, the staff were marvellous. Plans were hastily drawn up, weekend arrangements were cancelled, families were notified and round-the-clock work began. Parts were made, mended, cannibalised and, if not actually stolen, were appropriated from every conceivable source. I personally contacted the directors of a number of motor factors in the city of Portsmouth. They immediately agreed to stay open for us, morning, noon and night over the whole weekend. If they had it, we got it. No red tape, no documentation, no payment. That was all taken care of later.

There were people in, on, under and around every tractor. Refreshments were brought in and work continued ceaselessly day and night throughout the whole weekend.

I am delighted to say that on the Monday morning with great pride and more than a sigh of relief, I watched as the last of the tractors was craned aboard at one end of the ship as the Royal Marine Band was playing for her departure at the other.

The rest, as they say, is history.

****

Chapter 3 - The Journey South

For some vessels the 8,000 mile journey south to the Falklands Islands commenced in early April as soon as the prospect of military action was recognised. For most it was to be a three-week journey. Three nuclear submarines were dispatched immediately, while the first ships left UK dockyards in varying degrees of readiness on 5th April.

The rest of the fleet started their journey over the following days. Ships departed to sizeable waving crowds of friends and families, many not believing military action was likely.

For most service people on board, the majority of whom were young inexperienced men and women, their time was taken familiarising themselves with their new environment, keeping fit, and training. The fit-out of ships continued, while safety routines were practised regularly, all hoping they would never come into reality. Many ships stopped at Ascension Island or Freetown in Sierra Leone to collect stores and equipment.

Some light relief with the King Neptune ceremony to celebrate the crossing of the equator was enjoyed by many.

Most news came through the BBC and as the UN and US peace negotiations stumbled along with little progress, the belief that war could be averted reduced as the days ticked by. The recapture of South Georgia by Royal Marines from HMS *Antrim* on 25th April gave a boost to morale. However, with the news of the sinking of the cruiser *General Belgrano* by submarine HMS *Conqueror* with heavy casualties, the rejoicing was short lived with the realisation that British ships would soon be in the same area and could suffer the same fate.

Two days later HMS *Sheffield* was hit by an Exocet missile which started a fire in the control room. 20 men died – it was the first British warship to be sunk in the conflict. Practising for Air Raid Warning Red intensified as the harsh realities of the likelihood of war sank into everyone.

Andrew Cave, Seaman Missileman S(M) on HMS Hermes on the Weapon Direction Platform

Falklands Flagship - Getting Ready for War

On the 2nd April 1982, I was on HMS *Hermes* a 744-foot aircraft carrier which was in a dockyard assisted maintenance period in Portsmouth with half of her ship's company on leave who had to be recalled. She was covered in scaffolding from the top of her main mast to the deck and had great chunks of her main machinery off the ship being repaired in dockyard workshops ashore.

We were awoken with the normal call known as 'call the hands' and started to prepare for the day ahead as was normal onboard a warship. At about 0730 hours there was a pipe (tannoy message) instructing those of us onboard to clear lower deck and muster in the hangar where we were told by our Commander that all long leave was cancelled and that we were to prepare to sail for war as soon as possible. We were told that the Argentinians had invaded the Falkland Islands a British overseas territory 8,000 miles away in the South Atlantic. I like many others at the time had never heard of these islands!

At approximately 0900 hours the dockyard started to fill with lorries which were full of stores for our journey south and I, like many others, spent most of the weekend storing the ship.

On Monday 5th April, HMS *Hermes* sailed on time fully stored with 12 Sea Harriers and 18 Sea King helicopters and served as the Flagship during the Falklands war. Our journey south involved many exercises to prepare both the ship and crew for action stations which should be achieved in minutes. On hearing this ear-piercing alarm, you quickly put on your anti flash hood and gloves making sure that both your *'once only suit'* and lifejacket were attached to your respirator and made your way as quickly as possible to your action station. All watertight doors and hatches would be closed by the damage control parties to preserve watertight integrity once everybody was in position and reported to the captain. The ship was ready to fight with weapons ready and was now in the following condition: NBCD state 1 condition Zulu. Two alert Sea Harriers would be prepared for launch.

Before arriving at Ascension Island, we had a line crossing ceremony which commemorates a person's first crossing of the equator and is officiated by somebody playing King Neptune! There was a noticeable change in our surroundings with the temperature rising dramatically and the ocean becoming a calm vibrant blue playground for the many mischievous flying fish, turtles, dolphins, and hammerhead sharks that played below.

Whilst at Ascension there had been a lot of talk around the ship about all of those under 18 years of age which included me, being flown off the ship as we were considered too young to go to war. This did not happen. I also remember that during this time I became acutely aware through my duties of assistant gunner's yeoman that we were carrying nuclear depth charges.

As we got nearer to the TEZ it became obvious that we were going to have to fight so a great deal of time was spent preparing the ship for war, securing loose items, taping up mirrors and stowing infrequently used objects. Junior rates mess decks which were beneath the waterline were now ordered out of bounds due to possible torpedo attack.

I can also recall Rear Admiral Woodward who commanded the *Hermes* aircraft carrier group addressing the ship's company to prepare us for the task ahead. The only thing that I remember from this talk was him mentioning that not all of us would be going home!

Our working practices also changed from traditional watches to defence watches which were a six hours on six hours off system. Sleeping was very difficult when your mess deck is out of bounds, and you must try and rest in noisy passageways fully clothed in anti-flash gear whilst the other half of the ships company are going about their duties. I was exhausted after just a few days of this routine and can remember being called to action stations many times whilst off watch which resulted in rest periods being swallowed up. My defence watch position was as a member of the weapon direction platform (WDP) crew. This was an open lookout position above the bridge which left you exposed to both the freezing cold and the mountainous seas of the South Atlantic.

****

Alex Manning, Assistant Staff Minewarfare and Clearance Diving Officer (ASMCDO) on HMS Fearless

Preparing for Enemy Mines

Fearless herself was a very crowded ship, both personnel and stores-wise, to the extent that a one-way system existed on the main deck inside, carpeted and packed to the deck-head with boxes and sacks of dry rations! I recall the tremendous sense of purpose and involvement that seemed to attend everything, even though many thought a political settlement would be the eventual outcome. Everything was real. We were going to take on the Argies and beat them, all effort being to that one clear end until we were told otherwise.

I and our stoic and utterly dependable Chief Petty Officer (Minewarfare) Derek Ridley took away an LCVP (Landing Craft, Vehicle and Personnel, one of the ship's four smaller landing craft) for half a day trialling a portable commercial North Sea sonar set to see if it might be any use for minehunting i.e. locating ground mines – magnetic, acoustic, pressure-activated mines, also known as influence mines, laid on the sea bed. It wasn't, but it made for a nice day out! Another time, I had a long but purposefully enjoyable couple of days going round all the STUFT ships (Ships Taken Up From Trade), all the civilian ships, issuing boxes of anti-attack swimmer (frogmen) scare charges (1lb blast grenades) and showing their First Officers how to prime and use them and under what circumstances.

****

Stuart McCulloch, Radio Operator HMS Fearless

A 17 Year-Old Goes to War

Dad did national service in the navy in the 1950s and both brothers were in the navy (the eldest having just left) so, with little opportunity available to me locally, I decided to join up when I left school in 1981.

I did the training and passed out as a Radio Operator in March 1982 at HMS *Mercury* in Hampshire. I was about to go on two weeks' leave when the news came through about this place we'd never heard of, being invaded by Argentina and that some of us were being drafted onto ships to be readied to go, mine being HMS *Fearless* with a mate I'd been in training with.

I had the weekend to go home and then I joined HMS *Fearless* on the Monday. I was 17 years old. During that time at home, I found out that my brother on HMS *Arrow* was already on his way to the Falklands.

It was strange as this was my first draft out of training, and I had never been abroad before I joined the navy. I had to get used to life on board ship and the many duties that were shared, ship maintenance, cleaning, kitchen duties etc. as well as the roles behind our particular specialisms. I felt a bit like a fish out of water as I'm sure many do straight out of training.

The sad loss of the *General Belgrano* and other incidents at the time were greeted with glee and talk of how it will all be over before we even get there. Then we lost the *Sheffield* and our outlook changed!

****

Gary Mcilvenna, Royal Marine on HMS Fearless

Royal Marines Head South

At the time of the Falklands War, I was a 22 year-old Royal Marine serving in 4th Assault Squadron RM based on HMS

Fearless, (an amphibious assault ship), which carried four small landing craft – Landing Craft Vehicle Personnel (LCVP).

I joined *Fearless* in November 1981, by which time I had been in the Royal Marines for five years. I was at a wedding in Plymouth when news filtered through that Argentina had invaded the Falkland Islands. I reported to HMS *Fearless* on Sunday 4th April 1982 and we sailed for Ascension two days later.

Ascension 17th April

Upon arrival, along with numerous other ships (warships, merchant ships), one of my clearest memories was the intense heat and that we all bronzed well. Some of the lads went shark fishing and had shark steaks on the ship's menus. We took light tanks (Scimitar and Scorpion) from the Blues & Royals regiment and transporting them to the open sea, lowered our ramp and let them fire their main turret guns. This was a fire support practice manoeuvre in the event of an opposed landing.

7th May

Fearless sailed south from the Ascension Islands and we had various briefings on the capabilities of the Argentine airforce. I remember thinking to myself that the amphibious assault group could take a pounding from the Argentine Skyhawks, Mirages, the Exocet carrying Super Etendards and Pucara ground attack planes. Sadly, my fears were realised as one of our landing craft (LCU call sign Foxtrot 4) sank, losing six of her crew.

****

RO(G) Tony Lawrence, Radio Operator HMS Fearless

Radio Operator on HMS *Fearless*

I joined the Royal Navy in July 1981 straight from school at 16 years old, something I'd always wanted to do since I was in junior school. In March 1982 I passed out from HMS *Mercury* as a qualified but inexperienced Junior Radio Operator, awaiting my first sea draft. Two weeks later, Argentina invaded the Falkland Islands and I volunteered to join HMS *Fearless* as part of the communications department 'war complement'.

Being under 18 years of age, my parents had to give their permission for me to go. My father was a bit concerned about what might become of me, but my mother, with a sense of history and national pride, and a bit of 'Maggie' Thatcher British Bulldog Spirit, knew I really wanted to go, so gave her consent.

HMS *Fearless* was the command-and-control ship for the Amphibious Landings in San Carlos Water during the Falklands War. She was a large ship with over 500 crew onboard. Be that as it may, the fighting defence of the ship actually only fell to about 10 percent of the crew, manning Sea Cat missile launchers, Bofors guns and GPMG weapons on the upper deck. The rest were more often than not confined to their action stations below decks manning switchboards, Ops Rooms, communications and electronic sensors, Fire and Repair Posts, First Aid Stations, engineering compartments and the dock. Without sight and sound of the action going on above, there was great reliance on the 'pipes' and sitreps from the bridge and ops room to warn and alert everyone as to the ebb and flow of the battle going on outside…

****

Alex Manning, Assistant Staff Minewarfare and Clearance Diving Officer (ASMCDO) HMS Fearless

News of the Sinking of the *General Belgrano*

A short while later Captain Larken came back to tell us he'd now received reports that *Belgrano* was sinking and with possibly heavy casualties and that he'd keep us informed. Sure enough, about two hours later as I recall, he came back on and I'll never forget his words: "*This is the Captain. I can now confirm that Belgrano has sunk and that it has been, I'm afraid, with heavy loss of life;*

although we don't know the exact figure it's definitely high, likely to be 300 or more. I know we should all be relieved that the second most important unit of their navy has been taken out but we shouldn't take any pleasure in the loss of life that's gone with it - they were matelots just doing their job, like we are." Indeed they were; the final figure was 326, nearly a third of her crew, and we most certainly took no pleasure in it.

When it reached us, the Sun's infamous "*Gotcha!*" headline was treated with utter contempt and when, later in the conflict, some lads were told that a press man was going to visit them, their response was "*I hope he's not from the f------ Sun!*"

****

Steve Walsh, Royal Artillery on board the QE2

Luxury Liner to Troop Ship

On the 12th May, we left Lille Barracks in Aldershot for Southampton. When we arrived, the scale of the operation became obvious. There were numerous army units preparing to embark as well as masses of press and the public.

I was redirected to a cabin on 2 Deck. It was quite a sumptuous space with twin beds and an en suite bathroom and dressing room. Not too bad at all and not a bad way to go to war.

We looked down at the crowds who looked so small, dwarfed by the enormous ship. A military band played on the quayside as the ship manoeuvred from her moorings and gently turned toward the Solent. It felt like a carnival. The sky seemed to be full of news helicopters and a flotilla of small boats surrounded the ship. As we sailed into the setting sun, the flotilla gradually turned to return to Southampton but one boat and a lone wind surfer followed us for over an hour.

The ship had had a very quick refit in preparation for the journey and its unusual passengers. This seemed to have involved covering the carpets with thin sheets of wood and removing pictures and ornaments. That said, it still seemed very luxurious. One of the more substantial modifications was the fitting of a helicopter pad over the stern swimming pool area. A Sea King helicopter was now strapped down where normally there would be septuagenarians sipping cocktails and basting themselves in suntan oil.

I quickly discovered that if I pressed my bedside button in the cabin, a waiter would appear and bring anything we liked to eat 24 hours a day. I remember thinking that won't last – and it didn't. It quickly became obvious that this environment was not conducive with retaining fitness for the job in hand.

We spent hours every day running around the decks to maintain fitness levels. The constant pounding on the wooden decks with hundreds of soldiers in boots carrying rucksacks was causing the decorative wood panelling on the restaurant ceiling below to fall on the unsuspecting heads of those enjoying the culinary delights that Cunard were providing.

At frequent intervals, bags of rubbish were thrown over the stern and used for target practice to test and zero the weapons. The Sea King helicopter would often take off at night and circle the ship seeking any light escaping from the ship. Obviously, in its normal role the ship would be lit up like a Christmas tree.

There were periods of boredom and, as always, the army makes its own entertainment. There was a crossing the equator ceremony, which is an old navy tradition of dressing up like Neptune and Mermaids and throwing people into a pool of gunge. Strange people these navy types – an opinion that I would revise over the coming weeks.

Back out to sea now for the crossing to Ascension Island. We remained on board the ship but had a clear view of the airfield, which was buzzing with activity with numerous RAF aircraft positioned on the airfield. Whilst the US had declared themselves independent of the UK/Argentinian dispute, it was clear there was a great deal of US assistance being provided to us.

Over the next few days, the weather slowly began to change, the seas became grey and rough and the temperature began to drop. As we sailed through the 'roaring 40' latitudes, the seas became huge and even *QE2* seemed to struggle through the enormous waves. As each wave hit the bow, she was pushed back until she gathered momentum and moved forward again. At one point a navy warship sat off our starboard beam and I remember watching her bows burying into the waves that appeared to engulf her before she reappeared from the other side of each wave. This relentless motion continued for several days and many of the soldiers were suffering badly with seasickness. Jenks was confined to his bed for several days. The mood on board was still quite light-hearted and many of us began to think that diplomatic solutions would soon be found and we would be heading back to the UK.

****

Neil Maher, Signaller, Army Air Corps on board the QE2
Courtesy of the Army Flying Museum

'No More Room Service'

I got on board this ship, this massive ship, I'd never been on a cruise ship before in my life and being an NCO I was put in this two-man cabin, with this REME guy and we had an en-suite, a bed each with these fantastic sheets. I'd never felt anything like it, they were as 'soft as anything; at that time you got woolly blankets in the army, and I had this really soft duvet sheet, wonderful and I remember this person coming in saying '*Oh I am very sorry'* he was very apologetic, he says, '*I am very sorry, cos we've had to strip things out because we're taking you guys, the cruise has been stripped down so we won't be able to serve you in your room but what I'll do is I'll set up some cakes and things in the little galley at the end of the corridor'*. Lo and behold I went down to the galley and there were these little cakes and stuff.

We wandered round the ship trying to see, so we looked over the ship, there were loads of people, crowds and everything cheering you, and more and more troops coming on all the time and we set sail eventually into the Channel.

****

Garry Hearn, Lance Corporal, Royal Signals attached to the 1st Battalion Welsh Guards on board the QE2

Welsh Guards on the *QE2*

In 1982, I was a Royal Signals Lance Corporal attached to the 1st Battalion Welsh Guards providing specialist communications expertise in what was known as a Rear Link Detachment. My brother was in a similar role with the 2nd Battalion Scots Guards.

When told we were off to join the 1st Battalion Welsh Guards as a team of six communication experts we were not only confident in the job we had to do but we also wanted to beat them at communications and fitness. The Welsh Guards were rightly proud of their heritage and ability, and we were of ours.

Early May and we head off south on the *QE2* 'the' luxury liner of the time, a few soldier-resistant changes but still outstanding service and food. Oh, what a lovely war springs to mind. Go past Ascension Island in the mid-Atlantic and the rumour commences that we are being tailed by an Argentine submarine; generates a feeling of fatalism, '*better ignore that as there is nothing I can do.*'

Lectures on battlefield first aid, basic Spanish (including relevant swear words – that's how to get the attention of a soldier), PT and weapon firing. Pack kit, four magazines of 7.62m, two bandoliers of rounds, radio, 5.4m mast, radio batteries, personal kit, saline drip, rations. Lift backpack (robust canvas, unable to keep out water, but loved it) on to shoulders, no that doesn't work, leave back-pack on floor, lie back on top, slip arms through straps, and climb up rifle until erect; just. Now start tabbing around the deck; no that doesn't work, adopt a shuffle instead. Feelings of, got to be able to carry it, need to show the infantry we are as good or better, and there are no taxis or buses on the Islands so suck it up. Thank God we will have a radio borne land-rover though.

****

Phill Basey, 3rd Officer on tanker MV British Esk

Tanker MV *British Esk*

On the morning of 2nd April 1982 I went out on deck to relieve my opposite number on the 4 to 8 watch to be greeted with the news that the Argentinians had invaded the Falklands. At first we thought it was a late April Fool's joke! Seven weeks later the tanker *British Esk* would be leaving the task group heading north for Ascension with 200+ survivors from HMS *Sheffield.*

After leaving Hamburg we went directly to Portland to be fitted with our Stern Replenishment At Sea (RAS) equipment. After meetings with company representatives asking for volunteers the crew complement was culled to the minimum deemed necessary, approximately 30, to operate the ship. We were supplemented with six Royal Navy (RN), two Royal Airforce (RAF) and three Royal Fleet Auxiliary (RFA) personnel. Wives and girlfriends came to visit and say farewells, we took on as many provisions as we could store, filled up with as much diesel, heavy fuel oil, and aviation fuel as we could and within a week of hearing the news we headed south. To say that we were totally unprepared for what was to come would be a gross understatement.

During the long journey south, we did not call into Ascension we just plodded on by ourselves, the daily routine broken up with the occasional visit from an RAF Nimrod. Eventually we took up station at the southern refuelling station. During this initial period things were fairly mundane. Every couple of days or so RFA *Appleleaf* (Auxilliary Oiler) would come and pay us a visit, take off some cargo and then disappear back into the murky, very grey skies and rolling grey seas. RFA and RN ships are used to beam RAS but for me, and I suspect most merchant seaman, the first beam

RAS was terrifying. As we were to learn later *Appleleaf* was gentle with us, coming up slowly from astern, matching our speed and then gradually drifting closer, probably no more than 20 to 30 metres abeam; the RN ships were not so gentle. When everything had settled down and we had connected *Appleleaf's* refuelling rig to our pipework I remember looking down at the standing wave between us and *Appleleaf,* penguins were surfing in the wave!

After a week or so of working solely with *Appleleaf* we were informed that we were to join the main Task Group (TG), apparently one of the other RFAs, not *Appleleaf,* had contaminated her cargo and had to go north. We headed to rendezvous with the TG, the weather by this stage had improved, it was a bright sunny morning but with patches of dense fog. We had difficulty identifying ourselves with the fleet and it was very sobering seeing HMS *Glamorgan* emerge from the gloom with her 4.5" gun trained directly where I was standing. One single red, white and green funnel amongst a multitude of grey!

Life was a little different now, not only did we have regular visits from *Appleleaf,* but we also conducted our own stern RAS with smaller RN vessels. For a navigator my life now became slightly more exciting, I wouldn't say that 'Rules of the Road' didn't apply but they were definitely to be used for guidance only. Station keeping within the overall force disposition was also a new skill to be learned, however, we were 'politely asked' a number of times to regain our station. The air and submarine threats were ever present and on numerous occasions when we had to play catch-up to regain station, HMS *Hermes* was only ever a distant smudge to the east.

I usually had company on the bridge at this time, well during the daytime anyway. We were host to a detachment of SBS, whom, when they were not sleeping, liked to spend their time on the bridge watching what was going on. In the afternoon they would go for a nap prior to being picked up by a helicopter taxi later in the afternoon. They would arrive back with us the following morning. They never spoke about what they did but we would hear of their exploits on the BBC World Service.

Life continued roughly in the same manner for a while, we were detached with HMS *Plymouth* to recover an air drop from a Hercules. The drop zone was a couple of days NE of the main TG so off we went. At about 0700 hours on the first day all hell broke out, main gun, machine guns, mortars the lot. My captain, who had been in the shower, arrived on the bridge with a towel nowhere big enough, wanting to know what the hell was going on; I didn't know. It transpired that the captain of *Plymouth* liked to exercise his gun crews and 0700 hours seemed a good time. It would have been nice if he'd told us.

****

Arun Desai, Navigation Leader, 47 Squadron, Ascension Island

<u>47 Squadron to Ascension</u>

In April, we were briefed that flights to Ascension would take place almost immediately. These were flights with very heavy payload. We needed a refuelling stop en-route to Ascension. Initially, the flights were routed via Gibraltar but the short runway there did not allow the high payload we wished to carry.

Though Ascension had a 12,000 feet runway, there was not much infrastructure for the influx of the number of British Forces personnel who were sent to operate the base for the increased air activity. Normally, one RAF Hercules flight a month and one USAF C141 resupply flight per week were the regular visitors. These flights could be managed well. Such was the boredom factor amongst the few American civilians who worked at the airport that they called it Wideawake Airfield!

In short time, Ascension became a very busy airport. Helicopters which arrived in the back of Belfast aircraft were re-assembled and operated between the airfield and the ships of the fleet which had no time to stop. The Americans pulled out all stops to provide the fuel for the many aircraft that arrived on the island. Oilers berthed offshore at Georgetown to offload their cargo into the many underground tanks. So much for the fuel cuts imposed by our MOD!!

The small domestic area a couple of miles away from the airfield soon became a large accommodation area put up by the American military. The area came to be known as Concertina City as it was just that. Compressed packages flown in by the USAF were opened and out popped a rectangular tent for 10 people. Included in the contraption was an air conditioning unit. About 50 of these tents were erected very quicky to accommodate the British service personnel who were arriving to support the aeroplanes and ships. The Chow Hall and the Volcano Club were solid buildings. The Chow Hall was opened for round-the clock feeding and the Volcano Club provided the rather gassy and cold American beer such as Bud and Old Milwaukee. Spirits of all colours were in abundance.

The big drawback was the noise. To power the Concertina City, a huge generator was installed. The white noise of the generator could be heard for half a mile around the site.

****

Brian Short, Royal Marines Bandsman on Canberra

Extracts from Brian's book The Band that went to War

<u>Reality of War Suddenly Dawns</u>

When you join the Royal Marines Band as a young musician, you do not really expect to be called up to serve in a war. Yes, we have basic military training on joining, but nothing like the intense and comprehensive training our commando brothers go through. So, when we were recalled from Easter leave in the spring of 1982, we assumed we would be guarding our barracks whilst our 'roughty toughty' commandos would go off and sort out the Argentine problem. That assumption turned out to be very wrong, as within 24 hours we were on our way to Southampton to join the cruise ship *Canberra* as part of the medical squadron.

Once over the shock of 'going to war', once we sailed the band settled into a daily working routine of training alongside the marines and medics. We all wrongly assumed that the diplomatic efforts would be successful and that in a few weeks we would be back with a story, a tan, and a medal.

We headed for Ascension Island, where we met up with the rest of the Task Force. There was then a heavy workload of moving stores between the various Royal Navy, Royal Fleet Auxiliary and civilian ships, with some brief respites ashore for R&R on volcanic beaches. Due to the perceived submarine threat, *Canberra* sailed each night in various directions, and returned in the morning.

However, one evening after hearing the news about the sinking of the *General Belgrano,* we sailed for the last time, and we were definitely heading south. After also hearing about the loss of HMS *Sheffield*, we all knew we were in a shooting war and preparations stepped up several gears. Marines and Paras were running endless miles around the decks to keep up their fitness, and weapons training and zeroing was conducted from the stern of the ship.

****

Ade Thorne, RAF EOD (Explosive Ordnance Disposal) team on RFA Sir Bedivere. Extracts from 'My Falklands Diary'

How to Shower the Royal Navy Way

I joined the RAF in 1978 as a weapons mechanic.

Mid-April

I was working as part of an EOD team up at Otterburn ranges when we got the call to return to Wittering asap. There I was informed that I would be part of a team travelling south to the Falkland Islands,

We had two weeks to get the kit together, including one x 4 tonner complete with eight tons of gear including gallons of raccasan (toilet flush) and two x LWB Land Rovers with trailers. A team of eleven was assembled including Flt Lt Al Swan ("the boss") and myself, Jnr Tech Ade Thorne.

The Squadron brief was to to clear all areas of land required to operate the Harriers on portable operating strips once the ground was secure.

10th May

RFA *Sir Bedivere* sailed into Ascension. We managed to get aboard an RM Gemini and go out to the RFA. At this point we had to climb up the rope ladder dropped over the side. It was quite scary watching my 50-year-old WO attempt to pull his way up. We then set sail every night to avoid the Argentinian submarine threat. We had four times as many people on board than we should have.

Showers were something else. We got called forward by room to the showers. We went in four at a time and stood in the showers. A navy guy shouts, "W*ater on, armpit armpit, bollocks, arse out"*, then as we stepped back to apply soap another four moved into the showers. We applied soap to the four areas then swapped back over. This time we had double "*armpit armpit bollocks arse out"*, to rinse off.

****

Colin Hamilton, Lt. Commander, HMS Leeds Castle

Sector KILO

On 22nd April 1982, HMS *Leeds Castle* was recalled from our fishery protection patrol in the North Sea and ordered to return to Rosyth to prepare for operations in the South Atlantic as a Dispatch Vessel.

Following a furious 72-hour period of storing, including 50 tons of rations, increasing fuel and water capacity and fitting of a reverse osmosis water plant, we proceeded to Portsmouth to give 24 hours leave to all hands. We followed *Hermes* out of Portsmouth on 29th April.

Save a two-day stop at Ascension, during which we off-loaded the rations and embarked 40 helo loads of urgent stores and mail for the task force, we sailed alone and flat out for the TEZ. Our max speed was determined by the colour of the diesel's exhaust system. Bright orange OK, white a bit marginal. I wonder if this is the first time a ship's speed has been determined not by the bridge, but by the on-watch Tiff? Our maximum speed was regrettably interrupted for five days when a camshaft sheered. 72 hours later a new one was dropped in the water by RAF Hercules some 1500 miles south of Ascension and 36 hours later we were back up to bright orange. Incidentally, when HQ engineers asked the diesel manufacturer if they had a spare camshaft they were told '*No, but we can let you have a new engine'*.

We understand the staff officer then said, '*Well take the... camshaft out of the engine and have it delivered to Brize Norton tomorrow morning'*. Sadly, we never discovered his identity.

****

Philip Piper, Gazelle Pilot, 656 Army Air Corps aboard MV Nordic Diary extracts

656 Army Air Corps - Heading South

8th May

Boarded onto MV *Nordic*, Townsend Thoresen Ferry. Waved a fond farewell at 1300 hours.

13th May

Had another afternoon of getting the a/c (aircraft) up on deck and the procedures are now far smoother.

We hear on the news today that the Argies have lost 3 a/c, shot down by Sea Wolf (ground-to-air missiles). We lost yet another Sea King helicopter. Also hear that a frigate got hit in the attack but that no one was injured.

14th May

The decks looked like Brighton beach today; every conceivable flat space was taken up by scrawny/fat lily-white bodies

17th May

It has been very hot and humid today. The Flight started to get things organised at lunch time and we (Sgt Moran and myself) went flying for 6 minutes. At first it was slightly unnerving to fly off from and back onto a moving ship, especially as the flight deck was in front of the superstructure.

18th May

The crew put on a Neptune Party for all of us on the Flight Deck. It really was hilarious. I was eventually hauled up onto the platform, covered from head to foot in chocolate ice cream, smothered in kippers and then given a dunking in the pool (large canvas sack...!). Consolation prize was a can of beer.

22nd May

We learnt this morning that the Task Force has managed to land 1000 troops onto East Falkland: 4 dead and 29 injured at first count. We lost one Harrier and 2 RM Gazelles. We're awaiting further details.

Note: Flew with Sgt Moran at night and remember it being a terrifying experience with no horizon that night, no flying stabilisation equipment, no night vision goggles and having to fly past the superstructure before flying sideways at the speed of the ship to lower yourself down onto a rolling deck.

23rd May

We're told that a British Frigate was sunk in Falkland Sound and that 20 men were missing, presumed dead. We've also heard that three RM crew were killed in the 2 Gazelles that were shot down.

24th May
A lot of people are starting to get just a little bit itchy now especially as the Task Force has been on the Islands for the last three days. Think that by the time we get there it will all be over.

27th May
Sea temperature down to 12 deg C. Immersion suit weather. (Note: Immersion suits were a pig to get on and off and very uncomfortable to fly in with the only saving grace that you might survive a bit longer in cold water).

Tony (Bourne) and Sgt Sutherland went flying this afternoon. Tony loved it and Sgt Sutherland hated it. Visibility was down to about 1000 metres and the sea conditions were foul.

****

Nick Brotherton, 'Sea Cat Aimer', HMS Argonaut

Sea Cat Aimer on HMS *Argonaut*

In March 1982 I was drafted from HMS *Cleopatra* which was in drydock for a refit to HMS *Argonaut* as a temporary draft due to a ship's company being taken ill and leaving HMS *Argonaut*. I was a Sea Cat aimer but as HMS *Argonaut* already had a full compliment of aimers my "action station" was the for'ard magazine.

On the way south I was given the opportunity to fire/guide a Sea Cat missile which was a turning point for me as upon that test I was given the position as for'ard Sea Cat aimer as my "action station" which meant I was no longer in the for'ard magazine which saved my life in the weeks to come.

The trip south was long, only broken up by a welcome stop at the sunny and very hot Accension Island together with many other ships. The sea state grew progressively worse as did the weather. Eventually HMS *Argonaut* rendezvoused with the main group.

From my position in the Sea Cat director on the bridge roof I had a perfect view of all the ships as far as the eye could see. It reminded me of the Second World War convoys, it was a truly amazing sight.

Soon we received news that the *General Belgrano* had been sunk by one of our nuclear-powered submarines HMS *Conqueror*.

There was no turning back now, we were at war. The euphoria soon turned to sadness then to anger as the grim news came over the ship's tannoy that HMS *Sheffield* had been hit by an Argentine Exocet missile and was on fire and sinking.

****

Nigel Turner, Leading Cook on HMS Hermes

A Cook at War

I joined the Royal Navy aged 16 at HMS *Raleigh* on the 3rd August 1970 and served 23 and a half years, leaving on 25th December 1993 as a Petty Officer Cook.

We sailed on the morning of 5th April 1982. As we sailed south the ship began to practise ship-wide drills to hone fire-fighting and damage control skills. Action Stations and Defence watches were practised. Full lockdown and condition 1 Zulu Alpha practised as it was not known if the Argentinians had any chemical weapons. Ship knowledge became ever more important.

Admiral Woodward embarked from Gibralter with his staff and his Chief Cook 'Taff' Pringle so now there were three sharing the captain galley. From leaving Ascension our senses seemed to be heightened and geared up and positive because of the years of training for engaging in such an event.

Normal duties continued and we began to sleep on top of our bunks fully clothed with our respirator, Once Only Suit, lifejacket and Anti-flash stacked on the bottom of the bunk - close to hand. The further south we went, the more 'a state of alert' became second nature and every alarm, ship-wide broadcast, news bulletin was avidly listened to. Into the Total Exclusion Zone, we realised that the Argentines were in for a fight and a conflict became very real.

****

Tony Pitt, Commander, RFA Sir Percivale
Extracts from his personal diary

UK to Ascension - Preparing RFA *Sir Percivale*

This phase of the operation started at midnight on 6th April with a rendezvous with other vessels of the Task Force, off Eddystone Lighthouse. The period was spent working up the ship in all aspects of its task. A lot of time was spent with flying operations in order to familiarise the air crews with operations at sea. Many internal exercises were held dealing with the safety of the ship and those of the embarked force who were suitably trained were incorporated into the ship's organisation. Replenishment at Sea (RAS) approaches were also practised with other ships including stern RAS which was considered the most suitable method of refuelling in the waters of the South Atlantic.

On the maintenance front time was spent painting out any high visibility colours on the ship that stood out, including the white areas.

During the trip down we received various bits of information on future intentions, the most important of which was that the mix of ammunition and vehicles on all ships was unsatisfactory and there would be extensive reshuffling of cargo throughout the force. Whilst at Ascension the LSLs would be fitted with air defence weapons comprising Bofors 40/60 and GPMGs.

Official clearance was given to operate Sea King helicopters from the aft Flight Decks of LSLs.

On the ship defence side the armament was fitted … although the system had still to be tried we appeared to be ready to defend ourselves. Due to the foredeck configuration it was only possible to fit one Bofors 40/60.

It had been hoped that the embarked force would be able to put in some training but due to various circumstances only one exercise was completed. This involved helo transporting 7 Battery and their guns to the airfield for a mock assault. From the point of view of ship organisation it seemed to go very well.

On completion of watering at 0520 Z Friday 30th April the ship was, in all respects, ready to proceed to the Falkland Islands area.

Some passengers had been transferred before departure. We had lost 148 and 8 Batteries and 59 Cdo Sdn Condor Troop and embarked Cdo Log Reg Main B, total passengers were now 335.

****

Chris Clarke, Master, Europic Ferry

‘No Lights, no Radar’

Europic Ferry was a freight ferry normally employed on a voyage of no more than 9 hours between Southampton and Le Havre on a daily service. By that time *Europic Ferry* was fifteen years old so we never thought we would be involved. A week later all that was to change, and *Europic Ferry* was being converted for a military role and would be the equipment transport for the Second Battalion Parachute Regiment (2 Para) with 60 of their associated personnel. We also embarked a naval party to assist us with communications, refuelling at sea and flight deck operations etc.

On 22nd April after only three days of conversion the ship sailed to Portland for final stores and to be introduced to the ways of the Royal Navy aided by our embarked RN naval party. We had our first trial RAS (replenishment at sea), which I had always viewed as black art only understood by the RN and RFA, but soon to become routine for us. Helicopter operations were another novelty later to be hardly worth a second glance. We sailed from Portland to rendezvous with the container vessel *Atlantic Conveyor* off Plymouth and both ships proceeded south believing that we would hand our military hardware over to the real fighting sailors somewhere safe such as Ascension before returning to the UK. This assumption was supported by the fact that the ship's hull was painted bright orange, a colour chosen for its high visibility properties, and they had told me in Southampton that painting it grey wasn't necessary!

We did in fact arrive at Ascension and after only a day there, we were on our way again but now under very much a war footing. It was all very strange to a merchant navy shipmaster, no lights, no radar, being told what course to steer and at what speed and only military communications. All very obvious but a bit of a culture shock just the same.

As the force steered further into the South Atlantic the mood changed with the realisation that we would be involved in what had become a shooting war. The Paras lent us guns which they set up at various points around the decks to provide an element of self-defence.

****

Simon Sugden, Weapons Engineering Mechanic Ordnance HMS Coventry

<u>Issue of 'One Only Suits'</u>

My naval career started 20th October 1980, I was 16 years and seven months old. I can still remember the excitement and nerves but this is all I had ever wanted to do since about the age of 12. I went to HMS Collingwood where I would start my training to become a Weapons Engineering Mechanic (Ordnance). After six months at Collingwood having successfully passed my basic engineering courses, I received notice of my first sea draft, HMS *Coventry*.

A sense of "seriousness" soon took hold as wills were drafted, Geneva ID cards were issued and rank badges were removed from uniforms and the mass issuing of "once only suits" focused the mind. Although if our officers were to be believed we would sail over the horizon guns blazing and the Argies would pack up and sod off home. They told us that, yes, they had Exocet missiles but they didn't have the ability to fire them from planes.

Life on board was definitely starting to change as securing for action was taken to a whole new level and the relentless amount of damage control training now meant that most scenarios had been covered, well almost all.

****

Howard Johnson, Sgt Ammunition, MV Lycaon

30-Day Ammunition Resupply - MV *Lycaon*

On any military campaign the Task Force carries sufficient resources for the initial engagement with a follow up resupply. In the case of the Falklands it was 30 day resupply.

29th April A relatively small ship, MV *Lycaon,* hid in Southampton moored around the corner from the main task force and we loaded her up. Military onboard Naval Commander Stiles, me, RCT Port Maritime Staff Sgt G Horsley and a small detachment of Royal Marines. We loaded:

Ammunition	2,076 pallets (plts)
General Stores	118 plts
Compo	530 plts
Defence Stores	71 plts
105mm gun barrels	x 6
Wombat	x 1
Small arms weapons	5 plts

4th May fully loaded, at 0400 hours we quietly slipped out of Southampton waters.

15th May Arrived in the Ascension. We took on "Stuff" - loaded Sidewinder, 3-inch rockets (chaff) and general stores.
We sailed next day at 2359 hours and started a watch system with mounted LMGs (light machine guns) on the bridge wings. It all started to feel real.

****

Arun Desai, Navigation Leader, 47 Squadron, Ascension Island

Long-range Airdrops at Sea

All types of aircraft were arriving on the Island daily to perform duties over the South Atlantic.

The fleet sailed past Ascension taking on board more personnel and equipment. The helicopters provided sterling service undertaking this task. Soon, the fleet was out of range of the helicopters, so the Hercules took over the duties of equipment resupply by air drops. However, sailing at full speed, the fleet was beyond the reach and return of the Hercules. Air-to-air refuelling (AAR) became the option.

We could not use any airfield on the South American mainland routinely for diplomatic reasons so long-range flights with two refuelling brackets during the outbound leg were planned to keep the supply chain active. In addition to the normal five crew, the Hercules flew with an augmented crew of an extra captain and navigator and an air electronics operator (AEOp) from the Nimrod world. The ninth member was the air dispatcher from the Army air dispatch squadron.

I was sent to Ascension as a passenger on a VC10 to augment a crew.

Early call for these flights was mid-night with an Intelligence (int) briefing when we were told the location of the target ship to which we would drop the supplies. Supplies were mounted on honeycomb platforms which would take about one ton of supplies each. The freight bay had four extra fuel tanks which each had a capacity of 7,500 lbs. All these tanks were used for these flights. Aft of the tanks were placed the 12 One-Ton containers each with four parachutes. The plan was to drop these containers into the sea for the RN to retrieve them by helicopter or a rubber inflatable boat (RIB). Normally, all the containers would be dropped in one pass, but no helicopter or RIB would cope with 12 containers, so we dropped them one or two. The fuel plan allowed for one hour's loitering in the vicinity of the ship before setting heading for Ascension.

In preparation for the flight, the last point of call was the greasy spoon at the airfield where we tucked into a hearty meal at about 5.00 am. This was the last hot meal for over 24 hours.

With an extra 30,000 lbs of fuel, we staggered into the air on Runway 12 and when clear of the Island headed South-South-West (SSW) for 'THE' ship. The Victor tanker took off much later as it had the speed to catch up with the Hercules. We levelled off at 22,000 feet as the weight would not allow us to climb to a higher level.

About eight hours later, at the agreed time the Victor was in our vicinity. At least the first refuelling bracket was possible. There was no radio contact so as not to compromise our position. As the range closed in, the observer in the cupola identified the descending Victor in the 8 o'clock position. It overtook and positioned directly in front of us. Colin the captain relaxed his fingers and toes as both aircraft approached the start of the bracket. With the hose trailed from the Victor, we peered to the front for the green light for Colin to inch the Hercules probe into the basket of the Victor. The Victor was flying at just above its stalling speed whereas the Hercules was flying at a speed which was burning a lot more fuel. So, the two aircraft commenced a shallow dive of 200 feet per min. Fuel was taken on board to fill to maximum capacity. This toboggan technique was devised by the Victor and Hercules pilots during the qualifying flights in the UK.

The join and connect was in generally clear weather but as we descended through 15,000 feet the cloud built up and keeping visual with the Victor became tricky. Add to this the turbulence and it became quite dangerous, but we needed the fuel. The requisite amount was complete at about 2,000 feet where the uninviting South Atlantic showed off its sea horses. All our tanks were full as we climbed to 22,000 feet.

Some hours later this process was repeated at the second and last RV with a Victor tanker. After this refuelling, we continued to the target ship. Locating it was difficult in the murk of the South Atlantic winter, even though all eyes were looking out for the ship. After some loitering, the ship was located, and we made the pass for the mutual identification of each other. If we saw the helicopter was airborne and the RIB was in the water, then this was the indication to us to make several passes to drop the supplies onto the water. The ship would turn into wind so that the bridge crew could see the load, mounted on a honeycomb platform, to cushion the impact. We flew along the port side from aft to fore at a safe distance. The navigator put the GREEN light on, having allowed for the forward air throw and drift back because of the wind. The idea was for the load to land athwartships so that the helicopter or the RIB could retrieve the load and take it on board. On most instances, the anti-G mechanism on the top of the container would operate and disconnect the parachutes which would allow the helicopter winchman or the RIB party to hook the container and take on board. There were dis-heartening instances when losing containers, which had travelled 4,000 miles, failed to reach its destination.

After the last drop, we closed the rear ramp and door to indicate that there was no more to drop. With a cheery wave to the bridge, we set heading for Ascension, 4,000 miles away.

There remained a small matter of sustenance. Since the greasy spoon breakfast about 18 hours ago our food intake was limited to Pot Noodles.

We reached terra-firma around 8 am – some 26 hours after leaving it.

Our ops officer Pat, greeted us with a crate of cold tins which we took to the Greasy spoon where we debriefed the Int, Met and Engineering officers over a full fry up. The sun was well and truly up and heating the Island and we retired to the bungalow to sleep.

In a 12-day spell, the crew undertook four of these flights

I complete this narration on 2nd April 2022, 40 years after the invasion by the tin-pot regime which thought that it would be a walk-over. Well, it wasn't.

****

Falkland Island Defence Force 1972 (top left clockwise) Pat Lee, Brian Summers, Gerard Mackay, Capt DM Parkinson RM, Ian Cantlie.

Courtesy of Brian Summers

Lt Keith Mills with his Royal Marines contingent on South Georgia.

Courtesy of Keith Mills

Wreckage of Argentine Puma shot down by Royal Marines on South Georgia.
Courtesy of Keith Mills

The Union Jack flying once more on South Georgia.
Courtesy of Keith Mills

Ascension Island. An RN Sea King is lifting 7 Bty 105mm guns on *Sir Percivale*.
Photo Eddie Bairstow

Ready to refuel – view from the cupola.
Courtesy of Arun Desai

Crossing the Line Ceremony on RFA *Sir Percivale.* Rev Wynne Jones, 45's Padre was the judge. The Ship's Captain, Capt Pitt RFA, is the person in the blue cap in the middle. I gave my camera to someone before Neptune's guards got me. I am the person being hosed down and scrubbed by the Bears in white.

Photo Eddie Bairstow

RFA *Sir Percivale* from Gazelle helo flown by Capt Nick Pounds RM, OC M Flt.

Photo Eddie Bairstow

British Esk Heading South.
Courtesy of Phill Basey

Sea Harrier FRS1 landing. © MoD

The flight deck of HMS *Hermes*, 1982. © MoD

Chapter 4 - Into The War Zone

The creation of the 200-mile Total Exclusion Zone (TEZ) around the Falkland Islands by the British Government set a clear marker that the British meant business and were set on their mission to liberate the Islands unless the Argentinian Junta withdrew their forces unconditionally.

However, as the various ships moved south however, the early optimism that a peaceful solution would be found and everyone could turn round and head home started to dissipate. The mood matched the weather. From the heat of the equator, the weather deteriorated and the seas got bigger as the southern hemisphere winter approached.

On board the ships the training intensified and changed from physical fitness to preparedness for enemy attack and duties at action stations. The issue of Once Only Suits to prolong survival in the chilling waters only increased the tension and reality of likely conflict.

But it was the short-lived joy at the news of the sinking of the *General Belgrano* soon followed by the sinking of HMS *Sheffield* that really brought home to everyone that war would happen and that the Argentine forces would be no pushover. Ships went on a war footing as they entered the TEZ with everyone increasingly aware of the threat the Argentine Airforce posed.

On land, the Falkland Islanders were corralled under armed guard into various settlements around the Islands to begin several weeks of occupation and imprisonment. Meanwhile SAS and SBS forces landed and remained undercover providing intelligence to the Task Force commanders and Northwood.

****

Exocet Concerns

This is the place to remember the fourteen shipmates who died as a result of the Exocet attack on the ship on 12th June. We will remember them.

HMS *Glamorgan* had four Exocet missiles, fitted in their sealed canisters, just aft of the twin 4.5-inch gun turret on the fo'c'sle and we fully understood the characteristics and limitations of the system. The Exocet threat was real as we headed south, and we knew which Argentinian ships and aircraft were Exocet-capable and were in no doubt that they would deploy and use the missiles. One small part of defending oneself was to use chaff and place it relative to the ship such that the incoming missile would be seduced to attack the silver paper target generated by the chaff (a rocket-fired bloom of radar-deceving foil strips), fly through it and eventually run out of power and ditch harmlessly in the sea.

The missiles, in those days, had a range of twenty miles and they were launched in the general direction of a target and would then activate the inbuilt radar system at a point ten miles from the expected position of the target. The radar in the missile would then search from near to far and from left to right and would acquire and lock onto the first target it located. The missiles would fly at one of three pre-determined heights above the sea; this height being set by the launching vehicle and could not be changed once launched.

Clearly, the best place to position the chaff cloud was ahead of the ship and on the starboard bow. However, if your ship was steaming, at 28 knots, to attack a surface ship, such as the ARA *General Belgrano*, and there was a headwind of say, 25 knots, then the chaff would be moving aft at 53 knots (61 mph) and would be useless as a means of distraction after just a few moments. We needed to know how often to fire a new chaff distraction cloud ahead of the ship. I designed a plastic calculator with inputs of wind speed and relative direction and ship's speed, which produced the requisite firing rate.

We soon realised that we would run out of chaff, ahead of re-sully, if we were to face many such challenges and we needed a better solution. This is where the idea of deploying our Wessex helicopter came from and we fabricated a large metal radar reflector in the classic diamond-shape and suspended it from the airframe. The pilot flew to the appropriate spot ahead of the ship, on the starboard bow, and yes, we did remember to remind him of the three heights at which the Exocet could fly and suggested he flew slightly higher than the greatest of the three, suggesting he flew slightly higher than the highest of the three!

There was one other major concern I had and that was the matter of where an incoming Exocet might hit the ship. *Glamorgan* had a magazine full of Sea Slug missiles, laid flat, in a magazine that ran two-thirds the length of the ship on Number Two deck. These two-ton missiles, twenty feet in length, had one serious drawback in that the four wrap-round boost missiles were extremely sensitive to physical shock and shrapnel from a missile strike would almost certainly cause ignition. If one booster was ignited the consequences were probably going to be disastrous for the ship as there would be sympathetic ignitions from other nearby boosters. Although the magazine was divided by flash doors and the missile immediately behind was protected by a deflecting plate, no one was entirely certain if we would survive.

Having studied the height above the sea at which Exocet would fly in its terminal phase, I realised we did have two very strong parts of the ship, namely the bow and the stern, which would absorb a lot of the energy and, more importantly, waste a few precious milliseconds as the missile impacted. The Exocet has a fuse delay of 14 milliseconds from impact to detonation, to allow the missile to penetrate the ship's skin and, of course, cause more damage by expending thr energy of the explosion within the confines of the ship. If we could take the impact on the bows, then the enormous weight and bulk of the two anchors and the anchor cables in the cable locker would absorb a lot of the energy and take up the 14 milliseconds, so that most of the energy of the warhead was expended into fresh air. Similarly, at the stern, we had the massive steel structure on the quarterdeck of the Sea Slug launcher and behind that two thick blast doors angled at 45 degrees, which again would do the trick.

After many hours discussing the options, the Captain instructed all Officers of the Watch and Warfare Officers in the Operations Room, that if we were ever to detect an inbound Exocet missile we must turn either towards or away, depending on the relative angle of approach. On 12th June when we were tragically hit, it was the reaction of the watch-keeping team on the bridge that saved the day, as they saw the incoming missile just abaft the port beam and turned away at 28 knots. The turn to starboard, at that speed caused the ship to roll quite substantially and the spurn-water on the deck-edge on the portside, where the missile hit, was several feet closer to the sea and to the missile height than normal. If it had struck us when we were steaming normally, I am certain it would have penetrated the ship's hull instead of the helicopter hangar higher up and caused catastrophic damage.

The first day at war

On 1st May, just after the Vulcan bombing raid on Stanley airfield, we detached with the frigates HMS *Arrow* and HMS *Alacrity* to bombard the airport at Stanley. During the process we were attacked by four Argentine Mirage aircraft. We were operating close inshore at the time and two aircraft appeared from around a bluff and were upon us before we could react. The pilot of the attacking aircraft appeared to make a simple mistake in his bombing run by flicking his wings, as he approached from dead astern, to make both of the two 500lb bombs he was going to drop, strike the ship. He over-corrected and the two bombs criss-crossed the ship and exploded beneath the stern, displacing an enormous amount of water, making the ship temporarily unstable.

In the Operations Room, as the ship started to roll dramatically, I heard a high pitched and young voice from somewhere in the darkness say, "*We're going over*", followed immediately by a deeper and more mature response *"No we're not laddie. Just get on with your plotting job. There's a good lad."*

Meanwhile, damage control parties throughout the ship were searching for signs of damage inflicted by the bombs, particularly towards the stern. One matter of real concern was the welfare of the young Mechanical Engineering Rating closed up, on his own, in the cold, damp and lonely steering gear compartment, right aft beneath the water line, the 'Tiller Flat'. His task, should damage be caused to the steering gear, was to switch the system to emergency steering control. The Senior Engineer in the Machinery Control Room amidships was obviously concerned that the rating was unhurt after what must have been a traumatric experience with two 500lb bombs exploding very close to the stern and he also wished to check the state of the steering gear itself. He telephoned the Tiller Flat.

"Are you alright down there?" he asked.

After a short pause, he received a reassuring response from the young lad and was told that the equipment was functioning perfectly and there appeared to be no real damage apart from a few shattered light bulbs. He continued:

"Is there anything you need then?'

"A new pair of overalls would come in handy, Sir," came the reply.

****

George Birkett, Chief Engineering Mechanician, HMS Invincible

<u>First Day Inside the TEZ</u>

I joined the Royal Navy in February 1961 and left in 1985. During the Falklands war, I served as a Chief Engineering Mechanician responsible for the forward propulsion section. This included two of the four Olympus gas turbines and the associated gearbox and ancillary equipment.

1st May: After learning that bombing raids had been carried out on the airport at Stanley everyone onboard was feeling very tense and ready for anything. Despite this it still came as quite a shock when the Action Alarm sounded and the ship was piped to Action Stations.

A few of us had been having a coffee in 6Q (deck 6 section Q) when the alarm sounded and the effect was amazing. I had not realised I had so many joints in my legs; they were like rubber for a few seconds and then the self-preservation took over and we were off. That initial feeling will stay with me forever, a combination of fear, panic and, I guess, excitement, although I think the excitement level was fairly low.

Once closed up down the Forward Engine Room (FER) the pulse rate started to slow as the mind became totally absorbed with the various tasks to be undertaken to get the space closed down for action.

The next important task was to find what we thought would be the safest place to take cover should the ship come under attack. We never found out if we had made the right selection. We would have found out the hard way if it had not been.

We spent the rest of the day closed up and listened intently as numerous raids (some spurious) developed and then receded.

During this period, I was amazed at how fallible radar is with regards to object recognition. Heavy cloud formations, fog banks in fact almost any solid or semi-solid object gave off a reflection.

In the interim, we had "Action Messing" which was feeding in shifts. The food was fairly basic, but filling. There was a set time to eat it, and then return to your action station and let the next shift go. The system worked very well. We would also have "Action Snacks" which was usually a cup of coffee and a bun or something else just as lethal.

The rest of the time was spent doing the odd cleaning job, reading or just relaxing. I started reading Lord of the Rings. We finally fell out from Action Stations at 2030 hours.

Conversation down 6Q was fairly animated, particularly with our Fleet Air Arm (WAFUs), giving us blow-by-blow accounts of that day's action. The Harrier Squadron (801) had been heavily involved and had been claiming two or maybe three kills, one of them being the first recorded of the campaign. No doubt the "Fog of War" had clouded the issue and we would learn later the true figures.

Our three SBS (Special Boat Service) visitors sat and took it all in, asking for clarification on various points. The situation for them must have been totally alien; after all they would normally be the focal point of any action.

One of the three, Kiwi, was in training, and was going to try and break the world press-ups record, and he would spend some time in the 6Q training room perfecting his technique. Being in there with him was really awe-inspiring. For his rest period between sessions he would 'relax' by doing sit-ups.

We tried to keep all three supplied with "Nutty" (sweets/chocolate) it kept our energy levels up. Supplies of were limited so they really appreciated thrm.

Note 1: Compartments were designated from forward A to aft depending on the number of compartments. Q was fairly well aft of the ship, in fact if I remember correctly the final compartment designation was U.
Note 2: WAFU - Terms for Fleet Air Arm personnel - Nickname Wet and Flipping useless or Weapons and Fuel Users. There is also a much ruder version of the first term!

****

Neil Maher, Signaller, Army Air Corps. On board the QE2.
Courtesy of the Army Flying Museum

QE2 to the *Canberra*

Then to the SS *Canberra*. Coming the other way were the survivors from HMS *Sheffield*, so they'd obviously gone through a bit of a bad time and were entitled to a nice journey back on the *QE2* and we were just going to head the other way.

So, unfortunately for us the SS *Canberra,* although I am sure it is a lovely ship. It had had the marines on it prior to us and had already been down to San Carlos Water. Now in South Georgia to pick us up and it was probably not in its usually tip top condition. Having come from the *QE2* it was a bit of a drop in standards. Yeah, I ended up in a room of about six to eight of us in this cabin, just bunkbeds. We were escorted by HMS *Antrim* to meet up with the Task Force, and when you met up with the fleet you went out on deck and boy did it make you look and feel proud because you saw this big flotilla of ships and it was really impressive. It did make you feel proud.

We basically slept in our combats and all our webbing, and everything was all piled up in the middle of the room with our weapons and everything, just waiting.

****

Stuart McCulloch, Radio Operator, HMS Fearless

Arriving in the War Zone

When we arrived near the islands, the ship was in a lockdown situation where you only went above deck if your duties required you to.

We had been given our issue of equipment for the conflict – a gas mask (in case of a gas attack), anti-flash gear (a white balaclava and a pair of white gloves that we were to wear in case of an explosion and flash of flames to protect our head and hands) and our Once-Only Suit to be used if we needed to abandon ship. It was designed to help keep us warm for a couple of minutes in the water, any longer than that and chances of survival were slim. We had to make our own dog tags (which I still have) which said 'Seaman Rating' so that I could not be identified as a radio operator for fear of torture for information should I beome a POW.

There were updates from the captain on the situation and what we would be looking to do and, one evening, we were told that we would be landing the Task Force in San Carlos Water, on the north-west coats of East Falkland, overnight and that, for the duration of that, we would be going into radio silence. I wasn't on duty that night and it was weird waking up the next morning and finding that we had indeed landed troops whilst I'd been sleeping.

Then the air attacks started.

****

Andrew Cave, Seaman Missileman S(M) on HMS Hermes on the Weapon Direction Platform

Harriers in Action

On 1st May operating inside TEZ we went to dawn action stations knowing that a Vulcan bomber (Operation Blackbuck) was preparing to drop its payload on Stanley airfield. This was not an exercise and I remember making my ascent to the chaff rocket launchers through all the chaos, noise, and difficulties in navigating the many decks with others via ladders and kidney shaped hatches which were smaller hatches in the larger closed hatches.

Whilst at my action station (one of the chaff rocket launchers), I watched our 12 Harriers launch to attack the airfields at Stanley and Goose Green with 1,000lb bombs and BL755 cluster bombs, accompanied by eight more Harriers from HMS *Invincible.* About an hour later our jump jets returned through the mist and one by one they landed with one Harrier having a 20mm cannon shell hole through its tail fin from Argentinian anti-aircraft fire. This first attack by our Harriers led to BBC war correspondent Brian Hanrahan's now famous sentence. *"I'm not allowed to say how many planes joined the raid, but I counted them all out, and I counted them all back."*

We were now well and truly over the start line, and although I didn't know it at the time, but the next few months would have a massive impact on my later life. The very next day saw the

Argentine cruiser ARA *General Belgrano* torpedoed by HMS *Conqueror* with the loss of 323 lives.

****

Nigel Turner, Cook on HMS Hermes

Daily Action Stations

The sinking of the *General Belgrano* was met with an initial cheer, but soon became a reflective moment as that could easily have been us in the freezing water and life rafts. Senses became heightened as there was bound to be retaliation. Once again going to Action Stations as 'Air Raid Red' warning sounded out, myself and fellow cook Mark Say went into our routine of closing doors and hatches and taking our station either side of the large 2 Sierra (flat) compartment. We were both sited next to hose reels and a damage control phone connected to the after-section base.

Two days later at Action Stations the news arrived that HMS *Sheffield* had been hit by an Exocet missile flying at over 700mph and that casualties were being flown to *Hermes*. The most serious casualties were taken straight to the sickbay, and others into 2 Sierra flat where camp beds had been laid out for the injured. The sight of burnt blackened faces, shocked faces, staring eyes, smell of burnt clothing and the quietness of the injured seemingly accepting their fate. Myself feeling so helpless and yet angry. This is not a conflict - this is war - we could be killed and set me thinking more than ever about my wife and little girls.

But life on board carried on with daily Action Stations and air raids on the fleet and a heightened state of readiness 24/7. We had now been issued with fire retardant overalls to wear over our No.8s (action working dress) and to carry them at all times. The MOD in its cost cutting had replaced the all-cotton No. 8s with a polyester/cotton mix which had melted onto the skin of the *Sheffield* casualties causing severe burns.

Tom Rowan, Petty Officer Aircraft Mechanician for 899 Squadron on board HMS Hermes

Harrier Trouble on the Flight Deck

I was on the flight deck as this was my action station if not carrying out repairs/servicing on Sea Harriers and RAF Gr3 aircraft.

A Sea Harrier was recovering to the deck and dropped his nozzles to the hover position and from a perfectly normal recovery we had a huge cloud of smoke and steam emanating from the aircraft. The FDO (Flight Deck Officer) quickly got the aircraft on to the deck, the pilot raised the nozzles to the normal flight position and the smoke etc reduced immediately.

I got the FDO to position the aircraft into the area in front of the bridge called the "graveyard", an old-fashioned term because that was where 'dead' aircraft were positioned away from danger so that any damage could be assessed. A quick debrief of the pilot established that he may have been hit by ground fire, i.e small arms.

The aircraft was still smoking at the rear so I asked the "greenie" (electrical) guy, Bud Abbott, to remove the access panels to the equipment bay whilst I went up the rear hatch to remove the "LOX" pack which was a pressurised container of liquid oxygen to allow the pilot to breath at altitude. I have to point out that my headgear was painted in yellow and black stripes. Anyway, as soon as Bud removed the side panels, daylight flooded into the area where I was removing the potentially dangerous lox pack.

Apparently, the FDO had decided to observe our actions and was diligently standing by with a CO2 fire extinguisher!! In his defence, he must have glimpsed my yellow striped crash hat in the confined space I was in and let go with the CO2 right into my face! Well, CO2 immediately removes all oxygen and I literally fell out of the panel with 3 kilos of LOX pack in my hand!! And there I am lying on the deck temporarily unconscious with the equipment lying beside me!! I came to very quickly and realised that I had just been "gassed" by one of our officers!

I do admit I was a tad unhappy and expressed my displeasure in sparkling "Queen's English" and suggested that the FDO should remove himself from my general vicinity!!

I can laugh about it now, but as the saying goes, "*that's life in a blue suit.*"

****

Simon Sugden, Weapons Engineering Mechanic Ordnance, HMS Coventry

The Reality of War

1st May was to me, "D-Day". By this date the full Task Force had formed up, the Total Exclusion Zone was in place and ourselves, HMS *Sheffield* and HMS *Glasgow* formed up as the forward protection line to protect the carriers from air attack. This was it; this was real. David Hart-Dyke, our skipper, called the ship to Action Stations and I closed up at the Aft Damage Control Section Base. My role was to be part of a four man patrol whose job was to search for damage following an attack and to report back to the section base on fires, floods and/or structural damage.

Once the ship was closed up and in the highest state of readiness then we waited - and waited. What were we waiting for? One of those moments that goes down in history. We were waiting for the Vulcan strike. The Ops Room kept us informed as they tracked its progress and we were waiting for one word "*superfuse*", the code word for a successful attack on Stanley Airport. On hearing this the mood changed from one of trepidation to one of exhilaration - this was it, this was what we had trained for, and more excitement followed as the Harriers took their turn on the airport.

2nd May brought more news to cheer about, the sinking of the cruiser *General Belgrano*. As I say, something to cheer about after all, we were at war. Over the years I have thought about the lives lost and whilst it is saddening, I do feel that the order to sink her was justified. She could have changed course at a moment's notice and her big guns could have fired upon us at over 20 miles away, , not to mention the Exocets her escorts were carrying as well as, we now know, she was too.

Spirits were high until on the 4th May when the mood would change. Once again we were in formation with HMS *Sheffield* and HMS *Glasgow*. Earlier in the day one of our main radars had gone down, so we changed position with HMS *Sheffield*, putting us in a central position between the two other ships. Then came the broadcast "*Air Raid Warning Red, hands to action stations*".

Unfortunately, *Sheffield* was struck amidships and whilst a massive blow for us all, things could have been worse as it failed to explode. To see her ablaze on the horizon and to later hear that she had sunk whilst being towed to South Georgia for emergency repairs focused all our minds and made us realise that not only was this for real but we, too, were vulnerable.

A positive to come out of her sinking was that lessons had been learnt in the short period between the strike and her sinking. Not all doors and hatches had to be closed, in fact leaving certain hatches open would prevent them being buckled or twisted and hindering escape.

****

Mike Norman, First Lieutenant and Executive Officer, HMS Sheffield

Extracts from Mike Norman's memories on HMS Sheffield

<u>HMS *Sheffield* - Hit by an Exocet</u>

At approximately 1000 hours on 4th May, *Sheffield* was at defence watches (second degree readiness), the southernmost of three Type 42 destroyers (the others being HMS *Glasgow* and *Coventry*) operating as a forward anti-aircraft picket 18 to 30 miles (29 to 48 km) to the west of the main Task Force which were south-east of the Falklands.

I set off after lunch to carry out 'Rounds' of the ship, checking on watertight security and battle preparedness. We were now at the second degree of readiness in Defence Watch having been closed beforehand at Action Stations since dawn.

It was four days into the war, 4th May 1982. ARA *General Belgrano* had been sunk two days previously and with this came the realisation that we really now were at war with Argentina. I went the short distance aft from my cabin to the ladder down to 2 Deck. I was not sure what came first; whether it was the loud bang or the hammer-like blow to my chest, followed by all the air being sucked out of my lungs. I picked myself up off the deck.

"What the hell was that for Christ's sake", I thought? Had we been hit by something without warning? Certainly there was no '"Take Cover" broadcast from the Officer-on-Watch on the Bridge or from the Ops Room. Nor was I aware of any aircraft screaming low overhead. Was there something bad happening in one of the machinery spaces? Whatever it was had come out of nowhere.

I looked down at the wooden ladder and noticed it had disintegrated in the shock wave and lay in a heap of splintered wood on the deck below. I couldn't believe what I was looking at. I climbed down, somehow, to 2 Deck, to be met by a large amount of black acrid smoke filling the passageway fast. People were coming out of the Ops Room, shouting, coughing and spluttering, some with flash burns on the face and eyes streaming. My eyes started to stream too. Instinct kicked in. I crouched down low where the air was a little less thick with smoke and put on my AGR (anti-gas respirator). This at least protected the eyes and would give me some protection from the toxic smoke. The emergency lighting was next to useless in the circumstances. The best I could do at that moment was to lead survivors forward to the fo'cstle escape hatch, feeling my way along the cluttered bulkheads, past the ladder down to Gunners messdeck. On opening the hatch, light and air flooded into the darkness below. The fresh air was sweet and removing my AGR, I gulped in lungfuls.

Climbing out onto the foc'stle with some difficulty, due to all the survival kit I was carrying, and looking back I could see a huge column of black smoke billowing up the starboard side of the superstructure, obscuring the mainmast. I ran to the starboard side and it became all too apparent what had happened. There was a huge hole in the hull amidships about six feet above the waterline, belching fire and black smoke.

Then the word 'Exocet' flashed into my mind aboutwhich there had been a lot of talk and speculation. Trying not to think of the carnage inside the ship I grabbed a hose, and with others - I don't know who - we connected it to one of the foc'stle fire hydrants and turned the wheel. Nothing! We tried another hydrant in desperation - still no water. This was not good. Then I remembered the Emergency Rover Gas Turbine (RGT) Pump stored down aft near No2 Section base. I ran there via the port waist passageway to find that a couple of Chiefs had already got it onto the quarterdeck and were making preps to start it up. The starting handle was cranked up but then the bloody chain mechanism broke before it reached self–sustaining rpm. It had been tested every day without mishap. Typical. Now we really were f***ed, with our last real chance to tackle the fire having gone.

Climbing up the superstructure I reported this fact to the Captain, who I found on the bridge roof. The bridge had already been evacuated and the bridge wing doors clipped shut. A short discussion ensued and we realised from the outset we were a dead ship. We needed to tell the Admiral what had happened but with no communication with the outside world the Captain decided to send our Lynx with the Ops Officer, Lt Cdr Nick Batho, to tell the Admiral on HMS *Hermes* what had happened.

The Ops Officer arrived on the flight deck by which time the aircraft was 'burning and turning'. Apart from telling *Hermes* what had happened, emphasising that we had no firemain water or motive power worth speaking of and no communications, he was to ask in particular for firefighting equipment, Breathing Apparatus (BA) and emergency fire pumps plus what first-aid kit for burns they could quickly rustle up. He was also to request helo assistance to evacuate our wounded.

And then an eerie silence descended on the ship, save for the crackling black smoke and occasional muffled explosions coming from somewhere below decks. Amazingly, I noticed we were still underway on one Tyne gas turbine in a slow turn to port. The sea was calm with a low undulating swell. What to do now I thought? What of the ship's Company?

I rushed along the port waist again to arrive on the fo'castle to find there was quite a throng who had made their escape from below decks. Many were injured, some seriously, with varying degrees of burns. They were being attended to by the ship's Doctor, Surgeon Lieutenant David Ward and POMA 'Ged' Meagre. One man in particular caught my eye, MEM Harrington, who had apparently managed to climb up a 40 ft escape ladder in the FAMR where the missile explosion had occurred. His nylon clothing had melted and fused onto his skin in places and he was clearly in agony. I enquired if he had been given morphine. I needn't have asked. CERA Strange was equally in a bad way with 60% or more burns. The team was doing everything they could for them. I saw the 'Buffer',(Chief Botswain's Mate) CPO John Batting, briefly and asked him to get a small team together to go round all the upper deck hatches and bulkhead doors to make sure they were all clipped tightly shut, ventilation outlet trunking too, if he could. We needed to cut off the supply of air and oxygen to the fire as much as possible.

Then I heard a GPMG opening up on the bridge wing port side. "*Christ, are we under air attack again*?" I could see the gunner, Able Seaman Purcell, giving it what for at something in the distance. I strained to see what he was shooting at. "*Christ, it was one of our own, a Sea King*". I shouted, gesticulated and waved my arms at him to go 'guns tight'. "*That was a close shave*" I thought. But such is the fog of war. The Sea King was too far away to be concerned about this 'blue on blue'. They probably never knew they had been fired on by us anyway. They had obviously come to do a recce, guided by the pall of smoke on the horizon as seen from the rest of the Task Force way to our rear.

And so began 'my war' in earnest in a very distressing and ignominious way. As the saying goes 'War is 95% boredom and 5% terrifying. This was my 5% moment...'

Two days later...

It was a black chilly night in the South Atlantic as we stood on the quarterdeck of HMS *Hermes,* aware of the presence of others only from stifled coughs and the occasional 'sniffle'. The ship's Chaplain was doing his best to conduct the service from memory because no lights were allowed during darkened ship routine in case an enemy submarine should be close by. His words sounded detached from the reality around us, fading and returning as the rhythm and noise from machinery and the ship's wake competed for our attention in the darkness.

Somewhere to my right, under the cover of a Union Jack and stitched up in canvas, was the body of Petty Marine Engineering Mechanic David Briggs. We had recovered him from the fo'cstle of the ship earlier that same day. Two days previously he was alive and a valuable member of our close-knit ship's company. Now he was dead, asphyxiated by black toxic smoke as he tried selflessly to retrieve valuable firefighting equipment from within the for'ard part of the ship. He didn't have the proper breathing apparatus for protection and he made just one journey too many. Petty Officer Medical Assistant 'Ged' Meagre, having gone in to rescue him with no thought for his own safety, tried desperately to revive him but it was too late.

In the darkness my mind drifted back to the events of 4th May. Was it really only two days ago? It all seemed so unreal. And I had had very little sleep at all since those terrible moments of carnage, death and devastation. Our attempts to save our much-loved ship, in the end, were futile in the end, an impossible task with no means to fight the raging inferno below decks. When help did arrive after about an hour and a half in the form of pumps and BA it was too late. In reality it was probably too late from the outset but we had to try.

In the end our captain, Captain "Sam" Salt, a submariner by trade, decided to abandon ship to prevent further loss of life since the fire was spreading forward unchecked, towards the missile and shell magazines. There was a very real risk that the whole ship could blow up. So unceremoniously the crew jumped across to HMS *Arrow,* alongside on our port side, heaving up and down in the gentle South Atlantic swell, our hulls tortuously grinding together, metal to metal. Some of the crew had narrow escapes from being crushed between the two hulls.

After a while a Sea King arrived and it wasn't long before the captain, the MEO, Commander Bob Rowley and I, accompanied by Chief Electrician Mike Smith and Chief Gunnery Instructor, Charlie Adamson, were being winched up clear of the flight deck, our captain being the last to leave. And as I looked down on what had been our home for the last eight months, on fire and belching alternate black and white smoke from every orifice, I remember looking at my watch and being in disbelief that we had been fighting to save our ship for over four and a half hours. It seemed like only half an hour!

As we transited the fifteen or so miles to the Flagship, HMS *Hermes*, we survivors must have looked a very sorry bunch, sitting there cold, wet and dirty, staring blankly ahead and alone in our own thoughts and insecurities. For my part these were mostly thoughts of disbelief as to what had happened, coupled with a sense of inadequacy and failure. I expect the others felt much the same. We knew we were at war with Argentina. But suddenly it had become personal.

My mind returned to the present and the solemn matter in hand. The Padre was again competing for our attention above the noise of the sea and the vibration of the ship with the words of the naval hymn. We did our best to join in…

"Eternal Father strong to save
Whose arm hath bound the restless wave
Who bidd'st the mighty ocean deep
Its own appointed limits keep.
O hear us when we cry to Thee
For those in peril on the sea"

I could hardly get these words, and the verses that followed, out of my mouth and my eyes welled up with tears. But that didn't matter. This seemed to be the most fitting and poignant hymn in the circumstances we found ourselves. I stared as hard as I could in the direction of Petty Officer Briggs and even though my eyes had gained some of their 'night vision' the night was starless and still very black. All I could do was imagine what was happening as the Padre conducted the committal.

Then I heard a rasping 'whoosh' which I realised was the sound of canvas sliding on wood and a moment later a 'splash' as his body hit the sea twenty feet below. Nobody said anything after this sombre experience, deep in our own thoughts and conscious of our frailties. We dispersed wondering what tomorrow would bring.

That first evening was interrupted when the ship's main broadcast burst into life.

*"Do you hear there? Commander speaking. Just a quick update for you on the day's events. I expect most of you by now will have heard the terribly sad news that Sheffield, who was on Air Defence picket duty some 40 miles up-threat, was hit by an Exocet missile at about 1400 Zulu this afternoon. The Task Force defences including the Sea Harriers were unable to deter or prevent this attack. After four or more hours of heroic attempts to put out the fire the ship was abandoned to prevent further loss of life. We have a number of casualties onboard which are being treated in our Sick Bay, mainly for burns. There is no information available at this moment on casualties or survivors but I will let you know more as information becomes available. The other sad item of news today is that three Harriers of *** Squadron took off on a bombing raid on Argentine*

positions at Goose Green and sadly only two aircraft returned. So not a good day for the Task Force today. Finally, let me remind you that the submarine threat continues and that the ship's company should remain above the waterline unless their duties require otherwise. That is all".

The final toll was 19 missing presumed dead plus PO MEM Briggs whom we'd buried at sea earlier. 263 had survived. Of the survivors 26 were injured, six suffering serious burns. There were some incredibly heroic and miraculous escapes. Most of the injured were in *Hermes*' sick bay and the PMO allowed Captain 'Sam', Bob Rowley and myself to visit them yesterday evening. They were mostly remarkably cheerful. The strength of the human spirit in times of acute adversity never ceases to amaze me.

7th May – Three days after HMS *Sheffield* had been hit

And so it was that in the late forenoon, the MEO, Bob Rowley and I took off in a Sea King piloted by Keith Dudley again who had volunteered for the job. The sea was calm with a low undulating swell coming from the southwest.

Keith's voice came on the intercom saying that he had visual on *Sheffield* about two miles on the 'nose' and that she was upright and level in the water. I unstrapped my seat harness and standing up I put on the 'despatcher harness' that the aircrewman gave me, something I had done many times previously. He motioned me towards the open cabin door, clipping my harness to an overhead rail. I sat myself down in the doorway, feet resting on the outside cabin step. Leaning well forward I could see the ship ahead of us, shrouded in mist like some sort of '*Marie Celeste*'. She was indeed afloat and level in the gentle South Atlantic swell. We approached with caution coming up on her astern on the port side at about 100 yards distant just in case she chose this moment to explode.

The first thing I noticed was that the two AS12 Missiles we had unloaded from the Lynx two days before, had 'cooked off' in the intense heat of the fire in the hangar and had exploded. The hanger doors had blown out. I asked Keith to close in for a closer look and as we came to the hover and moving sideways towards her I could feel the heat coming off the hull and superstructure even at this distance. One could also see the shimmering heat haze above her. Everywhere I looked the paint had been badly blistered by internal fires from the waterline all the way up to the superstructure, radomes and masts. The only areas that were not blistered were the magazines in the bow, so the sprinkler system had indeed worked after all and had flooded the Sea Dart and 4.5inch shell magazines.

I asked Keith to do a slow circuit so that I could see the starboard side where the Exocet had entered the ship. Apart from the 18 foot by six feet jagged hole in the centre of the ship about six feet above the waterline, the blistered and blackened paint on the starboard side was just the same as the port side. So the ship had burnt from end to end except the magazines in the bow, for'ard of the fore screen. On closer inspection of the missile entry point one could clearly see that the hull plating was 'belled' outwards with considerable 'petalling' of the plating, consistent with our belief that the missile had indeed exploded inside the hull in the area of the FAMR and galley.

I then suggested to Keith that I thought it was safe enough for me to be lowered onto the fo'cstle. I could see Petty Officer Briggs' body by the Sea Dart Launcher under a cover of some sort.

The heat coming off the blackened and charred fore screen and the bridge was very noticeable despite the rotor downwash. What particularly caught my eye, curiously, as I began to be lowered down onto the fo'cstle was the very blackened and blistered paint on the port side of the fore screen, the other side of which was or had been my cabin. It must have been an inferno in there and all my belongings, some very much treasured like my Aircrew Flying Log Book, would now be burnt to a cinder.

I was now on deck in the foremost part of the fo'cstle. It was eerily quiet in the swirling mist and weak sunshine. I went over to Petty Officer Briggs' body and turned back the cover. He seemed at peace with the world. I pulled up the cover again out of respect.

He was a brave man who I hoped would be recognised at the appropriate time.

I motioned to Keith to come in closer and gave him the 'thumbs up' for the MEO to join me on the fo'cstle and motioned that I wanted the Neil Robertson stretcher, which is a canvas and bamboo contraption especially useful in confined spaces. The MEO came down on the winch wire with the stretcher clipped on as well. We laid out the stretcher on the deck beside Petty Officer Briggs and then lifted his body on to it. It never ceases to amaze me how much deadweight a body can be. I hooked on the stretcher and gave the 'thumbs up' to the crewman and up he went as I guided the stretcher clear of the guardrails until I saw that he was safely inside the cabin.

Finally, I took some photos of the fo'cstle area with the Hasselblad camera with a 127 roll of black and white film, borrowed from the Leading Phot in the aircraft. I asked Keith if we could do one complete circuit of the ship so that the Leading Phot could get his pics. As we manoeuvred around the ship at about 50 yards distant, I made mental notes of some of the less expected damaged areas like the upper superstructure, the charred radomes and masts. There was very little that escaped the inferno. Then we turned for home. It wasn't long before we were back onboard and shutting down the rotors. There was a reception party from the Sick Bay to take away the body and Bob Rowley and I went to debrief our Captain on what we had seen and found. It was 7th May, Doomsday plus 3!

Sheffield was taken under tow to South Georgia, but then the weather deteriorated and she rolled over and sank. The survivors were collected up and returned to Ascension Island via a returning BP Tanker *British Esk* and thence to the UK via 'Crab Air' the RAF!!

****

HMS *Sheffield* Ablaze

Tuesday 4th May (on *Alacrity*)

At 1800 hours we hear that the Captain of *Sheffield* has given the order to 'Abandon Ship'. It has been a long time since any RN Captain has had to issue such an order. We all received the news with great sadness. How can one of our modern ships be caught out like that? It is now confirmed that it was an Exocet missile, launched below the horizon that hit the ship. There are around 20 dead on board.

At 1820 hours we fall out of action stations and I meet up with NGFO3 (Naval Gunfire Forward Observer) who all look quite shocked. They have now stepped over that invisible line which divides exercise play from war. It is now 1930 hours and *Sheffield* is ablaze but it is thought she may not sink after all.

At 2015 hours we go to action stations again due to aircraft in the area. There is a renewed haste about closing up now and all upper deck lookouts suddenly develop 20-20 vision. The hostiles are once again chased off by our CAP. At 2115 hours we stand down again and all of us are left with our private thoughts. We have a quiet night with both sides licking their wounds. I find it hard to sleep because each noise sounds like something else and each wave that hits the ships side sounds like ... well, you can guess.

****

Alan Gratton, Steward, HMS Yarmouth

Helping HMS *Sheffield*

I was working in the officers' bar in HMS *Rooke* (Gibraltar) when I was summoned to the Supply Officers' office and informed that I was to join HMS *Yarmouth* in place of a steward. He had broken his arm and I had to do a temporary swop draft as I was one of the only single stewards on the base.

HMS *Yarmouth* was first to go to the aid of HMS *Sheffield* and took off the first casualties. I was a member of the first aid team. We later towed the ship before she sank. To see HMS *Sheffield* on fire will always remain so vivid. I had always felt so safe being onboard until that day. We didn't stay too long with *Sheffield* that day as there were reports that there might be a sub in the area.

The ship also helped HMS *Ardent* in Falkland Sound and later on 21st May when she was bombed, whilst protecting the San Carlos landings, our time was spent trying to hose her down. *Ardent* later sank.

****

Andrew Cave, Seaman Missileman S(M) on HMS Hermes on the Weapon Direction Platform

***Sheffield* Survivors**

On the 4th May we were called to action stations due to an air threat, and at some point, we became aware of a great deal of smoke coming from the horizon. This turned out to be HMS *Sheffield*, which had been hit on her starboard side by an air-launched Exocet missile. There was then a great deal of helicopter activity as firefighting teams and equipment was loaded and dispatched to *Sheffield*'s aid. Some time later these helicopters started to return carrying the brave injured survivors from *Sheffield* who were taken to our sickbay. I, like many others that day, saw things that you can never unsee including some terrible burn injuries. Some hours later

I can recall passing a group of survivors, some with what I believe to be cling film covering their burns, sitting quietly in a passageway clearly haunted by their recent experience. *Sheffield* lost 20 Sailors on this day with a further 26 injured and she sank six days later becoming a war grave.

****

Phill Basey, 3rd Officer on tanker MV British Esk

Taking *Sheffield* Survivors Home

By this time, we were running low on cargo, we were detached to meet up with the Amphibious Group coming south and conducted stern RAS with one of the RN Assault Ships, (I can't remember if it was HMS *Fearless* or HMS *Intrepid)* and a number of other ships.

We gave up the rest of our cargo to an RFA before heading north. Prior to departing we had 200+ survivors from *Sheffield* put on board. Every spare bit of cabin space, storage spaces, cupboard shelves was made into a bed space; I had an additional four POs in my cabin sleeping on camp beds. I was on good terms with the Chief Steward and even though we had been a dry ship for some weeks, I managed to get a bottle of rum from him every now and again, to leave in my cabin when I went on watch at night. When I returned to my cabin there was always a tot left on the side table. Strangely my bunk was also always pristine but warm.

Our journey north took a final twist when the Argentinian Air Force Intel 707 found us, circling round us at lowish level before disappearing. We didn't know what it was but the *Sheffield* guys did, so we headed east for a couple of days just in case.

We dropped the *Sheffield* survivors off at Ascension then we headed for Portsmouth. A quick few days with wives and girlfriends, refuel, more cargo, more provisions and then south again for round 2, this time with two T42 destroyers for company.

George Birkett, Chief Engineering Mechanician, HMS Invincible

Personal Links to HMS *Sheffield*

Tuesday 4th May

In total contrast to yesterday, the weather today was perfect for flying. The morning passed fairly quickly, and before closing up I had a walk up top and stood on one of the starboard side weather decks to enjoy the sun and the view, which consisted mainly of sea. One of the Petty Officer Mechanicians (Pete Gooch) joined me and we stood chatting about things in general and nothing in particular.

Our conversation was brought to an abrupt end by the Action Stations alarm sounding and the ship being piped to Action Stations. Within minutes of closing-up down in the FER we were "hitting the deck" as warnings of "missiles in flight" filled the air.

After a short time, we were informed over the main broadcast, that HMS *Sheffield* had been hit. Information at first was vague, and the means of attack i.e., torpedo or missile was not clear, although early indications favoured a missile attack. Later it was confirmed that the attack had been from an air launched Exocet.

Everything seemed so surreal and we carried on doing what we could, listening to the news that was put out from the Command or via the Ship Control Centre (SCC). The reality of the situation became very clear when it was announced that HMS *Sheffield* was being abandoned. Casualties had been flown to HMS *Hermes*, and HMS *Arrow* was alongside HMS *Sheffield* taking off the Ship's Company.

The saying "The first cut is the deepest" was certainly apt in this instance, and none of the future ship losses had quite the same effect as that of the *Sheffield*.

For myself and several others the feeling of loss was a little greater, as we had served on HMS *Sheffield* in the earlier years of her life, and still had good memories of our time onboard. I didn't know at the time, but a good friend of mine John Strange was a crew member. I wondered how the Commander of the Task Group felt, for Admiral Woodward as he was now, had been captain of HMS *Sheffield* during my time onboard.

The rest of the day was spent closed up, and we listened to reports on *Sheffield*, and later that evening when we fell out, it was still the main topic of conversation.

****

Ewen Southby-Tailyour, ***Major, Royal Marines***

A fuller account is provided in Ewen's book Reasons in Writing

My 1982 in a Nutshell

That Argentina invaded the Falkland Islands did not come as a surprise to anyone who had lived there before 1982. Then, the near-constant topic at private parties and public meetings, in Government House, across the settlements and in the pubs had never been 'if' but 'when and how'.

I had been appointed to command Naval Party 8901 between 1978 and 1979, in preparation for which I attended meetings in the MoD, the FCO and GCHQ. My orders, jointly, were clear. During 'our year' we were to disregard the previous plan which, on invasion, had us rushing in to the bare countryside to conduct 'guerrilla warfare'! We were now to propose and, if agreed at Cabinet level, practice a staunch defence of Stanley and especially Government House. This we began but there were two snags. First, we had no defence stores or weapons and, second, the Governor, Jim Parker, was being briefed by a different department within the FCO and one that supported his view that any invasion force should be met with cups of tea!

Thus, much of our training had to be conducted without the Governor knowing - and when he did know he forbad it. Bizarrely, these 'prohibitions' also restricted myself, my wife, Patricia, and our two young children Hamish and Hermione from mixing with most of Stanley society. Clearly this was impossible and culminated in a signal to the Secretary of State for Foreign Affairs from the

Governor, complaining about my military and social disobedience. Luckily, we had an ally in Rear-Admiral William Staveley, then Chief of Staff to the Commander in Chief Fleet, who wrote a personal and strongly worded letter to me offering full and total support for both my military and 'social' actions.

Reconnaissance Pre-War

One of our many requirements was the selection of a beach into which a SBS reconnaissance patrol could be landed by submarine in advance of any (possible) re-invasion by the British. I could not choose this in isolation and so needed to visit as many beaches as possible, not only to allay suspicion of what I was really up to, but to ensure that I had the widest selection from which to choose the best (eventually, Campa Menta Bay) from both the hydrographic point-of-view and the military perspective.

Using our 150-ton MV *Forrest*, under the command of the redoubtable Jack Sollis - and any visiting yachts - I instituted a series of patrols that, in addition to our duty of training the 'Settlement Volunteers', allowed me to 'survey' as much of the coastline as possible. I could not risk anyone, especially the Governor, knowing the 'secondary' reason for these visits and so was obliged to state that I was compiling a yachtsmen's guide for the various clubs of which I was a member. Of course, this did not amuse the Governor either!

At the end of the year, I had amassed over 1,000 photographs and filled a 120 page, A4 notebook with hand drawn charts, notes and sketches of the coastline. I had also annotated the eight Admiralty charts I had, almost all of which were dated 1833!

On my return to the United Kingdom I offered this work to the Chief Hydrographer of the Navy who commented, '*These are the amateur jottings of an itinerant yachtsman and are of no interest to this department.*' And there the matter lay until the morning of 2nd April 1982 when I was summoned to Headquarters 3 Commando Brigade and a very busy Brigadier Julian Thompson.

"*Tell me all you know about the Falkland Islands.*"

"I won't tell you a thing unless you take me with you!" We were long-standing friends.

"You're coming, now prepare a lecture for my HQ first thing tomorrow morning." I did and homed in on San Carlos, among others, as a 'place of interest'.

On joining HMS *Fearless* I was not expected so I set up my 'office' and cabin in a bathroom and the next morning pondered over how I was to play the immediate future. This needed careful handling to prevent my love affair with the islands clouding my advice. Eventually I explained to the Brigadier and Commodore Amphibious Warfare, Michael Clapp, that I would only offer facts and never (my very subjective) opinions. From then onwards I was on call throughout every 24 hours, often summoned at 0300 hours to watch a big toe point to a section of a large map spread across the brigadier's cabin carpet. *"There Ewen! What's that place like?"*

I would give a five-minute synopsis and if they thought the place needed further discussion would return with a slideshow and comprehensive brief. Added to this routine were my instructions to lecture to every military formation in the Task Force as it headed south, requiring numerous flights and night-stops across the fleet.

Only twice did I let my personal feelings creep into my advice. On one occasion I wanted to prevent a landing onto the islands' only king penguin colony (Volunteer Bay) and, on another, I needed to thwart the destruction of one of the most beautiful islands (Carcass Island) with a vast concrete runway. The commanders saw through each subterfuge and quietly ignored me!

Having sailed from Ascension Island, I briefed many ships' captains and commanding officers, including those of the SBS and the SAS; the latter two for a number of 'advance force' operations prior to the main landings. Subsequently it became clear that while the SBS took my advice on local conditions and planned accordingly, the SAS '*knew better*'. Hence the raid on the Pebble Island airstrip was inexcusably delayed for, against my guidance, the reconnaissance party was landed to the east of the notorious Tamar passage (with a tidal stream of up to ten knots) which they then decided to cross in canoes, the most inappropriate method of travel across the whole archipelago. I had advised them to land across a beach at the north of Pebble Island in inflatable craft launched from a frigate. As a result the SAS asked Rear-Admiral Woodward - the Battle Group Commander - for a delay which would have meant the raid taking place after the San Carlos landings. Woodward ordered them to *'get on with it'*.

Finally, on 13th May, yet with no final confirmation from Northwood but with an original list of 11 possible assault areas reduced to three, and on the assumption that San Carlos would be the chosen one of those three, the Brigade Commander gave his 'Orders Group'. The Commodore's pre-landing conference would follow.

Prior to this O Group I was, for the first time, asked for my personal opinion of San Carlos as our amphibious objective. Up to then, I had not been privy to the differing needs of the sea and land forces and could only comment as far as the topography was concerned. Now I could state that it was certainly the best anchorage that I knew of - land-locked, surrounded by hills and with useful beaches - from which to conduct further operations once the Commando Brigade had been established ashore. I played no part in choosing San Carlos: that final judgement was for those more senior than me to make, with all the facts and intelligence available to which I was not (totally) privy. Considerations ranged from the comparative strengths and capabilities of our and the Argentine forces (afloat, ashore, and in the air) together with the topography, weather and sea states, distances to Stanley, distances from the closest enemy airfields, logistic support areas, transport availability (mainly helicopters) and the rest.

I suppose it was inevitable that, as the senior landing craft officer in the Task Force and as one who knew the area well, I was tasked with leading the initial amphibious assault onto the chosen beaches within San Carlos Waters on the 21st May.

Then, in theory, my part in the saga ended but I remained on call for future tasks, one of which was the landing of the Scots Guards into Bluff Cove from HMS *Intrepid*. However, the ship did not launch its four laden landing craft in the position ordered by the commodore. This unforgiveable action led to a lengthy, open-sea journey with no charts, in the dark and in fast deteriorating weather during which the small, un-armed convoy was star-shelled, targeted by high explosive and frightened by the sudden appearance out of the darkness of two (friendly?) warships. It also led indirectly to the loss of a large number of Welsh Guardsmen (and others) in RFA *Sir Galahad*.

When the fighting ceased on 14th June I was detached to HMS *Avenger* and, with her helicopter, was to scout the western shores and islands for any enemy who may not have known that the 'war' was over. I was, also, a member of the tiny team that took the surrender, to the settlement's enormous relief, of Pebble Island (Argentine commanding officer, "*Oh good. My men will be pleased!*"). Our major task, though, was to search for any downed pilots. Sadly, we found a number of dead aircrew and tabulated their positions meticulously for recovery prior to formal, military burials. We also conducted a day-long, but fruitless, search for *Fearless's* lost landing craft *Foxtrot Four*.

On our return to Stanley I spent a riotous 36 hours visiting as many old Falkland friends as possible before it was time to leave.

Because I had not been in command of anyone my only duty on board *Canberra* was to write my Report of Proceedings of Landing Craft Operations for Major General Jeremy Moore. This was an easy task. All our years of training among Norway's Arctic fiords had paid off and thus there were few lessons to be learned other than that of 'command and control' should the long-proposed, 3 Commando Brigade's independent landing craft squadron become a permanent reality - which it did two years later as 539 Assault Squadron.

The long 'cruise' home in a 'luxury liner' (*Canberra*) was unforgettable with non-stop concerts, SODS operas (Ships Operatic and Dramatic Society!) and impromptu parties.

For me it had been a very personal 'crusade'

Neil Wookey, CPO 801 NAS Sea Harrier squadron on board HMS Invincible

Extracts from Neil's book 'From the Cradle to the Grave'

Missile Attack

I served on board HMS *Invincible* with 801 Naval Air Squadron (Sea Harriers) as a CPOAEA (Chief Petty Officer Aircraft Engineering Artificer).

It was during a second missile attack that I was caught in the hanger. The ship's tannoy again called, "*Air Raid Warning Red, hit the deck*".

I was with a couple of my buddies and we found ourselves lying on the deck in the centre hangar. I looked up and saw that our Chief Reggie, (Regulator – ship's policeman) Leon Smith, had got his clip board above his head. I said *"We're roughly midships and about half way up the ship's side, which means any missile is going to come in through that bulkhead, so I don't think a clip board is going to help, Leon".*

We decided this was not a safe place to shelter, so we ran to the forward hangar where a huge mound of bergens (rucksacks) used by the SBS were piled. We started to burrow our way in to give us some protection in case the missile hit, but a casual comment from a Special Forces (SBS) marine stopped us in our tracks. He was leaning casually against the AMCO (Aircraft Maintenance Control Office) door and said "*I wouldn't get in amongst that lot mate. It's mostly ammunitions and explosives*".

To quote from Monty Python's film The Holy Grail, *"Run away, Run away".* We decided not to cover ourselves with bergens full of explosives and instead be British about it and have a seat in the AMCO and maybe grab a coffee.

****

Under Air Attack

As we approached the Falklands, Captain Layman gathered as many that would fit into the junior rates' dining hall as possible for a final briefing. Captain Layman explained that the main Task Force landings and bridgehead would be at Port San Carlos (soon to be known as 'Bomb Alley') and that HMS *Argonaut* together with other ships would be there to protect the troops going ashore as well as the supply ships. We were going to act as "picket ships" to draw the enemy's fire which would be the Argentine Air Force.

Our own air cover would be thin due to the aircraft carriers, vital for the Task Force, trying to remain a distance outside the potential range of attack and. Someone asked when the *Argonaut* would be withdrawing from Falkland Sound, expecting to be within hours. The captain said that we would not be withdrawing, we were there for the duration. Picket ships are expendable and losses were to be expected.

21st May: Under Attack

The ship's company closed up for action stations early whilst it was still dark. Weapons system checks complete, missile launchers loaded, 40/60 Bofors manned and ready, together with many small-arms machine guns on the bridge wings and down each side of the ship. As dawn slowly broke, I could make out the land, East and West Falklands, with many Royal Navy ships protecting the landings.

The sunrise was stunning. Clear blue skies appeared overhead, all was peace and quiet. My first impression was the Falklands are just like Dartmoor but with sea surrounding it. Suddenly I think it was HMS *Antrim* opened up with her 4.5inch gun offering Naval Gun Support (NGS) and striking an Argentine observation post on top of Fanning Head, the highest point overlooking Falkland Sound and San Carlos. Huge explosions of high explosive shells sent large amounts of rock and debris into the air. I viewed this through my Sea Cat binoculars. Anyone under that barrage was in deep trouble.

HMS *Argonaut* was attacked by an undegtected Argentine Aermacchi which strafed the ship, put a rocket through the main radar and dropped a bomb off our port quarter just missing the flight deck. Three sailors were injured in that attack which included shrapnel wounds to the chest of the Master-at-Arms which very nearly killed him; one sailor had facial injuries including a large part of his nose taken off; a third lost an eye and part of his foot was blown off. The aircraft alerted the mainland and this was the start of a long and dangerous day.

Casualties evacuated, everyone on the upper deck was now very much switched on and waiting for the inevitable onslaught. Blind piped up (operations room). "Air Raid Warning Yellow", air attack probable. Next was "Air Raid Warning Red, Air Raid Warning Red", air attack imminent. "Bogeys (enemy aircraft) 60 miles closing", "Bogeys 40 miles closing", "Bogeys gone low" meaning they had dropped below our radar and could appear from any angle. Suddenly aircraft filled the sky with the Royal Navy ships engaging. Aircraft flew incredibly low and fast, the crew in the Sea Cat TS tried to "lock on" to the jets with the missile systems radar but were unable to do so due to "clutter".

The weapons radar could not identify the aircraft against the land mass of West or East Falkland. The weapon system is designed for open sea warfare not close inshore engagements. I was screaming "Aloft, Aloft" - I was asking for control of the director (which is what I was sat inside) and the missile launcher as I could see the threats all around and aircraft attacking us. Fortunately, the crew in the TS (Transmitting Station), who were below decks and unable to see the danger unfolding, gave me control. The missile launcher then tracked my every movement that I made from the director. I had the best seat in the house at the highest manned point on the ship on top of the bridge!

The *Argonaut* was moving at speed, turning sharply giving the missilemen and gunners the opportunity to engage the Argentine aircraft with everything we had. It was agreed that I would keep control in the "aloft" mode but I did not have the facility to fire any missiles, this would still have to be done from the Sea Cat TS crew way below decks. I would quickly evaluate the ever-changing targets, those that posed the biggest threat to the *Argonaut* and her crew. I would then shout '*Fire*' and the TS crew would hit the launch trigger. This was not how the system was designed to work but we had to come up with a working solution and quickly, which we did.

The Enemy Engagement rule book no longer existed; safety checklist ignored, it was all-out warfare. I shouted '*Fire!*' and a missile launched, I aimed it right over the top of HMS *Broadsword*, chasing an Argentine aircraft which it evaded. Next an aircraft flew higher than the rest, I got him into the view of my sights, shouted '*Fire*', and seconds later the aircraft was no more. A Dagger aircraft was hit by a Sea Wolf missile from one of the other ships, the aircraft was extremely close to *Argonaut*, I watched the pilot through his canopy fighting with his controls and trying to regain control. I watched the aircraft hit the sea at well over 600mph and explode on impact sending a massive plume of water skyward.

On the far side of Falkland Sound was HMS *Ardent*; she was being mercilessly attacked, and was on fire, smoke billowing and out of action. Still the attacks continued. Mirages flying so low and fast strafed *Ardent* and as the shells dropped short, huge plumes of water would rise up and the aircraft would fly through the spray.

HMS *Argonaut* had fought well but our luck was about to run out. I tracked and was preparing to engage an aircraft on our starboard side when a shout went up "*Alarm! Aircraft red 9 zero!*" I started to swing the missile system around to engage the threat when the Operations Room interrupted and said '*No, do not engage friendly aircraft, they are Harriers."* I swung back to the original threat on the starboard side without getting to see to port side. The yell went up again *'No, they are Skyhawks!!'* The aircraft on the starboard side suddenly broke off and banked away sharply, and the exact same moment the 40/60 Bofors engaged the incoming aircraft on the port side. HMS *Argonaut* turned sharply to starboard, a fully broadside to the attacking aircraft so that all the weaponry could engage. But the *Argonaut* was now a very large target. I swung the weapon system back to port but it was too late, I got as far as midships and looked to my left.

I saw five Skyhawks in a row. I was almost looking down on them. At this point everything happened in slow motion. I fully expected the aircrafts' cannons to open up and strafe us, but they didn't. They were on a bombing run and there was nothing we could do to stop them. The aircraft nearest to me released its bomb, it appeared to fall in slow motion, falling directly below me. I glanced at the Skyhawk that released the bomb, its height was level with me it was that low. I could see the pilot in his cockpit, I could see the yellow hazard stickers on the side, I could even see the saltwater streak marks on the rivets where they had flown so low from Argentina. This aircraft was flying at nearly 600 mph yet everything was in slow motion. At that point I knew I was going to die, my last words were "*please God, let it be quick*".

The explosions never came, however *Argonaut* reappeared from behind a curtain of five 1000lb bomb splashes, still alive but badly damaged, on fire, out of control at speed with no power heading straight for Fanning Head rocks at the mouth of San Carlos. Both anchors were dropped by quick-thinking crew saving us from further disaster. Five 1000lb bombs were dropped, three missed, one entered the boiler room just missing the main boiler, a second went into the for'ard fuel tanks and deflected into the for'ard Sea Cat magazine setting off ammunition including missile warheads and killing Matthew Stuart and Iain Boldy, fire engulfing the forward part of the ship. If either bomb had detonated then *Argonaut* would have been lost along with most of her crew. Although badly wounded, she would live to fight another day.

Argonaut was on fire, no power to the weapons systems, we were sitting ducks. We could hear aircraft all around but could not see them because of the smoke from the onboard fires. HMS *Plymouth* raced to our assistance and provided us with protection whilst some power was reinstated to the *Argonaut's* weapons systems. We were back in the fight!

HMS *Plymouth* stayed with us for the rest of the day fighting off Argentine aircraft desperate to finish us off. By nightfall the day's action was over for the time being. The gunners' mess and the adjacent mess deck were destroyed and all we had left were the clothes that we stood in. We had nowhere to sleep, nowhere to go, and were told to find somewhere, anywhere, to get some sleep - any compartment or space would do. I stood on the upper deck in the middle of the night with just the wind whistling through the superstructure. Ships are noisy there is always something running but no engine noise, no generators, nothing, it was really eerie. I stood for ages watching HMS *Ardent* burning on the other side of Falkland Sound thinking '*There but for the grace of God...*"

Finding somewhere to sleep was short-lived as sailors were being gathered on the forecastle to raise both anchors. Due to the ship's boiler being out of action the capstans usually used to raise the anchors in a matter of minutes were dead, so we sailors would raise the anchors using blocks and tackles. This would take hours, pulling in the anchor cable a few feet at a time by hand. HMS *Plymouth* came alongside, which was a dangerous move because if either 1000lb bomb detonated it would take out both ships and crew. With the cable and both anchors eventually safely stowed it was time for some breakfast even though it was about 4am. We in the anchor party hopped over the guardrail onto HMS *Plymouth* and headed down to the junior rates' dining space for our first hot meal in 24 hours. Thanks again, *Plymouth.*

Still in pitch darkness it was time for HMS *Plymouth* to move off and be replaced by two landing craft seconded to act as makeshift "tugs" secured either side of *Argonaut.* The landing craft towed *Argonaut* to a small inlet just inside San Carlos Water well away from the other ships due to the unexploded bombs. Stokers working flat-out throughout the night had restored some power to *Argonaut* and we dropped anchor and waited. The ship's gunners, all of whom had fought hard and bravely not slept for the past 24 hours, had resupplied ammunition from the aft magazine and completed weapons system checks. We waited silently in the darkness, waited for sunrise, waited for the inevitable air attacks.

The captain's ship's log summary of the *Argonaut's* first day: "*Two unexploded bombs lodged in vital areas…fires in ammunition magazine…. engines and steering out of action…. HMS Argonaut still fighting*".

****

Howard Johnson, Sgt Ammunition, MV Lycaon
MV Lycaon as a requisitioned cargo ship carried vast quantities of ammunition, rockets, fuel and everything else that the forces needed. Her job was to resupply ships of the fleet wherever things were needed.

<u>Resupplying the Fleet</u>
19th May
Ordered to head for South Georgia,

24th May
Engine breaks down amidst a submarine threat, crew started to get worried. Next day underway to Holding Area.
28th May
Anchored Stromness Bay and issued ammo to RFAs. Overnight Argentinian cargo plane drops (mortar?) bombs on the anchorage - we were quite lucky though.

29th May
Started Replenishment at Sea (RAS) 12 pallets of Rapier missiles, 87 pallets 105mm HE and eight pallets 81mm mortar to RFA *Blue Rover* via HMS *Cordella*.

30th May

Left Stromness due to air action, went into iceberg field and drifted for two days. On radar iceberg and ship looked the same, we moved around for nine days.

3rd June

RAS to RFA *Resource* 14x Sidewinder,79x3in chaff rockets, 30mm HE and SAA. (small arms ammunition).

The problem with moving ammunition in the Atlantic was the sea conditions (swell). As the ship moved the underslung pallet strops would go loose and then quickly tighten as the boat dropped on the waves. To hold the strops in position when slack and release them when under pressure required some dexterity; unfortunately, we lost one guy's fingers that got pinged off between the strop and the pallet. I think he lost three fingers.

8th June

Moved to Cumberland Bay, arrived Grytviken and went alongside support tanker RFA *Pearleaf.* Moved a couple of shoulder-fired 66mm HEAT rockets onto the bridge just in case.

10th June

Arrived at the TRALA (Tug, Repair and Logistics Area) in anticipation of going into San Carlos, also waiting was *Canberra, Atlantic Causeway, Elk* and *Glamorgan.*

12th June Night

Glamorgan went in to bombard Stanley but was badly damaged.

It was getting to the stage where the ammunition was needed ashore.

13th June

Under escort of HMS *Arrow,* we with MS *Baltic Ferry* and frigate HMS *Minerva* went into San Carlos Bay.

14th June
"Air Raid Warning Red1". HMS *Cardiff* shot plane down. We anchored alongside *Antelope* - one of her lifeboats was drifting around (empty).

****

Philip Piper, Gazelle Pilot, 656 Army Air Corps, aboard MV Nordic. Diary extracts

<u>South Atlantic Weather</u>

28th May
We've heard that the Paras and the Commandos are doing sterling stuff on the F.Is. Am doubting whether there will be very much work for us to do.

Am due to fly this afternoon but the weather is looking very grotty. Sea temp is now down to 5 deg C. Without an immersion suit the survival time is less than five minutes.

29th May
We now have real South Atlantic weather. The Nordic is rolling around like a sick pig. Many 'passengers' are looking somewhat peaky.

30th May
Went to the 'church' service today; not surprisingly there were quite a few people that turned up for the service. Spent the day going backwards and forwards from position Lola, which is very frustrating.

****

__RO(G) Anthony Lawrence, Radio Operator HMS Fearless__

War and Remembrance

"Well, I know we all came down here to fight,
And I realise it's no longer a 'bite',
It's so hard to keep this smile on my face,
When there's bombs falling all over the place,
Skyhawks to the left of me,
Daggers to the right, here I am,
Stuck in the middle with you
Yes, I'm trapped here below decks with you."

Adaptation of the 'Stealers' Wheel' classic "Stuck in the Middle with you"

****

San Carlos Water – 'Bomb Alley'

On the 21st May British forces launched an amphibious attack on the shore of San Carlos Water, an inlet into Easdt Falkland fron the north end of Falkland Sound. The area became known as "Bomb Alley" as the invading force and support ships came under heavy attack from the Argentine Air Force. The action took the Argentinian Army, much of it based in Stanley, by surprise. An Argentinian force at Fanning Head was neutralised by a heavily-armed SBS team put ashore in advance from HMS *Antrim*. Another Argentinian unit from Darwin was prevented from moving to San Carlos by the SAS.

The invasion force was able to land successfully and secure the beachhead, landing 3,000 men and 1,000 tons of equipment on the first day and consolidating the beachhead in the next few days. The surface-to-air missiles used by the escorting ships and the STOVL (Short Take-Off Vertical Landing) Sea Harriers from the carriers were able to protect the landing force from an even more intensive air attack. However, during the landings the supporting ships came under heavy fire from Argentine planes, including Pucaras from Goose Green and A-4 Skyhawks and IAI Daggers from the Argentine mainland. HMS *Ardent* was damaged badly on the 21st May and sank the day after. HMS *Antelope* was hit on 23rd May, received two unexploded bombs and when one exploded whilst being disarmed, caught fire and sank next day. MV *Atlantic Conveyor* was struck by an air-launched Exocet on 25th May and HMS *Coventry* bombed and sunk north of West Falkland. The loss of the four Chinook helicopters, supplies and airstrip landing equipment on board *Atlantic Conveyor* was to hamper the British force as it advanced out of the beachhead. However, the naval losses could have been greater as thirteen bombs hit British ships without detonating.

By the 25th May the British land forces were in a position to continue the battle on land.

Brian Short, Royal Marines Bandsman onboard Canberra
Extracts from Brian's book The Band That Went To War

First Air Attacks

Now committed to the landings, in the early hours of 21st May, *Canberra* and various other ships slipped quietly into San Carlos Water. When the dawn broke to a wonderful bright and crisp morning, we looked at the skyline of the surrounding headlands and many ships at anchor or patrolling around us in a protective pattern.

The peaceful scene did not last long as by mid-morning the Argentine Air Force began a series of intense and relentless air raids. In *Canberra* we had its own Air Defence Troop and they fired off shoulder-launched Blowpipe missiles, accompanied by the loud chatter of the twenty-six 7.62mm GPMGs (General Purpose Machine Guns) we had spaced around the ship's upper deck. Add to the bombing all the other weapons, guns and missiles from the other ships, and the sight and sounds were like every war film we had ever seen - but this time it was for real. San Carlos became known as "Bomb Alley", and not without good reason for the sheer number of bombs dropped.

I think there is a certain respect for the way the Argentine pilots pressed home their attacks in the relatively small and heavily defended anchorage and beachhhead, having only seconds to choose a target, drop their bombs and escape in one piece, or sometimes not, just disappearing in a puff of smoke. Some of the pilots that were hit did manage to eject and were captured, not surprised to be held at gunpoint by the people they had just been trying to kill but equally surprised at the medical treatment provided as required.

Having delivered our troops ashore, we then undertook loading tons of ammunition and other stores to be slung beneath a queue of waiting helicopters, each one hovering over the deck to then quickly hook up between the air raids. On some of the return journeys they brought with them their first casualties.

There were some terrified Argentine walking wounded, but also three deceased Royal Marines light helicopter pilots who had been shot down. Not content with shooting down the helicopters, the Argentines then shot at the men in the water as they swam ashore, only one badly wounded sergeat surviving. The war took on a different hue for me from then on and the Argentines were thereafter referred to as the enemy.

****

Alex Manning, Assistant Staff Minewarfare and Clearance Diving Officer (ASMCDO), HMS Fearless

Preparing for Landing at San Carlos

The final go-ahead from the War Cabinet for a landing at San Carlos on 21st May came on 18th May. At an RV with the Carrier Battle Group (CBG) on the 19th, well north-east of the Falklands the sea was criss-crossed by landing craft and the sky full of helicopters, most with underslung loads but the deadline was met and the Amphibious Task Group (ATG) ready to go.

If the specialist assault ships, *Fearless* and *Intrepid,* were crowded before, they were now very crowded indeed! Designed to carry, in normal course, 650 troops (i.e. a commando/battalion) with their stores and support elements, *Intrepid* now carried, in addition to the already-embarked 3 Commando Brigade HQ and Signals Squadron, 3 Para, Z Company of 45 Commando, elements of the Commando Logistic Regiment, the bulk of the SAS and SBS and God knows who else besides. With the ship's company of 600, a total of at least 1600 souls in all and probably even more.

Friday 21st May dawned bright and clear and there were the Falklands, the air so clean and the distances (and therefore the ranges) so deceptive you felt you could almost reach out and touch them. It looked for all the world to me like Dartmoor with a lot of water, deceptively peaceful and serene.

Things began in earnest from 0845 hours local time (12.45 GMT) onwards. We didn't have long to wait after that and from about 0935 hours the Daggers, Mirages and Skyhawks from the mainland came in with mind-concentrating regularity. Every available gun and missile in the anchorage started firing and aircraft started getting blown out of the sky. My pre-RN Royal Marine service and further commando service in the Navy had let me offer to take charge of *Intrepid's* GPMG battery, what had to pass for a basic (very basic!) close-in weapons system and the offer was gratefully accepted. We had seven GPMGs on the signal deck, three on fixed mounts on either side of the ship and one that we ran from side to side and rested on a sandbag, depending on which side the attacking aircraft were coming from – needs must! One round in five was a tracer so that we could see where our fire was going and the lead gun would put down a visible stream of fire in front of an aircraft but in its line of flight that the other three could then home in on and, if the range and height had been assessed correctly, create a concentrated zone of fire that it would fly into. Easier said than done of course and my main task was ensuring tight arcs of fire were kept as, with all the shipping in the anchorage and troops on the ground, there was otherwise a severe risk of us hitting our own side.

I will never forget *Intrepid's* Captain Peter Dingemans words when, over the main broadcast at dusk, he congratulated and thanked everybody for what they had endured and achieved that day. He wanted to reinforce this, he said, by reminding us of what Admiral Cunningham had said when his using the navy to get the army off Crete during WW2 had led to heavy losses and criticism of his continuing to do so: *"It takes three years to build a ship. It takes three hundred years to build a tradition*". I looked up at *Intrepid's* battle ensign, proudly flying, and just knew we were going to win, whatever it was going to take.

****

George Birkett, Chief Engineering Mechanician, HMS Invincible

Action Stations at San Carlos

Saturday 21st May

Today at 0730 hours the assault forces landed at Port San Carlos, San Carlos Settlement and Ajax Bay.

In no time the opposition turned up, carrying out almost continuous air raids on the ships in San Carlos Water. The ships renamed this area "Bomb Alley" a name which would become synonymous with ship damage and losses.

During all this we were closed up at action stations listening intently to any news from the command or the on-watch personnel.

Sitting below the waterline in these situations can be quite unnerving, but there was so much going on and the "Sitreps" (Situation Reports) were coming in so fast and furious, that there was not enough time to get concerned. Apart from that it was the job we had to do, and there was worse happening inshore.

****

Mick Fellows, FCPO Fleet Clearance Diving Team No1

Getting Aboard HMS *Antrim* - Unexploded Bomb

On the 21st May 1982, 'D Day' of the Falkland's campaign, I was the Fleet Chief Petty Officer Diver of the Fleet Clearance Diving Team No1, embarked on RFA *Sir Tristram* in San Carlos Water with HMS *Battleaxe* and four LSLs. (Landing Ships, Logistics). Around mid-day, after offloading troops and equipment onto Red Beach at Ajax Bay during numerous low-level attacks by Argentine aircraft, I was given a signal saying HMS *Antrim* has been hit by an unexploded weapon and required bomb disposal assistance.

A Wessex helicopter was dispatched to transfer us to *Antrim*. We skimmed the waves below attacking aircraft towards the San Carlos entrance and located *Canberra* with HMS *Antrim* doing figure-of-eights turns around her at high speed. The pilot's voice in my helmet intercom said, "*Right Mr Fellows, get yourself into the winch wire recovery strop and we will lower you onto the Antrim's flight deck*".

I complied and was lowered and left dangling in space just below the helicopter's cabin as we approached the *Antrim*.

Whilst looking down at *Antrim* I heard a loud engine roar from behind me and, looking up, saw two Argentine jets swooping in and firing rockets and cannon shells into her flight deck. The shells hit the hangar and the helicopter parked outside, wounding a number of the aircrew as well as a Royal Marine who was firing a machine gun from his hip. The screaming noise from the jets and their cannon fire was horrendous and a new experience for me. I bent my knees and lifted my legs up as the tracer trail from the cannon shells seemed to be passing just underneath me. Looking up as we violently swerved away from the ship's stern, I gave a frantic '*wind me up*' signal to the winch man.

I was dangling on the end of the winch wire being swept through the sky thinking, "*Christ, the pilot's forgotten me*". He hadn't of course and was now turning to port very sharply with his main blades just skimming the water to get away from the attacking enemy aircraft fire. His sharp and sudden exit strategy meant there was only one place I was going to end up and, as I hit the ice-cold waters of the South Atlantic. I received two jolts to my system; the first being the discharging electrostatic shock from the helicopter that whipped through my body in a most unpleasant manner but one that was only preceding the even worse shock of immersion into the freezing cold ocean. A sudden and numbing cold enveloped my entire body as I gasped for breath. I could feel my heart slowing and my peripheral vision dimming as its output dropped and my eyes became less focused.

The helicopter dragged me through the water for what felt like two hours but was, in reality, about thirty seconds. Enough time for me to say, to no-one in particular, "*Fuck this*", and to ditch the rucksack, with its heavy explosives content that I had, fortunately, slung over only one shoulder. As I was about to swallow my next dose of salt water, I shot out of that freezing environment and started to fly like a kite again. The helicopter pilot had now gained some height so the winchman was able to haul me back into the main cabin where someone immediately gave me a headset, and, before I could tell him exactly what I thought about his low flying skills, the pilot spoke first, saying,

"Sorry Mr Fellows, I'm heading back to Sir Tristram. I can't risk another run whilst the ship's under attack".

He obviously didn't really want to risk both his aircraft and crew's necks by having to make another attempt at landing me on the ship, and I didn't blame him.

There now seemed to be continual swarms of attacking aircraft coming in with smoke trails streaming from their rocket fire whilst *Antrim*'s defensive fire seemed to be all over the place. One Argie aircraft came in so low that it hit the communications whip aerial on the ship's port bridge wing. I pleaded with the pilot, in case he was not aware, why he'd been attempting to deliver me to the warship, that *Antrim* had an unexploded weapon on-board and desperately needed assistance to render it safe. If he was not able to deliver me, the bomb could explode and not only kill her entire crew but also lose a major warship asset leaving the *Canberra*, with its cargo of 3,000 soldiers unprotected.

He rather reluctantly agreed to make one more attempt. This time I decided to put my boot in the recovery strop and hold on to the lowering wire with gloved hands, rather than having it secured around my chest – so that when I got close to the flight deck, I could just step out and drop off. As we came in close to the stern of *Antrim*, I could see their firefighting team spraying foam over the flight deck to extinguish some small fires amidst the many patches of bright red blood covered areas where wounded victims had fallen.

As we swooped in, I removed my foot from the helicopter recovery strop and dropped onto the foam-covered flight deck.

Unexploded Bombs

A ship's officer took me straight to the unexploded bomb's location in the after-heads (toilets). It had entered the hull through the ship's stern by the after-missile doors, bounced off the Sea Slug missiles' magazine's deckhead, jinked up through the pyrotechnic magazine hitting the deck-head (ceiling) just below the flight deck before stopping in a horizontal position after demolishing the third toilet pan in the heads. The compartment was now illuminated only by its emergency lighting, was filled with smoke and flames could be seen through the entry hole in the bulkhead from where the bomb had damaged some flares in the adjacent pyrotechnics' magazine.

Beneath the tangled mass of broken metal fittings, I could see the dark green coloured shape of a large 500kg bomb. The ship's officer identified the location of the nearest telephone and damage control locker then disappeared, very quickly, down the central ship's passageway. Jan and Nigel started fighting the fires with CO_2 extinguishers taken from a damage control locker. I started removing loose debris from the toilet cubicle to gain visual access to the bomb in order to try and identify its country of origin, type and fusing system to evaluate the threat to the ship that was continuing to manoeuvre in a wild zigzag fashion in order to try to avoid further damage from the air.

The captain would announce over the tannoy system when an enemy attack was coming in and initially, like idiots, we all ran forward away from the bomb into a mess deck and took cover under plywood tables.

How much protection were we going to get from a plywood table if some Argie aircraft's rockets happened to hit it? Mind you, why we even bothered to run forward and take cover from the enemy aircraft's cannon fire when one slip of the hand or violent movement of the ship could have actuated the fusing mechanism of the bomb, something that would not only have killed us, but the 400 plus sailors who were on board the ship as well, only occurred to me afterwards.

Loose wreckage from the bathroom partitioning and broken pipe- work all around the bomb prohibited my view of the tail fuse. I knew I had to first stabilise the bomb from rolling along with any one of the ship's violent manoeuvres before clearing away the wreckage with a hack saw and cold chisel so I could examine the fuse. Once this was achieved, I saw that the drab green painted bomb had the words 'Made in Bilston, England' stencilled on it in bold white letters. The nose and tail ends of the bomb had been badly damaged by the flight through the ship's compartments, the tail fins had broken off and disappeared and the brass tail fuse was distorted out of recognition.

I could not see if the arming prong was in place in the fuse and therefore could not tell if the weapon was fully armed or not. Some wires were extending out of the damaged mechanical fuse though, and that puzzled me, making me think that perhaps the bomb was booby-trapped electronically in some way.

I taped up the bare wires with insulating tape to prevent them from shorting out on the surrounding metal bulkheads before informing the bridge by telephone of the identity of the unexploded weapon in the after-heads. The Captain was fighting for his ship as well as trying to protect the *Canberra* from Argie aircraft attack and was not too concerned about my report on the make and type of bomb.

As I had no way of removing the badly damaged fuse and, as there was no precedent in naval history for the situation we were in, and therefore no approved methodology or guidelines for such a situation, I felt more than a little alone in the world but was far too busy to start crying about it and, in doing so, showing a lack of confidence to my young assistants.

Had I encountered a modern unexploded bomb on shore, we had an assortment of tools and procedures immediately available to us. On this task we had a pair of pliers, a hammer and a cold chisel. By far the bigger challenge, as far as I was concerned, was installing confidence into the minds of my young nervous assistants, that I not only had the confidence but also the ability to render this weapon safe whilst, at the same time, operating in a violent unstable funfair-like and very rough ride environment without killing us and all of the 400 plus ship's company.

I sat astride the bomb and studied the surrounding environment, while my two young divers lay alongside the bomb with their backs against it and their feet, clad in heavy boots, pushed up against the toilet bulkhead. This was done in order to keep the bomb steady and to prevent it from rolling during the ship's ongoing and violent manoeuvres as it kept up its anti-aircraft attack whilst I located some wooden damage control wedges in order to secure it in a more stable position. Once it was securely held in place, I snipped away at what was left of the bomb's broken off tail section with a pair of pliers in an attempt to identify the partially hidden fuse and its arming fork condition.

It took six hours to clear the wreckage from around the bomb, cut an exit hole in the flight deck and rig the sheer legs (lifting spparatus) to lift the weapon. I was very worried that the violent manoeuvring of the ship as she came under what seemed like constant enemy aircraft attack was going to jolt the bomb during the lift and cause the fuse to commence the explosive detonation chain.

After approximately two or three hours working on the bomb, time flies when you're constantly thinking along the lines of 'am I taking the right action or am I about to commit mass execution of a few hundred men', a Petty Officer Telegraphist informed me

"The UK wants to communicate with you, on a secure speech line, to find out what nationality, type and fusing system the unexploded bomb has."

I could understand their concern as this was the first time an unexploded bomb had deposited itself on board one of our capital warships at sea in naval history let alone this particular conflict. Once inside the wireless office I was given a headset with microphone but before I said a single word a voice at the other end that said,

"Hello Mick, this is Hamish Loudon".

Hamish was the Lieutenant Commander Mine Warfare Clearance Diver in the Commander-in-Chief Fleet's Headquarters at Northwood.

"*What make and type of bomb have you got there? You can speak openly Mick; this is a very secure line*".

"*Hi, the weapon's a British 500 kg bomb*" I responded.

A slight pause before Hamish's sharp response.

"*British. Are you sure?*"

"*Yes – 100% positive*", I replied, adding, before he could ask how I could possibly know, "*…it has 'Made in England 1965'* stencilled on its side in white paint. It's coloured olive green and it has got a red band, the old NATO explosive colour marking around it".

"*Anything else?*" "*Well, there's graffiti roughly painted on it that confuses me: it has the words 'Na Negara' painted on the side. That probably means 'bugger off, filthy Englishmen', or something similar- but it would be handy to know what it means*".

"*Well how can we or DEODS-TIC help?*" asked Hamish. (Defence Explosive Ordnance Disposal School - Technical Information Centre)

"*These are my intentions…*" I replied, "*Really?*" he responded.

"*Well, that's my plan, unless you have a better one Sir*"

He didn't offer one and I didn't expect him to.

"*What I need to know is what does 'Na Negara' mean and can I safely move the bomb, as long as I keep it on a level plane and lift it very gently, without it detonating and killing me and Antrim's entire 400 plus crew?*"

After a short pause he replied, "*I'll pass you over to Tony Lombard at the Defence Explosive Ordnance Disposal Technical Information Centre*".

Tony, who I had known for many years and had worked for at Faslane and in the Far East Clearance Diving Team, came on the radio and said,

"*Sorry, Mick, my team of Explosive Ordnance Disposal Technicians, Army, Navy and Royal Air Force have listened to your conversation with Fleet and without knowing the type and condition of the damaged fuse, cannot say if your proposed methodology is sound or not. Good luck*".

This response did not surprise me.

Number 10

What I didn't know at that time, but found out later, was that my conversation to Fleet and DEODS was relayed on loudspeaker to the Cabinet Room in No. 10 Downing Street.

A few weeks later, when I had the honour and pleasure of meeting the Prime Minister at the State Victory Dinner, she said to me, "*Mr Fellows, do you recall the radio conversation you had with the Fleet MCDO and DEODS whilst dealing with the bomb on the Antrim?"*

"*Yes Ma'am, I do, it's engraved into my memory bank."*

I'll never forget her reply.

"*I thought myself an experienced lady of the world. My father owned a greengrocer's shop and I helped in the store where we sold beer and whisky until quite late on Friday nights to all the local heavy drinkers. I thought I knew just about every word and obscenity in the English language. You used naval phrases that I had never heard before"*.

Mrs Thatcher continued, *"I asked the Senior Naval Officer present, Admiral Fieldhouse, 'who is this man and where did we get him from?' The Admiral said he didn't know, to which I replied, 'Well, if he's still alive after the conflict, I would like to meet him.*

Much later, and as the only non-commissioned officer at the victory celebration dinner at Number Ten, I had the honour and extreme pleasure of such a meeting.

Removing the Bomb

The lifting operation had to be conducted very slowly without any jerking or twisting motions, an awkward procedure for a single operator. I had sent my two assistants forward with, albeit a minor chance of survival, in case of a mishap.

I commenced by pulling the unexploded bomb aft of its location and clear of a main electrical cable run above it. Once it was below the exit hole cut in the flight deck, I repositioned the chain lift and slowly raised the weapon, an operation that was prolonged by continually repositioning each block throughout the process.

I hoisted the bomb without jolting or altering its horizontal plane up through the hole that had been cut in the flight deck. Garry and Nigel now appeared from the helicopter hangar, (not the forecastle as ordered) pushing the ship's helicopter torpedo loading trolley. We carefully positioned the bomb on the trolley whilst keeping its horizontal attitude in place with wooden damage control wedges. Crossing the flight deck to the ship's gangway derrick on the starboard side, we attached a block and tackle to the strop secured around the bomb and hoisted it off the trolley.

Fearful that all of this movement may have inadvertently started the damaged fuse's detonation process, I contacted the captain and suggested that he should go full ahead on both engines turning the ship sharply to starboard kicking the stern over to port as I released the bomb on its long pulley rope thereby not fouling the starboard propeller.

As HMS *Antrim* went full ahead, and with a sharp knife in my hand, just in case of a hang up, the horrible thought went through my mind that, once I'd dropped the bomb overboard, the water pressure on its damaged fuse might actuate it before it was fully clear of the ship's hull. Trying to banish that thought from my mind, I released the rope pulley and the Argentinian bomb - but 100% British manufactured - was dropped to the seabed without any further problems - and a great deal of personal relief.

"*Mr Fellows…*" Captain Young called from the bridge on the ship's tannoy system, "*…we have just received another signal from DEODS stating, 'do not attempt to move the bomb as it may have an anti-disturbance device fitted'*

"*Thank you, Sir - too f***ing late*" was my verbal response over the ship's speaker system. We could now hear the relieved cheers from the ship's company mustered on the forecastle.

Note: Antrim's unique bomb removal methodology set the procedures employed for similar actions on four other warships and RFAs during the conflict.

****

Brum Richards, 148 Commando Battery Naval Gunfire Support

Bomb Alley on HMS *Plymouth*

Sunday, 23rd May

At 1000 hours we are back in Bomb Alley and at full action stations. Although we are still able to fire NGS we are set up in the anti-air role. At 1330 hours I am monitoring the air circuit and hear that two of our CAP have spotted three enemy Pumas operating in the sound and engage them. They manage to splash two of them and the third crashes into the hillside whilst attempting to manoeuvre his helo in a fashion not thought of by the designers. We do not know if they were carrying any troops aboard.

At 1645 hours we are attacked by four Skyhawks coming from the east. Two of them return for another attack on the *Antelope* specifically and one of them puts a bomb in her but as he passes very low over her clips her mast. A split second later a missile from *Brilliant* hits the aircraft and there is the most amazing explosion I have ever seen. I cannot see anything hit the water around the *Antelope*. An almighty cheer goes up from those of us on the bridge. The total raid was assessed as five Mirages (one splashed) and four Skyhawks (three splashed). If the one Skyhawk ever got home, we will never know.

The bomb that hit *Antelope* did not go off and so she moves into shallow water about 200 yards off our starboard beam. We get our fire-fighting gear ready to help if required. The bomb goes off at 2026 hours and we move in to help fight the fire which follows the explosion. The fire is getting out of control aboard *Antelope* and we are quite close to her. I am manning a fire hose on the quarterdeck.

Suddenly at 2147 hours her Sea Cat magazine explodes and we all have to take cover in a hurry

At 2200 hours the *Antelope* is abandoned and left to burn herself out. The Captain of the *Antelope* is brought aboard us and passes me on the quarterdeck. I simply look at him and say '*I am sorry sir'*. He just nods at me and rushes up to our bridge. I would rather not see any more ships die if at all possible.

****

RO(G) Anthony Lawrence, Radio Operator, HMS Fearless

'Air Raid Warning Red'

From the bridge comes, *"Air Raid Warning Red, Air Raid Warning Red, aircraft in the Sound; On Anti-Flash."*

The waiting is the worst bit and doesn't do anyone's nerves any good. You start to think how are you going to get out if we get hit? Would I even see the bomb come through the bulkhead and would it explode on impact or after it had entered? But you carry on working, transmitting and receiving signals, re-tuning equipment, always with one ear listening and waiting for news on the incoming raid.

> *"Air Raid Warning Red, raid coming in from the West on Port side. Same configuration as yesterday."*
>
> *"Aircraft closing fast -Take cover! Take cover! Brace, Brace, Brace!"*

We all take cover, lying face down on the deck, under teleprinter bays, under desks, head between arms, anti-flash on and hands over heads. It's hot, the air conditioning is off. No one speaks, the only sound in the Main Communications Office (MCO) is the constant chatter of the teleprinters as messages continue to arrive into the ship. Although we can't see what was going on outside, we hear the frigates opening up on the other side of the Sound. Looking around you can see the apprehension in people's eyes; they're looking at you and you're looking at them and we're all thinking the same - all hoping we don't get hit, and you think to yourself are there any other better places to take cover! One of the lads has taken to propping up a picture of his girlfriend next to him; he says that if we do get hit, he wants her to be the last thing he remembers. From where I'm lying my last image is going to be Radio Operator 'Spider' Kelly's backside!

"Attack from astern. Take cover! Take cover! Take cover! Brace, Brace, Brace!"

We listen to our Sea Cat missiles being launched, followed by the dull repetitive thud, thud, thud, of the Bofors guns on the bridge wings opening up as the aircraft close the range, and finally the General-Purpose Machine Guns (GPMGs) in sandbagged positions around the ship, going into action. Dust and paint flakes from the deck head and pipes above float down on to us, disturbed by the sudden vibrations running through the ship, (I remember thinking someone's going to get a rollicking from the Radio Supervisor later for not cleaning them properly – probably me!). Then there is a roar of jet engines as the aircraft pass close by. Heart and head pounding, we all wait for the impact and sound of explosions within the ship and the fires to come. You can't help but think that the 'Argies' are intent on destroying your own little world and you are their prime target. Remember your training. Escape Routes – what's the quickest way out to the upper deck? Where is the nearest fire-fighting equipment located? Time seems to stand still. Then there is the resounding clang of a shockwave that hits the ship's side as the bombs explode in the water.

"We've hit one plane flying away with smoke billowing out."

"Take cover! Take cover - Brace, Brace, Brace! Aircraft coming in forward of us; he flew right over us! Another coming in from astern; Brace, Brace, Brace!"

The sound of one more jet passing overhead followed by another clang and thud, very loud.

Firing abruptly ceases then it's *"Stand to – all compartments check for damage,"* with the Radio Supervisor and Leading Hands repeating the order. We check all around the Communications compartments and equipment and the reports come in; no damage and nobody hit – this time.

"Aircraft, bearing 310° opening north – CAP engaging. On the Fighter Control circuit 'Red Leader reports he has two Mirage visual and is going "buster."

"Air Raid Warning Yellow, relax Anti-Flash."

Thirty seconds later we're told an Argentine plane had just crashed in the water about a mile and a half up the Sound. I really didn't give much thought that the pilot had probably just died; all that mattered to me and everyone else at the time was that the gunners onboard and ashore, with their missiles and gunnery get as many planes as they could. After all, I doubt the pilot would have been giving me a second thought as Galtieri stuck a medal on his chest for sinking us!

However, even when the aircraft have disappeared or are reported to have been beaten off by the Combat Air Patrol (CAP) Sea Harriers, we have to stay at action stations for quite some time because you never know if there are more aircraft around, or if the ones that had just attacked are going to turn back around and come at us again…

Things have got a bit quiet again. No more reports of incoming raids so we manage to get a bite to eat. We each get a brown paper bag consisting mostly of corned beef sandwiches and chocolate bars with a bit of fruit thrown in. I decided to have a look up top to see what was going on, using the excuse that I was checking out one of my escape routes. The landscape looks a lot like the Highlands of Scotland, but it's a lot colder and bleaker. There is a smell of cordite in the air and up at the head of the bay RFA *Sir Lancelot* and RFA *Sir Galahad* have been hit by bombs that didn't explode. As yet we don't know of any casualties.

I can also see RFA *Sir Geraint* and it's strange to think that back in March during training, myself and the rest of my communications class at HMS *Mercury* had sailed on the RFA *Sir Geraint* to Antwerp for a weekend 'jolly', and now here we are, together again a few hundred yards away from each other, under completely different circumstances on the far side of the world, facing a barrage of shot and shell with me over here on HMS *Fearless* contemplating that perhaps I should have chosen a safer career, like alligator wrestling!

"Air Raid Warning Red, Threat report bearing 270 - range 100 miles, strength 3"

And so, the cycle begins again…

****

Alex Manning, Assistant Staff Minewarfare and Clearance Diving Officer (ASMCDO) HMS Fearless

Unexploding Bombs

Antelope had sunk on the 24th May, after an attempt to render safe the first of the two bombs she had taken the previous day had tragically failed and there were now unexploded bombs in *Sir Lancelot* and *Sir Galahad* from the 24th also. The reason why so many of the Argentine bombs were hitting our ships without exploding (doing damage of course) but passing straight through before exploding in the water) was not so much because, as is often claimed, their fuzes were incorrectly set but, rather, because the pilots were deliberately flying that low to present faster, harder targets for our missiles and guns.

We were more than a little upset, however, to hear the fuze story being broadcast to the world by the BBC! Although this may well have been due to some clown in the *Monastery of Defence* leaking it to them in the first place, the need to broadcast or publish the truth in a democracy is all very well but, when it puts lives at additional risk as a result, I think a degree of circumspection isn't out of order. To put it bluntly, we were incredulous, bloody angry and felt betrayed, the more so when the BBC then broadcast that 2 Para was advancing towards Goose Green, then that 3 Para and 45 Commando had left the beachhead and, shortly after that, that 5

Infantry Brigade was on the final leg of its journey to San Carlos! Having already let the world know that the ATG had sailed from Ascension, then that it had RV'd with the CBG and was poised to invade the Falkland Islands, is it any wonder we were asking "*With friends like that who need enemies?*", a comment that wasn't just aimed at the BBC.

***Antelope* Explodes**

The explosion started fires which, with the firemain ruptured and even with hoses plied from two of *Fearless'* LCUs, proved impossible to control, and as they moved towards the ship's Sea Cat magazines she was abandoned. Just 10 minutes later the fire reached and exploded the ready-use Sea Cat magazine, and when it reached the main Sea Cat and torpedo magazine shortly after that, *Antelope* blew up, the explosion providing one of the iconic images of the Falklands War and a sight none of us who saw it will ever forget (I remember looking at my watch, 18.47 hours local/22.47 GMT).

The ship burned through the night and into the next morning until a further major explosion, probably the second bomb, broke her back and she finally sank, bow and stern pointing skywards. Before she did, and as if the brilliant clear sky and sunshine of that day weren't enough, the huge column of white steam rising from her broken, burning middle formed a perfect location marker that was not at all welcome

After the experience with *Antelope,* the principle with all of them was now very definitely the Dutton Principle, which meant, in practice, "*Take 'em out the way they came in, the same way up, without disturbing their fuzes*", which was easier said than done, of course. With shipwright and engineering support provided from both *Fearless* and *Intrepid*, Bernie Bruen dealt first with *Galahad's* bomb, found in her battery store among broken batteries and spilt acid. On the morning of the 26th, having supervised the careful cutting of an exit route in the manner of Mick Fellows in *Antrim* earlier, he famously had the bomb lowered by crane into a gemini inflatable packed with boxes of corn flakes to cushion it while it was towed away and sunk in deeper water, after which *Galahad* was operational again.

The fact that the offending bombs were all British made was, perversely, some help as, with DSSS (satellite) communication back to the UK when necessary, the teams could know exactly what they were dealing with (not that that eased the strain on those dealing with them).

****

Nigel Turner, Leading Cook on HMS Hermes

Argentina's National Day

The mess decks on and below the waterline had been vacated due to the risk of torpedo attack and the sailors sleeping and making a new temporary home in the passageways running the length of the ship. Visits to the forward part of the ship became less frequent and being as quiet and careful as not to disturb those watch keepers asleep on the decks and in the twilight of reduced lighting. Not very comfortable for many - at least I had a bunk.

Ships being bombed and sunk and sailors killed, daily air raids on the fleet, and scanning the casualty lists to see who had been killed. Recognising many names of cooks that I had known and served with caused great sorrow within but was quickly put aside for another time. We still had a job to do - we were professionals, staying positive and mindful.

On the morning of 25th May the ship had just fallen out from Action stations. Phew - another Air raid survived - back into the captain's galley and get the kettle on for a brew.

The klaxon sounded – "*Quarters Stand To - Quarters Stand To - Incoming Missile - Take Cover*!" Grabbing our kit and running out of the galley, closing and clipping the door and hatch behind us, we dived into 2S flat and attached ourselves to the deck by the cabin bulkhead.

I was lying on my stomach with head between my arms and waiting for the explosion and fires to come. Heart pounding and listening, a few expletives, a quiet prayer. Others doing the same including the ships Padre – 'Rev Dev'. The ship's engines seemed to roar and the ship noisily vibrate as it began to turn, a Harrier engine seemed to scream right above us, hear chaff rockets being launched. Remembering our training. Seconds. Thinking of my wife and little girls. A huge calmness and stillness overcame me and everything would be alright. Seconds. The Excocet missile had missed us due to the defensive manoeuvres but had gone on to hit the *Atlantic Conveyor*.

A massive sigh of relief, and a bit hyper for a few moments, thanking God that I was alive to fight another day, but sadness for the defenceless *Atlantic Conveyor* that took our hit.

What now? After falling out from action stations back into the galley and thinking about the captain's lunch and dinner. News coming in that HMS *Coventry* had also been bombed and sunk. Will this ever end?

The daily air raids continued over the next three weeks, going to action stations sometimes twice/three times a day as the ground forces began their campaign of landings. The continuous noise of Harriers night and day to support the ground troops with air cover, punctuated my mess deck, which was just below the flight deck, with intense disruption to sleep, but hey ho, my discomfort meant that I was alive.

****

Gary Mcilvenna, Royal Marine, HMS Fearless

San Carlos Water

19th May

Our LCUs transferred 40 Commando from *Canberra* to HMS *Fearless* in preparation for the landing.

Landing Craft Go Ashore

20th May

Landing craft were prepared for landing troops in San Carlos Water and got some rest time before the early morning landings the following day. I remember lying on my bunk trying to get some shut eye but could not drop off as my mind was preoccupied with what may happen when we attempted to land on the Falkland Islands.

21st May

In the early hours, going down to the dock of *Fearless*, where the four big LCUs were housed, I vividly recall the red lighting and the smell of diesel exhaust fumes from the craft. We took on board 40 Commando but there was a problem with *Fearless*' ramp door, delaying departure.

Eventually, the hydraulic problem was rectified, and craft were able to leave. I remember feeling the fresh air on my face and looking upward at the clear sky, hearing the crack and thump of HMS *Plymouth* engaging an Argentine position on a hill feature called Fanning Head. Special Forces were also on the ground engaging the Argentine position with small arms fire. You could see the tracer from their general-purpose machine guns as they progressed. These actions were a wake-up call for me. This was not an exercise.

We proceeded on a seven- mile trip to the landing beaches. I felt extremely vulnerable, as I stood looking out of the cockpit window thinking a burst of enemy fire could take me, the coxswain and the naval mechanic out. My landing craft was the lead craft and the three LCUs and four LCVPs formed up behind us. There was radio silence and as the signaller, I had to flash messages using a pin prick light on my torch. Fortunately, and to my great relief, there were no Argentine forces on the beach that we landed on (Blue Beach 1).

All landing craft deployed their troops, and our next task was to go to HMS *Fearless*' sister ship, HMS *Intrepid,* also an amphibious assault ship with the same specifications as *Fearless*. We embarked 3 Para on board and proceeded to transport them to Green Beach, (at Port San Carlos at the northern end of San Carlos Water) by which time it was starting to get light. Thankfully, once again, there was no opposed landing.

We were now hearing air raid warning messages over the radio. By now, it was a nice, clear morning. Our landing craft took shelter in a bay, looking out at all the ships in anchorage in San Carlos Water. "Air Raid Warning Red" was announced over the radio and minutes later, Argentine Skyhawks attacked the warships. I could see small arms, Bofors guns and Sea Cat missiles targeting the Argentine aircraft. I saw a stray Sea Cat missile hit the back of one of HMS *Intrepid's* LCUs, deflecting into the sea. Over the coming days, our priorities were to get ammunition stores and vehicles ashore.

I witnessed numerous Argentine air attacks but particularly recall a Skyhawk getting shot down. HMS *Ardent* was sunk, losing 22 lives, after a good fight against massive air attacks. Also, HMS *Argonaut* was badly damaged and had lost all power. Three LCUs including mine and two others were tasked to tow the stricken ship back into San Carlos Water where it had protection from the rest of the fleet.

23rd May

HMS *Antelope* was hit by an unexploded bomb. Later that night, there was an explosion - my initial thought was that a mini-Argentine submarine had torpedoed one of the ships in the anchorage. We soon found out that the unexploded bomb had detonated whilst being defused by a bomb disposal officer. Landing craft made their way to the distressed ship with LCU F4 arriving first, rescuing the remaining crew. When my landing craft arrived, we helped to fight the fire with our fire-fighting equipment.

25th May

From my landing craft, I watched a Skyhawk being shot down over *Fearless* and I saw the pilot eject from the plane close to her.

He was rescued by one of *Fearless'* landing craft and taken back to the ship.

27th May

I witnessed an air strike on Blue Beach, where 3 CDO Brigade HQ was located. The Argentine Airforce were now arming their bombs, dropping them from a short height with the correct fuses. During the first days of the air raids, Task Force ships were being hit by bombs but not exploding due to them not having had enough time to be armed to detonate. I knew only too well that if these bombs had been correctly armed, we would have lost more ships during these air raids than we did.

****

Tony Pitt, Commander, RFA Sir Percivale
Extracts from his personal diary

'Our Ships Are Being Hit'
Saturday 22nd May

During the early hours of the morning HMS *Ardent* blew up and finally sank. The glow of the fire was visible in the sky over the hills to the west of San Carlos Water. During the night RFA *Sir Tristram* and the STUFT cleared the area to the Total Exclusion Zone.

Sunday 23rd May

Decided to shift anchor again a little closer to the shore to gain more protection from the land. Loaned the ship's welding machine to HMS *Argonaut* which had been damaged on Friday. Argentinian aircraft did not reach San Carlos Water until late afternoon and once again attacked in the north but all the "plums" had gone. HMS *Antelope* was hit during this attack but one aircraft was seen to explode in the air quite close which was good for morale. A very depressing sight, although it was good to see how disciplined the disembarkation was.

Monday 24th May

Shifted anchorage once again before first light to make room for the "big boys" arriving at first light. Took up a position to the south of No 16 berth in Fern Valley Creek. Quite cosy.

RFA *Fort Austin*, RFA *Resource* and RFA *Sir Tristram*, which arrived at first light, all anchored very close together abreast of each other in the middle of the inlet. It looked very precarious to us.

Further sustained air attacks occurred during the day when RFA *Sir Lancelot* and RFA *Sir Galahad* were badly hit by bombs that did not explode and RFA *Sir Bedivere* was also slightly damaged. *Sir Lancelot* and *Sir Galahad* were both evacuated until the bombs had been dealt with. *Sir Percivale* had two near misses and for the first time had a chance to open fire, with some hope of success but a fuse failed on the Bofors at the crucial moment and the chance was missed. The GPMG, however, had a hay day and all were convinced we had some hits but no damaged aircraft were claimed. For the first time the aircraft had attacked from the south up the valley with three LSLs in line and three larger ships at the end of the line in a T formation. It was very fortunate that the ammunition ships were not hit. When *Sir Percivale* had near misses the attacks came down the inlet from the north but the aircraft seemed to have trouble with the terrain.

During the day *Antelope* finally went to the bottom having eventually broken her back. Discharge of *Sir Percivale* was completed that evening and we were ordered to sail to the TEZ at 2100 hours. Our task was to pick up stores for vessels in the Amphibious Operating Area and return.

****

Neil Maher, Signaller, Army Air Corps.
Courtesy of the Army Flying Museum

Signallers Going Ashore

A small group of us had to go ashore first on this lifeboat. This signals detachment was made up of three other Signallers, and we were detailed to go ashore, through this hole in the side of the ship, into San Carlos Bay. This hole in the side of the ship - you come to it and you look down and the sea is, I don't know, 40+ feet below you and this little bright orange life boat bobbing around and as the waves came in it rose up and came close to you but then sank back down again 40 feet.

What we were told was as it came down you jumped and with your webbing on and your bergan and everything on. What happened was you jumped to the boat and because you had so much weight on you didn't bounce you just kind of hit the boat and then didn't move. Then there were two sailors, one on each side grabbing your webbing to lift you up and plonk you on the side of this seat on the rim of the lifeboat, waiting for the next guy.

So that was my journey to the shore on this bright day-glow orange lifeboat, putting along in this open water in the San Carlos Water. I was looking up at the sky thinking "*My God I've got all this webbing on and I'm so heavy that if this thing turns over I'm just going to sink like a stone1*"

We went ashore, and as a Signaller I had my webbing which must have been 40lbs with full ammunition, basic rations, and stuff. I had also a large pack which in total everything must have been about 100lbs, On top of this ridiculous weight, you've got your weapon, which the SR8 is not light and then I've got a radio in my other hand, which is 36+ lbs.

Getting settled in

Once we got there a few people had already arrived and we started digging as the bay had already been attacked a number of times, so I just dug in. I put a poncho over the shell-scrape for cover and just settled in for the night. Not the most salubrious location. I was just very thankful to be honest to be ashore and have some earth under my feet, rather than being stuck in a ship with no control of my circumstances. I was quite happy to dig in, a lot happier in this little trench, although it was freezing cold – Lord, it was cold! I can just say that throughout the rest of the campaign it was cold. We were equipped for European war not the Antarctic. Believe me, it was cold for those that weren't properly equipped.

****

Larry Jeram-Croft, Lynx Pilot, HMS Andromeda
Personal diary extracts

Lynx helicopter pilot on HMS *Andromeda*

Note: The phrase ESM AEW, the AEW means Airborne Early Warning. Because we had lost our fixed wing AEW the only way to get early detection of an Exocet raid was to send the Lynx out ahead of the force to listen for the enemy aircraft radar, which is what we were doing on 30th May.

30th May: A life changing day

The first sortie was uneventful. The second sortie wasn't. Nor for that matter was the third.

So there I was at 6,000 feet, way up ahead of the main force. Behind us in a line, on on anti-aircraft picket duty were three ships. *Andromeda* was to the north, *Exeter* in the middle and *Avenger* to the south. I can remember cruising along eating peanut treats and arguing with Bob about the shapes of various clouds. His mind was always more obscene than mine so it kept us laughing and passed the time. On several occasions, a Sea King turned on his radar and gave us palpitations but all seemed routine.

Then with no warning, all hell broke loose. The Orange Crop started beeping with a strange radar which was clearly 'Handbrake'. We immediately called the controller in *Hermes* and gave the bearing which was to the south of us. At the same time, one of the ships also called the radar and confirmed our alert. The Task Force went to Action Stations at the code word 'Zippo One' and started firing chaff and doing everything they could to defend against Exocet attack.

We had done our job, there was nothing else we could do as we were far too far away to deploy the jammer. We had already decided what to do next - run away! We knew it was possible that the Argies would have escorts for the Super Etendards and that we could get caught up with them. The only thing an unarmed helicopter could do was hide. I accelerated up to our maximum speed of 150 knots and headed for a nice big fat cumulus cloud back towards the force. We never got there.

Suddenly, a continuous tone screamed out from the Orange Crop. Bob immediately recognised it as a 909 radar lock on. He looked over his left shoulder and uttered those immortal words *"Shit they're firing at us!"*" I banked the aircraft hard left and looked. I actually saw the smoke trail of at least one Sea Dart coming up at us. I still have the odd nightmare about it. I knew we were dead.

To this day I have no idea if what I did next saved our lives but in an instinctive reaction I pushed the cyclic stick fully forward. We dived vertically. We pulled out at about two thousand feet, amazed we were still in one piece and just in time to see a long streak of flame on the horizon. I have no idea how fast we went but I'm certain that I broke the world speed record for a helicopter by some significant margin - even though I will never be able to claim it!

Just a little shaken, we realised that it had all suddenly gone quiet on the radio. To the north, I could see a ship with smoke pouring out of it and flashes of something. We gingerly went to investigate. It was *Exeter* and it was only smoke from her funnels and the sun glinting on her radars. Slowly everyone checked in and it was clear no one had been hit. We went down to *Avenger*, where a Wessex 5 had had the presence of mind to hide behind her bulk and then we saw some dye in the water. On investigation, we saw the remains of an aircraft and an ejection seat with a body still in it, sinking. The dye was from the survival kit in the seat.

Later we got the full story. The two Super Etendards had come in from the south, fired one missile, the last one in their arsenal and turned for home. They were accompanied by four A4s (Skyhawks).. Two were shot down by *Exeter*. The Sea Darts, we had got in the way of, were in fact aimed at them and the wreckage in the water was one of them. *Avenger* claimed to have shot down an Exocet with her 4.5-inch gun although it seems pretty unlikely and maybe they saw the flames of the crashing A4s, as I suspect we did.

However, one Exocet definitely locked on to *Andromeda*. They had the 'eyewater' radar of the missile on their own ESM and were tracking it with the Sea Wolf system. What's more, some of the crew on *Exeter* actually saw it crossing their stern and heading for *Andromeda*. Everyone had hit the deck and were praying that the Sea Wolf would do its job when the missile ran out of fuel and fell into the water just outside Sea Wolf engagement range. Relief was tempered by annoyance that we hadn't proved the system against an Exocet for real. So when we got back there was bugger all sympathy for us. And rightly so I guess. My senior Chief came out to meet me with a roll of toilet paper in his hand! Oh, and in *Exeter*, they knew all about us and that we were in the way of their firing solution on the A4s but, quite rightly they fired anyway...

So we got back on board for tea and no medals. Everyone was a little rattled, to the extent that that evening Bob and I broke our no drinking rule.

****

Stuart McCulloch, Radio Operator, HMS Fearless

Under Attack

We were one of many ships that sat in San Carlos Water being attacked by Argentine aircraft. There were so many air attacks during those few days that the bay was nicknamed "Bomb Alley". It seemed that there were times where no sooner was one raid over and we were stood down from action stations that another would come.

I spent all that time inside, either on duty in the comms room or resting or assigned other duties. My mess deck was near the front of the ship, just above the waterline. The comms room was near the top of the ship just in front of the mast. During action stations you stayed on duty doing your job but off duty meant a speedy ascent from the mess deck to a small room near the comms room where a lot of broadcast equipment was held in racks. We would cram into this space and sit and wait to hear what was going on. The escalation in these situations went from Amber Alert to Red Alert and finally to *"Take Cover!"* On the call of "*Take cover, take cover*" you would try to get as low as possible and put your hands over your head and hope to hell that you'd be okay.

If you were on duty in the comms room you'd be at your assigned station and continue to work until the order of *"Take cover!"*, when you'd dive under the equipment bench and stay low with your hands on your head. One time a couple of us anticipated it and dived down on Red Alert, only for the Radio Supervisor to give us a kick and tell us to get up and carry on!

We'd hear the whoosh of the jets flying by and the pom-pom-pom of the Bofors and other guns firing at them. Being inside all the time it was very difficult to get a real sense of what was happening outside as we couldn't see anything, only hearing those sounds.

Charlie Number 1

I mentioned the equipment we had been given for the conflict (gas mask, anti-flash gear and once-only suit). I will always remember a surreal situation I witnessed during one air raid as I was heading up to the comms room.

The onboard laundry and barber were, as it was on ships at that time, run by a contract with an organisation that provided Chinese workers. These guys worked and lived down in the depths doing the laundry except for the head guy, known as Charlie number 1 (a generic term and a sign of the times), who was the ship's barber. He sat in an area just below the comms deck with a chair and set of scissors and clippers and would do haircuts. He always wore flip-flops, white shorts and a white vest, I don't recall seeing him dressed any differently, rain or shine, war or peace.

I remember seeing him, as we were called to action stations and therefore heading up to the room with the comms equipment in it, sitting in his usual place with his usual flip-flops, shorts and vest with this white balaclava and white anti-flash gloves on and thinking – how on earth are those going to help him if we are hit?

Super Etendard

After the first few days, we would occasionally leave San Carlos Water to take on board more troops to deploy on land. *Fearless* was one of two assault ships with landing craft to take troops and equipment to shore. The sister ship was *Intrepid.*

On one of these trips I was on duty monitoring the broadcast equipment when a signal came in that made my blood run cold. There are levels of communications to indicate the priority of the message and one had come through to say a Super Etendard was in the region where we were. The significance of this is that these were the aircraft that carried and launched the Exocet missiles which could sink a ship. It was an Exocet that hit HMS *Sheffield.* I was terrified we were in the open South Atlantic with little protection and we had a potential ship-sinking plane spotted in the area. It didn't come to anything, but it was one of the few times that I stopped in my tracks and felt fear run through my whole body.

HMS *Antelope*

One of the most recognisable images from the Falklands is the time HMS *Antelope* exploded and was lost. It was hit by two bombs that did not explode immediately, one of them only when it was being defused and it lit up the sky. I didn't see the explosion, but I heard it as we weren't that far away. I remember a Marine and I sneaked out of the comms room and stood on deck for God knows how long just watching *Antelope* burn. It was weird as it looked like someone had taken a hot knife and sliced it down the middle as you could see different levels and crew members running through to congregate on deck to abandon ship, as it burned. It's an image I will never get out of my mind. HMS *Antelope* was a Type 21 frigate, the same as HMS *Arrow*, the ship that my brother was on.

****

Chris Clarke, Master, Europic Ferry

Conspicuous in San Carlos

Early next morning we entered San Carlos Water. This was my most memorable time during the whole deployment. *Europic Ferry* was one of only three STUFT (Ships Taken Up From Trade) to be involved in the initial landings, the other two being *Canberra* and *Norland*. Day was breaking as we entered the inlet on what looked like being a bright, sunny and clear day which would leave us liable to be attacked. I felt quite calm as everything seemed to be falling into place.

As we entered San Carlos we could see the tracer on Fanning Head at the entrance as the Special Forces dealt with an Argentine outpost on top of the headland and then we could see *Canberra* looking pristine and white, much as I had seen her during my early career with the P&O Company.

Even before we had reached our allocated anchorage we were getting on with our job, bidding good luck to our troops as they flew off to get on with their job, while other helicopters had started to lift off our cargo of munitions and military equipment. Once anchored, we carried on discharging our cargo when not being interrupted by Argentine air attacks.

There were times when the Argentine aircraft broke through to the anchorage inside San Carlos Water, where again the warships appeared to be the main target. The raids were over incredibly quickly as the aircraft were chased away by missiles and guns with lots of smoke and noise. They didn't come back for second runs!

Although our Paras had taken most of their weapons with them, we were still able to fire with the few remaining guns on board. I can't claim any hits but it was great for morale. Unlike warships, which have stops on their systems to limit the arc of fire to prevent hits on their own ship, we had no such refinements and had to be careful in our enthusiasm not to score an own goal by shooting our own ship!

In the middle of all this, we were told that *Europic Ferry* was very conspicuous with her orange hull and bright green funnel while surrounded by grey warships. Something had to be done so we mixed white with black paint to make grey and started to daub it over the hull and superstructure in an effort to merge into the background as a form of camouflage. The ship's crew were magnificent to a man during that frightening day, particularly as most of them spent their time below decks unable to see what was going on but still able to hear the sounds of what was happening outside. When the bosun complained that the messman hadn't swept the messroom, I knew I had nothing to worry about from that direction!

Eventually darkness fell and we were pleased we had played our part in the Navy's busiest day of action since the Second World War.

****

Barrie Jones, LRO(G) HMS Intrepid

'Inside a Tin Can'

I was an LRO(G) working in the main communications office on HMS *Intrepid* on watch or at action stations waiting in the transmitter and receiver rooms until called upon.

Like many others, I was inside a 'tin can' either on watch or at action station. You heard the whoosh of aircraft and missiles going by and the sound of machine guns firing a barrage of bullets, just wondering if anything was going to come through the deckhead or bulkhead and, if it did, hoping it would be quick and painless. Then you shook yourself out of it and got on with the job at hand. Same every time air raids came into San Carlos Water.

****

Ade Thorne, RAF EOD.

Extracts from my Falklands Diary

San Carlos Water - Going Ashore

23rd May

As I stood on the deck taking pictures, a marine on a mexefloat said, "*You won't be doing that at 2 p.m, mate. Argies come at 2.*" He wasn't wrong. I could have set my watch by it.

Suddenly all hell broke loose – metal tins being banged, ship's horns being blasted, lots of small arms fire, then a massive whoosh as a missile fired by one of the warships cracks past us. Our brief was to go back to our bunk and lie down, pushing mattresses against the bulkhead. On the way down I saw some Argentine Mirages, I think, go flashing past. They were so low. I remember thinking, "*Brave bastards*", because they were just met by a wall of small-arms tracers, and missiles from the ships, and they kept coming.

The running commentary from the bridge was absolutely brilliant, because you have no idea what is going on above decks and it's bloody frightening, I can tell you. We had a couple of bombs hit us but luckily they didn't explode. One bounced through the crane on the front, skipped off the water and into *Sir Galahad.* We were credited the kill of a Mirage, but we also put a volley from a GPMG through the wardroom of HMS *Fearless.*

The night before, HMS *Antelope* had exploded, unfortunately killing one of the RE guys trying to defuse a bomb. He was on Flt Lt Swan's and FS Doc Knight's EOD course. So, it was getting very close to home now, the reality was sinking in.

24th May

It was decided that we should move ashore, both us and the Navy Fleet Clearance Dive team. All of our explosives were too much of a target if we stayed onboard any longer. So, at 0200 hours we moved the vehicles out of the back of the RFA and onto a mexefloat. A few minutes later we arrived at Ajax Bay. Our 4-tonner got off okay, but unfortunately our first land rover jack-knifed as it drove off because the acute angle of the ramp and beach was too sharp. So, we had to sledgehammer off the towing hook.

It was totally dark, and we could only move the vehicles inshore a few hundred metres because that's when the road stopped. We slept in the vehicles for the rest of the night and in the morning we moved into the old sheep refrigeration factory, which became known as '*the Red and Green Life Machine*' (because the forward field hospital had been set up in it) and looked for somewhere to settle down.

The RSM from 45 Commando appeared outside and wasn't impressed as he looked around. *"Oh for f***'s sake the bloody Air Force has arrived. F*** me, only they would bring a 4-tonner decked in white Arctic camouflage and two land rovers with bright red wings and f***ing blue lights on top. Get them covered up now."* For the next few hours, we made a mud paste to cover up all the bright colours so we weren't such a target.

Over the next few days, with no EOD action involving our team, we doubled up as stretcher bearers as the helicopters came in. We went out to a few ships that had UXBs on and helped identify them, but it was mainly the navy boys that defused and dumped the bombs over the side. They did a great job there.

Of course, we all went down with Galtieri's Revenge at some point. The shit tent was just a 12' x 12' with a large trench dug inside it. You went in four at a time, hung onto the makeshift scaffolding pipe, dropped your trousers and leant back over the trench to do your business. It was obviously not the time to stop and chat. The rat pack toilet paper was like shiny paper too. Absolute nightmare.

On one of my many trips, as I pulled my trousers up, I saw my knife fly out of my top pocket and in slow motion do a couple of spins before going headlong down into the trench. It wouldn't have been so bad but it didn't even land in my own poo. I had to retrieve it because I only had the one knife.

****

Rob Shadbolt, CPO Lynx, HMS Antelope

HMS *Antelope*

I was a Chief Petty Officer in charge of the Lynx helicopter based on the Type 21 frigate, HMS *Antelope*. We sailed during the very early days of the conflict from Devonport and the journey south took us approximately three weeks.

Antelope played its part bravely, carrying out numerous operations around the islands. On 23rd May however, we were tasked to support disembarking troops in San Carlos Water and during this day we came under severe air attack taking two 1000lb bombs neither of which exploded. While a team worked on first of the bombs it went off, causing a massive explosion and fire throughout the ship and after a fruitless but brave attempt at putting out the fires the decision was taken to abandon ship.

As you will imagine this provided its own set of nightmares but eventually the crew was rescued predominately by Royal Marine landing craft taking us to a series of nearby ships. More air attacks took place the next day and then we were transferred to a North Sea ferry (MV *Norland*) which took us to South Georgia, from where we embarked on the *QE2* for passage back to Southampton. This was not the luxury cruise you think, of as the rumour every day was that we were being shadowed by an Argentine submarine, plus the fact we had no changes of clothing, money, toiletries or anything else as when you abandon ship you just leave with what you have on.

For many years I could not speak of those few days in May 1982, even to my wife and family but over time things in my memory have eased but will never be erased.

****

John Thain, Junior Ordinary Seaman on MV Monsunen. Story told by his son, Scott Thain (aged 14)

First published in The Falkland Islands Journal 2012 Vol 10

British Forces Land at San Carlos

On the 21st May the British landed at San Carlos and Port San Carlos. It was the early hours of the morning when Dad was woken by naval gunfire. The ships were bombarding Fanning Head where there was an Argentine outpost. This bombardment drove the Argentine troops away from Fanning Head and they passed through Port San Carlos settlement.

Shortly after daybreak the bulk of the land forces landed at Sandy Bay. There were lots of ships in San Carlos Water and also a lot of helicopter movements. Two of these helicopters flew too far in front of the British forces and were shot down by the then running Argentines. The first one shot down crashed into the water in front of the house Dad was living in. The crew both got out and the helicopter sank. The pilot, Sergeant Andy Evans, was seriously injured and his co-pilot, Sergeant Eddy Candlish, swam him ashore while the Argentines continued shooting at the airmen in the water.

Dad and some other people helped carry him to the house on a stretcher.

Several minutes later a second helicopter was shot down but this one crashed onto the hillside and both crewmen were killed. Both helicopters were Gazelles of the Royal Marines. Dad and the others got into the house and they tried giving the injured pilot first aid but unfortunately he died on the floor from his injuries. Dad then went with Fred Ford and Sergeant Candlish in Fred's Land Rover and took Sergeant Evans' body back to the beach where the British were still in the process of landing. Just as they arrived at the beach and handed the body over, the first of many air raids started.

On one particular time Dad remembers lying face down on the ground where a member of 3 Para had just started to dig a trench. It was about six inches deep. The Para lay on top of him – Dad said *"it was truly terrifying with the noise of aircraft flying around us shooting and the British shooting back"*. San Carlos became known to the British troops as Bomb Alley and to the Argentines as Death Valley.

For the next two nights, Dad and others worked with the troops ferrying their equipment into the hills using tractors and trailers. When news reached them saying the *Atlantic Conveyor* had been sunk and a lot of equipment was lost with her, Dad was asked if he would give up his treasured motorbike for use by the troops (Dad treasured his bike, which was new and he was always polishing it) – this he did without hesitation; it was a small price really.

On the 14th June, the day of the surrender, Dad flew into Stanley on a Chinook helicopter along with members of the British Forces and his treasured motorbike, which was returned to him several days later. He was suitably compensated – several months after the conflict he received a new motorbike as a gift.

****

Coventry / Atlantic Conveyor

Throughout the war, the Argentine Air Force demonstrated huge skill and resolve in attacking and inflicting casualties on the British ships in and around the Falkland Islands. San Carlos Water, between East and West Falkland, became known as Bomb Alley due to the ferocity of the battle as Royal Navy and merchant ships were attacked day after day.

Argentina's National Day, 25th May, always seemed likely to be one which would see every attempt by the Argentine airforce to inflict damage on the Task Force, so it came as no surprise that regular attacks were pressed home. Many ships were hit and damaged and two, HMS *Coventry* and the merchant ship *Atlantic Conveyor,* were fatally hit and sunk with considerable loss of life,

The descriptions of those aboard HMS *Coventry* and *Atlantic Conveyor* during the air attacks and when they were hit describe graphically the horrors they witnessed and endured, as well as the heroic efforts from other vessels to rescue them.

Both losses were tragic, but militarily the sinking of the *Atlantic Conveyor* had a huge effect on the future execution of the war as a great amounts of supplies were lost including a number of helicopters. With only one heavy lift Chinook available, the landing of men and supplies at Bluff Cove in early June had to be carried out by Royal Fleet Auxiliary ships RFA *Sir Galahad* and RFA *Sir Tristram.* The devastating consequences of this are told later in the book. These 'lost helicopters' would also have been used later in the conflict to transport ground forces towards the capital Stanley. Without them, many of the forces had to 'yomp' or 'tab' over the inhospitable landscape with all their equipment towards Stanley.

****

Simon Sugden, Weapons Engineering Mechanic Ordnance, HMS Coventry

Under Attack

We then reached the 25th May, Argentine's National Day. We expected this to be a difficult day, but little did we know how difficult!! As day dawned our worst fears were compounded by the blue skies and gentle swell, perfect flying conditions. We were stationed just north of Pebble Island and acting as a trap for aircraft who had attacked San Carlos and then took a route home north. This position was a risk as we were too far from Harrier protection but we had HMS *Broadsword* with us for close protection so we took comfort in that. The first attack of the day saw us use Sea Dart to take out a Skyhawk, the second attack saw yet another hit for *Coventry*, however as other aircraft had escaped us they reported our position.

As the attack came in we heard the whoosh of the Sea Dart, then for the first time during an attack the boom of the 4.5 gun and then the sound of close range weapons, this was not looking good.

Then from memory over the main broadcast came "*Brace Brace Brace*" the next two sounds were two deep thuds then silence for a couple of seconds then came the noise of the explosions that shook the whole ship; it felt as if I was being lifted off the deck, then a strange silence. My thoughts later assumed this was because a lot of the machinery had shutdown and the sound levels of a normal functioning ship at sea had become almost silent. This silence was broken by Chief Petty Officers shouting "*Patrol search for damage*".

This was when the training kicked in, like someone had inserted a data card into the brain of a robot, no fear, no panic. With the three other members of the patrol, we started to open up compartments. I remember going down into my own mess deck, 3P. No damage, then down into 4P and once again no damage. As I climbed back up the ladder into my mess deck I noticed the towels tied in knots to front of our locker doors were starting to hang away from the doors. My first thought was *"Great we are doing a high-speed turn"* then reality set in there was no noise coming from the props that were directly below us, we weren't turning we were listing.

We made our way back to the section base. Fighting against the list made it difficult, and smoke was now filling the passageways. There was only one thing left to do and that was to negotiate the swinging ladder that was our escape to the upper deck. Once on the upper deck I made my way to the flight deck where I would say there was a state of organised chaos. Our helicopter Lady G was chained down to the flight deck. I remember the pilot and observer trying to get the flight deck cleared of spent 7.62mm shells that covered areas of the deck. I believe their intention was to try and get the helicopter airborne, an impossible task given the situation.

The PO of the flight was one of the first people I met, his words to me were *"come on Molly get your Once Only Suit on"*. I released my gas mask bag from round my waist. All the training we had done on the way down, time and time again we practiced various scenarios unfortunately we hadn't once practised putting on a Once Only Suit and I got it wrong. I suppose my natural survival instincts kicked in and I pulled out my life jacket and placed it over my head, I then removed the once only suit from its bag slung underneath my life jacket I stepped into it and then pulled it up. It should go under the life jacket not over it but there was no time to change things so I just pulled it over the life jacket as best I could, sat on the side of the ship and slid into the South Atlantic. As soon as I hit the water my Once Only Suit started to fill up with water. Luckily, I could still swim so I headed for the nearest life raft which when I got there was filled with more than its capacity, so myself and one of my mess mates just managed to sit half in half out in the entrance.

Within a few minutes one of the older Chief Petty Officers was brought to the raft by a couple of the guys. He was in a bad way suffering very much from the cold and also in shock, and we had to get him out of the water and into the raft for him to have any chance of surviving. This meant me and my mess mate had to get back fully into the water. The abandon ship was very swift and well organised given that all the ship's main broadcast had been knocked out.

Life rafts now started to join together and it was soon realised as she went over further on to her port side the water being sucked into her was dragging us nearer to her so our main focus suddenly became to get as far away from her as possible. *Broadsword* had launched her sea boats and had already started to pick people up, as the helicopters reached us I still remember the feeling of relief we were now going to be okay. A Wessex 5 was soon hovering over us and within minutes I was being hoisted up. As I landed in the helicopter I remember asking the air crewman if he could cut the legs of my Once Only Suit as the ties had become extremely tight as the suit had filled with water.

Within a few minutes the helo was full and off we went but first we flew over what had been our home, a sad sight to see her now laid on her port side. All this had happened in what I remember was about 45 minutes.

The helo took us to RFA *Fort Austin* where we were given dry clothes, fed & watered and then allocated a bed which was very kindly given up by crew members of the *Fort Austin.* I remember waking up in the cabin to be greeted by two chefs whose cabin it was, one of them was not looking good at all, drip white. He suddenly ran out and was obviously going to be sick, I asked what was up and was told that they were both members of the ship's First Aid team and had spent most of the night treating our burns victims. Both were true heroes.

As the next day dawned there was the official duties that needed to be done, the roll call. It took some time to confirm that sadly we had lost 19 shipmates.

Our time on board RFA *Fort Austin* saw the majority of our ship mates join us from HMS *Broadsword* and this meant now having to deal with the reality that 19 of our shipmates would forever remain on watch. Three close mess mates and my Divisional Officer were among the nineteen, morale was low.

****

Chris Clarke, Master, Europic Ferry

Atlantic Conveyor

On 25th May we were again to go back to San Carlos in the company of the container ship *Atlantic Conveyor.* We were just about to join up when *Atlantic Conveyor* was hit by an Exocet missile and was subsequently abandoned. This left us just north of a force under attack with no escort as all concentration was naturally on rescuing the personnel from *Atlantic Conveyor.*

Eventually we were ordered "*Europic Ferry carry on*" which meant continuing to San Carlos. That's just what we did at top speed steering a zig-zag course in case of submarine attack, not an everyday situation for a cross-channel ferry! The loss of *Atlantic Conveyor* hit us hard, not only was she a fellow transport ship with which we had come a long way but there were some personal contacts too, especially among our ex-Cunard crew members. I had met Captain North on a few occasions when we discussed how we might use *Europic Ferry* as his "landing craft" in case the much larger *Atlantic Conveyor* couldn't get sufficiently close to shore.

****

David Baston, CO 848 Squadron on board Atlantic Conveyor

***Atlantic Conveyor* - 'Abandon Ship'**

I still feel that in getting sunk we in some way let the side down. That feeling will never change. Our aircraft and men would have been so useful to those already ashore.

I will go back to the moments before the missile strike in a little more detail. *Atlantic Conveyor*'s Cunard crew were simply amazing. They could not do enough for us in enabling things to happen on their merchant ship, the like of which they had never seen before, and much of it involving considerable risk to themselves and the ship itself. You only had to watch the fuel bags burst as the first bad weather arrived to get the idea! Huge bag tanks as used in the field were strapped into containers alongside the upper deck to provide aircraft fuel. Add a bit of pitch and roll and you can quickly get the notion that this was not a very good idea as the fuel sloshed back and forth until the bags burst and fuel poured all over the deck and down the sides of the ship. They dealt with all this alongside the servicemen aboard as though it was an everyday happening.

You get the idea – a crew of servicemen and merchant seamen led by a combined command of Capt Ian North of Cunard and Senior Naval Officer (SNO), Capt Michael Layard, to meld together the disparate needs of aviation and vital store ship roles. The banter and humour was truly amazing. Not much political correctness in the South Atlantic thank goodness, and I have to mention here that much of this wonderful ambience was down to Ian North and his First Officer – sterling chaps both of them.

We picked up some vital spares as we passed through Ascension – including a sunhat for me – bald head don't you know – but the crew of *Atlantic Conveyor* helped as well, providing Wellington boots, torches and other bits of equipment that would be so useful once disembarked.

The officers of the *Atlantic Conveyor* had invited the officers and senior rates of the embarked force for a drink on Cunard on the evening of the 25th May. We had a bell system that sounded alerts – the only one that was ever used was "Air raid warning" and this was what sounded as we were about to ruin Cunard's profits for the year. My action station was on the starboard bridge wing manning my 7.62 machine gun taken from a Wessex, ably assisted by my loader a Petty Officer armourer. I was on the bridge as I was commanding officer of the squadron and thus available to the command on aviation matters. Standing there on that evening, the weather grey and a bit forbidding with a fairly low swell, looking out at all those warships getting very excited indeed. Helicopters flashing around dropping chaff, rockets going off in all directions, and us not knowing what the hell was going on. Personally, I had no fear at all at that point – as my father, an army officer used to say "*Where there is no sense there is no feeling*"!!

As we stood around chatting about the dramatic scenes unfolding we had no idea that there were two Exocets on their way towards us. Decoyed away from several targets apparently, they finally fixed their beady little eyes on us and as we had (a) no idea they were coming and (b), there was nothing we could do about it, we stood about in blissful ignorance.

Then the amazing W-WHUMP. We looked at each other and said "*What the **** was that?*" almost in unison. We soon realised that not all was well as smoke started to appear extraordinarily quickly from the side vents that line the upper deck, ventilating the enormous holds below. Smoke also seemed to be coming from the port quarter where we soon learned that was where the missile or missiles had struck. At the time of the impact we had one Wessex airborne on an HDS sortie and one Chinook airborne on I think a test flight. We also had one Wessex spread on deck amidships facing aft and another on the stern deck. All the others were folded and tucked away. I discussed with the SNO whether I could perhaps get the spread Wessex airborne, but it very quickly became apparent that we were now two ships' companies. One was forward near the forward flight deck and the rest of us from the superstructure aft. Somewhere around now I thought it a good idea to put on my goonsuit that was in my cabin just below the bridge. I dragged it and my Mae West (life preserver for you young!) up to the bridge. I was very upset to find that it no longer fitted! I soon found out why as I had nicked my senior pilot's suit and he was very indignant!

Down below every effort was being made to fight the fires – but this was no warship – so no comprehensive fire main or water and fireproof doors. Jury rigged fire mains had been rigged and these were being used as best as possible. At about this point HMS *Alacrity* came alongside our starboard side and poured huge amounts of water in all directions in a truly brave and valiant attempt to help us. She just nudged up to us and stuck there. She eventually was ordered I believe, to leave us as there was a distinct danger that we might explode and take her with us. We were after all full of excitingly explosive bits of kit.

It was getting distinctly darker now and after much discussion between the SNO and the captain it was decided to order "*Abandon ship*". There was by this time no proper broadcast available to inform everyone of the decision, and so the SNO told me to go down to the main decks and encourage everyone to get off. I was lucky to be able to go down inside the island because as yet the smoke was not too thick to stop us using the main stairwell. The SNO and the captain had subsequently to climb down using the iron ladders on the exterior of the bridge – no joke. The port side of the ship was a no no and so starboard aft seemed to be the place and all the RN standard life rafts were thrown over the side, along with more rope ladders and ropes. Everyone had "once only" suits, those ghastly bulky bright orange things that are difficult to put on quickly let alone correctly – though everyone had been drilled in them and the life rafts on the way south. They also had 'board of trade' life vests.

When the life rafts were chucked over from the *Atlantic Conveyor* that had about a 50-foot main deck to sea height, they hung from their painters at about a 45-degree angle all on top of one another like a line of dominoes. This made boarding them a nightmare for those climbing and jumping from the ship. It must have been getting hot as the APU (auxiliary power unit) of the parked and rotorless Chinook on the after deck started up all on its own!

It was now getting dark and having passed the word to everyone around to go, it was time for me. The soles of my very smart Clark's desert boots having started to melt, it seemed a good time. I climbed down a rope ladder but about halfway down discovered that it had been cut off, probably by HMS *Alacrity* nudging alongside during her valiant efforts at fire suppression. It was not a time to hang around as the ship's side was starting to glow red and bits of hot stuff were pinging straight through the hull all around me. Discretion being the better part of valour, I let go!

I arrived in the water alongside a life raft that was tipped up at an angle and was helped aboard by one of my Royal Marine aircrewmen. I then got out my aircrew knife and cut the painter tying it to the next raft in line. I then hopped around a few rafts doing the same thing and reminding people where the survival knives were stowed in their rafts. After a while we had a few rafts in the water at the correct angle and some drifting off astern. One small problem at this stage was the shape of *Atlantic Conveyor's* hull down aft. Being a greyhound of the seas, she was beautifully streamlined with a "cruiser" stern. In the swells she was pitching up and down, and on the upstroke was sucking the rafts in underneath her and on the down stroke... Not a pleasant place to be.

HMS *Alacrity* was at this stage firing gunlines over the rafts to enable them to be dragged across and emptied of survivors. Gunlines are very thin nylon lines and bloody difficult to hang on to especially with cold hands. I was quite warm at this stage as I had my goon suit on and had been hopping about a bit. The time came to cut free from *Atlantic Conveyor* and get pulled over to *Alacrity*. (other life rafts were drifting off to other ships astern and I cannot recount their stories). I was tugging like mad to get us away from *Atlantic Conveyor* and by the time we eventually got alongside *Alacrity* I could not feel my hands having been clinging to this tiny wet gunline as though it was life itself. *Alacrity* had scrambling nets down all along her midships section of her port side and in turn we were trying to climb up. We had one or two bodies bobbing about which was not much fun. When it came to my turn to climb up, I got halfway and realised that without feeling in my hands, I was going to get no further. I fell off and landed in the water alongside one of *Alacrity's* ships divers who very calmly said "*Good evening Sir, may I help you?*" Oh what joy!! I looked up at the deck above and standing there was an old chum, a Jungly pilot doing time as First Lieutenant of *Alacrity*. They then threw scrambling nets down from the flight deck – much lower freeboard

– and used the flight deck crane to help hoist the tired and incapable to safety.

We stayed in *Alacrity* for a few days, my goodness they were kind to us, keeping out of the way whilst they dashed about fighting the war, and were eventually transferred to the BP tanker *British Tay*, to take us back to Ascension. We were no use in theatre as we had no aircraft, no kit and would have been a drag on the rations.

Fly home to Brize Norton from Ascension…and that's it.

****

Howard Ormerod, Atlantic Conveyor

'Air Raid Warning Red'

We prepared to offload the rest of the supplies –including kerosene, tent & equipment, landing pad construction equipment, vehicles, cluster bombs and Wessex helicopters. The major events of the day are well documented elsewhere. At the "emergency stations" call, I went to my nominated station, which just happened to be the bar! The next two calls were "*Air Raid Warning Red*" and "*Hit the Deck*" followed quickly by a thud and a distinct shudder of the ship. At the time, I thought that it was probably a bomb. Smoke seemed to be everywhere and getting worse. It wasn't long before the ship's tannoy stopped working. I went to the bridge to report hotspots. When I got there, I saw that some people were already wearing their orange survival suits. We were then told to reassemble on the deck so it was pretty obvious what was likely to happen.

The initial descent down the rope ladders to the sea was well controlled, despite at least one ladder being damaged and shortened which meant a longer drop. In fact, my own drop was quite long enough. I had probably got a third of the way down when someone shouted for me to jump (to speed up the process); someone else shouted not to jump as the ship's rolling could have sucked me under. So I compromised; went down to about halfway and then jumped.

As I swam to a life raft, a wave picked up the raft and landed it straight on me. I think that was the worst experience I had. It was dark, and some trailing lines such as the raft's own ladder made it more difficult to swim underwater to get clear. When I did, I was exhausted and was, and still am, grateful to the chaps who were already in the raft and helped me get in. After a short rest I was able to help others in. HMS *Alacrity* fired a gun line to us which we were then able to use to pull the raft alongside her; then it was a case of climbing up the scrambling net to get onboard and change into dry clothes. As an aside, in a previous job, I had been responsible for providing "survivors' clothing kits" for ships to carry for such a situation. Now I was wearing one.

Alacrity looked after us well that night. We knew that the names of the survivors had been signalled back to the UK, although it was a while afterwards that I heard that Liz, still deployed on *Uganda*, had been told that I had "no significant injuries". After *Alacrity*, we transferred by helicopter to the tanker *British Tay* where we descended to the deck, one by one, whilst the helicopter hovered above. Then it was back to the UK in an RAF TriStar.

****

Steve Regolo, General Communications, HMS Hermes

'We all hit the deck'

25th May

I joined the navy Oct 1977 and served on HMS *Hermes* from 1979 up until we got back from the Falklands in 1982. My main job was in General Communications basically a 'Sparker' dealing with providing communications for the fleet specialising in cryptology and secure communication nets and message handling.

I worked closely alongside our SAS communicators, 264 SAS Signals, during the conflict and was shocked to hear of the loss they suffered when cross-decking from *Hermes* to HMS *Intrepid* on the 19th May 1982.

I became close friends with a couple of the guys who perished that night. I recently visited St Martins Church in Hereford to lay a tribute to Cpl Mick Mchugh who in particular became a close buddy whilst down South.

One of my most poignant memories was the infamous date of 25th May 1982.

Whilst on duty down on 7 deck of HMS *Hermes* in the Communications Control Room I carried out my usual routine of setting up the 'complan' (Communications Plan). Anxiety and stress levels were running high as we were on heightened alert due to the fact that this day was in actual fact Argentina's May Day of Revolution.

I could sense the tension with some of my colleagues especially the POWEM(R) whose name escapes me but will never forget the fear on his face as we were ordered to 'Stand To'. We were closed down for action as we had been for most of the day, and when our Executive Officer Cmdr Locke screamed the order over the ship's tannoy system, we all hit the deck at the same time. We covered our heads with our forearms and I looked at the POWEM(R) who was staring back at me. His eyes were filled with terror. I couldn't help myself and started to snigger like a young schoolboy having been told off for laughing.

It seemed like forever before the All Clear was given. In that short period of time I couldn't help myself thinking of my family and how the hell I was going to escape a sinking Carrier seven decks below. Returning to my mess deck shortly after my shift was over I decided to go via the upper deck and the site that I witnessed will live with me for ever.

The *Atlantic Conveyor* had been struck by Exocet missiles and the scene was of utter chaos and destruction.

****

Tony Pitt, Commander, RFA St Percivale
Extracts from his personal diary

Assisting the *Atlantic Conveyor*
Tuesday 25th May

We met up with the Carrier Battle Group and took up station off *Sir Tristram* very pleased to be out of "Bomb Alley". A quiet day, we had hoped. However, there was an Air Raid Warning late evening and within one minute of the warning, *Atlantic Conveyor* had been hit by Exocet missile. She was stationed about two miles on our port quarter. We were sent to assist with the fire to leeward, the side of the hole. The wind was too strong for the water pressure in *Sir Percivale's* fire main to be effective.

A very large hole was visible port side of the engine room which was well ablaze. Moved the ship clear to windward where *Alacrity* was already picking up survivors. Remained in vicinity to assist if required but had difficulty avoiding all the helos that, by this time, had congregated and were looking for survivors. When it was obvious there was no way in which we could help we rejoined the rest of the group.

****

Colin Hamilton, Lt. Commander, HMS Leeds Castle

Sector KILO

Having received not a single signal from CTG on passage south, we had no idea where the Task Group was so, on 21st May we arrived in the TEZ in their last known position – some 12 hours old. No-one there! Luckily a surface search Lynx spotted us and after eyeing us with suspicion for some time, he closed and scribbled their range and bearing on a piece of paper!

We found the group that night and without further ado were assigned a sector on the anti-submarine screen, Sector KILO. The sector was 305-340 degrees from the main body, i.e almost directly up-threat. No nav lights, India band radar (our only radar) silent! An uncomfortable night followed. It was perfectly obvious why we were so stationed, but I don't remember anyone commenting!

During the next three days, we were dispatched around the group, passing stores and mail, returning to KILO in the evenings. Early on 25th April, we were sent to rendezvous with *British Trent* to transfer mail. Four hours after we departed, an Exocet missile flew directly through an empty KILO and struck *Atlantic Conveyor*, with the catastrophic and well-known consequences.

I have therefore wondered many times subsequently what would have happened had we remained in KILO. It is axiomatic that the impact of the loss of such a valuable cargo had very severe consequences and probably prolonged the war by many days. The question I have therefore always pondered is whether the loss of perhaps half our team and a minor war vessel would have been a very reasonable trade and the placement of an indefensible fish boat in that sector a justifiable decision. I believe so.

My occasional nightmare revolves around a man-overboard. While transferring stores and mail after dark with one of the tankers and with ships darkened, one of our rib crew was swept out of the boat by heavy seas. The water temperature was 1 deg C. Despite dropping markers from the ship (some distance from the boat), it took some time to find him, during which levels of anxiety rose swiftly!

He was 17 and we believed he was the youngest man deployed on Operation Corporate.

****

RO(G) Anthony Lawrence, Radio Operator, HMS Fearless

'Brace, Brace, Brace'

"Heads up, possible aircraft approaching from the south"

"Report from HMS Intrepid - Mirage – aircraft bearing red 45"

"Air Raid Warning Red; ship under possible air attack, HMS Intrepid over flown by jet."

From the Bridge comes *'Under missile attack from Dagger, engaging with Sea Cat. Brace, Brace, Brace!'* - my fresh mug of tea, (one sugar), goes flying upwards so everyone gets some! Out of the blue there is an immediate pipe for *"First Aid parties to the Port Bridge Wing at the rush!"* My immediate thought is 'we've been hit.' The front of the bridge has been strafed with cannon fire and three of the gunners and one of the lads on the Gun Direction Platform (all of them 17 or 18 years old) have been wounded by shrapnel, one seriously with a bad leg wound…

…RO 'Russ' Abbott and I get 'volunteered' by the Radio Supervisor to do the daily gash burn in the ship's incinerator located on the port waist. This is probably one of the smallest compartments on the ship and very claustrophobic. The task in hand is to flash up the incinerator and burn about three months' worth of un-required signals and other documents, making sure nothing is left but a pile of ash. Needless to say, there are thousands of bits of paper that we must burn. This job can only be done during daylight hours as the sparks coming out of the incinerator vent would give our position away at night. The downside is if there is an air raid, we have to stay confined in the smoke-filled compartment and hope we don't get stuck in there. The smoke gets so bad that we have to take a break for some fresh air every fifteen minutes. Luckily, we didn't get caught in any raids…

"Air Raid Warning Red, Air Raid Warning Red."

"Wave coming in at the top of the Sound now, Stand-by, Stand-by!"

"Attacking Broadsword who is fifteen miles north of us."

"Broadsword and Coventry are being attacked fifteen miles north."

…I was manning the inter-ship teletype circuit in the MCO when I received the two messages about HMS *Coventry* and *Atlantic Conveyor*. HMS *Coventry* is reported to have been hit by three bombs and is sinking and keeling over; helicopters are on scene taking off survivors. HMS *Broadsword*, despite her damage, is also picking up survivors.

Then the second signal that the *Atlantic Conveyor* had been hit by two Exocet missiles about ninety miles northeast of Stanley; obviously meant for HMS *Invincible* fired from two Super Etendards. You could have heard a pin drop when I read them out to the rest of the Watch in the office; everyone is stunned, how many more ships are we going to lose?

POW and Promotion

We got ourselves a POW! Two A4 Skyhawk fighters came in fast and low with one aircraft being shot down. The aircraft exploded about 50 feet above the ship, with the pilot ejecting just in time amidst a shower of broken cockpit canopy and pieces of debris which fell onto the upper deck. The plane broke up and fell into the water about 100 yards from the ship.

"LCUs picking up the pilot."

"Pilot is alive but suffering from shock, they're cutting the lines of his chute to get him into the boat."

The captain, or someone, said to him served him right for playing silly or stupid war games!

...I got promoted during one air raid! The Signals Communications Officer, Lieutenant Commander Whelan, came crawling through the MCO door as we were all lying flat out taking cover, to congratulate me that my promotion from Junior Radio Operator to Radio Operator 2nd Class, (equivalent to Ordinary Seaman), had been approved; dizzy heights indeed!

****

The attack on HMS *Coventry*

As a young Sub-Lieutenant aged 23, I had graduated in Naval Engineering from RNEC Manadon in June 1981. I reported onboard HMS *Coventry* in late February 1982.

Tuesday 25th May - Argentina's National Day - became a day to remember, and, for several ships of the Task Force, one never to be forgotten. Our Admiral had warned everyone to expect fierce attacks from the Argentine Air Force.

HMS Broadsword and HMS *Coventry* were told to take up position about 12 miles north of the northern-most entrance to Falkland Sound, just off Pebble Island. The day began well. After an attack on San Carlos, Sea Harriers chased two Mirages north out of the Sound towards us.

Nothing further of note happened until about 1730 hours when we received a 'Head Up West' warning of inbound aircraft, with an ETA in our vicinity of about 25 minutes. We passed this message to the ship's company, warning personnel that Action Stations would be piped at 1750 hours.

At 1745 hours the bridge personnel started to don their anti-flash gear (hoods and gloves) in preparation for Action Stations.

After being relieved on the bridge I had gone down to my Action Station once again and reported in to the WE Damage control Section Base in the Computer Room where both PO Fallow and I were closed up, and the compartment secured at 1Z. We both then checked over the sonar equipment to make sure there were no faults showing, and then settled down in the relative comfort of the adjacent 3F mess deck to read our novels.

We sat and waited. A group of four aircraft were finally detected at the maximum range of our 965, approaching the Falkland Islands from the west. The aircraft were tracked in until they disappeared from the screens as they crossed West Falkland – lost in the radar clutter of the land. It all went quiet, where were they? Suddenly two of the aircraft were detected as they burst from the nearby coastline, heading straight towards the ship. With only 12 miles of clear water between HMS *Coventry* and the land, and the aircraft flying at close to 250 knots, this gave us less than 5 seconds to lock on and engage. It simply wasn't enough time, and we knew it.

As the two aircraft approached, even though we didn't have missile lock-on, we launched a single Sea Dart missile as a deterrent. Our attempts to deter the aircraft seemed to be successful, both banked to the right away from us.... only to attack HMS *Broadsword* on her starboard quarter.

Below, we had heard and felt the 4.5-inch gun begin firing, loosing off several rounds, a pause, and then several more. The time was about 1815 hours. We could also hear the sound of the 20mm cannon and Light Machine Guns.

The attacking aircraft were flying extremely low and close together, I'm told that everyone dived for the deck, all except the gun crews, who kept on firing for all they were worth. Seconds stood still as both ships watched the aircraft release their 1000lb bombs, and there was a loud CLANG from the stern of *Broadsword*, which, allegedly, was heard from *Coventry*. No explosion came. Crew on both ships started cheering, but our celebrations were somewhat premature.

The two Skyhawk fighter-bombers each released two 1000lb bombs from their wing hard points, and moments later three of the four hit *Coventry*, amidships, on the port side. The effect was devastating.

Seconds after the impact, there were two almighty explosions close together, and the ship started to list immediately. We had felt the two distinct bangs in our 3F mess, with much vibration transmitted through the hull structure. I suspected that we might have been hit, twice, and this seemed to be confirmed when the lights abruptly went out and we were plunged into semi-darkness, broken only by the dim glow of the emergency lighting in the mess deck and SIS. PO Fallon and I made our way warily into the SIS compartment to check for damage but found none. Power to all the sonar cabinets was still on, as far as we could see.

As we returned to 3F we began to smell smoke, drifting down from other mess decks above us, wispy tendrils appearing around the edges of the escape hatch that we had left cracked open between the two compartments. I tried to contact the Computer Room using the internal telephone but the receiver was dead. No noise was coming from the ship's main broadcast speakers in the compartments, not even the low crackle of cross talk and interference that usually indicated the system was live. There was an eerie silence. Having no form of communication beyond the SIS and mess decks, and with increasing smoke building up in the compartments, I made the decision that PO Fallon and I should both leave via the open escape hatch.

It was about this time that we realised that the ship was listing to port by about 5 degrees. This time, however, we didn't seem to be straightening and then listing over to starboard in the opposite turn. There was something seriously wrong!

The incoming aircraft had caught the ship as she was weaving at speed, and one of the bombs unluckily hit the engine room area, close to the waterline as the ship was heeling to starboard. What had been on the waterline under helm was underwater when the ship righted. The second bomb penetrated the hull at 2-deck level, below the bridge, just where the Computer Room was located. The third bomb, almost unnecessary, penetrated the superstructure just about 01 deck, right where the OUTs 4-berth cabin was – My Cabin! This was personal! In one attack, and with just the first two bombs, HMS *Coventry* had lost her propulsion and weapons systems, and the fireball from the second explosion channelled up the hatch to the Ops Room, causing severe burns to the personnel manning that key compartment. It was from here that most of the injured personnel came. In a matter of minutes we had been rendered helpless, defenceless and without motive power. Even if *Coventry* had not been in imminent danger of capsizing, our fight was clearly over.

Back down below, a voice was shouting "*Come along, move for'd to the foc's'le Escape Hatch*". I joined the mass of stumbling bodies, and dutifully followed the instruction, moving forward.

The smoke was bad and beginning to catch in my throat. As the orderly file of personnel reached the forward cross-passage, the line split and there was a Senior Rate at each ladder, directing people upwards to the Foc's'le. I remember thinking how business-like the process was and had by this stage assumed that the captain had given the order to '*Abandon ship*'. I moved towards the Hydraulic Compartment hatch, up the ladder, and then out onto the Fo'c'sle, just abaft the breakwater screen.

In the meantime, the ship's list had increased to between 10 and 15 degrees, and I took up a position by the starboard side, to assist in feeding people forward, towards the bow, as they came up the ladders. After five minutes or so the flow of personnel from the escape hatches dried up, and I moved forward myself, intending to reassure people, help them with their life jackets, inflate them, and generally make sure there was continued order amongst the 20-30 people gathered there. I didn't really know what I was doing; didn't know what I should do, they didn't teach this at Dartmouth, or in the NBCD lectures.

Climbing nets had been thrown over the side further aft and people were clambering down these towards the rafts. Seeing the life rafts nearby, some of the crew at the bow had started to jump into the water.

As the list increased however, it became less of a jump, more a slide down the side of the hull. I yelled at a group of four or five figures that were obviously considering donning their survival suits, and encouraged them to just get off the ship, though my words were a little more colourful than was perhaps warranted. As the list had developed to almost 30 degrees by this stage, the bilge keels were becoming exposed, and crewmembers were hitting these as they slid down the hull to the water below. This was to cause some painful back injuries we were later to discover.

As the last crewmembers leapt from the fo'c'sle area and swam furiously to the life rafts, I found myself alone by the gun, and the rate of list seeming to have slowed down. Having actively encouraged several crew to jump in without their survival suits, I decided that it would be a good idea to put mine on! This was neither as easy nor as obvious as you might think, requiring me to take my lifejacket off in the process: in the circumstances you will appreciate this was not an act one considered lightly. In the end however, after 10 minutes of struggling, I had my survival suit on, my life-jacket belt with anti-gas respirator haversack firmly buckled round the waist once again, and the buoyancy portion of the life jacket inflated and round my neck and shoulders. I was ready for anything.

As I looked around for inspiration, I spotted two life rafts in the water on the port side of the ship. At the port side, water was lapping the guardrail stanchions, so there would be no jump, I could slip gently into the water in the lee of the ship.

Slipping gently into the sea as I had planned (wow, it was mightily cold) I swam slowly out to the little yellow dinghy, hauled myself into it, and looked around smugly at my new command!

I was now faced with a quandary as to what to do. The life raft had no oars, and yet I didn't want to stay where I was vis-à-vis the ship, which was listing very steeply to port, the bridge wing now touching the water. I needed to propel the life raft somehow. I tried the canvas lifejacket holder, but without success. It looked like I was trapped in the lee of the ship, right where HMS *Coventry* was slowly, but inexorably, capsizing.

I could see the occupants of the other life raft waving at me and shouting, though their words were unintelligible, something that should have served to indicate how far away they really were. I waved back to reassure them that I was all right. It was only later that I found out that they were not enquiring as to my wellbeing but trying to warn me that internal fires were raging towards the 4.5-inch magazine, about 20 feet from where I bobbed in blissful ignorance!

I found myself back adjacent to the Sea Dart launcher again, noting somewhat abstractedly how sharp the proximity fuse sensors on the end were. The list on the ship was now almost 60 degrees, and I was still no closer to finding a way out of my predicament.

The movement was brought to an abrupt halt and I looked round, only to discover with abject horror, that the life raft had collided with the end of the remaining Sea Dart missile, and that two of the sharp proximity fuse points were buried in the fabric of the dinghy! There was also an unmistakable hissing sound coming from the front of the dinghy, and the rubberised body of the life raft was definitely softening to the touch. I had become the first, and perhaps only, person to have his life raft sunk by a Sea Dart missile!

As the dinghy slowly deflated around me, sinking lower in the water, I realised that I would have to abandon ship a second time. So much for my first command! Faced with the necessity of taking to the water once more, I decided to try and swim away from the ship.

I struck out for the second life raft that I had seen earlier, watching as it bobbed into sight above the waves (they were not high, but my viewpoint was very low!). I can remember feeling the water seeping slowly into my survival suit, creeping up my legs, soaking my clothing, and the consequent loss of feeling in my limbs.

After an uncertain period of swimming (I really can't remember how long it was – five minutes, maybe even 10 or 20 minutes) I found that I had reached the other life raft, though I suspect that it must have made equal progress towards me. Considering that the occupants would have wanted to stand off from the ship as far as possible, in case the magazine blew, I was exceedingly grateful for their selfless action. I was hauled into the 25-man dinghy and found the captain, badly burned around the face and hands, the PWO(U) - Clive Gwillam, and Jamie Miller, together with a number of other faces, to whom I sadly couldn't put names. But I was safe, amongst friends, and things couldn't get any worse, surely?

HMS *Broadsword* set about the task of recovering the HMS *Covemtry* survivors, praying that no more aircraft would attack while the rescue was underway. They could see men were leaping into life rafts from the smoking, listing hull, and others were simply jumping into the icy water. It was imperative that the survivors were rescued as quickly as possible. Sea Harriers provided a protective umbrella as ships and helicopters worked to get everyone onboard before nightfall.

HMS *Broadsword*, holding a position some two or three hundred yards away, launched a Gemini which headed towards us, coming to our aid. The rescue attempts were hampered by dense clouds of black smoke billowing from our stricken ship, and the Gemini was clearly wary of approaching too closely just in case!

Helicopters now started to appear; their presence reassuring, but downdraft from their rotors interfering with further attempts to tow us away from the danger zone. We watched a helicopter touch down on the ship aft, two wheels on the point of the deck, the pilot holding his aircraft finely balanced as some figures were pulled into the body of the cab.

A second helicopter, an ASW Sea King as I recall, went into the hover over us, and a winch man appeared with a rescue strop above our life raft. The occupants were lifted off one by one, the injured ones first, others, like myself, with no immediate urgency of rescue or treatment, content to wait our turn, especially as I was one of only a few wearing a survival suit!

As the helicopter banked away to take us to safety we had our last sight of HMS *Coventry*, lying crippled in the chilly waters of the South Atlantic, her port side well under water. For months she had been my home; for others, it had been years. We had thought ourselves invincible; a compact self-contained community. And suddenly it was all over. I was left with a feeling of great sadness.

I can remember little of the immediate hours that followed, other than the helicopter ferried us to HMS *Broadsword*'s fo'c'sle, where we were winched down and led to a makeshift reception area within the ship, given a hot shower, and dry clothes and something to eat.

It emerged that almost all of the HMS *Coventry's* survivors were ferried to HMS *Broadsword*, which acted as primary casualty receiving ship. All were examined, given medical treatment if required, re-clothed, fed, and the more seriously injured flown onward to the hospital ship, the HMHS *Uganda*. The helicopters had proved to be invaluable.

With all the survivors rescued, HMS *Broadsword* returned to San Carlos where, under cover of darkness, we were put into landing craft from HMS *Fearless* and transferred to RFA *Fort Austin*, and later cross-decked to RFA *Stromness*.

The official statistics show that HMS *Coventry* had lost 19 killed in action, and a further 30 injured, the Captain, David Hart Dyke one of those most severely burned. It could be argued that out of total crew of circa 250, the loss of only 19 could be considered fortunate. That may be true, but the loss of just one life is a matter for great sadness, and many lost close friends and colleagues that day.

****

Jack Bedbrook, MD Devonport Dockyard
Courtesy of his widow Sylvia Bedbrook

Tribute to Captain Ian North of the *Atlantic Conveyor*

After a lifetime at sea, Ian North was about to be retired - a fact which caused him much concern. The Falklands War was his lifeline, and his service contract was extended. He was sent to Devonport to take command of the *Atlantic Conveyor*.

Ian North was a character, christened Captain Birds Eye by the dockyard workforce, and his spirit and enthusiasm was a tonic to the dockyard men working on the ship.

On completion, the ship, loaded with aircraft, helicopters and a large quantity of spares, sailed for the Falklands. Unfortunately, she was hit by Exocet missiles and sank.

HMS *Brilliant* went alongside the sinking ship to pick up survivors. Her Captain, John Coward, now a retired Vice Admiral, recently recounted to me that he saw Ian North in the water and although HMS *Brilliant* threw him a life-raft, he was too weak to clamber aboard and he drifted away.

A sad end to a gallant captain, but I am sure he would have wanted it this way rather than being retired. Ian North received a posthumous DSC.

****

Goose Green to Stanley

The landing at San Carlos Bay had been successful, but by 25th May British senior commanders at Northwood had become concerned about the lack of progress and break out from San Carlos Water. Brigadier Julian Thompson, land forces commander, considered that an immediate diversionary attack in the area was unnecessary and would draw men and arms away from the main thrust planned towards Stanley. However, he was ordered to plan an attack on the Argentinian forces at Goose Green and Darwin. It was hoped that this would keep up the momentum of the campaign and further improve support from the British media and the public.

The 2nd Battalion of the Parachute Regiment under the command of Colonel Herbert 'H' Jones were ordered to carry out a raid on Goose Green and capture it. On 28th May, the Paras marched the 13 miles from San Carlos to the forming up position as the transport helicopters had been lost on the *Atlantic Conveyor*. They were outnumbered and lacked artillery support. The Argentine forces were alerted to an attack by preliminary Naval Gunfire, an SAS raid on the Argentine forces at Darwin Ridge and almost unbelievably, a BBC report that Goose Green was going to be attacked. After a 13-hour hard-fought battle in which Colonel H Jones was killed leading an advance on an enemy machine gun post, the Paras captured Goose Green and the Darwin area at the cost of 18 killed and 65 wounded. Gallantry awards were given, including a posthumous Victoria Cross for Colonel 'H' Jones.

Taking Goose Green was an important event in the Falklands campaign, as it improved the morale of the British Forces and lessened the morale of the Argentines. At home it ensured the continuing support of the British Public. It allowed the British Forces to move decisively from the beachhead and plan forward movement towards Port Stanley. 42 Commando prepared to move by helicopter to Mount Kent, which would provide an advantageous position five miles West of Stanley. Here they met opposition from Argentine 602 Commando. For the next seven days the SAS G and D Squadrons and the Mountain and Arctic Warfare Cadre struggled to establish a position on Mt Kent allowing 3 Commando to advance. Eventually the Argentine forces withdrew.

By the 1st June, the 5th Infantry Brigade had arrived to reinforce an advance across the island. On the morning of 8th June Argentine air attacks from Skyhawk A-4s resulted in the deaths of 32 Welsh Guards on the RFA *Sir Galahad* and RFA *Sir Tristram* at Bluff Cove. A disagreement over whether the Guards should disembark or not resulted in them being sitting targets. LCU Foxtrot Four was also sunk. Total deaths in this incident were 56 killed and 150 wounded.

The harrowing images of the rescue operations from the burning vessels by helicopter crews and other ships were broadcast to the world. Much debate has since been made as to why the troops had remained on board rather than being 'dug in' on the shore in relative safety.

The casualties were the highest by any British military force in a single event or action since the Second World War and accounted for over one fifth of the British fatalities during the Falklands War. *Sir Galahad* was damaged beyond repair and was scuttled while *Sir Tristram* was repaired after the war.

On 11th June units of 3 Commando advanced on Mount Harriet, Two Sisters and Mount Longdon. They were supported by naval fire. HMS *Glamorgan* was hit by a land- based Exocet missile, sustaining 14 fatalities. The fighting was fierce as forces moved towards Stanley over the mountains. Both sides were fighting in harsh weather conditions as the winter set in, with heavy casualties. However, the superior British forces made progress and on 13th June, they took Wireless Ridge, then Mount Tumbledown resulting in the collapse of the Argentine defence of Stanley. White flags were seen flying from the hills overlooking Stanley.

A cease fire came into effect on 14th June and later that day Brigade General Mario Menendez surrendered to Major General Jeremy Moore.

****

Gerry Akhurst, Commander 7 (Sphinx) Commando Battery RA, part of 45 Commando Group

The Royal Artillery and the Falklands War

The Royal Artillery had a significant impact upon the Falklands campaign. It is safe to say that the light gun, together with the Sea Harrier were the battle winning equipments. Post-campaign discovery of the Argentine Commander's thoughts made it clear, it was our artillery that worried him most. When, three weeks after landing, our guns helped smash his defences, his worries were confirmed.

At every level of the campaign, there were Gunners. We fought in every battle; indeed, few set-piece engagements would start until adequate artillery was available. Gunners took their place in the close support of the Infantry: providing essential fire support advice; directing fire into the midst of the fight; and carrying the destruction directly onto and beyond enemy positions, to frustrate, harass and destroy.

Field artillery was fundamental to the attack, while air defence artillery defended against the Argentine air threat. Potent and well-equipped, its brave and talented pilots flying sophisticated aircraft caused havoc to our fleet. But once the Rapiers and Blowpipes were established ashore, they contributed mightily to the devastating toll inflicted upon the Argentine Air Force.

At every level the Gunners were fully integrated into the planning and fighting. Small patrols often took a forward observer (FO) with them. Company Commanders always had a captain FO to hand. Likewise, a Battery Commander (BC) at Battalion level constantly advised and provided fire support. And so on up through Brigade (Bde), to ultimately divisional level.

3 Commando Bde was swiftly sent to reconquer the Falklands. Comprising 40, 42, and 45 Commandos, with 29 Commando Regiment RA, they had sailed within three days. 29 comprised three-gun Batteries (Bty's), 7, 8, and 79. Each Bty had six 105mm Light Guns, capable of firing out to 17,000 metres. Batteries

provided a BC to the Commando tactical HQ, and an FO to each Rifle Company. A fourth Battery, 148, had five naval gunfire teams to direct heavy naval gunfire. These NGSFOs generally worked with the BC to beef up fire in support of an attack.

All in 29 Commando Regiment had completed the gruelling commando course. They were fully integrated with the Royal Marines; they exercised together and were often barracked together. Most of 29's soldiers spent their careers with the Commando Brigade, while some Officers were on their second or third tour.

Prior to sailing, the Brigade was reinforced with 3RD Battalion the Parachute Regiment. In turn they embarked with 29 Bty from 4th Field Regiment Royal Artillery. In a similar way to the Marines, the Battalion and Battery were well used to working together. They joined the adventure with gusto and swiftly got used to the eccentricities needed to work well together.

To further strengthen the Bde, 2ND Battalion the Parachute Regiment, complete with 97 Bty from 4 Regiment, were called up. They flew to Ascension Island and boarded the fleet as it paused there to consolidate.

Apart from a troop of first generation and cumbersome Blowpipe missiles, 3 Cdo Bde had no air defence capability. To correct this, 43 Bty from 32 Regt RA provided more Blowpipe sections. While T Bty, with its new, largely untested, and fragile Rapier missiles, were plucked from their camp in Lincolnshire and added to the force. They knew little about the Cdo Bde, less of the Royal Navy, and had never been transported by ship or helicopter before. Intense training was therefore essential and would only be learnt on the voyage south.

Finally, two weeks after the San Carlos landings, 5 Bde, a hurriedly gathered formation of thrown together units, followed in the Marines' footsteps by landing in the Falklands. As part of this Bde, RHQ of 4 Regt could now largely take back control of 29 and 97 Batteries. However, to provide BC and FO parties for the now eight Commando/Battalions, the Artillery scoured units in the UK and Germany. In common with the Bde, these were hastily assembled, had little knowledge of their affiliated infantry, nor the ground they would soldier on. To further supplement the air defence, more Blowpipe sections were added from 21 Bty in Germany. RHQ 12 Regt arrived and took on the coordination of all land-based air defence assets. Now, at every HQ, from Coy to Bn and Bde, and now the nascent Divisional HQ, there were Gunners.

The War

Prior to the main landings Argentine locations were struck with naval gunfire. The Cdo and Paras stormed ashore with their attendant Gunners already registering targets. Within hours the guns were flown ashore and shooting started. As a priority the Rapiers were landed around the bay and were quickly in action against the Argentine Air Force. The latter directed their attacks at the mass of shipping but were aware of the Rapier and naval air defence presence. This threat alone forced them to fly their attack at angles that favoured us.

That said, they were relentless and courageous in their attacks and scored many vital hits. But as time passed and equipment bedded in, the Gunners shot down more and more aircraft.

By now it was clear that the main Argentine defences were concentrated in a ring around Stanley's surrounding mountains. Now that the Marines were consolidated, and supplies of ammunition, fuel and food were stockpiled, it was time to advance. However, the arrival of 5 Bde, and the destruction of reinforcing helicopters, meant a reduction of transport. Accordingly, it was decided that 2 Para would attack the garrison at Goose Green, while 45 Cdo and 3 Para broke out, planning now to march to the attack on Stanley.

A troop of three guns and limited ammunition from 8 Bty was flown forward to support the 2 Para attack. The remainder of 29 Regt covered the breakout and ongoing build up.

The battle for Goose Green is well known and ultimately a huge victory, however the artillery contribution was limited by shortage of ammunition and the infantry therefore had a much tougher job. The lesson was not lost.

45 Commando and 3 Para soon marched beyond the range of the guns. To correct this, and to force an artillery attack, three guns from 7 Bty were flown forward in the one surviving Chinook. In a driving blizzard, into pitch darkness, the pilots flew the guns to Mt Kent. In appalling conditions and guided by the SAS a tentative Gunner hold was established. They immediately started to shell the enemy positions around Stanley while also responding to calls for fire from the advancing Marines.

While this spirited advance was continuing, a series of raids was conducted. One such was that on Pebble Island. The SAS with an NGSFO from 148 fired naval gunfire and placed explosive charges to destroy 11 Pucara ground attack aircraft.

As 45 Cdo and 3 Para closed on Mt Kent they were joined by 42 Cdo, and the remaining guns of 29 and 4 Regt, all now flown in. Helicopters flew in stocks of ammunition for the ensuing battles, and the serious business of patrolling and subsequent planning started. Aggressive fighting patrols infested the mountains to the front. In every action Gunners accompanied the Infantry and frequently engaged the enemy. This probing allowed intelligence to be gathered, while unsettling the Argentines.

From positions of observation BCs and FOs fired at the enemy. This constant and devastating harassment shocked those on the receiving end, preparing them by artillery power, for what was to come.

With patrolling complete, and information assessed, with orders given, and crucially the artillery well stocked with ammunition, the attacks began. The five main battles each had their own character and were fought with tenacity and valour. The stubbornness of the Argentine defenders, who fought well in ground favouring defence, could only be broken by skilled infantry supported by ferocious artillery targeting.

Aggressive BCs and FOs directed fire just beyond our attacking infantry's targets, anything to break the enemy in the close battle.

The crescendo of battle: the noise, the shouts and screams, the explosions, ear splitting, fizzing, terrifying; the sparks, the colour, the lights; the smell, the fear; although there was no fear: adrenalin kicks in and drives men forward. Close quarter battle can be compared to a car crash. A car crash that goes on and on, until suddenly it stops, and seemingly, in what feels like minutes, hours have passed.

And then the enemy were fleeing, they had broken under our assault. Now the FOs could fire and destroy lucrative targets: an airfield, complete with helicopters, supply ships and depots, and the retreating Argentines. But humanity ended this slaughter, and a cease fire was overtaken by their surrender.

The battles were over. The victors were determined infantrymen and aggressive artillery. The air attacks were fought off by technology operated by well trained artillerymen with sound common sense. All delivered by steady leadership, sharp intelligence and professionalism. Attributes the Royal Artillery has practised for centuries.

****

Darwin and Goose Green

Jim Love, 2 Para

Darwin Hill

The bodies lay in rows, at the bottom of the hill, to the left of the re-entry, near the Regimental Aid Post (RAP). I crawled back into the burning gorse. Just to try and keep warm. The smoke, and smell, that seeped into your clothes, and total being, of your body, would stay with you for ever. We sat in little groups, saddened by the fact that the CO and other officers and blokes had been killed that day. The wounded still lay, where they had fallen, their wounds tended to, by their comrades. They were now quietly waiting to be casevac'd out and away from the fighting that was still going on around us. Dinger had administered first aid to Monster Adams, using up all the available first field dressings we had at the time. Dinger was later to get a commendation, for his treatment of the wounded under fire.

All our spare warm clothing had been given to the wounded who were now dressed in a rag tag affair of thermal quilted trousers/jackets and waterproofs. Others lay in exposed inaccessible slopes where they were overseen by the enemy trenches, making it impossible to retrieve them or to administer first aid. We had been taught that it was better to leave the wounded and fight on through and to capture the objective. Returning later to check casualties, and dress wounds where necessary. Unfortunately, we had progressed no further than where the injured had fallen. Held up by the deep positions of the Argie trenches.

During the assault of Darwin Hill I had become separated from the main body and had only managed to regroup after some period of time. Helping to spot for a couple of GPMGs with the laser binos we had managed to obtain while on board the *Norland*. Dinger, PJ, and me had managed to collect some of the enemy's grenades, which lay strewn all around their positions. They were black, Bakelite affairs with two fuse settings. The pins had been removed and the firing levers were held down with elastic bands. We had managed to amass quite a considerable amount of these grenades and were eagerly awaiting the opportunity to use them.

It was shortly after Adjt. Capt Woods, was killed, leading to yet another assault on the enemy trenches, that we saw an Argentine officer attempt to throw one of the grenades like we had been collecting. It had only travelled a matter of inches from him as it arced in the air when it went off covering his body with burning phosphorous turning him into a human fire ball.

Apparently, the two fuse settings must have been today and yesterday. Gingerly, we emptied our pockets and pouches of the offending grenades. Leaving them in little piles for the engineers to defuse or safely detonate. There were already considerable numbers of British grenades strewn about us which also had failed to detonate. It was a task I did not envy them.

Eventually, the lads managed to capture or take out the row of enemy trenches which had thwarted us. The top of Darwin Hill was flat for a couple of hundred metres then yet another row of gorse bushes where it then dropped down to the airfield and the settlement of Goose Green. The row of gorse obscured anyone on the top from view. But the forward slope down to the settlement, apart from a few gullies, was totally bare-arsed. The enemy anti-aircraft gunners had turned their guns to the forward slope and the crest of the hill. Where they merrily raked from left to right and back again every exposed piece of ground. Their heavy, 50cals and 47mms taking a heavy toll on our advancing troops. Dinger and Captain Watson had disappeared up the slope through the smoky haze. Shortly before this Captain Dent had also been killed going up the same part of the gully. I did not honestly expect to see either of them again.

The CO's signaller, myself, and three others, went off up the hill. It was to recover H, the CO, and bring him back down for a casevac by chopper. When we got to him it was soon apparent that he was already dead. He sat with his quilted jacket on, hands clutching his stomach, a slightly dazed, and shocked, expression, on his face. His trousers had been loosened to administer the saline drip. We carried him none too ceremoniously on the upturned roof from one of the trenches, still hoping that perhaps some miracle could be performed by the medics. The corrugated iron unfortunately split like bomb doors on an aircraft causing us to stop and make another improvised stretcher with FN rifles and waterproofs. When we got back to the main position others took over from us and took him to the RAP.

PJ and I set about with some of the others under the direction of the CSM Colin Price to start with and check and clear the trenches of the enemy dead, gathering what suitable ammo there was. We apparently were running a bit low. I flipped back the corrugated-iron roof covering from the first trench while PJ covered me. As I flicked off the second piece, we could see two bodies in the trench. One was lying face down on the left-hand end of the trench. The other in a semi-sitting position on the right with a big hole in his right leg, about where the kneecap should be. He was wearing one of those silly deputy dog hats that we'd been told not to wear in case it caused a blue-on-blue situation. His head was forward, chin on chest, the greyish blue pallor of death filled his face. Nodding at PJ, I jumped down in the trench. I then slung my weapon round my back as I needed both hands free and my SMG was getting in the way. PJ was still covering me and there wasn't a lot of room in the trench anyway.

I bent down again in the bottom of the trench. As I leaned forward to check the body which was in the sitting position, his eyes opened. I fell back on my arse. I was frantically trying to grab the pistol butt of my SMG but couldn't as it was now dug into the side of the trench, which I had thrown myself back against. He raised his hands, palms extended to show he didn't have a weapon, crying in Spanish. He was asking for his mother, and mercy. What saved his life was that something in the trench fell striking metal on metal. Me, seeing his open hands, and thinking grenade decided to leave the trench, and, like, now! Without any further thinking involved, I was up, and out rolling down the slope, shouting, "grenade". I crossed straight through PJ's arcs, and at the cry of grenade, he too rolled back from the edge.

When there was no explosion or any sound other than the wounded soldier crying in the bottom of the trench, we went back for a look. Judging it safe, I jumped back down in the trench. It turned out he wasn't armed any more. His weapon was in the far end of the trench near the body of his friend. He had been shot in the knee, by his own officer, to stop him from running away, while the officer buggered off himself back to the safety of Goose Green leaving the rest, leaderless, and to their fate, against the advancing British Paras. All the enemy wounded were taken down the hill, to the Regimental Aid Post, to sort them out. The dead were laid out in rows near our own.

Meanwhile, Dinger had come back down from the forward ridgeline. PJ and I went off to take his place, with Capt. Watson. Major Rice, the artillery Battery Commander (BC), and his crew were now up there assessing the situation. He now had command of the battalion, being the senior officer. PJ went towards the gorse, where Capt. Watson, and Major Rice, the BC, were. I joined Bob McGoldrick, the BC's signaller, who was sitting in a small fold in the ground making a brew. Directly behind us, there was a Royal Marine, with a Blowpipe, a hand-held ground-to-air missile.

Although we were below the 50cal and 47mm. fire, we were being subjected to mortar, and 105mm howitzer fire. It seemed that the fire was sporadic at the time, but we had a couple of 105mm rounds to our left and right, with another going over the top of us. Typical method of adjustment for artillery fire. Bob had a hole in his helmet where a round had struck, then zipped round the inside, and came out the other side. He like me was still wearing one of the old, steel Para helmets, having more faith in it, than the new plastic ones. The rest of them, were now making their way back from the ridge, and heading, at a fair rate of knots, for the reverse slope.

Bob needed no bidding and was also gathering up his bits and pieces making sure he didn't spill or waste the brew he'd been making. Water was still in short supply so we couldn't afford to throw it away. Besides, it was nearly ready to drink. We called to the lone Marine, who was now standing in a small gap in the gorse, totally sky-lined on the ridge, his Blowpipe on his shoulder. Even from where we were we heard the pop of the front plate and saw the launcher dip. He was trying to engage one or some of the aircraft that were still taking off, from the airfield at Goose Green. There was an explosion and then a plume of black smoke rose in the air. We called again to him that we were leaving but he was now jumping up and down waving his arms in the air. Doing a little victory dance all by himself. He'd got one. We turned off and headed for the others, the whistling of rounds in the air as yet even more 105 mm rounds headed our way.

It was only still day one of the battle for Darwin, and Goose Green.

****

Philip Piper, Gazelle Pilot, 656 Army Air Corps, aboard MV *Nordic Diary extracts*

Searching for an Argentine Radar Site

3rd June

Got off the ship late evening on the 2nd June and flew to the 'camp' just outside San Carlos or 'Blue Beach' as it is called.

The camp is surrounded by lots of other little camps and the place is teeming with soldiers. The countryside is just like Scotland but without the trees; peaty and boggy and it hasn't stopped raining since we arrived.

5th June

Spent most of the day transiting between San Carlos and Darwin/Goose Green. Spent an hour looking for an Argentine radar site. The Gazelle Flight moved out of San Carlos water this evening into Goose Green settlement, which is simply a couple of dozen houses scattered around a jetty and littered with a lot of misused or unused military hardware. The airfield, which is just a grass strip, has a U/S (unserviceable) Pucara aircraft and two dumps of Napalm bombs. (This was hearsay and not verified by me at the time).

There are still 240 prisoners in the wool sheds here in the settlement. Apparently, they are all being very well behaved and with the Gurkhas guarding them - think this is a wise move.

We are very fortunate to have taken over a wee house here. All the houses here are prefab and although they are pretty sparse it is 100% better than living in a grotty trench. I had a lovely hot wash this evening and feeling much more civilised now. This house has only got two bedrooms and there are actually 28 of us sleeping here tonight, v cosy! There are still a lot of booby traps around the place, so one has to be v careful.

6th June

A tragic day. We eventually turned in at around 0230 hours only to be woken at 0430 hours to hear the news that Staff Sgt Chris Griffin's aircraft had been seen by a distant Observation Post to explode in mid-air. *(Note: it was later established Sgt Griffin's Gazelle had been hit by 'friendly fire'.*

7th June

S/Sgt Chris Griffin and LCpl Simon Cockton were buried today; Sgt Sutherland and LCpl Long were in attendance.

The eventual outcome of the incident is that we (helicopter crews) had captured eight Argentine solders. The fact that they were very scared and quite honestly hadn't got their hearts in it was neither here nor there. To be honest it was a bloody scary experience and not to be repeated, I hope.

****

Ade Thorne, RAF EOD.
Extracts from my Falklands Diary

Goose Green

The next day the ammunition stack had cooled down enough for us to start clearing up the area, which was an important helicopter pad, both for outgoing stores and incoming casualties from Goose Green. In teams of four we picked up stretchers and gingerly walked up and down picking up anything we could find, such as ammo boxes with all the heads of rounds poking through the sides, grenades, rockets, and mortars which had been propelled out but not gone off. A similar job in peace time would never have been done like that, but time was of the essence so needs must. I have to say it was a bit arse-tightening to start with, but there was so much to do we just got on and did it. I remember a Marine coming up and saying, "F*air play dude that was nonchalant but cool.*" If only he knew…

Goose Green was now in the hands of the Paras, but at some cost. Helicopter after helicopter brought in many casualties, and then the bodies. Sat in our room, a medic come through and asked for anybody who was blood type A Positive to come forward. I knew I was A Pos. Anyway, they got me to lay down, checked my dog tags, put a needle in, and I watched my blood disappear off behind a screen.

Next day I can remember all the Paras that had been killed during the taking of Goose Green being carried to a large mass grave on a hillock overlooking the sheds, and us all gathering up there for a small service. It was in total silence apart from the sound of the helicopters continuing to and fro between the ships and bridge heads. We also witnessed a Mirage being taken out by a Rapier missile. Finally, when the burial was over, we helped to construct a POW compound for the expected 1500 Argies from Goose Green.

27th May

The building we were housed in was the Field Hospital, but it had been decided not to paint a Red Cross on the top because of the close vicinity of all our supplies and ammunition, which were being offloaded every day.

Back in our room we all were munching away when the air raid sirens started going, banging of metal tins etc. I thought, "*Blimey they're late tonight*". Next thing small-arms fire opened up, and there was an almighty bang, a loss of air, and a rush of wind whistled past us. All the lights went out, the air was full of dust, and various people were shouting and screaming. Scrambling around for my tin lid and rifle I tried to crawl towards the door in pitch darkness, struggling to breathe because of the dust. I can remember the smell of explosives. I love that smell. "*Get up, get down!*" was being shouted. Obviously lots of confusion. I felt down my left leg and it was very wet, warm and sticky, but I could feel no pain, so I thought I had to keep going. Eventually we were all outside in a huddle. Looking to the back of the building there was a large fire where the Marines' galley was. It was not a good scene; 26 men were injured and were being treated for some bad blast injuries, and unfortunately five men lost their lives in that attack.

In the half-light I looked at my leg and I was relieved to see that the cause of the wetness was Mick Sidwell's rice pudding. At that point there was another almighty bang and we all dived for cover. A Sea King was lifting a double stack of ammo to go to the front line at the time of the air raid, so he just cut the rope. Somehow this stack had now ignited, and as it grew hotter the ammunition started to cook off. Suddenly we had mortars, rounds, 66mm rockets whizzing all over the place.

While this was going on Al Swan came up and said it was two Skyhawks. One dropped its stick of four down on the shoreline and the navy were dealing with them. For our four, we had one bomb go off, one had gone right though the building and was up on the hill unexploded, and the other two were lodged inside the building.

One was in the metalwork which ran inside the wall, the other was in the roof.

For the next two hours alongside the navy lads, we carried sandbag after sandbag up from the beach to try and put a block between the bombs and the operating theatres, which were still 100% functioning. Somebody found some old railway sleepers which we managed to put up under the now bulging ceiling and this seemed to do the trick. Al Swan and Dave Fields climbed up into the roof to try and identify the bombs. They were French with what they believed were impact fuses which had malfunctioned, probably because they were dropped so low and so fast that the retard didn't have time to function correctly. This fact was reported on the BBC World Service much to our disgust a few days later. Throughout the night. Al, and Doc I think, climbed up the hill to find our fourth UXB and detonated it, which lit up the night sky and alarmed a few people who hadn't been told what was happening.

****

Tony Pitt, Commander RFA Sir Percivale
Extracts from his personal diary

Argentine POWs
Sunday 30th May

Shifted anchor berth again to position east of 16 close in shore. During the afternoon and evening embarked over 300 Argentine prisoners from the surrender at Goose Green and Darwin. There were so many POWs that those in power were at a loss as to where to keep them. RFA *Sir Percivale* was used as a temporary haven. Commenced dropping scare charges as defence against underwater swimmers. POWs not over keen. Very noisy on tank deck.

****

Opening a Southern Flank to Stanley

A day after the surrender at Goose Green, we woke to a light covering of snow as far as the eye could see, accompanied by the unceasing Falklands' wind rarely below 30 kph during daylight hours. As I walked down from A Company's defensive position on Darwin Hill to the settlement below - passing a sheep pen littered with empty shell cases from the enemy's mortars, and an abandoned .50 machine-gun mounted on a Mercedes jeep - a man emerged from Darwin House and hailed me.

Brook Hardcastle - and his wife Eileen - had only just returned to their home after a month-long incarceration in Goose Green's schoolhouse. They wanted to know what they could do for my soldiers. It was a welcome opportunity to rotate my men through the settlement for a modicum of shelter and rest and was immediately set in train. Brook also extended an invitation for me to have supper with them that evening; since I knew that John Crosland (OC B Coy) planned to liaise later that afternoon, he too was invited.

Gathering local information is an opportunity never to be missed in war; this was the first occasion that I had met an Islander. At the time, Brook was the farm's manager for the Falkland Islands Company - a considerable responsibility. Apart from learning a great deal about life on the Islands, two of his observations were of tactical interest: first, he described watching through binoculars as the Argentine forces lowered an observation hut by Chinook onto Mt Osborne prior to our landing. That explained how the Argentines had continued to bring effective artillery fire on the battalion after A Coy had captured Darwin Hill. Secondly, as we discussed the prospects for moving forward to our ultimate goal - the recapture of Stanley - nhe told us of the phone link between Swan Inlet House, fifteen miles to our East, and the settlement at Fitzroy, which would take us to within eighteen miles of Stanley.

Ron Binnie, manager in Fitzroy, would likely know current enemy locations.

Crosland determined to call on the brigade commander at the first available opportunity, proposing to lead an armed recce to establish the presence of Argentine troops on the southern approach to Stanley.

On 2nd June, B Coy's recce force set off in three Scout helicopters armed with SS11 missiles. To exploit the situation, A Coy had been ordered to wait on the Goose Green helipad at one hour's notice to move. The mission was clear: secure the settlement at Bluff Cove by heliborne assault. As to the enemy dispositions, Ron Binnie made clear to OC B that Argentine troops had recently left Fitzroy and Bluff Cove. What wasn't clear was the enemy's new location; whether they had withdrawn to the ring of hills around Port Stanley or remained within striking distance of the settlements was uncertain. A Coy, I determined, should prepare for a counter-attack at first light if not before.

Short of time, I gave orders to the whole company. Weary from a hard-fought battle, they were nonetheless keen to press on as winter secured its grip. We would get one lift only from the sole surviving Chinook, call-sign Bravo November. A key question for me was how many men it would lift. The acting CO's concern was also to get an element of B Coy into Fitzroy before nightfall; they too would embark in a single lift, after our task was complete. The remainder of the battalion was to be ferried forward to the two settlements the following morning.

The RAF crew embraced the task. "*Fill 'em up, boss,*" was the pilot's response to my question. Eighty men in fighting order, including a mortar section, crammed into the back, while I squeezed in behind the pilot and navigator. We held our breath! Then, with a lurch or two, we took off, flanked by two Scout helicopters, flying nap-of-the-earth twenty-eight miles across no man's land to our target. Unbeknown to us, a failure of communication between HQ 5 Brigade and HQ 3 Cdo Brigade meant that a fire mission was laid on our target, called off at the last moment when the accompanying Scout helicopters were spotted by a RM patrol.

Approaching the target, I saw the welcome LS marker provided by a team from 2 Para's patrols who had deployed half an hour earlier. On the ground for a matter of seconds while we disembarked, the helicopters were quickly on their way back to Goose Green. In the silence that followed, with daylight fading, I confirmed defensive positions and arcs of fire with the platoon commanders, encouraging them to get going - conscious that the enemy would surely have spotted our arrival.

Leaving them to get on with it, I went to say hello to the Islanders who lived in Bluff Cove. A small boy rushed out to greet me. He informed me that it was his eighth birthday; he even told his parents he wouldn't go to bed until the British Army arrived. "*Well that was lucky*," I replied, after wishing him a '*Happy Birthday*.' Without doubt, we had 'arrived' on a wing and a prayer!

Not long after, I met the Kilmartin family. Their proposal to me was astonishing, a kindness of an exceptional nature. Switching off a generator which ensured winter supplies of frozen food, they offered to feed A Company during that long night. Accordingly, in groups of four, my men ate their first fresh rations in nearly a fortnight.

While the night was uneventful - we dug and prepared our defensive position - the following morning saw the remainder of A Coy joining us, with D Coy flying two miles further up the road towards Stanley, only to be shelled by enemy 155 mm artillery. 2 Para's position was certainly precarious, once again devoid of artillery or effective all arms supporting fire - a challenge for the brigade commander. He resolved it by bringing fresh forces to relieve us at Bluff Cove, enabling 2 Para to regroup for a day or two in the sheep-sheds at Fitzroy.

****

Neil Maher, Signaller, Army Air Corps.
Courtesy of the Army Flying Museum

<u>Setting up Comms at Goose Green</u>

The unit had moved forward to Darwin in Goose Green. The helicopter duly arrived, and it picked up our Land Rover and trailer and off it went. We were still left there, then the heavens opened, and it was like a monsoon, the rain came down in buckets and buckets for hours and we were probably stuck on the side of that hill for four hours. Although I had waterproofs, I was still wet through just all damp, cold and miserable. Eventually the helicopter did come and pick us up and dropped us off at Goose Green,

In the far, far, distance were the hills heading towards Stanley base and there were still Argentine Observation Posts (OPs) on top of those hills. And I'd just been dropped off cold and miserable, disorientated, and damp and asked to lay a line to Brigade HQ as we'd lost comms or something. Ok well where is it? It was in the open on the other side of the hills. I know that snipers like people with pips on the shoulders and anybody carrying aerials and radios, so I picked up this drum of cable and my weapon and off I went. I went off at a reasonable pace I'd say, headed towards this house non-stop and I turned up at this house but HQ wasn't there, so I had to divert to another house where the Brigade HQ was, anyway I set up communications and it worked.

There was a little shed nearby with a generator in. It was as noisy as anything and nobody was there because it was noisy, but it was producing electricity and more importantly, warmth. So, I put cotton wool in my ears and dried my clothes off. I hadn't eaten all this time, for about 24 hours so I had two days' worth of meals in my mess tins. Just filled the thing up to the top, cooked it and ate the lot. I had warmth in my belly, it was full, and I was in a warm room although it was extremely noisy, anyway I was out. It was the best sleep I'd had throughout the conflict. I was out for the count.

****

Ade Thorne, RAF EOD

Extracts from my Falklands Diary

Clearing Ordnance at Goose Green

Early June

Now it was our turn to move on to Goose Green. When we arrived, we managed to get set up in the old school house. As the prisoners were moved back to Ajax, we moved up onto the airfield to sort out the mess left behind. The grass strip was littered with helmets, rifles, and fighting kit. We just moved them all into similar piles. Lots of different agencies then picked up what they wanted to take.

Pucara aircraft littered the skyline. We weren't sure if they were booby trapped, so a decision was made to pull out all the ejection seats. This was taken after an earlier explosion had killed an Argentine who had been tasked with moving boxes of ammunition by the sheep-shearing sheds. Unfortunately, as an ammunition box exploded, he was trapped in a fierce fireball and subsequently died. We obviously didn't know if the box was booby trapped or just unstable. Coupled with things like rocket launchers strapped onto the kiddies' slide, 1000lb bombs wired up on the shoreline like mines, and numerous other weird and wonderful items, the decision to pull the seats was made.

After we had completed that job, we moved onto the napalm clearance. There were loads of tanks on the airfield, but we were summoned to a couple of people's sheds/outhouses where there were lots of containers with a weeping liquid crusted around the lids and another set of liquid containers. Not nice stuff. We commandeered a tractor with a sledge and transported them extremely carefully up to the airfield where we started constructing a large bonfire.

After we had cleared and tidied up the airfield, the sheep sheds, and the properties in and around Goose Green, we set about clearing up the cluster bomblets which were strewn all over the place. For every CBU (cluster bomb unit) dropped, on average fourteen bomblets did not explode for whatever reason. There were some still inside CBUs that were either jettisoned or belonged to a Harrier that had piled in. Over 600 bomblets were recovered this way between Goose and Darwin. These were placed on top of the napalm and other items, linked with det-cord, ready for the big blow.

Our final task at Goose Green was to check over thousands of Argentine 105mm rounds to see if they looked serviceable. They did and were airlifted up onto the front line for future use.

The number of minefields littered everywhere was a nightmare, but again we did not have time to do anything about them apart from mark them as best we could and move on.

It was now time to ignite the bonfire. A few minutes later the bonfire ignited – about 300m wide and at least a quarter of a mile high were the estimates. It certainly was a massive fireball with all that napalm.

Whilst at Goose we heard on the BBC World Service that the end was near, and the final battles were commencing. So, we packed up our kit ready to go. Then we heard that the white flag was flying over Stanley.

****

Bluff Cove and Fitzroy

Steve Walsh, Bombardier, Royal Artillery onboard RFA Sir Galahad

Attack on *Sir Galahad*

Once back at Fitzroy, it was decided that the Welsh Guards would be moved forward to Bluff Cove via sea. We accompanied them as we boarded *Sir Galahad*, a flat bottom troop ship. Accompanied by a second troop ship, RFA *Sir Tristram*, we sailed, under the cover of darkness, the short distance to Bluff Cove. We were quite happy aboard the ship, it allowed us to dry out our kit and get some hot food. Unfortunately, in retrospect, our happiness was both naive and short-lived.

Our team had managed to find a small room in the hold of the ship where ropes were kept. It was big enough for four of us and our kit. Captain Johnson had managed to find himself a decent cabin and presumably a seat at the captain's table. As the morning progressed, one company of Welsh Guards departed the ship and we remained on-board awaiting further orders. We remained in good spirits and had no idea just how much danger we were in. I left Moctor, Jenks and Woody briefly and went up the stairwell from the hold to the galley to get a hot drink. As I reached the penultimate deck level, there was a huge flash and bang and the ship felt as though it had been physically thrown. The noise of one or more Argentine fighter aircraft roared overhead. Within a few seconds, the PA system broke the messages "*Air Attack Warning Red*" immediately followed by "*Abandon ship*".

Initially, it was deathly quiet and then voices began to break through the silence. In the stairwell with me were around 20 soldiers, some had minor injuries but there didn't appear to be any serious injuries. Some flash burns and some minor injuries from falling over in the stairwell. There was a leadership vacuum and I encouraged those around me to follow me through a door into a corridor that ran port to starboard across the ship. I kept them all moving to one end, hoping for an exit onto the outside deck. When we reached the end, the door and surrounding bulkheads were twisted metal and there was no way out. There was an element of panic amongst some of the soldiers as smoke filled the corridor. Some of the Chinese crew had now emerged from cabin doors into the corridor and joined our small party. I encouraged them all to turn around and move to the opposite end of the corridor in order to find an alternative exit onto the outside deck, (although in reality I didn't really have a clue how to get out). One young Guardsman had become hysterical and I had to shout at him to get him moving. More by luck than good judgement, there was a usable door at the far end of the corridor and we emerged onto the outside deck.

Once on the deck, there followed scenes too gruesome to include in this writing (or even recall) and I will omit the next 30 minutes. As a poet wrote *"Emotion and dread lay underneath but on the surface, it is not to be seen"*.

Suffice to say there was fire, explosions and smoke billowing around the ship.

My own priority was to locate my crew and help anyone that we could. I miraculously stumbled across my crew on the deck and they all appeared to be remarkably unscathed considering they had been in the bottom of the ship, where it appeared that at least one of the bombs had exploded. It appeared that locating ourselves in the small rope room had been a pivotal decision. If we had remained in the main hold, the outcome would have been very different. We couldn't locate Captain Johnson, but we heard that one bomb had entered the officers' wardroom area. It was clear that the wardroom area was badly damaged and a fire was raging, so we decided that it was unlikely he would have survived. We moved together towards the bow of the ship, where there was less smoke. We stood there for a few minutes gathering our thoughts. The ship was exploding beneath our feet and we could clearly feel the heat rising upwards. We were ordered to climb down ropes to inflatable life rafts tied to the side of the ship. We did this very carefully, since we all knew that if we fell into the sea, we would only have two or three minutes in the freezing temperature before we would be overcome.

Moctor and Woody had climbed into an adjacent life raft but Jenks was with me in another. Once in the life raft, I looked around. There were around a dozen Guardsmen including two junior officers and a couple of *Sir Galahad's* crew. I let go of the rope tethering us to *Sir Galahad* and had a better opportunity to review our situation. Some of the Guardsmen had burns injuries but our major concern was for the Chinese crewmembers who both had severe burns, one of whom was slipping in and out of consciousness.

Jenks and me positioned ourselves by the small opening. To my great concern, in the lee of the wind, we had simply floated further down the side of the ship and continued to move towards the increasing fire and smoke. We searched the raft for oars, in order that we could propel ourselves away from the ship but to no avail.

Helicopters had begun to appear on the scene and one of the Sea King crews had spotted our precarious situation. I will always be impressed by the helicopter pilot's quick thinking, as he positioned the helicopter in such a way as to blow the rotors downdraft against the ship's hull which then gently blew us away from the erupting ship. Once a small distance had opened up between the ship and the life raft, the helicopter swung around behind us and blew us further away from the ship. The helicopter then hovered above us and the loadmaster leaned out of the door. In very simple hand signals, I was able to indicate that two of the men in the life raft were in a serious condition. The loadmaster understood my signals and lowered a winch to the lift raft. Jenks and I moved the men over to the opening of the life raft and fastened them onto the winch strap. The helicopter winched them away and I will never know who they were or if they survived.

48 soldiers and crew died that day on Sir Galahad and many more suffered life-changing injuries.

We floated around a safe distance from the ship until a powered lifeboat from the ship came around and collected a few of the life rafts, towing them all toward the Bluff Cove beach. On the beach, there were numerous soldiers primarily from the Parachute Regiment waist deep in the freezing water helping to lift the injured from the lifeboats.

Once on land, we moved along with the casualties toward the small settlement at Bluff Cove. To my surprise, when I looked down I still had my cup in my hand that I had taken for a cup of tea some two hours previously! We were all dressed in what we were wearing on the warm ship and all our equipment and weapons remained on the ship. That said, I don't remember being cold at all – I think the events had dulled all senses.

The Argentine air raid continued and we could clearly see around four enemy jets flying around San Carlos Bay dropping bombs on the British ships in the bay. Everyone in the area who had any kind of weapon was firing into the sky. I found myself reloading a machine gun for a chap leaning on a fence firing into the sky.

As night fell, it became clear that we were not equipped to see the night through in such cold temperatures without even combat jackets. I hardly slept and was constantly and deliberately waking my crew to make sure none of them slipped into hypothermia in their sleep. A very very cold night.

Argentine air raids continued through the day and we could clearly see ships in San Carlos Bay, which had become known as 'Bomb Alley', burning. It started to concern me that we were 8,000 miles from the UK and our naval support was reducing in numbers as the days passed.

We were offered additional clothing at Bluff Cove. We were directed to a pile of discarded kit. I found a reasonable condition parachute smock to keep me warm but as I held it up, I saw that the back of it had a six-inch hole in it. It became obvious that this kit had belonged to soldiers who had been casualties during the battle for Goose Green.

****

Philip Piper, Gazelle Pilot, 656 Army Air Corps, aboard MV Nordic Diary extracts: 'Musings from the Cockpit'

***Sir Galahad* is Hit**

8th June

A frantic morning was spent trying to move the Squadron to Fitzroy under our own steam, which is difficult at the best of times. Early afternoon we saw our first air attack, which was a number of Skyhawks coming in low over the bay and bombing the two Landing Ship Logistics (LSLs). Both were hit.

RFA *Sir Galahad* started to burn quickly and the ship was swiftly abandoned. *Sir Tristram* wasn't hit so badly however the fires quickly spread and she too was abandoned. Most of the troops jumped the rails but a number were unable to get out of the hull of RFA *Sir Galahad.* In total there were 40 dead and over 100 casualties.

We saw the explosions from Darwin and quickly flew to Fitzroy to help with the casualty evacuation. In all we did three runs from Fitzroy to Ajax Bay (Red Beach medical centre). Returning from our second trip to Fitzroy we witnessed a further attack by four Skyhawks on the settlement but fortunately this time all the bombs missed. HMS *Plymouth* was also hit, however the sitrep on her had yet to filter back.

Got back to San Carlos in the dark which wasn't too pleasant and then spent an awful night in some barn. Had bodies walking over me all night and my sleeping bag got absolutely soaked.

Everyone remains remarkably cheery despite all the tragedies. Hoping to recapture Stanley sometime this week.

11th June

Spent the morning looking after the Rapier Battery; they are located all around Fitzroy and Bluff Cove. The gun batteries have been pounding the Argentine positions on the high ground South of Stanley all day.

Spent the rest of the day taking Major Tim Marsh around the various locations; he is the Deputy Quartermaster for 5 Inf Bde. The poor chap really has a job and a half on his hands as over half of the Bde stores went down with the LSLs in Fitzroy Sound. *Sir Tristram* is still burning away on the water.

****

Gary Mcilvenna, Royal Marine on HMS Fearless

<u>Fitzroy Cove</u>

6th June

HMS *Fearless* undertook a night transit to Elephant Island to disembark two LCUs (F4, F1) with half a battalion of Welsh Guards, conveying the troops to Fitzroy Cove.

7th June

Following the arrival of LSL *Sir Tristram* in Fitzroy Cove, we were then tasked to unload troops and vehicles.

8th June

On this morning, LSL *Sir Galahad* arrived in Fitzroy Cove along with the rest of the Welsh Guards battalion. We RV'd with LCU *Foxtrot 4*, mooring alongside them. They were tasked to go to Darwin to collect urgently needed radio vehicles whilst my landing crafts job was to offload troops and vehicles from LSL *Sir Tristram.* In the meantime, *Sir Galahad* arrived at our location with the remainder of the Welsh Guards Battalion and we were then tasked to start unloading troops and equipment. Unfortunately, our ramp developed a hydraulic problem so we could not lower it and were unable to go to the rear stern ramp of RFA *Sir Galahad,* so we used the portside rear to unload stores and troops instead.

Whilst undertaking these tasks, *Sir Galahad* and *Sir Tristram* were attacked by Argentine aircraft. Three bombs hit the port rear side of *Sir Galahad,* causing a fire. At the time of this attack, I was standing in the cockpit of our landing craft, looking up to see the tail burners of the Skyhawk as it roared past. A Welsh Guardsman in the tank deck managed to fire a burst of machine gun fire at the attacking jet. We then took the walking wounded onto our landing craft, horrified at the shocking sight of their burnt, blackened exposed skin and charred uniforms.

We rescued over 100 casualties, taking them ashore where they were conveyed to a first aid post. Later that afternoon, we heard the sad news that call sign *Foxtrot 4* had been attacked by four Skyhawks. Six of the crew had lost their lives, two survived along with 12 army ranks who were located on the tank deck of the craft.

Later that night, we were tasked with trying to locate the stricken craft, our task made more daunting by the darkness of the night, but we could not find *Foxtrot 4*. This was quite possibly one of the most traumatic days that I recall.

****

RO(G) Anthony Lawrence, Radio Operator HMS Fearless

<u>The Tragedy of Foxtrot 4</u>

8th June 1982 will always be remembered for the disaster at Fitzroy when Argentine Skyhawks attacked and bombed *Sir Galahad* and *Sir Tristram* and the resultant loss of life to those onboard, in particular the Welsh Guards. What tends to be forgotten or mentioned as an afterthought in many histories written about the Falklands War is the loss of the Landing Craft *Foxtrot 4* This oversight still rankles many of the crew of HMS *Fearless* today. The sinking was a tragic and personal loss of six shipmates to all onboard…

We'd just fallen out from Action Stations after all having been up for some 19 hours without a break, when the captain came on the main broadcast system and gave us the bad news. *Foxtrot 4,* whilst transporting men and equipment for 5 Infantry Brigade, had been caught in daylight in open water by Argentine Skyhawks and hit by a 500lb bomb, killing six of the crew. The silence onboard was deafening and a terrible blow to our morale. The ship had been comparatively lucky up till now. The shock of it really brought it home to us youngsters that war isn't a game; none of us are invincible and that those nearest to us, or even ourselves, could just as easily be taken from this life in the blink of an eye. Everyone was very quiet and subdued that evening.

I never thought I would see Royal Marines crying but they did in our mess-deck when they heard the news that their friends on the LCU would not be coming back. The captain went down to see the marine sergeants in their messdeck; apparently, he'd taken the loss hard as he was so very proud of all his sailors and marines and what they had achieved.

The surviving army passengers and two crew were rescued by a helicopter and the wrecked landing craft left to drift in the gathering dusk and eventually sink. *Foxtrot 4* is the only Royal Navy vessel lost in the war with no known grave. For the crew of HMS *Fearless,* 8th June was the darkest day of the war.

****

Garry Hearn, Lance Corporal, Royal Signals attached to 1st Battalion Welsh Guards

Landing at Bluff Cove

Up Sussex Mountains, we are on the move, God it is good to get out of that miserable hole in the ground, we are moving forward, what a great feeling. Five miles later, turnaround and head for the hole again. Thankfully short-lived and on to HMS *Intrepid* for a trip around to Bluff Cove, instead of four landing craft there are only two, we have to split the Rear Link Detachment into three elements of which one group comprising me, Jerry and Ian Haines "Hainsey" will go first in the two landing craft and the others would go back and try again the next night. My Best Man, Barry Wilmore, plus two of the Welsh Guards Signallers with whom we had bonded on the journey south, Nigel Rowberry (ex-Royal Signals and a proud Welshman) and Thomas 'two-numbers' (a large humorous pianist of renown in the clubs of London) head back. Into the landing craft for a hypothermia-inducing hour-on-hour pitch-black scud across the waves of the South Atlantic with icy water constantly splashing into the open top boat; can't wait to get to land and start moving again.

Ashore at last, dig another trench, slightly dryer than the last but trying to dig into rock strewn land is not fun. Bonus, the HQ is in the middle of a block of disused porta-cabins and has been…camouflaged; guess which one the HQ is in! Decide to try to spend as much time in the trench as possible. Rations arrive, only type available is a pack for ten men which has to be shared between the three of us, a tin of ten sausages causes difficulties as three into ten doesn't go; we decide to have a fight to settle the distribution of the final sausage, it is what soldiers do.

Incoming shells, earth erupts before any sound of the explosion, fatalism returns, *"oh well nothing I can do if those land directly on my head as I won't hear",* despite clear evidence to the contrary it is a feeling contradictorily combined with a belief that you don't die at 21. Air Raid Warning Red and the Argentine air attack is on us within minutes, firing a rifle may not actually do much damage but it offers a feeling of doing something. A huge explosion and a plume of thick black smoke is filling the sky beyond the bluff. Fifty-six dead and hundreds wounded, most of whom are the Welsh Guards coming to join from the second night, a proud Welshman and a pianist are lost but thankfully I still have a Best Man; my theory of age 21 is on very shaky ground.

My brother calls on the Brigade radio net using veiled speech to see if I am safe, we connect and it feels good. My wife waits and is eventually contacted by the Regimental UK based duty officer, no Hearn on the list, joy for her then incredible sadness. The battalion is devastated but the decision is to keep going, reconstituted with two companies of Royal Marines; there are no taxis or buses.

Burial at Sea

At 1840 hours *Sir Galahad* is beached and abandoned. The UXB is lodged next to 200 tons of explosives. Our task for the night is to conduct a RAS (L) owing to the fact we are low on fuel and also we are given the task of burying at sea the two young sailors who were killed on *Argonaut*. At last light we slip out of Bomb Alley bearing the two bodies that are placed on the quarter deck, draped in the Union Flag and with two sailors in full dress uniform to guard over them.

The captain makes a broadcast to the ship',s company to the effect the burial will take place at 2230 hours from the starboard side aft and anyone who would like to pay their respects may do so. At 2215 hours the quarter deck is packed with all non-essential personnel in smart clothes one of whom is me. It is a very moving sight. I am right next to the guard rail where the bodies will be committed to the sea and the captain is opposite me. One of the sailors was 18 years old and the other 21. At 2230 hours we come to slow ahead for the ceremony and the CofE padre conducts his service. We are not allowed to show any lights which makes the ceremony, using shaded torches, even more eerie.

When the padre finishes the body is committed to the deep right in front of me. The RC chaplain is next to conduct his service which is more dramatic than the previous one. Finally, the other body is committed to the deep and I look up at the captain who has tears streaming down his face. It is only then I notice so have I. Nobody seems to want to fall out and we all stand there at attention for ages. Everyone is stunned by this service and there are not many dry eyes. At last some begin to move away and go back to their duties.

****

Bluff Cove

8th June

RFA *Sir Galahad* and RFA *Sir Tristram* had been bombed. I watched the news eagerly, saddened by the disaster. I was heartened when I saw some familiar faces on the lifeboats. Some of the RCT lads on board were flown home via Ascension. One lad got back to Marchwood and was dressed in the same borrowed RN blues for about two weeks. I'd often see him about and wondered when he was going to change? War affects people in different ways; I wasn't in a position to judge others.

****

Historian Nick Brazil

A Hero of Fitzroy - Hugh Clark

In the mid 1980s, I was living with my family in the Sultanate of Oman. Both my wife and I were keen thespians, so we had joined the local amateur dramatic society. If my memory serves me correctly, it was known as The Muscat Players. The group was popular amongst many expatriates, including the fair number of military personnel stationed in that Gulf State. One of these was a quietly spoken man aged 38 who was serving on loan from the Royal Navy to the Sultan's navy. His name was Hugh Clark.

To say that I knew Hugh well would be overstating it. However, we did have a couple of conversations, one of which I still remember thirty-five years later. I had been reading a book called "*With The Sultan In Oman*" by James Morrison (later to become Jan Morris). In it, Morrison related that in the Second World War, a Japanese submarine managed to sink a Norwegian merchant ship in Muscat Harbour. I was curious to know how anyone could possibly know the submarine was Japanese. In the course of conversation, I asked Hugh Clark about this. "*Intelligence,*" he replied quietly with a smile. Yes, that was Hugh as I remember him, soft spoken and self-effacing. One of nature's gentlemen. Quite by chance, another member of the Players had seen service with Hugh in the Falklands War. In fact, he revealed to me once, that he had been a winchman in the Sea King piloted by Hugh in that bitter little conflict.

As all good things must, our time in Oman came to an end. My family and I returned to England never to see Hugh Clark or any other members of the Players again. It was only a year or two later that I learned of Hugh Clark's heroic role in The Falklands War. It was in a book relating the history of the War. In the account of the sinking of the troopship, RFA *Sir Galahad*, it described how Hugh Clark flew his Sea King helicopter close to the blazing ship to save many troops. Whenever I watched the film clips of those choppers flying into harm's way, I always thought of Commander Hugh Clark and his great bravery. However, it was only researching the BMMHS book on the Falklands that I learned the full story of Hugh Clark.

On 8th June 1982, Hugh Clark's Sea King helicopter was at the little settlement of Fitzroy. By chance, the landing ship RFA *Sir Galahad* was in the bay at the same time. She was preparing to unload the Welsh Guardsmen who were on board. At about two o'clock in the afternoon a flight of A4 Skyhawks from the Argentine Fifth Air Brigade streaked down the Sound and attacked RFA *Sir Galahad* and her sister ship RFA *Sir Tristram.* RFA *Sir Galahad* was hit by three 500lb bombs. This was not the first time this troopship had been hit by an enemy bomb. On 24th May, a 1000lb bomb hit the ship but failed to explode. This time all three bombs detonated setting the RFA *Sir Galahad* and her ammunition ablaze.

Alerting all the helicopters in the area, Hugh Clark flew his Sea King into the thick black smoke billowing up from the inferno. Despite the danger from the flames and exploding ammunition, Clark lowered his helicopter down towards the deck of the stricken vessel. He and his crew winched many men to safety who would otherwise have died in the blazing wreck. The downdraft from the Sea King's rotor blades also pushed liferafts carrying survivors away from the burning vessel. Forty-seven men were killed in the bombing of *Sir Galahad* making it the highest British death toll of any action of the Falklands War. However, many more would have died had it not been for Hugh Clark's bravery. For these he was awarded the DSC for these actions and his "major contribution to the support of the troops".

Although his role in the rescue of troops is the one for which Hugh Clark is best known, it was not the only time he diced with the Grim Reaper during this conflict. In the Battle for Mount Kent, Clark was supplying ammunition to the troops slung under his Sea King. A sudden down draft caught his aircraft threatening to dash it on the rocky terrain. Thanks to his flying skills he controlled the helicopter narrowly avoiding a fiery death for him and his crew.

After the Falklands War, Hugh Clark was promoted Commander and served on loan to the Sultan of Oman's navy in Muscat. This was where I met him. Sadly, he died of cancer at the early age of 62 in 2010. His ashes were scattered in an ancient woodland near Devizes that he owned and loved.

R.I.P. to a very brave man.

****

Alex Manning, Assistant Staff Minewarfare and Clearance Diving Officer (ASMCDO), HMS Fearless

Treating the Casualties at Fitzroy

There were far more injured than Ajax Bay could cope with at once, so to enable it to concentrate on the most serious cases and minimize the waiting time for the others, some 75 of these "less seriously injured" (an entirely relative term, for their injuries and pain, too, were considerable) were taken by LCU to *Fearless, Intrepid* and *Atlantic Causeway*, each of which had sufficient medical facilities, staff and space to receive and treat them until they could be delivered, via Ajax Bay again, to the *Uganda*. Each ship took 25 and in *Intrepid* (and I understand this was also the case in the other two) there were so many volunteers to help that they were having to be turned away.

My abiding memory is of attending to and comforting a burned Welsh Guardsman who was sufficiently alert to be taking stock of his surroundings and ask what my rank epaulettes meant. When I told him they meant I was a naval lieutenant (at which he still looked blank until I explained it was the equivalent of a captain in the army) he actually stiffened to attention on his mattress, believe it or not, and said, "*Sorry, Sir, didn't know. Thank you for 'elpin' me though, it's really good of you.*" Having assured him that it wouldn't have mattered if I was the Archangel Gabriel, I went outside afterwards feeling thoroughly humble in the presence of such people and cried (discreetly, I hope; but I didn't worry about not pulling my weight anymore).

The aftermath of Fitzroy. *Sir Tristram* beached and *Sir Galahad* still burning, eight days later.

****

San Carlos Water pm 21st May 1982 taken from HMS *Intrepid*. *Canberra* offloading 42 Commando protected by *Antrim* and *intrepid*. (*Antrim* already with an unexploded bomb on board).

Alex Manning archive

San Carlos Water.

Courtesy of Ade Thorne

Under atttack. Mirage overhead.
Tony Lawrence archive

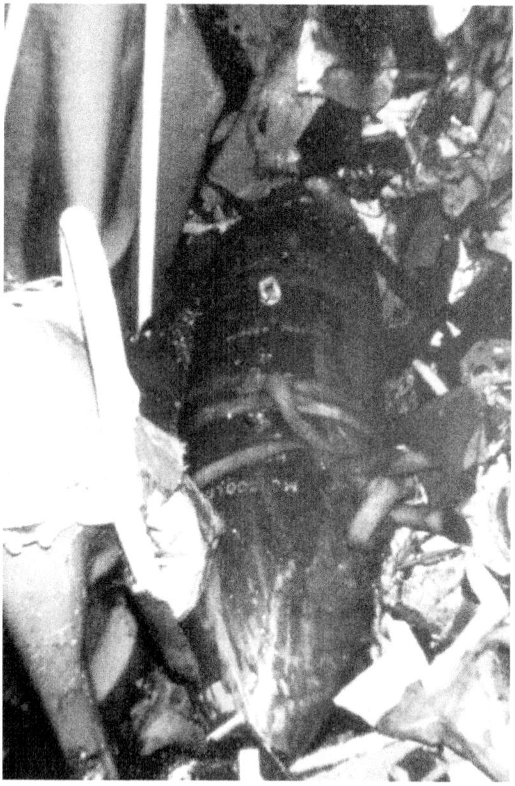

Unexploded bomb in HMS *Argonaut's* magazine. Lt Cdr Dutton and his team helped remove to bomb.
Courtesy of Tony Groom

21st May. Late afternoon, San Carlos Water. HQ Coy B Echelon leave RFA *Sir Percivale.* Landing craft to Ajax Bay, Red Beach.

Photo Eddie Bairstow

22nd/23rd May - 45 Cdo Gp, Ajax Bay. Royal Navy Moustaches. L-R. Doc, Dentist, MA, Schoolie, Padre, POMA. Dave Griffiths, Nigel Sturgeon, Paul Youngman, Eddie Bairstow, Rev Wynne Jones, Colin Jones.

Photo Eddie Bairstow

3 Cdo Bde boarding a Sea King.
Tony Lawrence archive

22nd/23rd May - Ajax Bay. L-R Mexefloat, Landing Craft, Rigid Raider. Ships LSL and *Fearless* or *Intrepid.*
Photo Eddie Bairstow

24th May - 45 Cdo HQ position above Ajax Bay. *HMS Antelope* sinking. Field Hospital on left shoreline. LSL on right.
Photo Eddie Bairstow

Looking down on San Carlos Water.
Courtesy of Gerry Akhurst

HMS *Fearless*. Lynx on deck HMS *Antelope* armed with Sea Skua missiles.
Tony Lawrence archive

Casualty evacuation on Darwin by 656 Sqn Army Air Corps.
Courtesy of Chris Nunn

27th May - 45 Cdo Yomp Day 1. Landing craft Ajax Bay to Port San Carlos (top left). Stop to adjust bergens (not size). 22km covered on day 1. Air attack on Ajax Bay after yomp started. 5 members of 45 Cdo Gp killed. (4 on 27th May. 1 died of wounds 10th June). 14 wounded in action. Some unit stores and ammunition destroyed.

Photo Eddie Bairstow

3rd-4th June - Two day move for 45 Cdo from Teal Inlet to patrol base near Mount Kent. Fighting order and sleeping bags. Volvo BV202E over-snow vehicle on the track.

Photo Eddie Bairstow

4th-11th June - 45 Cdo HQ patrol base west of Mount Kent. Volvo BV202E left. Gazelle Helo above. Ration packs right. Recce and fighting patrols in surrounding area as final plans and preparations made for 45 Cdo's attack on Two Sisters overnight 11th/12th June.

Photo Eddie Bairstow

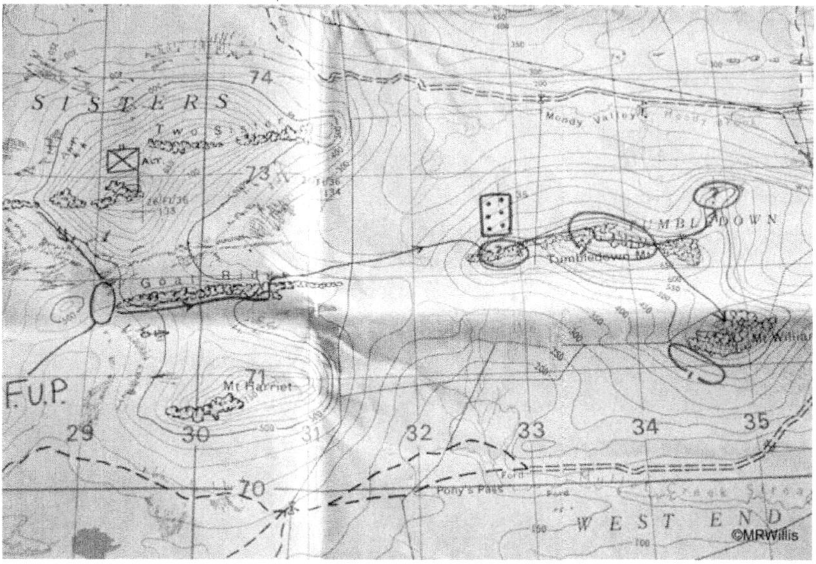

Map of Goat Ridge to Tumbledown.
Courtesy of Mark Willis

The long view from Tumbledown, looking west along Goat Ridge towards Two Sisters.
Courtesy of David Willis

Neil Maher, Signaller, Army Air Corps

Courtesy of the Army Flying Museum

Ashore at Fitzroy

We had good communications to the step up which was some distance away at Fitzroy so I was quite chuffed with myself. We were told to stand by anyway and we were going to go on the RFA *Sir Galahad* to be moved to Bluff Cove. We started to prepare to move and also one of the radio vehicles and trailer, the crew, the driver, were going forward too, went on the landing craft with the Marines, that set off and we were stood down. We were told we'd be taken by Helicopters so that was slightly disappointing but quite fortunate in hindsight because our departure by helicopter lift was obviously delayed because of what had happened in Bluff Cove. The Argentines hit the *Sir Galahad* and *Sir Tristram* badly.

During this same incident the trailer was being airlifted across but (not surprisingly) the pilot of that helicopter after seeing the Skyhawks coming in went to ground. It was their form of defence so they would drop the trailer which ended up in the middle of a mine field, so that was all lost. We'd lost the radio vehicle with the signal equipment on the vessel, the communications instructions too and pretty much everything. So, when we did turn up at Fitzroy, we were pretty depleted on the comms side.

Laying Line in Minefields

Back at Fitzroy we had line all over the place but fortunately I went across this track and they had this Scimitar tank that kept ripping up the line, we had to lay another so I thought I'm going to do another route. Now, I was obviously commander so I gave instructions. We will follow this fence line and you will go across the road. I gave him the brief and off he went, he's laying line and I'm following up tying the line quite securely at different points to make sure we don't have any more breaks and we can protect it as much as possible. So, I'm tying this line securing it all up at various points.

Next thing I hear he's shouting, there's this hullabaloo so I thought 'what's going on here?' I go forward and he's stuck in this little minefield. No idea how he got there but sometimes when you're laying line you go backwards so I guess he'd gone over the fence and not looked, and he was stuck.

I got there and there's all these mines, fortunately the Argentines at times laid mines on top of the ground. I came over and took control so he started listening to me, then I gave him instructions and got him out the minefield as if it was just an everyday thing. I remember a number of years later he came to my 40th birthday party.

****

The Battle for the Mountains

Brum Richards, 148 Commando Battery Naval Gunfire Support

Target Mount Harriet

Wednesday, 9th – 10th June on *Yarmouth*

At 0230 hours we are on station and ready for NGFO3 to give us our targets. He gives six which he cannot spot due to the distance. These targets are all to the enemy rear in Mt Harriet. We begin to engage at 0300 hours and at 0330 hours have completed all six targets. That is the slickest bombardment I have ever seen. We depart from the area jubilant.

At 0100 hours I have good comms with NGFO3 (Sgt Thomas & Gnr Pennington) and they ask me to engage three more targets than that previously asked for. I explain about the 100 max salvoes we are allowed, which we cannot exceed but they say these targets are gun Btys which have been causing some problems. I am quite prepared to do what they ask but we are restricted to 100 salvoes. They have no idea that we are running out of 4.5inch ammo down here. The UK is running out of it and cannot get it down to us quickly enough. There is even talk of trying to dive on the ships that have sunk in shallow water to see if they can recover any more.

The captain and I are restricted to 100 max but also want to engage what we are asked. The BC says engage the lot.

After a while he agrees to authorise the extra but for us to use the CO of 29 Regt's name as authority. At 0300 hours NGFO3 are in position and we begin to engage the four targets he can see.

The visibility is good and the crew on the GDP can see our salvoes landing. All four targets are on Mt Harriet. As we engage the second target we hit what is believed to be a missile site which erupts in a ball of fire. We pour a few more salvoes into the area and then continue with the other two targets. Sgt Thomas estimates 50 casualties which he can quite clearly see because of the fire raging.

On completion of the spotted targets we engage the three Gun Bty positions. As we engage them Sgt Thomas takes a bearing on the fall of shot and confirms they are in the target area. We fire 25 salvoes into each gun position.

0430 hours we cease firing. We are told our fall of shot is devastatingly accurate, which is a great boost to our gun crews. In fact the whole ship's company keeps congratulating me as if I were responsible but I have to assure them it is a total team effort. This is a very happy and professional crew.

****

Steve Walsh, Bombardier, Royal Artillery

Advancing onto Mount Harriet

All during that day, a single Argentine artillery gun targeted our position and shells landed randomly. An army priest came to our trench (from where, I have no idea) and held a short prayer session behind the rocks with Moctor and myself, who were both Catholic. The shells continued to fall. All very surreal.

I went to the briefing when we were told we would be moving forward to launch an attack on Mount Harriet under the cover of darkness. As night fell, we moved off in single file northwards.

I would stay at the rear of the Commando Company with Moctor. Captain Johnson would be toward the front with Jenks and Woody. As we moved forward in a boulder field, I tripped in the dark and my weapon dropped onto the rocks making a real racket. There was some whispered cursing directed at the idiot making the noise. Luckily for me, in the dark, no one could identify who the idiot was! Within an hour or so, there was a loud bang and the sound of one of the Royal Marines screaming filled the air. He had stood on a landmine and lost a foot. We were ordered to stand very still – sometimes an order is not required!

It was starting to snow and the wind was howling. Moctor and I stood together trying to shelter from the weather when our old friend, the Argentine artillery gun woke up. The shells landed randomly and fortunately off target around us.

A Gazelle helicopter came in very low with no lights and landed in the middle of the minefield – very brave stuff from the crew and within seconds it was gone, with the casualty safely aboard.

Eventually a couple of engineers made their way from the rear, very gingerly, up the line of soldiers to clear a path for us through the minefield. We arrived at a position at the bottom of Mount Harriet. We dug shell scrapes (shallow trenches) and tried to sleep for a couple of hours as the snow fell.

Moctor and I got our sleeping bags out and shared them with two Royal Marines but in the early hours, as dawn was breaking, it became obvious that we were in full view of the Argentine positions on Mount Harriet. We were ordered to 'bug out' fast. Within seconds the two Marines were gone and Moctor and I were left digging our weapons out of the snow and packing up our sleeping bags. Good move by the Marines – must remember to use someone else's sleeping bag next time! That said, we were only two minutes behind and soon caught up as we returned, at speed, to our original position a couple of miles north of Mount Harriet.

****

Mick Southall, Private 3 Para

Mount Longdon

On the 11th June 1982, I was a 17 year-old private in 5 Platoon B Coy 3 Para serving in the Falklands War. I had only been with 3 Para a matter of a few weeks.

3 Para were tasked with assaulting Mount Longdon. We marched some 10 miles to the start line at the base of the mountain. We were ordered to fix bayonets and move forward. After a few steps I heard a loud bang from the right and a man screaming. This was Cpl Brian Milne who had trodden on a mine causing him to lose a leg.

I heard someone shout '*run!*', so I ran to the rocks some 30m in front of me. I found myself alone. I looked around and tried to get my bearings. I peered around the rocks, and someone engaged me from around 20m away.

I then decided to move down to my left, where after a short period of time, around five minutes, I was reunited with my Section under the command of Cpl Ian Bailey. I was obviously relieved to be back with my colleagues.

We then started moving through the rocks where we found ourselves in a very narrow corridor when the Argentines started dropping grenades on us, this corridor became known as *Grenade Alley*!!!

When we eventually cleared through grenade alley, we found ourselves at a large boulder. I was to the left of the boulder. I peered around to see a figure around 10 feet in front of me, he was holding an FN Rifle and scanning the area where we were. I informed my Section that there was somebody out there, to which someone replied, "*well, fucking shoot him then*". Without hesitation I moved around the rock and for a split second everything stopped and before I had time to think my training kicked in and I engaged the figure with some four or five rounds before he had chance to fire back. He cried out and hit the floor.

We then moved forward as a Section, and I passed the figure on the ground and searched him to make sure he did not have any information on him and to ensure he was dead. Someone patted me on the back and said "*well done Babycakes*" (My nickname at the time).

I did not have time to reflect or think about what had happened as the battle was now well and truly on!! Over the years I have thought a lot about that incident and am comfortable with the notion it was him or me!

As the battle continued, we moved as a Section through the very difficult terrain. At this point 5 Platoon had split into two because of the difficulty of the terrain.

To our right was 4 Platoon who were trying to get a foothold on the mountain the same as us. As we moved through, we were engaged by two enemy bunkers. We returned fire and Cpls Bailey and McLaughlin decided that the best course of action would be to use the 84mm Anti-Tank weapon to neutralise the threat.

The meassage was passed to get the 84mm into a position where it could engage the bunkers. I had the 84mm and was told to crawl into a position where I could see the bunkers. I can't remember who, probably one of the Cpls told me to *"get this fucking right mate"* or something like that.

I slowly moved with my No2, Boots Meredith, to a fire position. I identified the bunkers some 50m or so away. I had no night sight so did my best with the standard iron sight.

I focused hard and when I was sure I had acquired the target I fired. The noise was unbelievable!!! I was very disorientated and deaf!! I had almost injured L/Cpl Colin Edwards as he was in the backblast when I fired, not sure if that was my fault or his!!!! Thankfully I hit the bunker and told my No2 to reload.

Boots did this and I focused on the other bunker. I was sure I was going to hit so fired. Nothing happened!!!! I had a misfire. I knew the drill was to wait 60secs to see if the round would go off. This was not a good idea!!!

The enemy had now acquired our position because of the noise and the flash from the 84mm. They started to engage us and someone grabbed me and dragged me into cover. I was then told to throw the 84mm away, so I did. The HEAT (high explosive anti-tank) round was still in it!!!!

I was quite happy to see the back of it as it weighed a ton!!!!!!

****

Steve Walsh, Bombardier, Royal Artillery

<u>Viewing the Fighting on Mount Longdon</u>

That night we stood on a hilltop watching the battle for Mount Longdon. We had a clear view of our artillery shells landing on the hilltop, which appeared to be glowing in the dark like a volcano. Tracer ammunition lit up the sky and I could only imagine the horror that was unfolding.

A group of marines escorted a large number of Argentine prisoners into the echelon area in almost pitch dark. They looked like a bedraggled group and I am certain that they were glad that their part was played out. In the confusion of the dark and noise, one of the marines came up behind Woody and tried, at gunpoint, to push him into the group of prisoners, assuming that he was an Argentine. We had to leap to his defence and explain that he was British. Oh, how we all laughed - except Woody!

****

Mick Southall, Private 3 Para

Mount Longdon - Heavy Fighting and Casualties

As the battle raged 5 Platoon (Pltn) and 4 Platoon joined forces to make up a more effective subunit. After a short time, we came under heavy effective enemy fire pinning us down. The commanders decided to find a route for us to take to attack these enemy positions.

Lt Bickerdike, Sgt Mckay and Cpl Bailey were trying to find a route when they came under heavy fire. Lt Bickerdike was injured, and Sgt Mckay and Cpl Bailey decided to turn the Recce into an assault. They charged forward together.

As they moved around some rocks they came under very heavy fire. Cpl Bailey was hit three times. Sgt Mckay continued the assault alone. The noise was incredible as the assault went in and the remainder of us gave covering fire. I have no idea how long the assault lasted, but eventually everything went silent.

After a sort time it was decided that someone should find out what happened. L/Cpl John Lewis of 4 Pltn decided to move forward. He reached out and grabbed the first person he could, which was me, and then told Pte Sulle Alhaji to join us.

We moved around the rocks and found Cpl Bailey who was seriously wounded. He had been shot in the hip, hand, and neck. We administered first aid and L/Cpl Lewis then decided that Sulle should remain with Cpl Bailey and look after him while me and him would locate Sgt Mckay.

I followed L/Cpl Lewis through some rocks until we came upon the body of Sgt Mckay. He was dead. We then came under fire so we moved back to Sulle to assist him and to ensure Cpl Bailey was ok.

Sgt Mckay was my Platoon Sgt in training. He was a brilliant bloke and would always ask how things were going if we bumped into each other. His actions changed the fortunes of B Coy and 3 Para and we were instrumental in being able to continue the assault on Mount Longdon. For his selfless act Sgt Mckay was awarded a posthumous Victoria Cross.

After the Sgt Mckay incident it was decided that we would evacuate any casualties we had suffered. Cpl McLaughlin and CSM John Weeks were shouting and encouraging us to get our guys back to the RAP.

I threw my webbing down and went out to find a casualty. It was at this stage that I learned things had gone very badly for the young friends I joined the army with.

Jason Burt aged 17 had been killed very early on in the battle. He was a great lad, a proud Londoner and a great laugh to be around. I was very sad to hear this news but had to forget about that as our guys needed help!!

I ended up next to Neil Grose who had been seriously injured, it was his 18th birthday. Mark Eyelles-Thomas was with Neil. Mark was also only 17 or just turned 18. Next to Neil was the body of Ian Scrivens who was also 17; it was clear that he was dead. He had been shot through the neck while trying to help Neil, poor Mark had seen all this. He was obviously shaken and desperately trying to help Neil. We tried to treat him but it was clear he needed some serious assistance. The small of group of guys helping Neil included Steve Jelf, another 17 year-old who had joined the army with us.

We put Neil onto a poncho and tried to carry him. Unfortunately, Neil was in a lot of discomfort and very scared. We were all trying to calm him down and keep him on the poncho so we could get him to the RAP, I don't think it was that far but carrying a casualty at night over that terrain was very time consuming and difficult. Eventually we arrived at the RAP and put Neil down. He was struggling a lot as he was very badly injured. Mark was at his head while I tried to hold his legs and feet in an attempt to make him more comfortable. Mark and myself tried our very best to reassure him but his injuries were so severe, he was in fact dying in front of us. After a short time Neil went quiet. It was obvious that he had unfortunately passed. I asked the medic, Phil Proberts if there was anything that could be done, he told us that we had done all we could.

This was the worst thing that happened for me on Mount Longdon. I know it affected others as well. All these very young lads had done our best for our wounded friend. We had carried him, done all we could and he still died on the side of that mountain.

I am still in touch with Neil's family and see them whenever there is an event surrounding the Falklands War.

At approximately 5am in the morning of 12th June the battalion had been engaged on Mount Longdon for five hours, attempting to shift the Argentine defenders out of their bunkers and therefore secure the position. Resistance had been far tougher than expected and casualties on both sides had been high.

As the fighting reached the rear edge of the position, a bunker was located that was impossible to knock out from the high rocks where most of us had ended up, intermingled with all sorts from other platoons and detachments.

Naval gunfire was brought in but landed on our position instead. It was decided to work our way around the side of Mount Longdon to reach the bunker which at that stage appeared to be one of the last holding out. Led by Lieutenant Cox and his radio man Steve Philips, a column of us were moving along the side of a rocky slope when a burst of fire went down the line from the front.

Johnnie Crow was killed instantly, and Lennie Carver was badly wounded in the chest. An Argentine soldier had come out of the bunker and fired, before running back in to cover. Individuals and groups of us crawled forward and returned fire on the bunker before Cpl. Stewart McLaughlin stood up and fired a 66mm anti- tank rocket, over the top of us and straight in through the aperture of the bunker, killing the occupants. In semi-darkness and amid the fire that was going on, it was a superb shot.

At this stage Dom Gray and Ben Gough from 2 Section ran up to clear the bunker and to check for enemy occupants. It was now getting light and as they were standing in front of the bunker. A burst of fire came in from across the open ground in front of where we now were. As Dominic and Ben instinctively dropped down, a round passed through Dom's helmet and cut a groove across the top of his scalp, causing a serious head wound. Dom was still exposed to enemy fire and was dazed with blood running down his face.

As Dom sat there with blood pouring from the wound to his head and before anyone else could move or do anything, I broke cover and ran out to rescue Dom.

I immediately grabbed Dom by the scruff of his smock and dragged him out of the fire zone to safety before the enemy had another chance to engage Dom and at this point myself.

It was pure instinct to dash out and grab Dom, I just didn't think.

****

Colin 'Taff' Edwards, Lance Corporal, 5 Platoon, B Company, 3 Para

<u>Ten Minutes on Mount Longdon</u>

I was Stuart (Scouse) McLaughlin's 2i/c and my job in the section was as a machine gun controller. I had to creep forward and find positions for my GPMG team so that they could give covering fire as the rest of the section advanced.

Somehow in the mayhem I got separated from my gun team but had met up with Terry Mulgrew from another section and we were soon joined by a young lad called Tony who was also from another section. The three of us found ourselves up against a rock face with a big gap and a large sloping rock. From the other side of the rock and about 15 metres away we could see gunfire being directed towards 4 Platoon who were still making their way out of the minefield.

Me and Terry crept as far forward as we could and could see the bunker where the muzzle flashes were coming from. I had one grenade left (we were all issued with two) as I had thrown one earlier in the advance. I pulled the pin and threw it and I heard it go off, but the fire still continued, I asked the other two if they still had their grenades. Tony the young lad (who had been seconded from the officer's mess to bulk up numbers), said he still had his, so I told him to get up where I had been and throw them at the bunker, to which he replied, "*You do it corporal, you're a PTI and got bigger arms*", to which all three of us had a chuckle.

I climbed back to the gap in the sloping rock and threw the two grenades, one after the other. I didn't realise until 35 years later when I went back on a pilgrimage that above the bunker was a rocky outcrop providing extra cover for the bunker and at least two of the three grenades had bounced off it.

As soon as the second one went off we dashed through the gap for the 15 metres and took cover in the rocks which formed the front of the bunker only to find that we, just me and Terry, were in the "shit pit" that the occupants of the bunker had been using as their toilet. It stank and we were both covered in toilet paper again this was worthy of a FFS, *('for fuck's sake')* and a chuckle.

The firing from the bunker had stopped, whether it was one of my grenades or fire that was being directed to the bunker from the flanks I will never know. Terry mentioned that he was gasping for a fag, so we crawled into the now silenced bunker and there were two dead Argentines inside. We took this opportunity to have a quick smoke, until we heard Scouse shouting for us to Reorg on him, so we doused our fags and made our way to the voice.

Once again, we were all together as a section, but still pinned down. Scouse told me to follow him ..."*Follow me lads, I'm FUCKING bulletproof*" - to see if we could find a way forward and as we passed a rock concealing another bunker an Argentine soldier pointed his weapon out towards where the rest of the section were still pinned down. Scouse shot him in the head at point blank range and I was splattered with blood, he was that close. So in the space of 10 minutes, I had been covered in shit and blood. We re-joined the section and moved across the gap and continued the advance.

****

Garry Hearn, Lance Corporal Royal Signals attached to the 1st Battalion Welsh Guards

Mount Harriet - 'No Buses or Taxis'

On the move, off to secure a start-line for 42 Commando attack on Mount Harriet. My friend the immense load is on my back, I shuffle and stumble over rocks, screes, and 'babies heads' huge clumps of grass tufts; no taxis or buses, keep going. Air Raid Warning Red, lie on our backs, load provides a place of rest but also an anchor to movement, faces look to the sky, if nothing else we can put the Argentines off with the sight of a hundred upside down turtles staring upwards as they seek out their target; clearly not turtles this time.

Climb up the rifle, on the move again and into a minefield, now pitch black and freezing cold, inching forward in single file, hour after hour; two Royal Marines are lost. Radio is tuned to the Brigade net, an encoded FLASH message, the highest possible warning, this is the real deal. Take down the message, immediately followed by a tell-tale repetitive 'shushing' noise in the headset, battery is dead. Comms lost, in a minefield, pitch black, moving forward toward the enemy, and with a FLASH message to decode – fuck, don't panic, there are no buses or taxis, just have to get on with it. Teamwork with the RSO and we are back in comms, didn't feel the cold.

On the start line, absolutely freezing, the tentacles of frost creep over Jerry and I as we lay on the rock-hard hillside. Minimal trailing wire antenna, low power, no comms, try a ground spike antenna, comms established, the enemy are above us on Mount Harriet. Artillery, from both sides, and naval gunfire from our ships smack into the hill, incredible red, white, green, blue colours exploding, flying shards of rock thankfully all of it is above us on the hill, incredible noise.

Petrified Argentine soldiers run into the position, POWs, grab them, and...give them a biscuit, humanity even in the height of war, how is that natural? A streak of white light shoots across the horizon to the south, another streak seeks to intercept it, but doesn't. We hear later it is thirteen killed and many more injured on HMS *Glamorgan* as a land-based Exocet missile found its target.

Closing in. A heliborne assault to the foot of Sapper Hill, the final high ground prior to Stanley. Weapon, radio, ammo, batteries, pack of Rolos, boiled sweets, and a sleeping bag (never leave that). The Wessex helicopter, noise reverberating from the open door, cling on to anything as it screams along inches from the ground, fan out and land...into another minefield, leap out the door, sporadic fire from the Argentine defenders, shouts of "*Get onto the track it isn't mined*". Run and hope; it works. Antenna up, comms established, and apparently resistance has ceased. Shake out and move forward, ready to take cover when needed. Argentine gun emplacement hit by counter-battery fire, two dead, half a head, no arm, glance, looks like we have won, and carry on; not much humanity there.

The night of victory and comms are still needed so stag on with Jerry and Hainsey plus a Welsh Guards signaller who has decided to wait until victory before developing acute appendicitis. Snowing, blowing a gale, and after three attempts to get a heli extraction, hexamine blocks simply don't provide enough light in the South Atlantic blizzard, we talk the pilot on to our position. Two days later, can't walk, feet are suffering from the constant cold and damp, back to shuffling but without the load; there might even be the odd bus or taxi.

****

Andy Tubb, Recce Troop 45 Commando Royal Marines

Two Sisters

Fresh out of the training box June 1980 within a few weeks of joining 45 Commando X-Ray Rifle Company, I applied to do a selection course for a PW3 (Snipers). And in 1981 and during the deployment I applied and was selected for Recce Troop as they were looking for snipers. I headed south as part of Recce Troop 45 Commando Royal Marines as part of 62 Foxtrot commanded by Marty Wilkes (section commander), Taff Crawford (radio operator) and my bivvy partner Mick Turns (gunner).

Objective: Two Sisters

Two Sisters was the 45 Commando's objective and Lt Col Whitehead knew he needed intelligence on the objective which led to Recce Troop doing multiple patrols on the peaks to secure best information for him. As a result, I found myself on the slopes of the Sisters five times.

Once we had arrived at Mount Kent, reconnaissance patrols were stepped up. Two Sisters became our regular patrol objective, conduct reconnaissance and leading fighting patrols to the peaks. On one occasion we returned to HQ and were given a warning order to leave in four hours to return to the Sisters. On this occasion two sections and the boss Lt. Chris Fox embarked on a patrol to gather information on enemy positions.

Leaving Mount Kent on 5th June, the nine of us headed out. In terms of distance Two Sisters was not far, I believe it was six miles yomp but hell the terrain made it feel like twenty miles with the stone runs and the wet moors. On top of that I was so knackered that if we took five miniutes'rest, I would take a knee rather than a prone just to stop fatigue taking over.

As we neared the Murrell River the fog had rolled in like something out of a Hitchcock film. Visibility was down and in our favour. Knowing what was on the other side there's a feeling that you become aware of. It is a feeling that is hard to explain but those who have experienced it will know. Maybe it's the numbness, or the fear of letting your oppo down. The dependable is the default of training and giving a 100% to that, the comfort blanket.

Crossing the river, we made slow progress up the slope. Due to the poor visibility, it was hard to see the man in front of you. Our spacing closed, not wanting to be separated from those who are constant to you and a potential lifeline. Expecting a contact from any direction of the compass at any moment is a scary feeling that increases the senses, with perceptual distortion starting to play tricks. The big one for me was time I had no sense of time. Not to mention it had closed in so much the possibility of just stumbling, stepping on an Argie or even falling into an enemy trench.

It was hard to tell how high we had climbed as there were no reference points to refer to. The decision was made to hunker up as it was perceived we were close to their lines and did not want contact due to the difficult exit and having obtained no intelligence.

At this point we should have been on our way back not squirrelled away in between two rock ridges that protruded like razors from the slope with four metres between them. It was so damn cold, we were just in fighting order, unable to brew up due to light discipline made our static stay on the slopes one cold miserable night.

As dawn approached and the fog cleared, the true reality hit us. During the night we had climbed past their front defensive positions and our layup spot for the night was amongst them. With senses being heightened I became aware of the slightest noise. The best option was to head down that evening to avoid detection.

For one thing, we had a good position to call down some artillery fire from the Commando's Battery. Our position enabled us to direct some spot-on airbursts on to them. All was going well until that airburst was above us, *"Check, Check, Check Fire"* was put out on the radio. Somehow Murphy's Law had come into play.

Around this time, we became aware of Argies carrying crates below us, these crates appeared to be heavy as two men were moving them. It wasn't long before it was surmised, they were getting ready to lay mines.

Suddenly and uninvited, because trust me we had been as still and quiet as humanly possible, we had an Argie with rifle slung and belt order over his shoulder stroll into what I guess he thought was the perfect ablutions spot.

He was engaged just as he became aware of us about four metres out. All hell was about to break out. The section laying the mines had a good fix on our position and we started to receive incoming small arms fire. It was time to leave and our route home was from their lines and now through the mine laying section.

As I mention training took over and we instantly broke down into small groups knowing our axis we started pepper-potting for about 400 metres towards home. Argies were getting organized and launched a counter. With rounds from the front and rear starting to find their way towards us, with the rocks being struck and raining small stone fragments on you. We fought our way down the slope using every drop of munitions we had, even 66mm rockets at them.

We got down to same level on the slope as the mine field section. I found myself checking round a rockface and coming face to face with the enemy. I pulled back behind the rockface and quickly lobbed a grenade around the corner. Finding ourselves all together, the last hurdle in our way was one of their gunners. With another grenade our passage was clear. With a quick reorg and charging a few mags, we got artillery again to smoke us out.

With the aid of smoke we got down to Murrell River, there was no pausing, distance was going to be our friend and I drew upon the pure adrenaline, pushing as hard as possible to make my legs pump as fast as possible on the wet terrain.

Surprisingly there was no artillery placed on us. We cleared the flat ground getting into cover and were able to regroup before the yomp home.

The yomp home was uneventful, which was welcome as there was not much ammunition between the nine of us. With the exception of the point man putting us to ground, he had spotted a small rock cluster ahead that had been fashioned into a shelter with wriggle tin for a roof. A white phosphorous grenade was used but it was all clear with no one inside.

Back at commando HQ, debrief, a warm, wet, scran (food) and head down.

****

Final Push to Stanley

Peter McManners, Lieutenant and Troop Commander 9 Para Sqn, Royal Engineers

Tumbledown

During the Falklands War of 1982, I was a young lieutenant and troop commander with 9 Parachute Squadron Royal Engineers. When the Argentines invaded in early April, I was on standby for the parachute contingency force. My personal equipment was packed and I was ready to go anywhere at short notice. Our most recent exercise had been a large-scale hostage evacuation. This took place on Salisbury Plain, but the storyline painted the training area as some far-flung country from which British personnel needed rescuing. The Falkland Islands was not on our list of possible places which might need our services. However, it is to this sleepy outpost where we deployed to fight.

As sappers, we are the minefield experts so it was our role to lead the infantry through the minefields laid by the Argentine forces. The terrain was wide and open and there had not been long to lay the mines. The chances of stepping on a mine were low but the psychological barrier was much greater. It was up to us to instil confidence in the infantry and maintain momentum despite the risk.

I was supporting the Scots Guards in the battle for Tumbledown Mountain. One task for my troop was to support the diversionary attack to the south flank of Tumbledown. The objective was to make a lot of noise and convince the enemy that this was the main axis of attack. There were minefields to cross so my men took the lead. One of my soldiers was killed, not by the mines but by machine gun fire. The name of LCpl Pashley is immortalised in stone at the Falkland Islands Chapel at Pangbourne College. He was a brave young man killed in the prime of life and will forever be remembered.

A subsidiary task which fell to my troop was to lead the Gurkha battalion through a mined area to their start line for the next battle beyond Tumbledown. I allocated one of my sections to this unenviable task. This would take place at night whilst the battle for Tumbledown was raging. There would not be time to carefully clear the route of mines. All my men could do is check for tripwires and take their chances of stepping on a mine. The whole battalion of Gurkhas followed as a long snaking line walking in the footsteps of my sappers. It was the luck of this occasion that they did not lose a life or a limb.

The task complete, the section reported back to me on Tumbledown Mountain. I could not have been more pleased to see them. In this second incident no one was killed or injured, so in the way that history is recorded it was of little significance. Such terrifying small tasks require enormous bravery. The job was done without casualties.

As Troop Commander, it was my prime concern was to get the job done and bring my men home. I was only partly successful.

****

Capt Sam Drennan and L Cpl Jay Rigg, Scout Helicopter crew from 656 Squadron Army Air Corps on Mount Tumbledown, courtesy of Major Fred Greenhow

Major Greenhow recounts the actions and words of his uncle Captain Sam Drennan, who flew on casevac operations on Mount Tumbledown with his co-pilot Lance Corporal Jay Rigg. The father of the badly injured Scots Guards officer, Lt Rob Lawrence, rescued by them on Tumbledown wrote a letter of thanks to Sam Drennan for saving their son.

Battle for Mount Tumbledown

Corporal Jay Rigg, my air gunner and co-pilot, and I arrived in the Falklands on 1st June. That was our first aggressive contact with the enemy. From the day we arrived we were really preparing for the big push on Stanley. Drennan and Rigg's aircraft – a Scout helicopter - was tasked to support the Scots Guards attack on Mount Tumbledown, a key enemy position which was strongly defended by some of the best-trained and led regular Argentine troops and Marines.

"Big Guy Fawkes Night" - Landing in a Minefield

Drennan and Rigg's aircraft was pre-positioned about fifteen miles from Mount Tumbledown before the British night attack went in. As we moved to our briefing we could see it all going on - it really looked and sounded like a big Guy Fawkes night. We were briefed by the Squadron Commander, and told that things were not terribly healthy up there, but would we like to give it a go? He was wearing his worried face! He said, *"Look, this is the score. The baddies are here, they're resisting fiercely, but we've got a casualty here and one there, who are both badly hurt and need to come out."* The aircraft were sitting outside ready to go. It was pitch black, no moon, and we didn't have night-sights. It was going to be an interesting night! So off we went to Tumbledown."

After we reached Goat Ridge we looked over the ridge and Jay pointed out where the first casualty was. I realised that no helicopter had been that far forward on Tumbledown. The Argentines then opened fire on us. They were using all that they had, including artillery shells, missiles, machine-guns and small-arms fire. My big fear wasn't getting hit by a shell, because if you get hit by a shell, you die and that's the end of the story. But if you see a missile heading towards you, and you can tell by the smoke, you can avoid it if you're fast. So I said to Jay, *"If you see a missile, give me a shout,"* which was greeted with raised eyebrows and a wry smile - apparently something had just passed our tail and I hadn't seen it!

The first casualty to be picked up and evacuated was a Gurkha. I went quite slowly down the side of this hill, at about fifty knots, because I'd decided that if we saw the smoke track of a missile coming towards us, I'd put the aircraft on the ground bloody quickly. Jay was keeping his eyes open. I was concentrating on missing the rocks on the way down and all the time there were puffs of smoke where shells were landing, which was quite spectacular - some were quite close to us. We found the Gurkha and they lifted him into the pod. We were using pods, like coffins, on the side of the helicopter, so we could get more casualties in. The back was open because Jay was in and out all the time. There was a little puff of a shell landing here and a little puff there, and I thought, *"Christ, I hope there's not a little puff here soon."*

I was worried about the Scots Guardsman that we had to pick up as well, because I couldn't see him anywhere. It transpired that the injured Guardsman was lying in a minefield. I'd got plastic armour underneath my seat, so if I'd hit a mine, it would have to go through the aircraft and the armour on the floor and on my seat before it blasted a hole in me and I might have survived. Not so Jay: he was on the skid! If we'd hit a mine he'd have got killed. It was our job to pick up this soldier and we did. We then lifted off, turned round and went like a bat out of hell for the safety of the ridge behind Tumbledown. We went whizzing back to the MDS (Main Dressing Station) where the two casualties went to the surgeons straight away. We'd managed to get in and get out again without getting killed. Then the floodgates opened.

Floodgates Open - Back to Tumbledown again and again

We heard by radio that the Scots Guards had been in very close combat and had suffered casualties. We went whizzing back out. I, who had been a Scots Guards officer before moving to the Army Air Corps and landed at the Scots Guards' Regimental Aid Post to get the latest information. I came across an old friend of mine, Colour Sergeant Archie Baird. I said, *"Hello Archie. How's it going?"* He said, *"Not so good,"* and turned back to the doctor and spoke about one of the men who was lying injured in the middle of the battlefield. *"He's gone into a deep coma, and it looks like he's had it.*' Both Jay and I sparked at the same time and thought, *'No, he bloody hasn't."*

Where we had to get to was right at the front end of Tumbledown. We sneaked along the northern side of Tumbledown. We couldn't actually land because it was too steep, and just to our right were the Argentines who were having a real go at us with their machine guns. The rounds were cracking over the top and some were bouncing off rock. We landed on this steep slope and before I knew what happened, Jay had gone. He was out and he was loading these injured soldiers, one into the pod and one inside. The longer we stayed there the closer the bullets got.

We had two casualties, both badly hurt. We managed to get Lieutenant Bob Lawrence into the back to be looked after by Jay, and the other one, with severe chest and gut injuries, we put in the pod. Unfortunately, Bob Lawrence was badly placed in the aircraft and had his head, which had a bullet lodged in it, very exposed to the bitter cold air. Jay had this young lad's injured head on his knee. Unbelievably he was still conscious and looking up at Jay and muttering. Jay pulled him round a bit and put his body in front of him. We were very determined that this brave lad wasn't going to die because even with injuries of such severity he was still fighting to live.

The casualties were delivered to the surgeons at Fitzroy MDS, which was a twelve-minute round trip from Tumbledown, and we went as fast as the Scout would travel. After three trips to the nasty area we'd taken out six casualties. Jay was in and out of the helicopter loading the wounded and looking after them in a way like a man possessed. It was quite incredible. Neither of us had slept all night, but then neither had those lads who were fighting and we weren't going to stop until they did. We went back again to pick up some more casualties.

As we got closer to Tumbledown, I heard over the radio that they'd found a soldier who had been severely injured. We'd been knocking the hell out of our aircraft for two hours and they hadn't killed us, so we thought, *'Let's get him out, let's go.'*

When we got there this poor lad was really in a bad way. He'd obviously got separated from his platoon, got badly shot up, fallen behind some rocks, and had been lying there for some hours before he was found. We got him on board and he was just lying there, like a rag doll covered in gore, looking up at Jay with big, frightened, staring eyes. He was in a terrible state. Although it was freezing cold, Jay took off his gloves and held his hand really tight. All the time he never let go of Jay's hand. Those terrible, big, staring eyes had gone into a look of death. I thought, *'He's never going to make it,'* but I'd underestimated just how fast a Scout can go, because that time she flew very fast indeed. When a man's blood is ebbing out of him, every second is vital until the doctors get a needle into him. Indelibly printed in my mind is Jay holding this dying lad's hand. He looked as if he was willing his strength to go from him into the other guy - and this lad did survive. Jay, who was twenty-one at the time, told me later that he was determined that he wouldn't let him die. He said, *"To see a guy the same age as me, with so much life left in him, dying - I couldn't let that happen!"*

The casevac flights continued through the day of the Argentine surrender and included flying enemy casualties to receive proper medical care. I remember an Argentine casualty who was obviously in great pain as he'd been badly shot up. He was just an eighteen year-old lad of peasant stock. He looked bewildered and terribly afraid. He was well strapped up, so Jay put him on the litter, but the noise of the helicopter rotors and all the rest of it must have really scared him. He was in a hell of a state, so Jay just leaned over and pinched his cheek and gave it a gentle shake and a pat. This lad's whole face lit up with relief.

Drennan was awarded the DFC and Rigg was Mentioned in Despatches for their joint gallantry at Tumbledown.

****

Brum Richards, 148 Commando Battery Naval Gunfire Support

<u>Supporting the Scots Guards on Tumbledown</u>

Saturday, 12th June on *Yarmouth*

At 0126 hours the Scots Guards are on their start line at Tumbledown and almost ready to move out. At 0138 hours we begin to engage targets in direct support of 2 SG. The first target we engage we hit with the first salvo and then put 20 more into it. NGFO2 come up and ask us to hit a Gun Bty which is causing 2 Para some casualties, so we oblige by pouring 20 salvoes into it and then returning to NGFO5. He has another target which is a MG position and is holding up the 2 SG advance. Once again, we hit it with our first salvo and destroy it. This is like a fairground shoot. *Avenger* now turns up and joins in so we give her to 2 Para. She also keeps pounding away at Sapper Hill during missions. By 0400 hours there are four ships all engaging targets at once. It is a spectacular and very noisy sight. Surely the enemy cannot hold on much longer. The results of ammo expenditure are: - *Active* – 288; *Yarmouth* – 244; *Ambuscade* – 228; *Avenger* – 156. Grand total 916. I hate to think what it would have been like on the receiving end of that.

We must have done a lot of damage. I know at one stage Captain McCracken was calling down rounds as close as 50 yds to own troops. The fighting continues all day, but the enemy broke at 1556 hours when white flags were seen outside Stanley. NGFO2 were with 2 Para as they entered the outskirts of Stanley. At 2059 hours we hear that General Menendez has signed the instrument of surrender. The air force say they will continue with the fight.

****

Nigel Turner, Leading Cook on HMS Hermes

Saluting HMS *Glamorgan*

News came in that HMS *Glamorgan* had been hit by a land-based Exocet and many killed but the ship had survived. On her way home after repairs HMS *Glamorgan* steamed past HMS *Hermes* and I and many of the ship's company lined the gantries and walkways and cheered and whooped for the brave sailors of war. The damage to the ship was clearly visible. God Speed and safe journey. More cooks killed.

The Chinese laundryman who tried to jump ship

Immediately after the Exocet hit on 12th June, we were in all sorts of trouble and one area of concern was the fact there were two Sea Slug missiles on the launcher very close to the fire that was raging in the hangar. We needed to get helicopters on to the flight deck to evacuate the wounded to HMS *Hermes* and there was a real possibility that the two missiles might be at risk or perhaps endanger the helicopters with their tail rotors a few yards from the launcher. Having sought the captain's approval and checked we were on a safe bearing, we decided to jettison the missiles by firing them into the sea at a safe range.

Meanwhile one of the Chinese laundrymen, Cheung Yu, decided that he had had enough and was going to leave the ship by jumping overboard. The sea was very rough and extremely cold, it was still dark and there was no chance of survival if he had made it. Luckily, the No 1 Chinese laundryman, Chan Lok Wing, had realized that Cheung Yu was in a state of total panic and so chased him as he made his way down two decks towards the quarterdeck, where the Sea Slug missiles were about to be fired.

In the operations room, having made the final checks, I ordered the Missile Officer to fire both missiles. At this exact moment, Cheung Yu had made his way to the guardrail, right aft on the quarterdeck, immediately below the missile launcher and was trying to get one foot on to the top guardrail to jump into the wake. However, Chan Lok Wing had just managed to catch up with Cheung Yu and grabbed him around the thighs in almost perfect rugger tackle. He managed to stop him jumping and started to pull him backwards to the safety of the deck, when the first missile roared past, followed immediately by the other.

A Sea Slug missile weighs in at two tons and by virtue of the four booster rockets, accelerates to Mach 2 almost instantaneously. No one had ever before stood within 100 yards of the flightpath of a Sea Slug at launch, but Cheung Yu had now set a new record by being about ten feet from one. Luckily, No 1 laundryman was reasonably protected by Cheung Yu's body and was relatively unharmed, but Cheung Yu was not so fortunate, suffering an immediate loss of hearing as well as losing most of his hair and part of his clothing.

The next day, when things had settled down a bit and the repairs to the damage were well underway, the captain enquired after Cheung Yu's welfare and suggested that we should invite him to the captain's cabin for a cup of tea and to ensure that he was being looked after properly. The captain also suggested that since I had fired the missiles, I should be present. When Chan Lok Wing and Cheung Yu arrived, it is fair to say that the captain and I were rather apprehensive in case this incident might cause repercussions around the fleet by Chinese laundrymen deciding to seek safer employment.

The captain and I had decided to create a reasonably relaxed atmosphere and had removed our anti-flash protective headgear and gloves before they were shown in. Before either the captain or I could even offer the laundrymen a chair, Chan Lok Wing took centre stage.

"Before we start, Sir," he said, *"we wish to make statement"*.

This didn't sound too good, I thought, but nodded and said that we were listening and asked No 1 to continue.

"We have meeting in laundry today and we think Cheung Yu fr....ing idiot. He lose his hearing and his hair because he not wearing his anti-frash."

Poor Cheung Yu, who still could not hear a single thing, saw our broad smiles and our faces portraying a mixture of relief and hilarity, and so he burst out laughing, which got us all going and we then got down to the serious business of tea drinking.

I am very glad to say that Cheung Yu did recover his hearing and his hair grew back.

****

On to Sapper Hill

We looked at our surroundings and quickly realised we were about 12 in number and the hills to our north, about three hundred metres away, were covered with hundreds of Argentines. Given there was no other cover available on the road and the surrounding area was mined, we took up defensive positions on the road behind our bergens. If the Argentines had still been up for the fight, they could have slaughtered us with machine gun fire from their dug-in positions. As I tried to calculate the Argentine position on the map and prepared a fire mission for the guns, helicopters began to arrive and more marines disembarked and very quickly our numbers swelled. At that point, we were almost certainly the closest British troops to Stanley.

As I scanned the hills with my binoculars, it was clear that Argentines were withdrawing down the hill towards Stanley. We set off, running up the road - chasing them. As we went, there were bodies of Argentine soldiers lying in the road like roadkill on a dual carriageway. Some soldiers stopped to take their weapons or other trophies. Within minutes we were told to cease firing since there were white flags flying over Stanley. For me the relief was palpable but there were some amongst us who wanted it to continue and had clearly found their calling. I didn't and will never understand that.

We moved onto the top of Sapper Hill and had our first view of Stanley – it looked like a small English fishing town and reminded me of Whitby in North Yorkshire. I was hugely relieved as it looked like the conflict had ended.

We spent the night in the trenches so recently vacated by the Argentines and we had a close-up view of the conditions that they had been living in for months. Clearly they didn’t have the field discipline that we were accustomed to, since there was rubbish, clothing, weapons and ammunition lying around. We were very careful not to move anything that could have been booby-trapped.

It was the 14th June and my 24th birthday. We had found an empty Argentine trench and huddled down. I slept like a log for about four or five hours, which was the longest sleep that I had for a long time.

The next day, we moved to the bottom of the hill but did not have clearance to enter Stanley. From there our team was moved by helicopter back to our gun position. It was good to see everyone. Then followed a few days of clearing the gun positions of ammunition. We managed to find a shed to sleep in at the side of a house and I began to feel very ill. It felt like food poisoning and I took to my sleeping bag.

****

David Chaundler, Lieutenant Colonel, 2 Para

Battle for Wireless Ridge and Stanley

The Second Battalion of The Parachute Regiment's last battle was the capture of Wireless Ridge. We crossed the Start Line at quarter past mid-night on 14th June 1982 for a four-phase attack supported by an artillery battery of 105mm Light Guns, the 81mm Mortar Platoons from both 2 and 3 Paras, a frigate – HMS *Ambuscade* – and four light tanks from the Blues & Royals. It was our third night without sleep, we had not seen a ration pack for 72 hours, and we fought all night in high winds and driving snow flurries with the temperature well below zero. Just before H-Hour a captured Argentine map was brought up to me showing a minefield right across our main axis of attack. It was too late to do anything about it if we were to capture our objectives that night; so we carried on. (The minefield was still there when I visited 20 years later).

As dawn broke, we captured the final objective – Wireless Ridge – and we could see Stanley. We were counter-attacked twice when suddenly in the valley below us the Argentine Army broke. Our tanks and machine guns were firing into the valley as were the mortars and the artillery when something inside me said STOP, you are slaughtering these people to no good purpose. (There is a moral dimension in war). I ordered a ceasefire. This was some seven hours before the official ceasefire.

I realised that we must get into Stanley before the Argentines had time to reorganise, but communications were poor and I could not get any sense over the radio. I got fed-up and ordered an advance into Stanley. First John Crosland's B Company onto the high ground to the south of the Moody Brook/Stanley road, then Dair Farrar-Hockley's A Company onto the road with Phil Neame's D Company with the tanks and the Machine Gun Platoon ready to give covering fire across the creek.

I was standing out on the forward slope of the ridge feeling pretty pleased with life when a helicopter landed behind the ridge. The Brigade Commander, Brigadier Julian Thompson, no doubt as frustrated as I was by the lack of radio communications, had come to look for himself. He crawled-up behind the ridge, saw me standing in the open and obviously thought, "*My God I have already lost one Commanding Officer from 2 Para*". He rushed out and rugger tackled me. As we got up I said, "*It's all right Brigadier it's all over, we must get in there (Stanley)*".

We walked off the ridge together behind A Company and onto the Stanley road. He left me to go to his Tactical Headquarters; and I then started to get orders to stop. *"Stop on the 93 Easting"*. "Anyone see the 93 Easting on the map?" I said. "*Oh dear we have passed it*". We continued on into Stanley. No shots were fired by either side. My reasoning for a ceasefire was not only that it was morally correct, but I believed the Argentines to have had enough and if we fired on them there was a danger that they would fire back and then we would be back into a firefight.

"*Stop now*". Again I was being ordered to stop. I told Corporal Cooper, my radio operator, to switch off his radio. The order to stop then came over the artillery radio net, which I ignored. I did eventually stop the Battalion on the tactically sound position of the Old War Memorial in Stanley. Also it was in line with Government

House where the Argentine General Menendez had his Headquarters. It would have made negotiating a surrender more difficult if we had overrun his Headquarters.

We had gone far enough. The war was over. For the record, despite popular myth, there were no white flags flying over Stanley!

****

Mark Willis, Captain (Adjutant of the 1st Battalion) in the 7th Gurkha Rifles

The Gurkhas in the Falklands

The main players in the land-based actions of the Falklands war were (in most people's eyes) the Parachute Regiment and the Royal Marines. Much glory is indeed due to them, but it's good sometimes to recognise the contributions made by some less high-profile participants. In this category I place the regiment in which I served – 7th Gurkha Rifles.

The 1st Battalion, 7th Gurkha Rifles (1/7GR) was a major unit within the ill-fated 5 Infantry Brigade, which was thrust into action woefully ill-prepared. Two of the brigade's three infantry battalions were taken away to reinforce the marines in 3 Commando Brigade, leaving only us. All the other brigade assets (e.g., artillery, signals, medics etc) were "cobbled together" at short notice and mostly under-provisioned – for example we initially had only one artillery battery (six guns) in support. We had precious little opportunity to train with the replacement units added to the brigade. However, in the best traditions of the service, we did the best we could!

1/7GR travelled most of the way to the theatre of operations in relative luxury aboard the Cunard liner *QE2*, continuing to train as we went, but we made the final part of the journey on MV *Norland*.

Going ashore on 1st June (with only the vaguest idea about what we were supposed to do, due to the absence of clear orders from above), our unit was unceremoniously dumped – piecemeal - by helicopter in and around Darwin and Goose Green. The following day we were able to re-group and take over from 2 Para, freeing them up for their subsequent "audacious" advance to Fitzroy and beyond. At the time, we were surprised that we (1/7GR), a fresh, fit, well-trained and numerically strong unit, were not used for the Eastward advance and 2 Para allowed to recuperate after its recent tough battle at Goose Green. The move forward by 2 Para was seen by some as a bold move, but by others as a big mistake (due to the logistical problems it caused) which ultimately led to the disaster at Bluff Cove.

Anyway, for the time being 1/7GR settled in at Goose Green, preparing defences against a possible counter-attack, guarding prisoners prior to their removal back to Ajax Bay, clearing rubbish and battlefield debris, and carrying out patrols to look for pockets of Argentine troops who might still be in the area. Most of these patrols were inserted / recovered by helicopter. One such foray resulted in the capture of 10 Argentines, equipped with SAM-7 shoulder-launched anti-aircraft missiles.

Once Phase 2 of the overall British plan was decided, troops began to be ferried forward to the new area of operations. This is when the Bluff Cove incident happened, causing severe casualties – mostly within the First Battalion Welsh Guards (1WG). I'm not going to describe it because I have no first-hand information about it. Suffice it to say that one of our companies (D) was also taken forward to the Fitzroy area by sea at this time, using the local coaster MV Monsunen, but plans to move the rest of the battalion by this means were cancelled after the Bluff Cove affair had demonstrated the acute vulnerability of troops carried in small, unarmed vessels. 1/7GR moved forward by helicopter, leaving one company (C) to guard Goose Green.

On the orders of HQ 5 Bde, we spent a couple of days in the area of Little Wether Ground, East of Fitzroy. Unfortunately, this area was in sight of enemy forces on Mount Kent, who directed long-range (155mm) artillery fire against us. We lost an officer and three men wounded here.

In the Phase 2 attacks, which now took place, the Marines captured the Two Sisters and Mount Harriet, and 3 Para took Mount Longdon. 5 Inf Bde got ready to carry out Phase 3. Second Battalion Scots Guards (2SG) were to take Tumbledown, and once their mission was achieved, 1/7GR was to pass through them and take Mount William. Elements of the depleted 1WG were to mount a diversionary attack to the South of Mount William. I should perhaps mention that all the infantry attacks mounted by the British in the Falklands war took place at night-time, with all the extra difficulties this entails

In order to maintain momentum, the 5 Inf Bde attack was initially scheduled to take place on 12th June (the day after the Phase 2 attacks mentioned above), but lack of helicopter availability meant that it proved impossible to move the men and their equipment forward in time for this, and the attack was postponed 24 hours. Even so, we all felt rushed – we had very little time to prepare and re-organise for the task. Even as we came in by helicopter to our Assembly Area at the west end of Goat Ridge we came under enemy artillery fire once more, so the element of surprise was non-existent. Our battalion plan of attack was necessarily pitched at quite high level because we had little idea of what the situation would be when our turn to go into the assault finally came: much depended on how 2SG fared.

Late in the evening of 13th June, we set off, crossing the Start Line in one immensely long single file, inching forward along the South side of Goat Ridge. We witnessed the artillery, naval gunfire, mortar and machinegun fire pounding Tumbledown, while listening intently to the radio traffic and trying to understand how 2SG were getting on. Their attack went very slowly, and our CO (Lt Col David Morgan) became increasingly worried, because it looked ever more likely that our assault on Mount William would have to be carried out in daylight, across very exposed terrain.

As we moved up the lower slopes of Tumbledown, we came under more artillery fire and lost a further eight men wounded. Fortunately, the shelling was of short duration (though it didn't seem like it at the time!) and we were able to evacuate our casualties and continue the advance.

Eventually 2SG prevailed in their mission and the Argentine forces crumbled, fleeing towards Stanley in an undignified mass. Our attached Gunners joined in with a "shoot" to send the enemy on his way. The enemy garrison on Mount William joined in the mass exodus too, and when we finally came to mount our (daylight) attack, it was unopposed. This latter fact was viewed by some as a disappointment ("the Gurkhas never got their moment of glory like the other units did") but others breathed a sigh of relief that further bloodshed was avoided.

As we all know, shortly after the battle for Tumbledown was concluded, the overall Argentine resistance collapsed (our battalion 2ic was seen on the BBC announcing gleefully *"There's a white flag flying over Stanley, tee-hee!"*). Most of the Para and Marines units headed pell-mell into Stanley, but 5 Inf Bde was ordered to stand fast in its current positions. We remained out on those wind-swept and snow-covered hills for two nights until finally recovered back to Goose Green by the ever-industrious helicopter fleet.

****

Chapter 5 - Medics, Padres ... and a Lawyer

Often overlooked, but behind the scenes, the roles of the 'vocations' played an important role in all aspects of the war, saving lives, comforting the wounded and providing spiritual solace and hope for all. HMHS *Uganda*, a schools' cruise ship beforehand, was swiftly converted into a fully-fledged hospital ship, with wards, operating theatres, treating British and Argentine casualties alike. *Canberra* and *QE2* were also fitted with hospital facilities, while a small fleet of smaller vessels including HMS *Hydra* became 'ambulances' to convey injured servicemen who were recovering to be taken tu Uruguay for flights home to the UK. The bravery and dedication of the medical staff have been widely commended by all they cared for.

On land the remarkable work by regimental medics, not least Rick Jolly's team in the *'Red and Green Life Machine'*, saving many lives, putting themselves in the firing line to retrieve casualties and give initial treatment on the battlefield. Along with Royal Marines bandsmen and others acting as stretcher bearers, casualties were evacuated often by helicopter to field hospitals in Ajax Bay or to *Uganda* or *Canberra* for treatment. The bravery of helicopter crews and many ships' crews in picking up survivors and casualties, often in hugely dangerous situations, should not be overlooked or underestimated.

Many Royal Navy ships had their own chaplain or padre, as did most regiments. Their role to support and give courage to their flock was much appreciated and noticeably, as war appeared more likely, the attendance at on-board services increased considerably. Theirs was also the sad task to conduct the numerous funeral services at sea or on land for those who were killed.

Only one lawyer accompanied the Task Force, Major Richard Spencer. Amongst other legal niceties, his main role was the orderly and appropriate handling of the many Argentine POWs and their repatriation to Argentina at the end of the war in line with Geneva Convention guidelines.

Liz Ormerod, Senior Nursing Officer, QARNNS on HMHS Uganda

HMHS *Uganda* in the Falklands War

In April 1982 I was working as a Senior Nursing Officer on the Intensive Care Unit at RNH *Stonehouse* in Plymouth. I had just completed a week of night duty and was expecting to have seven days off. That first evening I received a phone call telling me I was going to the Falklands and needed to report to the Naval Hospital within the hour. Several of my colleagues had also been ordered to the hospital and during the following hours we received lectures on the care of injuries which were likely to occur during a conflict. These included gunshot injuries, bomb blast trauma, burns and drownings. Initially it was thought that we would work ashore but subsequently it was decided that we would be better utilised on a hospital ship.

After flying to Gibraltar on 15th April, we gained our first sight of HMHS *Uganda* which, amongst other things, was having a flight deck installed. All the medical and nursing staff which by then, included staff from both UK naval hospitals, were accommodated in the cabins normally used by adult fare–paying passengers. These proved to be comfortable and relatively spacious. The lower deck dormitory accommodation, usually occupied by school children on educational cruises, was allocated for the use of 'walking wounded'. I was allocated to the intended Intensive Care Unit (ICU), a former cocktail lounge situated amidships, taking advantage of the relative stability of that position.

We sailed from Gibraltar on 19th April having been loaded up with many boxes of Field Hospital equipment. The journey to Ascension Island was spent opening and distributing the contents of the boxes to the appropriate areas, storing equipment and erecting beds. We had 20 beds on ICU plus 44 beds on an acute ward at the stern of the ship. There was also an operating theatre with three tables, laboratory, X-ray and dispensary facilities. We also had use of the ship's own medical facilities if needed. We were conscious of the need to maximise the use of the supplies given the uncertainty of the duration of requirement and difficulties in re-stocking. We also identified another major issue – that of limited fresh water. During cruising *Uganda* was not normally long out of port where she could obtain water, but now, it was obvious that we would require the facility to make our own water and, to this end, we had two desalination plants sent to us at Ascension Island.

We also spent time in training the teams with whom we would be working although up to this point we were hopeful that the situation could be resolved diplomatically.

Having thought I had left my fiancé, Howard, safely back in UK, it came as a shock to receive a letter at Ascension telling me he was also on his way down on *Atlantic Conveyor*. A subsequent letter told of their greatest fear of the Exocet missile which turned out to be quite prophetic!

Our first major involvement followed the loss of HMS *Sheffield*; we received our first casualties from there on 13th May.

Despite the work, there were several recreational activities organised to maintain morale. We had a Royal Marines Band embarked to act as stretcher bearers and ancillary staff and they also put on concerts to entertain us. We also had games nights and film nights.

The range of injuries was vast covering head injury, chest injury, burns, loss of limbs, drowning, smoke inhalation etc. We nursed both British and Argentine servicemen side by side without issue and the atmosphere remained one of cheerful acceptance.

After HMS *Sheffield*, there followed a succession of naval encounters which resulted in our being utilised to the full. We worked sea going watches of 'Four hours on' in three teams. However, because we could receive casualties only in daylight hours and with the limited number of staff, we often had to get up and help with reception of large numbers. We did eventually receive extra staff from HMS *Hermes*.

On the morning of 26th May, I was taken aside to be informed that *Atlantic Conveyor* had been hit and sunk by an Exocet missile.

As *Uganda* was covered by the terms of the Geneva convention, which meant that we weren't allowed to receive signals directly from the Task Force, we had to radio back to UK for information. This process took a total of 18 hours before I was told that Howard was a survivor and uninjured. Having previously been reluctant to set a date for our wedding, I resolved that I wouldn't hesitate now having been given this second chance!

In order to free up beds on the ship, we reviewed the medical condition of the patients to ascertain who was fit for transfer to one of the survey vessels which were used as ambulance ships to transfer the injured via Montevideo back to the UK. Gangways were put between the two ships meaning that transfer could only take place when weather permitted.

The weather conditions were variable with cold temperatures, ice, snow and heavy seas. Despite this, seasickness was not a major problem for either patients or staff.

Whilst awaiting transfer, the troops were encouraged, by the Red Cross representatives who came on board, to do some occupational therapy. I'm not sure that sewing cuddly toys is exactly what they had in mind, but they entered willingly into the activity.

Following the surrender on 14th June, the numbers of casualties decreased. Instead of being in the Total Exclusion Zone where we had been positioned, we anchored in the outer harbour of Stanley. Many of the casualties we received were injured by land mines discovered during searches of the streets and beaches around the capital.

The following few weeks were quite difficult as we watched many of the ships leave for home. We were required to remain there because the civilian hospital was still damaged after being bombed and the runway at the airport was also not usable. Eventually the hospital was sufficiently repaired and staffed with the help of the Army Medical Services and the runway recommissioned.

During the wait, many of the staff on HMHS *Uganda* got a trip ashore to Stanley. It was good to set foot on dry land and to see the Islands for which so much had been sacrificed. We finally transferred the last of our patients on 17th July and *Uganda* was deregistered as a hospital ship. This enabled us to bring back some remaining troops to the UK.

We had, by then, dismantled the beds and re-stowed the medical equipment leaving a few stains on the carpets and many memories. Over 700 casualties were treated on *Uganda*, 150 of them Argentines. We had three deaths on board. I will always remember the names of those, the bravery of the men whose lives would be forever changed by physical or mental trauma, the remarkable recoveries witnessed against all the odds of the sailors so nearly drowned from the ships lost in the hostilities. We finally returned to Southampton on 9th August.

The events in the South Atlantic changed us all. The journey home gave us chance for reflection and to put things in perspective. The friendships made during Operation Corporate were special in that they were borne out of a shared sense of danger, fear and uncertainty. For me personally, it taught me much about human nature and about myself. It also gained me an opportunity to finally set a date for the wedding – which we did on 2nd October that year.

Lester May, Supply Officer on HMS Hydra

HMS *Hydra* - An Ambulance Ship at War

I was 30 years of age and had joined HMS *Hydra* as Purser. She was one of the four H class ocean hydrographic survey vessels built in the mid-1960s.

General Leopoldo Galtieri clearly decided to spoil my plans by invading the Falkland Islands. We watched some of the Task Force sail.

Our unarmed survey ship, all white bar the buff funnel, surely had no role in the Falkland Islands so far away, nor the west of Scotland (Falkirk). Soon the ship was allocated as a hospital ship and the buff funnel became white, red crosses appeared, crypto was landed as required by the International Committee of the Red Cross

(ICRC) and chippies built 'hospital bunks'. A second medical officer and other naval medical staff joined the ship.

HMS *Herald*, recently returned from Gulf surveys, was also converted in Portsmouth and HMS *Hecla* was converted to a hospital ship in Gibraltar. HMS *Hecate* was in refit so not involved. HMS *Hydra* (Commander Richard Campbell RN) sailed on 23rd April 1982, with HMS *Herald* (Commander Robert Halliday RN) in company, the junior ship having fitted a flashing blue light on the upper deck.

Getting Ready and Heading South

At this stage, few expected other than a diplomatic solution, and like all ships going Down South, we hoped that Ascension Island might be the furthest south we'd reach. Ship's company training continued apace, but with an emphasis on medical training and giving blood. Damage control was always a challenge in H class ships, bulk survey stores and other spaces for'd were huge. Our bearded captain cleared lower deck and he told us, *inter alia*, that we would use all our water in three weeks without resupply and, of course, demands for water by the medics would increase usage.

He suggested our all ceasing to shave and only about a dozen of the 129 on board chose to ignore that call. The young doctors, both at sea for their first time, decided how many of the ship's company they required for medical duties, the captain halving that number as he advised that he required men for running the ship – no ship, no hospital of course, a small point missed by our red but green doctors in our life machine! A quarter of the ship's company were trained as auxiliary medical assistants, carrying out a range of duties, often unsupervised.

Arrival in War Zone

HMS *Hydra* reached the internationally-declared Red Cross Box on 21st May– a four-week passage south for our small, rather slow ship.

It soon became clear how the medical aspects of Operation Corporate were organised. Casualties were taken either to the Field Hospital at Ajax Bay (run by the estimable Surgeon Commander Rick Jolly) or perhaps directly to HMHS *Uganda*, requisitioned as a hospital ship. The H class trio were used as ambulance ships and, as soon as patients from HMHS *Uganda* were well enough to move, thus releasing urgently needed hospital beds, they were transferred to an H class, each ship taking some forty to eighty men on a four-day one-way trip to Montevideo, where they were transferred in a fleet of Uruguayan ambulances to an airport, where an RAF VC10 aircraft flew them home to the RAF's Princess Alexandra Hospital.

HMS *Hecla* made the first such trip soon followed by HMS *Hydra*, departing 'Red Cross Box 2' on 30th May for Montevideo. HMS *Hydra* made four such 'lifts' carrying 251 patients all told, the last on 7th July 1982.

A few notable 'highlights' include:

- Taking nine patients from SS *Canberra* and another transfer with MV *Norland* – I recall one Royal Marines sergeant among them, furious to miss out on the action, his having sprained his ankle falling down a ladder in the liner in very heavy weather.
- 'Saturday Night at Sea' for officer patients in the wardroom, whether it was a Saturday night or not – morale boosting stuff for all who dined. Patients with hands and wrists covered with flamazine and plastic bags such that one had to cut food and feed them and take them to the heads …
- Taking ICRC (International Red Cross Committee) staff, including boss Philippe Eberlin (who absolutely understood the patient benefits of Saturday Night at Sea), from Montevideo to FI
- Landing an Argentine helicopter from one of their two hospital ships (which carried a resupply of missiles for their navy – ICRC pragmatism prevailed, M. Eberlin aware of the

impossibility of their ever reaching an Argentine warship) – the helo was transferring ICRC officials

- Being inspected by two Argentine naval officers who embarked in the River Plate estuary
- Our ancient Can Man, not a star in the Naval Canteen Service, one evening after the surrender, drunk as a lord behind his shop counter – ship's company theatre, like a one-man Punch & Judy show, cheered up matelots and patients alike and no harm done!
- The Uruguayan *clarete* from the food contractor and the strawberries from the British lady ambassador were much appreciated
- I think we were without mail for over a month at one point – some had been lost – but one letter provided tears of joy. It told me that my seven-year-old nephew was learning about the war from *John Craven's Newsround* on TV and was concerned as to how an Argie submarine would know we were a hospital ship – were there Red Crosses on the bottom of the hull, he asked?
- The 70 year-old Geordie, Monsignor Daniel Spraggon, was a jolly Mill Hill missionary father, and his tales of occupation, large congregations, three Argentine RC bishops visiting (all properly approved by Rome), his hearing the confessions of conscripts and his suggesting that they should lay down their arms to save their own lives, especially his telling them that the Gurkhas were coming in the *QE2*, will stay long in my memory. I confess that my motivation had more to do with getting off the ship for an hour or so than with praying, but I am so pleased I met Monsignor Spraggon, a good priest indeed. He was made OBE in the FI Honours List Oct 1982. He told me that many an Argentine conscript, often Patagonian farmers' boys, could not comprehend that an Englishman could be a Catholic and few of these often-frightened youngsters knew

anything about '*Las Malvinas*'. His untimely death came after a fire in the FI hospital.

After our fourth and final trip to Montevideo, we were to be a stand-by medical facility in and around the islands.

At the end of June, a case of Swiss wine awaited the purser – a gift for the wardroom from Philippe Eberlin, the ICRC boss who had so much enjoyed Saturday Night at Sea. Awaiting all of us was a letter from Admiral Sir John Fieldhouse, forwarding a letter he had received from the MOiC of the RAF hospital – a BZ (*see note*) for HMS *Hydra* in particular as he reported the comments of a badly burned SNCO who was on board for one of our four 'lifts'

We stored ship from the SS *Avelona Star*, took on fuel and water. We sailed round the islands, carried the Civil Commissioner Rex Hunt, the former Governor, from one small port to another, carried a couple of cocks from one farm to another, had tea in farmsteads, a wardroom banyan *(see note)* ashore where no warlike activity had taken place and hosted a children's party on board for the children of Goose Green and Darwin. How lucky we were to see the islands and meet some of the Islanders. HMS *Hydra* even features on a rare First Day Cover for the first Falkland Island postage stamp issued after the surrender, on 16th August 1982, when the ship was then at anchor in Fox Bay.

Arrival Home

We sailed north at the end of August and the ship could not be early because of what awaited us in Portsmouth, as HMS *Hydra* was the last HM Ship to return home from Down South.

As we sailed into Portsmouth Harbour, the welcome was extraordinary. *"Hi-de-Hydra"* read a sign from a minor war vessel alongside HMS *Vernon*. Particularly memorable was the sight of USS *Mount Whitney* alongside at South Railway Jetty. HMS *Hydra* was flying the flag of a Rear Admiral and the US command ship the flag of Vice Admiral 'Ace' Lyons; her men lined the rails and, as we prepared to salute the senior ship, he ordered his flagship to pipe our ship first, a signal tribute that makes my eyes water with pride even now.

I had a pretty comfortable time, my large starboard-side cabin even having two scuttles. Just pity, though, my captain, 49-year-old Commander Richard Campbell, who had to put up with me for nearly 27 months as his purser, but I salute you Sir – submariner, droggy, steady as a rock and just the sea captain to make sure his ship avoided such a feature on an Admiralty chart, just the captain to sail into a war theatre with.

Note: The combination of the Bravo and Zulu nautical signal flags, i.e., Bravo Zulu, also referred to as "BZ," is a naval signal, typically conveyed by flaghoist or voice radio, meaning "Well Done" with regard to actions, operations or performance.

Note: Banyans is a time for the crews of Royal Navy ships to enjoy some downtime during long deployments at sea.

****

Geraldine Carty, QARNNS nurse on HMHS Uganda

Trepidation, Anxiety, Fear of the unknown

The ship had red crosses painted on it and it was frightening learning afterwards the Argentines were planning to attack the ship as they thought the red crosses were targets. It was after reflecting on what could have happened, that reminded me that I and my colleagues were in a war zone.

I looked after many men from the army. One man had a brain injury. Various staff members were managing to get patients onto the helicopters waiting to transport the casualties, but this man was proving to be difficult. Eventually after some discussion I managed to get him on the helicopter. It was a relief because he wasn't going without his green uniform.

When the RFA *Sir Galahad* and RFA *SirTristram* were bombed, I had gone to bed after a night shift. I was wakened by the tannoy asking for all hands to turn to. It was gruelling at times; I was awake for 72 hours doing what I had been trained to do. Young men from the military with all types of burns being catheterised, treated for trench foot, having strong analgesia to ease the pain, re-dressing wounds. This was constant. Starting at patient one to the end of the line and back again in the dormitories of the ship.

Another experience was looking after a few Argentine soldiers who needed treatment and were Prisoners of War. As per the Geneva Convention, they were treated with respect and dignity. It was strange having a couple of armed Royal Marines on the stairs protecting nursing staff and guarding the POWs. This was a scary time for me. I was paired with one of the nursing sisters and we went to do our medicine round. One of the Marines was also with us in the lower decks whilst we gave medication. Who was scared the most? Probably all of us had some trepidation.

****

David Jackson, Commanding No.1 Field Surgical Team attached to 16 Field Ambulance, deployed with 5 Infantry Brigade

'They shall grow not old'

"Sorry sir. I cannot survive this. It's too much; it's too bloody much". The anguished young Guardsman had interrupted me as I explained what I proposed to do in order to try and save him.

On the morning of 13th June, the Scots Guards were moved by helicopter from their position at Bluff Cove to an assembly area near Goat Ridge, west of Mount Tumbledown in the Falkland Islands. Guardsman CCT, a dispatch rider from the 1st Welsh Guards, was mortally wounded by Argentine shellfire directed from Tumbledown.

He was brought into our Field Surgical Team (FST) in a terrible state. He was still alive when he arrived, but had lost both feet, his legs were at unnatural angles and he was bleeding to death internally. It was a very severe blast injury. There was some hope for him, if I could arrest the bleeding, but this young, brave soldier knew there was no hope. He knew that better than I did.

His haunting words are not ones that I can ever forget, nor do I really want to, because they epitomised the spirit of the soldiers, who know when they have been injured beyond recovery and can accept their own death, even at their tender ages, with the same courage that they had faced the enemy. He was right. He had massive intra-abdominal and pelvic bleeding. His vena cava, the main vein in the body, had ruptured beyond repair and he died on the operating table.

As I closed his abdomen, I realised that I was never going to be as immune to the injuries of these young men as I hoped to be. I could divorce myself from the sufferings and the injuries whilst I had to do something about them, but in the dark moments, in the quiet moments, it got to me. It may be the case that his parents or family read this account and recognise this young Guardsman, who I have anonymised. He died bravely, with no hope, but no pain, on my operating table.

When I had finished sewing him up, I went on to my next casualty, who fortunately would recover from his comparatively light wounds. This patient was a young Argentine and he looked about 15 years old. He had been wounded by a fragment which had entered his upper right abdomen, but he was stable as I opened him up. Fortunately, the fragment had missed all the important anatomy; there was no bile, faeces or much blood for that matter. He had a small hole in the substance of his liver which I closed with a circular suture and no exit wound that I could ascertain. I assumed that the penetration of his abdominal wall had taken the sting out of this injury. I left a drain in for safety's sake and closed him up. He was shipped off back to Argentina. The padre knew the Spanish word for liver, so I wrote a note to accompany him, saying *"Higado – OK"*.

****

Senior Nursing Officer Nicci Pugh, QARNNS (Queen Alexandra's Royal Naval Nursing Service) on HMHS Uganda

'The Ties That Bind Us'

In 2019, following the publication of an improved & revised edition of *White Ship – Red Crosses*, I received a unique and very moving handwritten letter from a lady who lived in the Falkland Islands called Clara McKay. I had not met this lady, by then aged 95, but I had heard a great deal about her.

I also knew that one of our former patients on board the hospital ship in 1982, BLESMA member Robert ('Ossie') Osborn had stayed with Clara McKay on his two return trips to the Falkland Islands and we realised what a unique, interesting and moving series of links with the Falklands War this would all make.

So here is Falkland Islander Clara McKay's letter (see image of original) and how this all links to a seriously injured and courageous injured British soldier who lost his left leg in the battle for Mount Tumbledown on 13th June 1982.

Letter to Nicci Pugh from Mrs Clara McKay
Falkland Islands, South Atlantic *May 2019*

Dear Nicci,

*For years I have been going to write to you and thank you so very much for your book of years ago (*White Ship - Red Crosses*). I love the book and have read it several times, as it relates to the awful conflict. What you all did was wonderful, and I can't thank you enough. We, 22 of us, were locked in one room, so we know what Freedom means.*

The Invaders who locked us up cut the telephone lines and took all our radios and our 2 metre sets, so we had no way of knowing that the Task Force had arrived, did not know ships were in San Carlos waters, and had no idea (British) troops were ashore.

Forty-one Argentines ruled over us at Douglas Station.

If they needed me to get them beer from our farm shop, I always had a bayonet in my back.

When we saw the British walking over the Cavodi we thought it was more Argentines.

It's a long story. I don't think we have recovered.

*Last week in a café here, I saw a lady and gent at a table – I guessed they were from MPA (*Mount Pleasant Airport, also known as Mount Pleasant Complex*) so I went over to them and said: "I want to thank you for keeping us safe". They stood up, gave me a hug each, and said: "You have made our day". I said: "You have made mine. I am a Falkland Islander born and bred and I will be 96 in June".*

We are all so very grateful to the Task Force. We love to see all who visit back here. More and more come, and we can't thank them enough.

*I will close this scribble for now and put it in with Sheila Osborn's envelope with the hope that (*her son*) Ossie Osborn can pass this on to you.*

With all the 'Thanks in the World' for your part in 1982.

God Bless.

Very best wishes always

From

Clara X

Note from Nicci Pugh: Douglas Station that Clara mentions is often called Douglas Settlement. It is a large sheep station on East Falkland Island, situated on the western arm of Salvador Water. It was the first objective for 45 Commando Royal Marines in their epic yomp east from San Carlos Water towards the battlegrounds approaching Stanley; this is well covered in Ian Gardiner's The Yompers published by Pen & Sword 2012.

Clara McKay's letter leads on to the next 'Tie that Binds us' from Scots Guardsman Robert 'Ossie'Osborn:

In 1982 I was a twenty-one-year-old guardsman in 13 Platoon Left Flank, 2nd Battalion Scots Guards. The Battalion had recently returned to public duties in the UK from a six-month tour in Northern Ireland.

We left Southampton on May 12th on the *QE2* and sailed to Grytviken (South Georgia) via Freetown in Sierra Leone and Ascension Island. Off Grytviken we cross-decked onto the Canberra to get us into San Carlos Water. After a few days in San Carlos, we boarded the Landing Ship HMS *Intrepid* to sail round to just north of Lively Island, followed by a run into Bluff Cove in Landing Craft.

We arrived in Bluff Cove on June 6th the day before the Welsh Guards came round from San Carlos in *Sir Galahad.* Although Bluff Cove Settlement is within the same inlet as Fitzroy, it is about 15 miles to the north by land – there is a small settlement at each inlet.

On June 13th we moved by helicopter to our FUA (Forming-Up Area) on Goat Ridge prior to our planned attack on Mount Tumbledown.

After Left Flank had completed its part of the attack, I was detailed to act as security screen for a stretcher party returning to the RAP (Regimental Aid Post). After a short distance we stopped and swapped places, with the stretcher-bearers becoming the screen and the screen becoming the bearers. Five seconds after we re-started we were hit by enemy mortar fire - the person I swapped with, Guardsman David Malcomson, was killed outright and my left leg was badly injured. Another party from Left Flank returning from the RAP were the first to reach us. They carried those of us who were unable to walk back to the RAP, from where I was helicoptered first to Fitzroy and then to the field hospital at Ajax Bay, where I heard of the Argentine surrender on June 14th.

From Ajax Bay I was helicoptered out to the hospital ship *Uganda*, (official title Her Majesty's Hospital Ship *Uganda*), which was anchored nearby in Grantham Sound at that time receiving casualties from all the battlefields.

On the sixth day on board the hospital ship, RN Surgeon Lieutenant Warner explained the full extent of my injuries and that

I was going to have to lose the injured leg. My left leg was then amputated two days later under general anaesthetic. I remember signing the consent form with RN Surgeon Commander Peter Bull (Consultant Anaesthetist for the Task Force) and QARNNS (Queen Alexandra's Royal Naval Nursing Service) Operating Theatre Sister Nicci Pugh whilst I was on the operating table. They were both very kind and seemed to care about every patient individually, which is quite something considering the job they were doing and the rate of casualties going through their Operating Theatres at the time.

Some days later I started my return journey to UK. I was transferred to the Royal Navy 'survey-converted-to-ambulance-ship' HMS *Hydra* and then up to Montevideo in Uruguay. (I was one of very few patients who managed to sneak crutches off the *Uganda* and still use them to this day).

From the port in Montevideo we were transported individually to the international airport to fly back to the UK on an RAF VC10 via Ascension Island for re-fuelling. From RAF Brize Norton we were transferred to RAF Hospital Wroughton for post-flight medicals and my parents were able to visit.

From RAF Wroughton we were helicoptered to the Queen Elizabeth Military Hospital (QEMH) at Woolwich. I was offered rehabilitation (rehab) at either Chessington or Headley Court in Surrey, but with help from a friend and advice from Roehampton I made good progress from my home.

I stayed in the army completing just short of 24 years in total, working as a swimming instructor and in the Physical and Adventurous Training Office.

After I left the army in 2001, I was appointed the Cannon Master to His Grace the Duke of Rutland at Belvoir Castle. This is an honorary position, of which I am extremely proud. I fire the eighteenth-century cannons from the castle roof tops at the Duke's request for events, anniversaries, etc. On June 14th 2008 we had a special 'seven-cannon-firing' to commemorate the 26th anniversary of the liberation of the Falkland Islands, and this has been continued every year on this date to the present day.

I became involved in all sorts of other sports from volleyball to field athletics and competed in countless international competitive shooting events over the years. It may seem a funny way of looking at things, but I very much doubt if I would have achieved so much in these highly competitive fields if my life had not changed so dramatically in 1982...Like all of us injured in this way in war, once I knew the leg had to go I had to face up to a new and different way of life. I've just carried on working hard, enjoying competing in all these sports and making new friends all over the world.

Nicci has mentioned my membership of BLESMA earlier in this article; BLESMA have helped me a great deal in many different ways over the years.

The BLESMA charity is closely aligned with Blind Veterans UK, so it is a privilege to contribute to the Falklands War coverage in this way from another long-standing and hugely respected injured servicemen's charity.

After the 2007 larger national commemorations around the UK for the 25th anniversary year of the Falklands War, I heard through BLESMA of the first Hospital Ship *Uganda* Reunion, which was being held on board a cruise ship in April 2008. This was the first occasion all the many different personnel from the hospital ship had reunited and was unique in that all the former patients were included. Amazing! I signed up straight away, and soon discovered that the former Operating Theatre Sister, Nicci Pugh, who had organised my leg surgery all those years ago in the South Atlantic, was running the whole event. It was a brilliant and very special weekend. People travelled from all over the UK and from further afield to enjoy several hours of hospitality and reminiscing on board the P&O cruise ship *Aurora*, while the ship was on a cruise ship changeover in Southampton.

After six other similar maritime events, the group is still going strong and (Covid permitting) we hope to complete eight reunions this year in 2022 to commemorate the fortieth anniversary of the Falklands War.

I like Nicci's theme and title 'The Ties That Bind Us' there's no doubt war can be a nasty and destructive business, but it can also create amazing camaraderie and friendships that can help and strengthen us all over the years. My meeting with Clara and Bill McKay in the Falkland Islands so many years after the war is just one small example of 'the ties that bind us'...

In 2002 and again in 2007 I travelled back to the Falkland Islands and stayed with Clara McKay and her husband Bill in Stanley on both occasions. Bill, Clara and their family have since become very good friends; they opened their house and their hearts to me, a total stranger, and it made an enormous difference knowing what they had also been through in 1982. It is wonderful how kind everyone in The Islands is to returning veterans.

Robert 'Ossie' Osborn.
Assistant Curator The Royal Lancers and Nottinghamshire Yeomanry Museum, Nottinghamshire. December 2021.

**BLESMA: Formerly, The British Limbless Ex-Servicemen's Association founded in 1920. Now called The Limbless Veterans Charity. Registered UK Charity number: 1084189 www.blesma.org*

****

Senior Registrar and RAMC Major James Ryan onboard the QE2, then later RFA Sir Galahad

<u>Reminiscences of a Distant War - A Medic at War</u>

In 1982 I was 37 year-old and a lecturer in surgery, an honorary senior registrar in my final year of training as well as also a Major in the Royal Army Medical Corps (RAMC). Like all my contemporaries, military and civilian, at that time I had a unique and lengthy training, which today would raise eyebrows, but was a good preparation for war. Penetrating ballistic missiles do not respect anatomical boundaries or surgical sub speciality interests, particularly when deployed as a single-handed surgeon on campaign service.

Outbreak of war

This was a wholly unexpected event. My generation of military surgeons was fully expecting a general war in North-West Europe following an invasion by the Warsaw Pact. With no warning, Argentina invaded the Falkland Islands on 2nd April having landed on South Georgia a few hours earlier.

My warning to deploy on active duty took effect on 12th May when I embarked on the great Cunard ship *QE2* at Southampton. My Field Surgical Team, designated 55 FST, was to be part of the surgical support for 5 Brigade consisting of Welsh and Scots Guards, Gurkhas and Support Arms. Some of the Guards were aloof and unfriendly to the RAMC Medics and largely ignored us. One group of Guards officers would not come to RAMC doctors for treatment. Instead, they came to a private arrangement with the on-board Cunard medical staff that were more to their liking, which I found quite hurtful. They would change their attitude when we next encountered them during the war.

On a lighter note, the first intended anaesthetist for my FST was one Major H Hannah. That is until it was realised that this was Helen Hannah – a woman. Not just any woman, but the widely admired and redoubtable Major Helen Hannah RAMC. This caused some consternation. The British Armed Forces were not yet ready for a woman on their battlefield and she was quickly replaced by the equally well-known and redoubtable Lt Col Jim Anderson RAMC who would soon be appointed OC 55 FST. At our first O Group we were told without humour that the ship had been re-designated LPLL – Landing Platform, Luxury Liner. She put to sea at 1600 hours with no one believing that the team would get much further than the English Channel.

In preparation for war service, engineers in Southampton installed two helicopter pads, transformed public lounges into dormitories, further installed fuel pipes that ran through the ship down to the engine room to allow for refuelling at sea, and they covered carpets with 2,000 sheets of hardboard. A quarter of the ship's length was reinforced with steel plating, and an anti-magnetic coil was fitted to combat naval mines. Over 650 Cunard crew members volunteered for the voyage, to look after the 3,000 members of 5 Brigade.

The journey south took 15 days, leaving ample time for exercises and training with unfamiliar equipment. There was also ample time for pleasure. The author kept a diary throughout the campaign and it helps to illustrate the surreal atmosphere on board. It seemed bizarre to go to war on the world's finest luxury liner.

A few diary entries reflect the mood on board.

"12th May ...retired to the 1st class bar for large gins at 2100 hrs – retired to bed at 2330 hrs!

13th May ...Lifeboat drill ad nauseam...Superb lunch – fresh salmon yesterday – fresh crab today - and wonderful wines.

15th May...My first operation at sea – an appendectomy on a young combat engineer in the QE2's operating theatre.

17th May ...Captain's cocktail party followed by a steeplechase in QE2's Officers Wardroom!" It became increasingly easy to imagine that all were on a holiday cruise, at least for the officers."

Into the War Zone

Reality checked in when active service conditions were declared as we approached Grytviken in South Georgia. The *QE2*, initially bound for the Falkland Islands, had unexpectedly turned away and headed for South Georgia – a distance of over 7,500 miles from Southampton. Why? The given explanation was a threat from submarines. This would lead later to a spectacular insult by the crew of the P&O vessel SS *Canberra* which went directly to the Falkland Islands to off load her troops. Some time later her crew hung a sheet over the side of *Canberra* with the ditty – *"P&O cruises where Cunard refuses"*! Whether Cunard's *QE2* was not to be risked, or whether there was a genuine submarine threat is for historians to decide. All who cruised on the *QE2* retain an enormous affection for her. (In 1985 while on tour in Hong Kong the author had a chance to reboard the ship and explore familiar surroundings).

We arrived in Grytviken in South Georgia on 27th May. Troops and equipment were cross decked from the liner to an awaiting North Sea ferry, MV *Norland.* Our adventure on the luxury liner was over. Oh, how we had come down in the world.

We departed South Georgia for the Falklands that evening in an overcrowded ship in appalling weather and rough seas.

Sir Galahad* and *Sir Tristram

55 FST had an uneventful first week on the Falkland Islands. Bad weather kept the Argentine Air Force at bay resulting in a deceptive calm. With both infantry Brigades ashore assaults on Argentine positions could now proceed and land the force in an area to the south of Stanley. The area chosen was at Fitzroy and nearby Bluff Cove. 55 FST was assigned to provide surgical support to the force.

Our CO, Lt Col Jim Anderson, attended the Brigade briefing and was told that his FST should board the logistic landing ship *Sir Galahad* that afternoon. It became immediately clear that Brigade Staff Officers envisaged that the surgical teams would simply board *Sir Galahad* carrying their medical kit in their hand luggage. Col Anderson then informed the Brigade staff the 55 FST comprising over 20 personnel, numerous vehicles and trailers, furniture for operating theatres and wards and a considerable requirement for shelter, water, food and heating that this would take some hours to achieve. The Brigade staff were appalled and a heated discussion followed. This was to be the first of many adverse events, which delayed the departure of *Sir Galahad* and 5 Brigade.

Sir Galahad eventually sailed for Fitzroy at night of 7th June and arrived in Bluff Cove in broad daylight on the morning of 8th June. She anchored alongside her sister ship *Sir Tristram*, which had arrived the day before. To arrive in daylight effectively behind enemy lines and to begin unloading troops is an invitation for the enemy to attack. This was to be just one of a number of tactical and operational errors that led to a disaster at Fitzroy/Bluff Cove. Worse would follow.

A battery of surface-to-air missiles that was to cover the deployment of troops was not operational, and air cover had been drawn away from the area by what turned out to be a decoy flight of Argentine jets. Finally, it took many hours to begin unloading *Sir Galahad* because there was no room to dock the ship and unload directly onto to terra firma. Landing craft were also in short supply and there were critical equipment failures on board. The Argentines had plenty of time to call in a lethal air attack on what was effectively a sitting duck.

One of our surgical teams had just got ashore with its equipment when, at about 1400 hours, two waves of Argentine fighter-bombers bombed and strafed the ships lying motionless in the water. My team were still aboard and the officers were having gins in the wardroom and watching a very tasteless 8 mm movie on a TV monitor.

After the hits by bombs and bullets I ended up on the floor but my gin had not spilt. We were in total darkness and all exits were buckled. A remarkable quietness ensued and people just sat still and in silence. After a seemingly lengthy period we heard the unmistakably posh voice of a young Guards officer. He had explored behind the small wardroom bar and found a trapdoor leading outside – this, we were told later was used to restock the bar with beer barrels. The officer, who turned out later to be a very young second lieutenant in the Welsh Guards, was cool and collected. He ushered us all out to safety, only leaving when we were all safe.

Days later I related this tale to the Guards RSM and wondered if the officer should be put forward for an award. He shook his head and said that the young man had just done what would be expected of a Guards officer – no recommendation was made.

Out on deck was pandemonium. Our second in command was dead. Col Anderson had severe damage to his shoulder. They had both been outside bird watching when the attack came in. Col Anderson refused all medical attention. He simply made a makeshift sling for his left arm and carried on working for the rest of the war. Life rafts were deployed and helicopters hovered over the burning ship taking and winching people off the deck. The butcher's bill was appalling – 56 dead and 150 wounded.

We were brought ashore having lost all personal equipment and dressed only in shirts and combat trousers. We had also lost our personal weapons, cameras and in some cases our wallets and ID cards. The Royal Navy has a term for people like us - we are labelled 'survivors' and unfit for any duty. My FST was assembled, boarded on a helicopter, and evacuated back to the Red and Green Field Hospital at San Carlos where we were equipped and set to work on the continuing flow of wounded. We stayed with the Red and Green Life Machine until war's end.

****

Dr John Burgess, Regimental Medical Officer 3 Para

<u>A Medic with 3 Para</u>

To begin this reflection, I wish to pay tribute to my medical staff working alongside me in the Falklands. Many I had known a long time, but of the eight when we left UK, I only returned with four. L/Cpl Lovett and Pte Dodsworth were killed. Sgt Bradley and Pte Kennedy were wounded.

On Good Friday 1982 we sailed down Southampton Water on the *Canberra* and the send-off was terrific, from the dockside and past Southsea. The *Canberra* and her willing P&O staff looked after us superbly and it was a delightful way to go to war.

On the way south we trained others in first aid and enlarged the medical team. We practiced landings on Ascension and life was good. When we sailed south from there the mood changed in an instant. A blood donor session indicated that we might be involved in land conflict. The nights got darker, the seas rougher and colder. The sinking of the *General Belgrano* elicited no joy, rather the fear of swimming in those waters. We then had news of the loss of the HMS *Sheffield* and we knew we would be landing and fighting.

On D-2 we transdecked from *Canberra* to HMS *Intrepid.* We did it at night in the South Atlantic swell, out from the side of the ship, down scramble nets with full kit into a landing craft. Amazingly we did not lose anyone. Enroute to HMS *Intrepid* we saw the silhouette of the carrier HMS *Hermes* close by, putting up the Harriers that protected us from above.

D Day saw us in landing craft assaulting the beach at Port San Carlos. It was daylight as we went ashore and we expected to be shot as the ramp went down. Luckily, we were unopposed and after wading through the deep and cold water we made our way to the local settlement. We set up our medical facility in the bunk house, a community facility for farmers as they moved across the island. We were made most welcome and it was good both to be ashore and to talk to the Islanders.

We received our first casualty, aircrew from a downed helicopter, but the war was mainly overhead and aimed at the ships in the sound and offshore. On D+2 we had a dreadful incident with nine of 3 Para being wounded. I flew to the site with my medical team and others but in a glancing blow the Sea King struck its rear rotor on the ground. After gaining height again and spinning uncontrollably, the helicopter crashed a second time. Luckily it was into the soft ground, allowing us to get out safely and treat the wounded.

We evacuated the wounded on further helicopters and returned to Port San Carlos. There, that Sunday morning, we had our worst bombing raids. I have huge admiration for the Argentine Air Force and what they did in their fast jets, flying so low down the valley into our fire, knowing that they often had insufficient fuel to return to Argentina.

We heard of the success of 2 Para in Goose Green and had orders to move forward to Teal Inlet. My medical team walked, but I was offered a trip in a helicopter. We set up in an empty house, dug an excellent air raid shelter and waited until morning. That night it snowed heavily.

The following day it was onwards to Estancia House. The farm owners were superb, helping us set up in their house with others outside. Many of our casualties were suffering from the effects of having permanently wet feet, made worse by the cold. We had some medical supplies, but our best news was the arrival of Captain Mike Von Bertele and two of his medics.

On the glorious sunny afternoon before the assault on Mount Longdon, I and my team left on a flatbed behind a tractor, carrying stores as well as people. Capt Von Bertele and his team would travel up afterwards in a tracked vehicle as soon as possible. We lay low in the grass as the sun set and once darkness was established, we set out for the silent march east to Mount Longdon. It was a calm and clear night and we could see the silhouette of Two Sisters to the south of us. In line we crossed the Murrell River on ladders and continued to the western edge of Mount Longdon.

The quietness was suddenly broken with the first landmine detonation and injury. We were greeted with flares and machine guns. On that signal we ran up the west side of Longdon and I managed to find the comparatively safe gulley later depicted in the RAMC painting of Mount Longdon. It was only in retrospect that we realised we had run up the side of the mountain, over the rocks, carrying full kit, with no body armour, into a minefield and direct enemy fire. Not all made it.

Casualties arrived fast and we treated them as best we could in the dark and cold and constant fire. The mortars were the worst as we had no protection. From the small and sheltered gulley, the tracer passed safely overhead. Mike Von Bertele then arrived with his team to provide excellent support. We were able to get some casualties out in the few Bandvagn (BV) available. With daylight we were helped by the occasional helicopter, but regrettably we had to hold many patients in our location before they could be evacuated.

Many casualties occurred on the rocks just above and to the sides of our gulley. Many were gunshot wounds, but we also had frequent injuries and deaths from mortars. Capt. Von Bertele was inspirational in the way he left the gulley, collecting patients and bringing them back to comparative safety. The noise was tremendous, enemy fire close by and with our own artillery inward onto the hills. We could also hear the naval guns firing from offshore, with impact on the hills around.

Life on the mountain was grim. It was the middle of winter and I remember it being dark most of the time. Although the mountains were low in altitude, the wind and weather would come off the South Atlantic and Antarctica. As the fighting quietened, my medical sergeant, Sgt Bradley, went out in a BV to retrieve casualties just south of us. Regrettably they hit a minefield and after he got back, he could give no more.

On the second night 3 Para, assisted by 2 Para, made better progress and as day broke it was apparent that the enemy were retreating. Orders were given for the entry to Stanley and Mike and I decided that on this occasion he should lead on foot and I and my team would follow up in a vehicle as soon as possible. When it soon became apparent that the enemy were capitulating, I left in a BV and headed to Moody Brook. I somewhere overtook Mike and a helicopter saw us as the leading vehicle and dropped off the 3 Para regimental flag. We attached it to a Bangalore torpedo and I carried it into the western edge of Stanley where I rightly handed it to a regimental officer to carry forward.

Stanley was a mess. We moved into a damaged house with no electricity, and little food or water. My medics managed to acquire an Argentine G Wagen and located Argentine rations. Mike soon arrived and we plotted to relieve the Falkland Islands' hospital. This was in the then Argentine sector, separated by a white line. That night, he and I, with a medic apiece, "relieved" the hospital. The reception we had from Falkland Islands staff was terrific and we spoke as fellow professionals with the doctors and other Argentine healthcare staff.

A few days later the HMHS *Uganda* anchored in Stanley Sound. She was the main hospital ship and I and Colour Sergeant Faulkner, who had re-joined my team, were able to get aboard. As well as a most welcome shower and meal, we were able to meet some of our patients. I well recall a soldier who had been shot in the right shoulder with an injury to his neck. He had a tracheostomy and could not speak, his right arm was immobilised and with that he could not write, but slowly with his left hand in pencil and on a notepad he wrote: *"Thank you doc and colour for saving my life"*. Tremendous soldiers.

****

Dr Linda Parker, Historian and Author

<u>Military Chaplains in the Falklands</u>

The Task Force deployed to the Falklands Islands in April/ May 1982 was accompanied by military chaplains who were present with their men on board ship and in the fighting on land throughout the conflict. They offered spiritual, material and practical help, taking services, performing funerals and assisting with medical care.

On the ships going south there were naval chaplains, attached to each ship's crew, and army chaplains accompanying the land forces. There were four chaplains on the *SS Canberra* and three on the *QE2,* both of which had been 'taken up from trade'. The chaplains took interdenominational services which were well attended, followed by smaller Holy Communion services. Daily services were held and smaller groups prayed regularly, such as the group led by the Revd Peter Brooke of the Welsh Guards: *"Significant for me was a small group of six or seven of us who met for prayer each morning between breakfast sittings. One who prayed with us did not return. How can we measure the spiritual importance of these sacred moments for him?"*

The Easter Sunday service on the *Hermes* in 1982 was covered by Brian Hanrahan on the BBC and he quoted the chaplain, the Revd Roger Devonshire's sermon: *"In his sermon he said that everybody had to achieve a personal victory over their own fears or feeling. In the service prayers were offered for those the ship's company had left behind with little time to say goodbye."*

The Revd David Cooper, padre to 2 Para, tried to prepare his men for the conflict ahead. He explained:

I couldn't say anything I didn't believe. I couldn't tell them what happens after death, I had no idea, but I could tell them that I believe in a God who has the power to care beyond death. That they mattered and whatever happened they would still matter to God. But I didn't believe in a God who would divert the path of a bullet, so they had to accept what was coming and remember their training.

The Revd Richard Sigrist recalled the funeral of the Argentine submariner who he buried at Grytviken after the marines had regained South Georgia: *"We buried him on South Georgia in the grave we dug next to Shackleton's grave in the old whalers' cemetery there. It was a very moving occasion; the sailors turn out in full dress uniform ... I conducted the funeral and the Argentine Captain gave the eulogy. Anyway, at the end of it he threw his arms around me, in tears and said "well what is this all about? "It was very moving"*

The Revd Wynne Jones was the chaplain attached to 45 Commando in the fight towards Stanley. His presence was welcomed by the commanding officer Ian Gardener, who agreed with the often repeated maxim of Jones "*I am interested in the living not the dead*" and concluded that "*The chaplain's real job is to offer spiritual comfort to men facing death- to help marines do their jobs* "

Once ashore chaplains took services as and when possible. The Revd Derek Heaver remembered the second Sunday that he was on the islands and took a service at San Carlos, which was attended by civilians from the settlement, as well as the few soldiers who were not under orders to move. On Sunday 13th June, he and his regiment were in the thick of the fighting on Mount Longdon, where they lost 23 men:

That was a full day of shelling; we were so busy with the wounded and the dead. I found myself looking after the dead, caring for them, making them decent, putting them to one side, preparing them, taking personal possessions from them, documenting them. I thought of taking a service, but with the constant shelling, it didn't arise on that Sunday. But one thing that I did do that day was to get back by helicopter to Teal Inlet. In the late afternoon we buried eighteen Paras, sharing the service with the Marines and in the end there were 24 buried at that service.

The Revd Jake Watson RN, chaplain on HMS *Broadsword,* commented on the position of the naval chaplains: *"At sea the ship is the front line. We are all literally in the same boat."* The naval chaplains at action stations tended to be attached to the medical staff but took the opportunity when the ship was not closed down to move around the ship during operations.

The chaplains were involved with burials on land and at sea. Few readers who remember the Falklands conflict can forget the television news report from 2 Para at Ajax Bay of the temporary burial in a mass grave of the casualties by Chaplain David Cooper. He was later mentioned in despatches for his role as chaplain to the men of 2 Para.

Another vital role played by the naval and army chaplains at home on UK bases, was notifying the next of kin and providing pastoral care to the bereaved families.

BBC reporter Robert Fox praised the unit padres who *"had been quite outstanding in their service .... they do a lot of good for the health, care and welfare of the troops."*

The Revd Devonshire summed up the role of the chaplains during the Falklands War: *"we have to be witnesses to reality in the midst of what is unreal, to bring normality when all is abnormal, and in a crazy world be a contact with the eternal sanity of God."*

****

Revd Jake Watson, Chaplain HMS Broadsword

A Chaplain at War - Reflection

Forty-year-old memories are not always the most accurate, but when the memory is of something as traumatic as the Falklands War, it is as if those memories were branded into the consciousness. The possibility of being obliterated by a missile, injured, maimed, or trapped raises all kinds of conflicting emotions. It also motivates people to assess their priorities and what they hold dear in life. Chaplains of other services may have some choice as to how close they go to the front line. In the RN we don't have that luxury because the ship is the front line.

I was onboard HMS *Broadsword.* We were 'goalkeeper' on *Hermes*. Goalkeeper, that's sanitised MOD language for a suicide mission, if it came to it. *Hermes* was indispensable, we weren't, if a missile got through and our system couldn't take it out, our duty like *Brilliant* with the other carrier, was to take the 'hit'… and we would, that's what we were there for. It was our duty.

We were half a mile from *Ardent* when she was sunk and went to her aid. Their doctor had been blown into the freezing water. He was in the water for 10 minutes and it took us 4 hours to get his temperature back to normal. We were about a quarter of a mile from the A*ntelope* when she was hit and only yards from the plane which bombed her, as it pitched into the sea, because it was flying so low it clipped the *Antelope's* mast.

We were 400 yards behind *Coventry* when she took her bombs and were busy into the early hours assisting her survivors. Minutes before *Coventry* was hit, a 500lb bomb skimmed across the water and hit our ship's side. It took a scenic excursion through the innards, hitting a steel pipe and being deflected upwards (If it had gone downwards the consequences would have been far more serious). The bomb exited on the flight deck decapitating our helicopter in the process and snapping in two the live torpedo that was loaded on the helicopter at the time.

At this point the chemical alarm went off, indicating we may be under a chemical attack. It was, I think, the only time I had taken off my survival belt holding my respirator. In the five nanoseconds it took me to get to it, someone else had put it on. Fortunately, there was no chemical attack. The spilled fuel from the broken torpedo had set off the alarm.

During defence watches when things were quiet, I'd visit all parts of the ship from the bridge (and I still claim to be the first to observe the first direct attack against us.) and especially to the machinery and other spaces below the water line where nerves were quite frail. I also helped the watch keepers by doing a 2nd Officer of the watch, which was useful from a chaplain's point of view because I encountered people in the middle of the night I may not otherwise have seen.

A chaplain's action station is with one of the first aid teams. We were in and around Bomb Alley for the full period of the air war. I held the hand of a young sailor whose back had been peppered with shrapnel and who'd lost his nerve and was to be evacuated. Until the evening of the first day our Doc was a bit miffed because I'd pulled a larger piece of shrapnel out of a casualty than he had.

The day *Coventry* was hit we had our own damage to deal with. We then stood by *Coventry* in case there were further attacks and to deal with her casualties. *Coventry* was unfortunate, our Sea Wolf missiles were tracking the two planes that were attacking her. At 5km the missiles would have fired but for whatever reason *Coventry* pulled across our bow and the missile system went back to default and *Coventry* took three bombs. She exploded and during the next 45 minutes she turned over and sank.

The lucky survivors were those who were lifted off by helicopter and arrived aboard *Broadsword* dry. Most of the others at some point ended up in the freezing water. The first thing to do was to cut their bitterly cold clothes off them and get them into a hot shower. Some were 'walking wounded', others needed assistance and one or two were carried like babies. While trying to be 'light-hearted' with a survivor, whose back had been completely burned, and while trying to dress the burns with totally inadequate dressings, the thought occurred to me that this was never covered in the Pastoral Theology course I attended.

By the middle of the night when the survivors had been treated and fed, and with the more seriously wounded having been evacuated by helicopter to the medical facilities ashore, it was then time to discharge the *Coventry* crew for their journey home. As *Broadsword* was darkened and they were unfamiliar with the layout, I led them to the upper deck encouraging them as we went. Once in the landing craft they gave three cheers in appreciation of what *Broadsword* had done for them. It was quite moving as we had only done our duty.

20 years later the captain at HMS *Drake* was giving a lunch for three Frigate captains who had once been his students. Halfway through the meal, one of them asked if I'd been 'down south' on the *Broadsword*. He had been one of the *Coventry* survivors and had recognised my voice from when he was guided through the ship.

There were chaplains who yomped all the way with their units and stayed with the companies they thought would take the most casualties. Chaplains who were involved with casualties at every level of treatment, even assisting in operations and the respectful treatment of the dead and collecting body parts for burial. Chaplains who maintained some level of normality in a crazy world and others who helped people to control temporary fear. A brave man is not one who doesn't recognise fear, but one who can and still does his duty. It was some of my Catholic colleagues who, because of their shared faith, were able to calm prisoners of war and assure them that they wouldn't be abused or mistreated.

The first priority was people and not religious ritual, although it has a place. So long as chaplains are provided, no matter how hazardous some of the decisions may be, people are still being treated as human beings and not just cannon fodder.

****

Richard Spencer, MOD Lawyer on board Canberra

A Legal View of the South Atlantic Conflict

In 1982 when I went south I was the only lawyer who deployed on Operation Corporate, as a recently promoted major.

Apparently when the gunner told Major General Jeremy Moore that he was entitled to take a bugler with him, there was a small explosion, and the word went out that nobody else was joining the Headquarters, so I was told to relax and just to come over to main building if I was needed!

Somebody senior got the idea that crew members on STUFT ships (Ships Taken Up From Trade ie former merchant ships and civilioan vessels seconded for the duration), when they reached Ascension, might decide that they didn't really want to get involved in a war, and jump ship. It was decided to declare "Active Service", which would have the effect of making the civvies subject to the Naval Discipline Act 1957. I duly typed out the signal and was just about to sign it and send it, when I was told that it was for CDS to sign, not me! I typed it out again, and took it upstairs, where a full Colonel clerk checked my spelling, and then handed it to a Brigadier who went behind the curtain, and then returned with an impressive signature on it. I headed swiftly to the Commcen and rapped on the window. "*Flash Signal!*" I said, excitedly (to be fair it was the first I'd ever seen) – the guy yawned and said, "*Oh, another!*"

Then, as a result of an innocent misunderstanding, a Royal Marine Corporal shot and killed a protected prisoner of war, Sub-Official Primero Felix Artuso, of the Argentine Navy. The Red Cross would not be pleased! We might lose our no claims bonus! Abruptly it was decided that the Task Force needed a lawyer immediately, and I was given 24 hours to get myself to South Cerney.

At Ascension I was greeted without enthusiasm, and after a while was moved by chopper to RFA *Bayleaf,* where I was made very welcome.

I transferred, again by chopper, to a naval vessel, which made best speed for San Carlos Water – on the way, the BBC World Service news was patched into the ship's PA system, to tell us that the war was over. I was invited to send a "FamilyGram", which I think was the predecessor of the e-bluey.

I wrote, "*There is snow on the hills. Boredom the worst enemy"*, which I thought was clear enough, that I'd arrived, and that nobody was shooting at me. Herself didn't see it that way, and, bless her, belted into Guildford and invested in a slab of M&S's Swiss Chocolate, and a couple of pairs of nice woolly socks, which she wrapped round the "nutty", and posted it off to me. The mail bag rested on hot concrete at ASI for long enough for the choc to melt and flow into the socks!

I transferred to HMS *Fearless*, I was then moved to Government House in Stanley, which General Mario Menendez had left in good order, with it well stocked with excellent Argentine cheese and red vino. The following day, I walked down Ross Road, and fortunately bumped into Captain Chris Burne, RN, who I knew from the Wilton Hash. He said he had a Red Cross Delegate on board, and what should he do with him. I said, *"Get a lawyer, Sir*!" and he replied, "*Come aboard".*

Argentine POWs

Among many more important bits of kit that had been lost when an Argentine Exocet had taken *Atlantic Conveyor*, was the complete POW Camp Kit – tents, and record keeping kit and all! The Argentine surrender had made us responsible for the welfare of several thousand of their cold, wet, filthy and unhappy soldiery. It was essential to get most of them back home as swiftly as possible.

Canberra and *Norland* were pressed into service to ferry them back. A "cruise" to Puerto Madryn in Argentina followed. One tiny problem surfaced – some of the brighter Argentine squaddies spotted that having given their name, rank, date of birth and army number (if any!) they got a fresh white bread roll, and a paper cup of hot soup, probably the best meal they'd had for a week! So quite a few circulated, and joined the queue, gave another name, and received more bread and soup. This left us with a nominal roll of POWs that listed more people than we were carrying. Here the Red Cross delegate, Hugo Berchthold, came in useful, and sorted it out with the Argentine side!

Once the rank and file had been sent home, the Argentine Senior Officers were moved onto the British Rail Ferry *St Edmund*, which raised a problem. During the Napoleonic wars, the Brits had kept French POWs in rotting hulks of old wooden warships moored in malarial swamps along the south coast! Not surprisingly they died like flies, and when it came, a while later, to draft the Geneva Conventions, one thing that France insisted on was that POW Camps must be on land, but we didn't have the kit, and in any case a tented camp would probably have been blown away. London kept putting off the idea of sending the seniors home, until the Argentine Government said that the war had ended, but the Junta had fallen, and their successors wouldn't say it! The Red Cross delegates were getting twitchy – they knew that *St Edmund* was the best accommodation available, but it wasn't on land!

My major contribution to the campaign was to coin the phrase, "*embarked, pending passage*". The Red Cross liked this, and we didn't lose our NCB!

I had one more involvement with the POWs – I was told that there was a complaint! I went on board *St Edmund,* where I met the charming Vice Commodoro Eugenio J Miari, of the Argentine Airforce Legal Branch. I had an open Int Corps interpreter, and a covert one, dressed as a British Rail Steward (the outfit was a bit small for him). My opposite number said, in accented English, "*I have a complaint! Wai wicktise!*" My official interpreter said he didn't understand, and the disguised one said "*More coffee, Sir? I don't know what he's on about!*" After a moment, I realised that the good Vice Commodoro was older and more senior than me, and he'd learned his Latin before I'd learned mine! *Vae Victis*! *Woe to the vanquished*! All he was saying was that being defeated was absolutely bloody!

After that we got to talk normally – as the surrender had come into force, he'd wrapped his law books up carefully in carpet, and stashed them in a cupboard in the Secretariat. Could I, please, find his books for him? Alas, they'd been dumped, to give the Paras shelter and somewhere to kip! I could feel for him!

The Task Force sailed home, without me – I don't think I was on the nominal roll! One day, I queued up for my lunch in the rather dodgy building which British aid had built as a hostel for kids from the camp going to the secondary school in Stanley, and the Argentine Air Force had used as a field hospital. As well as a slab of sea trout, the aimiable Corporal Artley, of HQ LFFI (Land Forces, Falkland |Islands), dropped, with a clang, a South Atlantic Medal into my steel tray, and said, *"I think this is for you, Sir!"* No ceremony down there!

Note 1: Richard Spencer was the only British lawyer deployed during Operation Corporate

Note 2: Petty Officer Chief Engineer Felix Artuso was shot dead on 27th April 1982, whilst a POW by a Royal Marine when mistakenly thought to be sabotaging the Argentine submarine Santa Fe. He was buried with full military honours and his grave is on South Georgia in the same grounds as the grave of Ernest Shackleton.

****

Chapter 6 – The Islanders under Occupation

From the moment Argentine forces landed on the Falkland Islands on 2nd April 1982, the small community of Falkland Islanders were subject to military occupation. Severe restrictions were placed on everyone, and all forms of radio and other communication were forbidden.

Groups of Islanders were corralled in various places around the island for several weeks, with one being at Fox Bay housing 114 people of all ages. Food was limited, water in short supply, movement was restricted and the continued patrolling by aggressive occupying troops put great fear into many.

The only news came from the BBC World Service on radios hidden away in people's houses. News of successes, setbacks and casualties were shared only among adults for fear of disclosing the whereabouts of the radios.

Once British forces landed on the islands and bombardment and air attacks on key military positions began, the dangers intensified with many Islanders sleeping in basements and cellars for their own safety. With the increased fighting on the islands, the attitude of the Argentine occupiers became more agitated and threatening as the likelihood of defeat increased.

As progress towards victory was made and various settlements were liberated by British soldiers, not only was there great relief amongst the islanders, but immense gratitude for the liberating forces. This led to the development of friendships that have remained strong even to this day.

For many, once the Argentine surrender was announced on 14th June 1982, they were able to go home for the first time for weeks to see their families and friends, to celebrate their freedom and to resume their lives that had been so rudely interrupted. Many found their homes in a state of disrepair and in a disgusting state after the Argentine troops departed.

Three Falkland Islanders were killed during the fighting.

Many of the accounts from the Islanders are from interviews carried out by local school children doing projects about the war over the last four decades. Special thanks are given to Jim McAdam and the Falkland Islands Journal for his assistance and permission to use parts of these accounts.

****

Brian Summers, Falkland Islands Defence Force
Audio transcript courtesy of the Falkland Islands Museum

Occupation - Fox Bay East

Towards the end of April after the liberation of South Georgia, we started to prepare for things getting tougher. Behind our house was an old peat hole, and we put a roof on it as protection against the stray bullets that were being fired at night. We also put blankets in it too.

About this time, heavily armed Argentine soldiers surrounded the Cable and Wireless (C&W) building, and Stuart Wallace and I were told we were being taken away for our own safety, as it couldn't be guaranteed in Stanley. We were told to pack a small bag and bring our passports, and then taken to the airport. General Menendez arrived while we were in the departure lounge and a huge Hercules aircraft was backed up to the building. We thought we were to be taken off the Falkland Islands. However, we were put on Puma helicopters and taken to Fox Bay West.

Eventually, we were moved to Fox Bay East with several other people, and in no time we ran out of water. Between us we managed to dig up a spring which had very clear, clean water at the back of the house, and we stored the water in an old oil drum buried in the ground. We had to use a bucket on a chain to fill the tank in the loft several times a day.

Things started to become more uncomfortable the day after the *General Belgrano* was sunk, and all radios were confiscated. But we had prepared for such an eventuality and had hidden an aerial round the cladding, ceiling and chimney with the radio itself hidden behind bales of wool. Another was hidden in the toilet.

We would secretly listen to the radio, but never spoke about it or of any news in front of the children. We gave a daily briefing to the adults.

For much of the time, life was very boring and we would spend lots of time walking round and round the yard – hours and hours.

Under Fire

With regular naval and air attacks on any Argentine ships at the nearby Fox Bay jetty, we spent most nights sheltering and sleeping in the foundations of the house. We received a 'hit' when a shell went through the roof and lodged in the foundations by the deep freezers, without exploding. Luckily it missed the tray of bread rolls that had been baked for breakfast next morning, but it did hit a case of Carlsberg.

We had no idea if the shell was still live and dangerous and were worried that the power to the deep freezers might set it off. I decided I would be the one to remove it as I was the only single person there. I lay on the floor with pliers in a very enclosed space and eventually managed to extract the shell, which proved to be empty. It weighed 32lbs.

On the day of 2 Para attack on Goose Green, we were rounded up in the house and herded into the shearing shed. The Argentines were really serious that day and told us that if we crossed a line outside the shed, we would be shot. They also told us that the British had bombed a house in Goose Green and a whole family had been killed.

We could look across the bay in the morning and see Fox Bay West and a cemetery the Argentines had made for their dead. An almost daily basis, we could see additional crosses as their casualties mounted up. We could also see their defensive positions including mortar pits.

One of the mortar pits blew up, I am not sure why, and an Argentine soldier was critically injured in his leg. Dr Haines offered to treat the soldier as they did not have any of their own doctors there. The soldier's leg needed amputation. Dr Haines had no medical instruments and no anaesthetic and the plan was to use hacksaw blades sterilised in boiling water and an ether-based automotive solvent 'Pilot-Start' to carry out the operation. However, in the end the Argentines didn't like or trust Dr Haines and his services were declined. We learned later that the soldier died that night.

****

Marvin Clarke, Falkland Islander

Occupation - Major Patricio Dowling

Whilst in a state of shock and numbness, we settled into the routine of having been invaded and now occupied. I now encountered the infamous and feared Major Patricio Dowling. Needless to say, the encounter was not an experience I would wish to go through again. The exchange of varied and heated views resulted in Dowling going out to the back of the Police Station, returning with another member of his staff who had a prominent scar down the side of his face, hustled me up against the wall, at which point I felt something against the side of my face/neck, followed by the courteous advice, "*We know who you are, you're not very clever and if you know what's good for you, shut your mouth and go away or I will cut your throat*". I vacated the building with some haste.

Early in the occupation, many residents adopted the practice of carrying a sturdy pair of pliers or wire cutters as many miles of comms cable had been laid by the Argentines and if you got tangled in such cables, you just might need to extricate yourself by cutting the cables. Needless to say, the opportunity was taken to cut as many cables as possible en route. One such occasion resulted in a bit of heightened tension, but we managed to convince the somewhat upset soldiers in the Moody Brook area that the horses had got entangled and that there was no option. The fact that many Argentine soldiers spoke little or no English and we spoke little if any Spanish, was always a compounding factor during such exchanges.

We also took the opportunity to pass on information about Argentine activities, dispositions, weapons and anything else considered useful for future reference.

What became clear was that I was one of a number of residents who were subjected to being arrested at gunpoint on numerous occasions and wheeled off down to the Police Station or Gymnasium, held under armed guard and questioned. We were reminded that they knew who we were, then the priests would arrive and, after some time, we would be released.

Towards the end of April, the Argentine authorities suggested via the medical department that it would be a goodwill gesture to airlift all pregnant women to Argentina for their protection and safety with the airlift to take place around the 5th May. However, any early consideration given to this offer was short lived as a result of the Vulcan bombing of Stanley airport and subsequent Harrier activity. From the outset, Trudi, my wife, had made it clear that she would not be taking up the offer - who would want to be in Argentina at such a time as this, with the Task Force so close and an end in sight?

As the war progressed and the number of British casualties and dead started to increase, there was a feeling of guilt at such losses, compounded by the fact that we were in the middle and unable to do anything meaningful to bring this dreadful war to an end.

****

Gerald Cheek, Falkland Islander and member of the Falkland Islands Defence Force (FIDF)

Under Occupation

Later that day I was taken to the airport. It was extremely distressing to see all the Argentine activity, especially their flag flying from the flagpole. On the way back to Stanley, one of the Cable and Wireless engineers managed to inform us that Maggie Thatcher had announced that a Task Force was being prepared to sail to the Islands and evict the Argentines. I remember being considerably happier at hearing that news.

During the day the Argentines issued many announcements, edicts and instructions, one of the first being that a curfew was in place and if anyone needed to leave their homes they would have to wave a white flag out of the window and an Argentine soldier would come and ask what was required. No mention was made of the language problem.

The curfew was soon lifted, and Argentine troops were posted on all roads out of town.

On the 27th April, one of their (Argentine) Mercedes jeeps arrived and four military police came into my house in a very excited state. They demanded in English that we were being taken away. We were not allowed to use the telephone and told to pack what I wanted. Was I about to be flown to Argentina and join the many disappeared persons? The soldiers agreed that only I would go with them… and after 20 minutes it came time to leave. A difficult farewell to say the least. Thinking back, it was probably one of the most distressing moments of my life.

When we arrived at the airport, a Hercules aircraft was running up its engines…my immediate thoughts were we would be going to Argentina. However, I was taken to the terminal where a total of 14 people were waiting. We were put on a Puma helicopter...and headed west over the harbour to Fox Bay West just a short distance away. We were then taken overland to Fox Bay East. We learned later that at Fox Bay the Argentines comprised a company of engineers and some 900 or so soldiers.

All was fairly quiet for the first few days but then the intial attacks by the British forces occurred. This was the bombing of Stanley airport by a Vulcan bomber and the Royal Navy Sea Harriers, which quite understandably upset the Argentines at Fox Bay. We heard about these raids via the BBC radio, and a number of soldiers turned up and took the radio away.

During the seven weeks we were at Fox Bay, life obviously became a mixture of boredom, worry about how our families and friends were faring back in Stanley and ... our concern for the British forces. It was particularly sad to hear about the losses and...we felt we were somewhat to blame...

We also experienced fear for our own safety at times when the British forces were attacking Argentine positions around the settlement. This consisted of occasional shell fire from the Royal Navy at night and a number of Harrier bombings during the day.

The Argentine freighter *Bahia Buen Suceso* was moored at the Fox Bay jetty. This was the ship that took the scrap merchants to South Georgia a few months earlier. The ship brought in ammunition and helicopter fuel for their forces.

During one of the Harrier raids, it was hit by a number of cannon rounds and the crew hastily abandoned ship. We learned after that one of the holds was full of 105mm field gun ammunition. Given the position of the ship about a hundred metres away, I expect the settlement would have been destroyed. We also later found out that an explosive charge had been set amongst the ammunition but fortunately the timer failed... I guess we were lucky on both these counts.

A day or two later a group of soldiers surrounded the house...and we were marched to the shearing shed...and he (the officer) ordered a number of officers to guard us. We learned later that he had also ordered them to shoot us if we attempted to move from the area.

During another Harrier raid, their cannon shells struck a nearby hut used to store aviation fuel...in 40-gallon barrels which ignited and exploded coming through the roof of the building…like a Roman candle some twenty feet into the air. That was also quite alarming as the fuel store was only fifty metres in front of the house.

****

Nathaniel Cockwell (year 6)

From: The Falkland Islands Journal 2021 Vol 11

Fox Bay East during the Falklands War

The Argentine military forces invaded Stanley on the night of 1st-2nd April 1982. Fox Bay's invasion was a few days later. In the meantime, everyone waited. They were sure the Argentines would come because Fox Bay East had a post office and a radio station. The Argentines did eventually arrive on the 5th April and it was very frightening for the residents of Fox Bay.

My Granny described this in her diary from the time: "Richard told me and the children to stay indoors, but I'm afraid I peeped round the yard gate because I couldn't bear not to watch him. He couldn't find a white hanky, so he took some goose feathers to have something white to wave when he went to meet the 20-odd Argentine soldiers off the helicopter. They were darting about, dropping down, darting about some more. Anyway, they finally got here. Four of them came in and searched the house. They were very nervous and as a result the sergeant (I think he must have been) was rather belligerent. However, they went through everything. The kids were stood in the passage with a soldier guarding them with a gun – their eyes were out on stalks. The soldier was really young, about 17, and so nervous that the sweat was running down his face. I was too angry to speak, it felt as if my jaws had been wired together, and I just marched around with them prodding my back with a gun. If I could have taken the soldier who was pointing a gun at my kids and torn him apart I'd have done it with my bare hands."

Grandad explained: "Everybody at Fox Bay was finding it so difficult to carry on as normal – which is what the Argentines wanted us to do – but there were armed soldiers everywhere and they used to scream at people all the time if they tried to go anywhere. The locals didn't speak Spanish and only the Argentine officers spoke English and it was chaos".

Under Occupation

Granny and Grandad decided to create a bunker under the house in case things got too dangerous. Granny wrote in her diary: "Richard dug the hole in the foundations under the sitting room floor, much to the excitement of the children. It's distinctly cuddly under there but good solid stone walls and enough room for short periods (about 2'6" high), a wide-ish space under the sitting room – narrow passage past the chimney and a big space under the office, with more height there – about 4') where we will make another hole in the floor.

As part of daily life during the occupation, Grandad had to keep the farm running and this meant having to work alongside the Argentines. He kept water and generators running so they had some electricity – but the Argentines used the water and electricity too. The water came from a spring and had to be pumped but having so many people in the settlement put a lot of pressure on the system and it needed to be worked on a lot. The generators struggled to cope too. Grandad described how they coped with their food: "We had quite a bit of flour and essentials in the store and the Argentine soldiers weren't allowed in there. I was sent off to bring sheep in to kill – every time I brought a cut of sheep in (I'd bring in about 200 sheep each time) all the menfolk would rush out and grab a sheep each and we killed our own mutton in our yard. That's how we got our meat."

Harrier Attack

On 16th May, the Cockwells' house was clearly marked as Argentine Headquarters, which would have made it a target for the British to bomb. The adults in the household were worried that the house could be bombed so hung children's clothes on the washing line outside and painted 'Civilian' on the side of the house. The bunker under the house started to be used more frequently from then on. Granny wrote in her diary: "Wham bam, two Harriers came up from the south west at a hell of a clip. By the time we realised what was happening they were firing cannons at the "*Buen Suceso*" (Argentine ship on the jetty). We didn't actually see anything – bolted down the hole with considerable speed, as one may imagine! That cannon fire is the most terrifying sound – like a very loud tearing or ripping. We saw the effects afterwards though – they have put several cannon shells through the *"Buen Suceso"*. The chippie shop was blazing - there was a lot of fuel and paint in there and it went off with a series of loud explosions and burned furiously".

Granny wrote about it in her diary: "Last night was very disturbed – we all went to bed about 10.15pm or thereabouts. I hadn't completely gone to sleep when I heard what sounded like someone walking about on the floor above, nearby, very heavily! Both of us came wide awake with a jerk and the realisation that it was shellfire. Richard got straight up to get all the others down the hole – although we had started by all sleeping down there.

We were woken again at about 1.10am with further shelling. Both times it came in short bursts 8 to 10 shots then a pause – then 8 to 10 shots somewhere else. Several times over a period of about 15 minutes. We were stranded here – shells landed on the point to start with and then several bursts were over the top of the house. We could clearly hear the shells whistling as they passed over.

The doctor's house had a direct hit, as did the generator shed – luckily they missed the water supply and only one battery was knocked out. We have done all the washing and got ourselves all clean in case the water supply is damaged tonight!"

****

Bragnae Nannig-Wallace (aged 11)
From: The Falkland Islands Journal 2019 Vol 11

Held Hostage

This is a story of my family on my mum's side coped with the fact that they were under house arrest with 14 other people and that their enemy was literally right outside their door.

It was the 27th April and my Grandad was working at Cable and Wireless until a group of Argentine soldiers surrounded the building. The Colonel entered and said that they would take my Grandad and Brian Summers away because they were part of the Defence Force. The two men went in separate vehicles.

When they arrived, the Colonel went up to him and said in Spanish: "*I don't know why you are here but most of the people here I have had to shoot so I hope I don't have to shoot you*". They only spent one night at Fox Bay West until Richard Cockwell came over and offered for them to stay at his house at Fox Bay East and so they did. They stayed in that house with 14 other people.

Entertainment

The children had Lego, Battleships, and various other games and each other to play with. My mum had only her ragdoll, there was nothing else she had brought from home. The ragdoll was made from scraps of material that was given to my Nan by Grizelda Cockwell. The adults had a radio and books. The radio channel they would listen to was BBC because it would give you updates about who had died and who had killed the most and so on.

They were allowed outside, but only for half an hour. They had to stay within the boundaries of the fence. There had at least to be an adult to accompany the children as there were Argentine soldiers guarding the area.

Rations and Water

The Cockwell family started off with plenty of food and water until they allowed 14 other people into their house. There was then a shortage of water but amazingly not food. The food they had was mostly meat, potatoes and vegetables. As the Argentine soldiers had occupied the area they slowly ran out of water for cleaning dishes, having a bath and to drink. The water had got so bad to the point that the families had to share baths (separately). They still had plenty of food left when the war ended.

'Move and I Will Shoot'

One day the soldiers took everyone out of the house and led them into the shearing shed. They lined them all up and pointed guns at them and said in Spanish: "If you move I will shoot". As the adults weren't allowed to listen to the radio they used to take it to pieces and hide them around the house so the pieces by themselves would not look like a radio but broken pieces of machinery. Whilst the soldiers searched the house, fortunately they found nothing and allowed everyone back into the house in one piece. From that day on everyone in the house was scared stiff as this was a close encounter with their enemy.

What It Was Like as a Kid

There were eight children including my one-year-old Uncle. Most of them were around the age of four to six They were old enough to remember what happened but were still young so they didn't know what was going on. As the conflict carried on they grew more conscious of the fact that a war was on. My Mum said that she could sense that the adults were scared and anxious therefore she too was scared and anxious. Adam was six therefore he was the most spooked child there.

What It Was Like as an Adult

As an adult they knew what was going on and were absolutely petrified. But the adults who had children had to hide their fear, otherwise the children would get nervous or anxious and it would possibly turn into a mad house. Most adults came out of the war shell-shocked or depressed, for they had seen horrible things during the war. But the most heart-warming was the mothers always caring for their little ones and putting at risk their own lives to save their little ones.

Surrender: Returning Home

They arrived home one day after the Argentines had accepted their defeat. A Sea King helicopter had arrived to come and pick up the doctor, but as my Mum, Nan, Grandad and Uncle and six other people were trying to get back to Stanley, they offered them a free ride back home.

They returned to the old Woodbine Café and the house had been trashed; the soldiers had put a hole in the floor for an open fire and my Nan's cook books had been ripped apart and spread across the floor. As they lived in Fox Bay during the war no one was supervising the house and the house had caught fire and a man singlehandedly took all the furniture out of the house and put the fire out. They never returned to their old house on Davis Street and it has remained that way for all these years.

What It Was Like After the War

The soldiers had left Stanley in a horrible state. There were corpses lying on the ground and litter everywhere. Most of Stanley had been bombed and there were tents left behind. Most of the children were still too scared to leave their house as you can imagine because of the corpses that lie motionless on the ground. But they had to go to school eventually and therefore went to school and as you could imagine the children had a traumatic experience, but Stanley thankfully had slowly started to get rid of the litter and corpses. It is a more pristine environment now (2018). But we still remember those who fought with bravery.

****

Richard Cockwell, Falkland Islander

Extracts from Richard's diary 'An Interesting Life'

Unwelcome Invaders

In 1982, I was the manager of Packe Brothers and Co's farms at Fox Bay East, Dunnose Head and Packes Port Howard. Fox Bay was occupied, Dunnose Head was bombed by Harriers under the mistaken belief that the airstrip was being used by the Argentines and Packes Port Howard was where Captain Hamilton was killed.

5th April

The Argentines had invaded Stanley three days ago and in Fox Bay East on West Falkland we recognised that having a Government Radio Station and Post Office on the farm we could expect 'visitors'. Today ships had been seen off Fox Bay and later loud explosions were heard from out at sea. It was a calm and sunny day and everything and was quiet, but there was a tension in the air while everybody waited to see what would happen. We actually went picking mushrooms!

About 1.30pm a large helicopter flew over and landed behind the hill, so realising that something was about to happen, I made sure that everybody went to their houses and I walked out into the Bottom Rough Sheep Paddock (below the hill) and waited. After a while, I noticed helmeted heads appearing over the hill and became aware that there were a number of soldiers crawling towards me on their stomachs. They all had guns including at least two machine guns that were pointing at me. By that time I remember that a broadcast instruction on the radio had instructed everybody who wanted to contact the troops should wave a white flag. Unfortunately, the only thing I had in my pocket was a red spotted handkerchief!

Looking around I spotted a dead upland goose gander, so it having white feathers I picked it up and waved it at them! The majority of the troops stood up and came slowly down the hill towards me with their guns and the machine guns remaining pointed at me. The soldiers were visibly nervous with most of them having their camouflage dissolving into streaks caused by the sweat running down their faces! They appeared to be well armed with automatic FN rifles and the odd bazooka. In charge was a rather short but self-important looking officer bristling with weapons, including two hand grenades clipped to his chest, a pistol, a bayonet and a folding butt rifle attached to his belt.

He introduced himself as Major Minorini Lima and spoke very good English. (I later discovered that he had attended college in the USA). His first words after introducing himself were: '*My job is killing Communists, I hope that I don't have to kill you*'!

I could not recollect if I had ever been threatened with death before but I agreed with him. (Minorini Lima and I had an interesting relationship from then on but more of that later!)

After being interrogated as to whether there were any Royal Marines in the settlement and then trying to photograph me shaking hands - which I refused to do having seen a photographer recording what was happening - I was allowed to return to my house and family. When I went into the house, I found two very young and very nervous soldiers holding my two children (six and seven years old) against the wall at gun point with bayonets fixed. I regret to say that I lost my temper which made the soldiers even more nervous! I then discovered that other troops were making my wife lead them round the house at gun point and pushing her in to every room first. I summoned Minorini Lima and demanded that this would stop. It was this at time that I discovered that the troops could understand if you were angry or frightened, but if you spoke quietly and firmly they did not know how to cope with you! I used this tactic for the remaining time that we were occupied with frequent success!

****

Unexpected Visitor - Hector Hugo Luna

In 1982 Teal River was an "outside shepherd's house" belonging to Hill Cove station where a young couple, Paul and Dae Peck lived.

Hector Luna was shot down north-west of Teal River house on Friday 21st May. He ejected at very low level. His parachute was found in some sheep pens nearby and it is assumed that he made his way there to spend the night in what was very sparse shelter.

Late next morning, Saturday 22nd, he was seen approaching Teal River House, limping along very slowly. Paul Peck rang Tim Blake, the then manager of Hill Cove, to ask for advice. Tim asked him to offer help to the pilot. At Teal River that day were Jen Harvey, and Gerard 'Fred' Robson, a schoolteacher who spoke some Spanish, and they, along with Paul, collected Luna and took him to Teal River House. Dae Peck had been an auxiliary nurse at the King Edward Memorial Hospital in Stanley before she married, and she attended to Luna's broken right arm. His right knee was also damaged, but not broken.

Jen Harvey and Fred Robson brought Luna up to Hill Cove settlement. There were no roads then, and one can only imagine what the effect on a broken arm of the jolting of cross-country travel for several hours must have been. Upon arrival at Tim and Sally Blake's house at Hill Cove, Luna was given tea and then Tim helped him to get out of his clothes, some of which had to be cut off, and to have a bath. He then went to bed.

At this time there was only a single-line telephone between settlements on West Falkland, and the main communications to Stanley and East Falkland were by radio, the use of which the Argentines had forbidden. By dint of calling on the radio for some time saying who I was, where I was, and that we had a shot-down pilot with us and I would like to speak to a doctor, an answer came from an Argentine radio operator (at Fox Bay) whose English was quite good. Now at least they knew where the pilot was, although the doctor (an Argentine and speaking from Stanley) was no help at all,. So I took penicillin tablets from the farm medicine chest and started him on those. Luna was now coughing badly and I was afraid that he might get pneumonia.

Next day, Sunday 23rd, Luna seemed better and was able to sit by the fire in the sitting room. We were fairly sure that the Argentines would come to get him as soon as they could.

Hill Cove settlement is divided into two parts, the Point and the Top, about a mile apart. When the Argentine helicopter (dark green with a red cross painted on the side) arrived in the late afternoon, a group of heavily armed men jumped out and took up stations around the helicopter, while two or three men who we assumed to be medics came into the house. They carried side arms. At this stage a line of Land Rovers came over the hill from the Point where the recreation hall was and where a film was being shown – everyone wanted to look at the helicopter and see Hector Luna go away. This alarmed the guards round the helicopter and we were lucky that they did not open fire.

Hector Luna arrived back in Argentina safely. He was killed in an air crash in 1991 while practising for a fly past.

****

Christine Hewitt, Falkland Islander

Extracts from Christine's article 'Locked Up' published in the Falkland Islands Journal 2000 Vol 7

Locked Up - Goose Green Community Hall

When Argentine troops invaded, 115 civilians were locked up in the Community Hall at Goose Green on the 1st May. Everyone was very frightened. They were liberated by the 2nd Battalion Parachute Regiment on the 29th May 1982. Here are some of the people's memories:

Brook Hardcastle: The Argentine authorities told us we had been put in the hall for our own protection and we had nothing to fear;

they had come to free us from colonialism. We thought we were to be used as hostages and so worried about our future.

June McMullen Not having a bath or change of clothes. No privacy. Not being able to go for a walk or listen to the radio. I was also scared that Matthew, who was only four months old, would become sick as conditions in the Hall were far from hygienic for a small baby to be in. It was also a struggle to keep his clothes washed and to get them dry. Hearing the '*Sheffield*' had been sunk was one of the worst moments. I realised then that perhaps the Argies could do the Task Force some serious damage.

Amy Pole-Evans We were let out for a few minutes each day and chased around in a circle for some exercise, but we were not allowed to make any noise. It was very difficult to keep clean - but we all were feeling smelly and dirty. The children were all very good as they were stuck in with very little to do - we played cards and had a few board games to play. Some of the Argentines were very scared and when they were guarding you with a gun in their hand you did not know if they might shoot you. On the night of the fighting we slept under the floor and I think that for me that was one of the most frightening times of all.

Eileen Jaffray Overcrowding - scared - and after being outside for 10 minutes the Hall was very smelly.

Brian Hewitt Having to get used to small meals in the beginning, as we had to make the food last. Getting shot at when going out to round up sheep to kill for mutton, then being arrested and flown back to Goose Green in the Argentine helicopter. Towards the end there were constant naval bombardments. We had to make the best of a bad situation. After the radio was repaired it was good to listen to BBC news. The children learned not to be fussy with food. We watched the Paras advance on Goose Green and watched the old Darwin School burn down in minutes after a mortar attack.

Patricia Gray Living with 114 people in such a small room was not pleasant. We had to try and get food and blankets. We had very little water so we couldn't wash ourselves. We used water for the toilets and to clean our clothes whenever it was possible.

Paula Pole-Evans I remember being very scared. We had Argies guarding the hall all of the time. No one knew how long we would be there for or what would happen to us. The night that the British came and we all slept under the floor. We could hear all the guns and bombs going off and thinking the next bomb could hit us.

Tony McMullen I was the blackout man. There is a spire in the hall. I used to get up there each night and make sure that no light was getting out. One day the Argies came in the hall, put us up one end, took us into the billiard room a couple at a time and searched us. They thought that we were transmitting to the British and they were looking for a transmitter.

Kenneth Jaffray I remember Darwin School burning down. I can also remember an Argentine soldier being shot on the green. I remember the noise of the naval bombardment.

Ian Jaffray I remember the first day of the bombing of the airstrip with pictures falling off the walls and windows breaking.

Willie Bowles My memories are of learning Spanish fast and translating for the people in the hall. Explaining the problems to the Argentines and seeking medical help when needed. Obtaining food and drink as and when required. Trying to keep people calm and patient as much as possible. I was very busy. With hindsight and all the luck I was glad to be there. Faith, prayer and hope played a large part during the whole situation. It is a scar in your lifetime you cannot forget. The complete silence after the battle was eerie and the calm was an absolute relief.

Eileen Hardcastle Being surrounded by armed soldiers in the hall. Argentines filling a 40-gallon drum with sea water to flush the toilets. Thirty-four children - three months to 14 years and there being very few tears or squabbles amongst them. Many things were missing from our house, but I was delighted my engagement ring was found under the gratings in the wool shed where the Argentine prisoners were held, one month after we were liberated.

Shirley Goss What are my memories? Not good - Argentine forces parading around the settlement. Not being able to get out of the Community Hall to breathe fresh air for days. Not being able to walk freely anywhere for a long time in case of unexploded ordnance, mine fields, the mess the Argentines had left everywhere.

Lisa Jaffray We were allowed out for about 15 minutes a day to play football, oranges and lemons, things like that. We used to get counted in and out every time. I remember diving under the snooker table during bombing raids. When we went under the floor of the hall into the foundations, there was a little hole that we could see out of. I can remember five or six soldiers standing by the old milk shed - they always seemed to be there. I also remember that there were never enough toilets! When the English soldiers arrived, we children took around sweets and drinks to them, I can always remember seeing my first really coloured person. When we went back to our house it was like a pig sty. I think the Argentines must have wrecked it and dirtied it close to the surrender, as I'm sure no one could live like that.

John Pole-Evans I remember being scared, hungry and dirty. I was most scared during the air raids and when the Argies were firing at the British with the rocket launcher on the slide in the playing field as that was used to fire the rockets over the roof of the Hall. We didn't have much to eat and the water all had to be boiled before we could drink it. I only had a couple of baths and very few clean clothes. Whilst the Paras were fighting and the naval bombardment was going on just before the surrender, I was under the floor below the bar. I was very scared and did not think I would get out alive. I was relieved when the fighting finally stopped. I was glad to be alive, but at the same time sad to find out that some of the Paras had been killed. I will never forget the mess that the Argies had made in the houses and buildings.

Eric Goss My memories are of my efforts in getting food supply organised, keeping the settlement water supply going, passive resistance by turning water supply off to houses occupied by Argentine troops. Eventually being party to arranging the surrender. The wrecked farm. Broken aircraft and machinery of war was all over the place, and the general mess and filth. Accommodating the British forces in the aftermath of war. Clearing all the ordnance from the shearing shed and press well. Many dangerous items were removed by hand. Marking the minefields and making everyone aware of the danger of cluster bomblets that were scattered over the farm. Repairing the damaged houses took a lot of time and effort.

David Gray We were scared with very little food. Some people had very few clothes. We ran out of water and only had two toilets for all the people. We were bombed by Harriers and shelled by ships most nights. We slept on the floor with no blankets. It was a sad time with the death of young men on both sides and the agony and long-term effects of war. Some memories fade, but some people still have bad dreams. We are free.

****

Alicia Shepherd, (aged 11) Falkland Islander
Extracts from: the Falkland Islands Journal 2020 Vol 11

The Brave Battle 1982

I have lived at Goose Green since I was born. I now live part time in Stanley for school and get to go home on weekends and holidays. I love living at Goose Green. This battle happened to keep the Falklands and my settlement free, although my family and family friends were held as prisoner in the Goose Green Social Club. We all are so grateful for the sacrifice of 2 Para and other soldiers who fought and the ones who lost their lives.

Hazel Ford: I ate cream crackers, salami and a spoon of beans after that they made stew. The salami was from the store and hidden; they used to bring it in in pots. I slept in the hall on the floor. It wasn't nice being locked up. I was 26. Hazel also shared a story with me. She had to clean out the dog kennels and when the bombs went off there would be a fox hole. When she had done the dogs, she had an Argentine standing right next to her with a gun and the bombs went off and she had to get into the fox hole. She refused because there was a spider at the bottom of it and she was terrified so she said: "*I am not getting in there*!" After she tried saying *"No"* the soldier raised his gun to her head and forcefully pushed her into the hole. She also said they used to have a handheld radio that they had hidden in the club. Each family held a small part of the handset and every night at a certain time they would piece it back together to listen to the news and updates.

My family's story

My Grandad (David Shepherd), Granny (Elizabeth Shepherd), Aunty Sylv (Sylvia Shepherd) and Daddy (Colin Shepherd) were held as prisoners in the Social Club. They used to live at the dairy (as you come into the settlement you pass the dairy). Daddy and Aunty Sylv were only little 7 and 12; she said that it was such a horrible thing looking out the window and seeing soldiers fighting and dying everywhere, but daddy being a typical boy said he found seeing the soldiers exciting. They said they will NEVER eat spam and crackers again in their lives!!

They used to sleep in the bar. Grandad used to be marched to the dairy to get milk for everyone. He'd be taken by Argentine soldiers with guns! Their house was struck by a bomb and burnt down during the battle. They went home to rubble, almost everything they owned had burnt and gone forever. So sad yet they were so grateful to the 2 Para for saving their lives!

What happened to the pets and animals during the battle? Obviously, the people couldn't take their pets with them when they were taken prisoner. So they were left behind to fend for themselves. Sadly, when the battle was over and the people went home, they found most of their cats and dogs lying dead on the ground. Some people say the Argentine soldiers must've been so hungry that they ate the pets. Pet ducks and tame geese flew and swam across to the island to hide out the storm. Horses, cows and sheep were left to themselves and some sheep were also eaten by soldiers. Always in our hearts, NEVER forgotten!

****

Emma Neilson, (aged 11)

Extracts from the Falkland Islands Journal 2020 Vol 11

Pole-Evans Family in 1982 - Saunders Island

We tried to keep going as normal on Saunders, doing the everyday jobs on the farm. We had a twin tub washing machine for washing the clothes. I can remember during the War that one day the SBS soldiers came to the settlement. They had been hiding on the mountain above the settlement. They were watching us and checking no Argentine soldiers were there. They came and stayed for the night and then went back up the mountain because it was safer for us in case Argentine soldiers came. During the war we let people stay with us after Dunnose Head got bombed.

John Pole-Evans, Age 10 in 1982

When the Argentines invaded I was in Stanley. I was very frightened. I didn't know if they were going to shoot me or what was going to happen. Then on the 1st May the Argies took us and held us prisoner in the Goose Green Hall, where we had to stay until the British troops freed us on the 29th May. Just being so scared and not knowing what was going to happen to us. Then while the battle was going on we were under the floor, in case the hall was hit.

Whilst we were held prisoners in the hall we couldn't do much. I remember we had some packets of cards so we used to play cards, but most of the time we just wanted to see if we were going to get out. Some days the Argies let some of the women go over to the Galley (where the Galley café is now) to cook a meal for us, but I remember some days we didn't get food or maybe just a couple of crackers or some beans, we were all very hungry. Some days we didn't have much water to drink either. We didn't clean our clothes as we had no means of cleaning them nor any clean clothes to change into and, as there was sometimes no running water. Sometimes we couldn't use the toilet so we had a bucket for a toilet. We had no beds so we slept in family groups on the floor.

Lisa Pole-Evans, Age 8 in 1982

When the Argentines invaded I was on Saunders Island with my two brothers. We were staying with my uncle David and his girlfriend Suzan because our parents were in Stanley for medical treatment. I was very frightened. I didn't know if I would ever see my Mum and Dad again.

I was very frightened of the Pucara planes that came and flew really low over the settlement. We saw lots of planes flying around and some helicopters too. Everyone tried to carry on as normal, but we were not allowed to communicate with people in other parts of the Falklands (there were no telephones then, only two-metre radios or ham radios). We had some supplies in the farm store, but we had no idea when we might be able to get more. I had my 9th birthday on the 8th June. My Mum was not able to buy me a present, so she made me a complete set of bedding and clothes for my doll. It was very special to me and I still have it.

Also, on the day of my birthday, four SBS men, that had been watching the settlement for a few days, came and told us that they were there. We were very glad to see the British. During the war, we sometimes played outside, but I was very frightened of the planes, so I did not like it very much. I did not have any schooling, because the teacher was not able to visit.

Ginny Forster, Age 30

I was living at Dunnose Head farm in 1982 with my husband Jimmy, and our three children. Sarah, the youngest, was only four months old. We stayed at Dunnose Head for most of the war. I did feel frightened. We were lucky because the Argentines never did come to Dunnose Head, but the British thought that they might have been using the grass airstrip, so on 23rd May the British sent four Harrier planes to bomb the airstrip. Some of the bombs missed and hit the settlement. They damaged two houses, the little schoolhouse, the carpenter's shop and the farm store.

We left after the bombing and went to stay with friends at Hill Cove for a while to begin with, then we went on to Saunders Island until the end of the war. It was very frightening when the bombs went off. The windows in our house smashed in the porch and the door post broke. Tim Miller was in another house with two other people and he lost the sight in one eye due to getting shrapnel in it. We carried on with everyday jobs until the bombing, and we were able to carry on with normal things such as washing clothes in the twin tub washing machine. Once the store had been bombed though, we had no supplies so that's why we left then.

****

Liberation

Craig Lewis, aged 11
Extracts from: the Falkland Islands Journal 2014 Vol 10

Newhouse by Glamis

In 1982 the Argentines took over Newhouse and insisted that everyone in the outside houses went to Douglas. There was Billy and Clara and five older Stanley residents escaping the Argentines from Stanley. They all had to go into one house in Douglas which was very tight. At one point everyone in Douglas was escorted to the social club at Douglas by forty Argentine soldiers with bayonets attached to their guns. They were locked in the social club for four days. When they were released back into the settlement, Douglas Station had been vandalized and looted for anything valuable - mainly clothes.

The Argentines had taken all the food and vandalised everything in sight. In the years that followed, Billy and Clara found a lot of abandoned Argentine equipment on Newhouse land. There was ammunition, torches, batteries and wirelesses. The dogs would find hoards of equipment and the EOD (bomb disposal team) would be called out to dispose of it.

After 1982 there was a military base at Port San Carlos. The soldiers from the base would come and do regular patrols around the North Camp and would stop at Newhouse for a few nights. Clara would cook a large stew for them when they arrived and let them sleep on the floor inside. Clara and Billy would swap their home baking for the soldiers' compo. It was a change to their usual diet.

****

Keon Kennedy, (aged 14)

Extracts from the Falkland Islands Journal 2018 Vol 11

The Jaffray Family Experience at Goose Green

My family who were locked up in Goose Green Hall in 1982. On the morning of 1st May, British Harriers bombed Goose Green airfield where there were Argentine planes. A piece of a bomb landed in my grandparents' conservatory, next to the room mum and gran were sleeping in.

My family including my Mum, Grandparents, Uncles and Aunts along with Great Gran Ellen McCullum, who was 82, were then very quickly rounded up by the Argentine soldiers and locked in Goose Green Social Club as POWs.

We were put in the hall not knowing what was happening. We slept on the floor which was very uncomfortable. We were able to go home in the next few days to get 170 sleeping bags and blankets and some clothing but no personal belongings as we were under armed guard all the time.

There were 114 people locked up, with Great Gran Ellen McCullum being the oldest at 82. She slept on a camping bed to give her a bit of comfort as she suffered with hip complaints. Conditions weren't great. There were two toilets, one for male and one for females, two sinks and hygiene was very poor. Our main diet was one spoon of baked beans or spaghetti, one cream cracker and a slice of tinned meat, for a while, which was rationed. Our parents ate less so we could have more to eat.

After a while they allowed four women, who were walked from the hall to the galley (cookhouse) under armed guard, to cook hot meals for all locked up. The women rotated every three to four days. Once a day for 10 to 30 minutes, depending on the mood of the Argentines, all prisoners were allowed out for exercise within our boundaries, under armed guard.

We used to watch the Argentine soldiers have their meals through the window. They would take their helmets off, strip the inside out and put a scoop of yellow stuff into their helmets. They would eat it, then put the inside back in their helmets and put them back on their heads.

A decision was made when the battle for Goose Green started that everyone would go under the floor of the hall for safety reasons. When we got down the Argentine soldiers were posted at each exit so that no one could escape. Towards the evening most people went back up into the hall.

Watching the battle at night from the window was scary and amazing, with tracer bullets flying through the air. During the day we saw napalm being dropped on Darwin Hill, just below where the Para memorial is now, massive bright balls of orange yellow fire. During the battle Darwin School burnt to the ground.

Major Chris Keeble came into the hall late on the evening of the 29th May to inform us the Argentines had surrendered. The next day Major Keeble and the 2nd Battalion Parachute Regiment walked up the Green. They were greeted with cheers from very relieved prisoners of war.

We were able to go back to our houses once they had been checked by the Paras. We knew our house was safe to enter if there was a playing card nailed to the door. Our house was a disgusting mess. In the bathroom there was a 40-gallon drum in the middle of the floor full of used toilet paper. The kitchen was like a pigsty. They had totally destroyed or stolen our belongings.

The freezer had defrosted and had half a horse in it. Dad's garage was booby trapped with wire and a clothes peg attached to a grenade. The bomb disposal guys were called in to defuse the device.

****

Nathaniel Cockwell, (year 6)
From: The Falkland Islands Journal 2021 Vol 11

Last days of the war

The events happening on East Falklands made the Argentines at Fox Bay very nervous. After the British won the battle for Goose Green, they rounded up the civilians. Grandad explained: "They surrounded the house and came through all the doors with their guns and hand grenades. They rounded us up and put us in the shearing shed. The sergeant who was in charge – who was actually a decent bloke – had tears in his eyes and said, *"You must tell these people not to move as these men have been told to shoot you if you try to move."*

Life settled down again for a few days until the 5th June, when Fox Bay was hit by British naval gunfire. Granny wrote: *"At that point shells started exploding in the vicinity so we stayed put in our hole again. The children were excited - especially Adam who had slept through everything else. He made such a noise asking questions and making comments that we didn't hear much of the barrage, which was only about half an hour, spasmodic too. Some close, some further away."*

I'm sure Fox Bay West must have got some (shelling) too this time. We got another barrage starting at roughly 3am. Some of them were pretty close and each also was preceded by a starshell – quite a different noise. Daniel saw one of them hit something round the airstrip which went up in a sheet of flame – ammunition or petrol. They seemed very close and one of the last ones seemed to land very close – really shook the ground. Daniel woke us at 4.45am and said there was an unexploded shell in the house, so that caused a bit of excitement. It came through the roof in the dairy, ripped out a jagged long slot in the pantry wall (we were planning to demolish it anyway) missing the freezer and some cases of beer. The cans all looked all right on the outside, but the beer inside never recovered – every can just fizzed out when you opened it!,

The civilians all listened to the BBC World Service and heard about the bombings of *Sir Galahad* and *Sir Tristram* near Bluff Cove – it was difficult for them to hear about the deaths of the British men. In her diary Granny called it a "terrible, terrible thing."

Liberation

Granny described the news as "*A wonderful feeling, like waking up from a bad dream!*" She said it was also a sad time with many deaths on both sides and three civilians killed: "*We'll have to make a good job of it now, and never forget. It'll be so different.*"

Fox Bay was not actually liberated until the next day, on the 15th June. Granny wrote: *"In the morning a Lynx helicopter landed up on the Argentine helicopter pad and disgorged some Navy blokes. That was our liberation!"* Major Ewen Southby-Tailyour from the Royal Marines visited Fox Bay that day and, in his book, Reasons in Writing, he described the visit. He wrote: "*I had no time to bang on the door before it was opened. Even less time to say 'Hello Grizelda' and she was crying on my shoulder. How nice to be welcomed in such a way; unwarranted for I had done so little to help in their freedom compared with those further east, who were still suffering fearful privations and awful weather conditions*".

****

Brian Summers, Falkland Islands Defence Force

Audio transcript courtesy of the Falkland Islands Museum

<u>Liberation Day</u>

On 14th June, the news on the BBC was good and things were progressing well. However, we didn't know whether the Argentines on West Falkland would surrender or fight on, but we knew things were coming to a conclusion and we started to come back from under the floor. It was then Richard Cockwell advised us that the Argentines had agreed to surrender.

Next day a helicopter arrived and five RN servicemen appeared and took the surrender of the 300 Argentine soldiers at Fox Bay East. The surrender at Fox Bay West of nearly 1000 Argentines followed swiftly afterwards.

Weatherwise, it was one hell of a day – blowing, cold and wet – but it was our first day out for seven weeks, so we went out for a walk, but only for 10 minutes.

Another British helicopter arrived with Major General Jeremy Moore on board. He spent some time with us and explained what was happening. Not long after we scrounged a lift on another helicopter and flew back to Stanley and went home for the first time for nearly two months.

****

Nathaniel Cockwell, (year 6)

Extracts from the Falkland Islands Journal 2021 Vol 11

An Unexpected Visitor

Granny and Grandad's house was very full on the night of Fox Bay's liberation and even included some Argentine visitors. Granny wrote in her diary: *"Tuesday night was most chaotic – in addition to the Stanley people there were the five Navy people. After dark and quite late, although I can't remember the exact time, most of the people had gone to bed, when one of the Navy blokes came through to the kitchen and said, 'There's someone knocking at the door'.*

It was the Argentine Major and Captain Marina – they came in and produced a bottle of champagne and the Major said to Richard, *'I told you we would drink champagne on the occasion of the victory – the victory is yours – here is the champagne!'* This was so bizarre as to be almost unbelievable, but they came in and sat in the kitchen with us and one or two of the others and we all drank the champagne and toasted the British victory. Strange, strange thing."

Grandad and Major Southby-Tailyour went for a walk around the settlement. The Major wrote: "*The sight was depressing and mirrored that which I had found elsewhere. The community hall was a shambles and vandalised in the most repulsive manner. Human excreta in piles against the walls, puddles of urine, lewd drawings, smashed and broken furniture and fittings. Richard was visibly shaken. There was little structural damage, other than to plaster, windows and doors, but it was a disturbing sensation to witness such obscene abuse of a place in which a whole village lived, danced, drank and sang; in which couples married and children were christened; from where the elderly were buried; a place in which the Christian festivals were celebrated and which formed the focus for all that kept such tight communities together and vibrant.*"

****

Kerri Anne Ross, (Age 11)

First published in the Falkland Islands Journal 1997 Vol 7

'Lady, We are the Government'

When the British troops landed at San Carlos, every now and then they would pass messages over the radio as they neared Stanley. Then a few days before the surrender a call came through - '*The British Navy calling Stanley*' it was brilliant to hear them and they called every day afterwards asking to speak to '*someone in authority*' - nobody in the Argentine army would talk to them.

The RT station made history in the last few days of the war, as it was where the Argentines negotiated their surrender to the British. A couple of weeks after the surrender, normal hours of work started again. The radio was very busy and one day the Army was so loud on the farm channel that the operator had to ask them to move to a different channel as this was the Government channel for the farms to use. A voice came back over the radio saying '*Lady we are the Government!!*' But they did change channel.

For her services during the war Mrs Eileen Vidal, *'the Voice of the Falklands'*, was awarded the BEM.

****

Macaulay Middleton, (aged 14)
Extracts from the Falkland Islands Journal 2011 Vol 9

My Gran - So Far! Joan Eliza Middleton

On 13th June 1982, Dad and Mum went home around one o'clock in the afternoon after visiting Grandad & Nanny Coutts and found Gran under the table kneading the bread because there was lots of shrapnel landing on the roof of the house. Dad told her he thought it was time for her to go to the safe house next door but Gran insisted on staying where she was until the bread was cooked – and she did.

When the British soldiers poured into Stanley after Liberation Day, 14th June 1982, Uncle Gary, who was a Royal Marine, also arrived and brought a load of his mates to Gran's house to stay. They enjoyed Gran's cooking and just about exhausted her little old Servis washing machine.

After Liberation, Gran had British soldiers to stay at the house from the REME and other units. Gran also had RAF.soldiers based at Stanley airport up to the house to let them have a bath. Before they moved to Mount Pleasant Airport, they had a party at Stanley airport and presented her with a wall clock as a thank you.

Gran cooked bread every day for the British soldiers as there was no bakery for them when they first arrived. Even after a bakery was established, the soldiers still got yeast for Gran so she could make them bread. Gran is still a brilliant cook and she always has her cake tins full so that we have a choice for tea every day. Gran was a keen listener to the BBC World Service and when the 150th Anniversary for British Rule was celebrated in 1983, Gran knitted a thank you banner for Peter King, the main newsreader.

Gran has knitted all her life and says that her mother taught her. After the war she knitted hundreds of hats for soldiers and their families back home. She has also knitted lots and lots of sweaters over the years for her grandchildren. Many of the sweaters had cartoons or pictures that were popular at the time on them. Following Liberation and the opening of the Town Hall, Gran along with Betty Ford and Daisy McKay organized dances and raffles to raise money for the Forces.

****

Gerald Cheek, Falkland Islands Defence Force

End of the war

The end of the war came to us about midnight on 13th June. The news of the actual surrender was relayed to us by an Argentine Major. He knocked on the door...to report to his colonel and said the war was over and suggested we should take down the Argentine flag and replace it with the British one. As soon as the Argentine officer had left, the manager switched on his stereo record player and played some rousing tunes such as Land of Hope and Glory and Rule Britannia at maximum volume and we drank to British victory.

At around 9 o'clock next morning HMS *Avenger* came into harbour ... and a landing party came to take the surrender of the Argentines. Later that day, 14th June, a helicopter arrived carrying some senior British officers, including Major General Jeremy Moore, the commander of the British land forces. He was visiting settlements to see how people had fared throughout the occupation. We all had a cup of tea together briefly discussing the events of the war. An officer and two or three ratings from *Avenger* spent the evening with us, when there was a knock at the door.

The manager answered it and it was the Argentine major and his captain. The major produced a bottle of wine ... and he proposed a toast. He toasted the victory, the victors the vanquished and especially all those who had lost their lives and the many more who had been injured as a result of this totally unnecessary war.

****

Marvin Clarke, Falkland Islander

Surrender - Major General Jeremy Moore Visits

There was an air of very nervous hope that maybe, just maybe, the shooting was over, but nobody actually knew what was actually going on. Some time later word started to spread that a ceasefire and/or surrender was being negotiated, but no one really knew. Whilst I wasn't actually at the West Store, some time later there was a knock at the door, in walked Major General Jeremy Moore and his entourage, the surrender was signed the shooting war was over.

Later that night as tensions remained high, I found myself along with other volunteer firemen responding to numerous fires. It was soon evident that they were British forces, and that they were taking advantage of the fire to warm up and dry off. Pending further direction, after a brief chat, the fire was left to burn - '*it was deemed beyond our capability*' - so we returned to the Fire Station. That night and the next few days were spent responding to fires, many of which were now being started by Argentine forces, expressing dissatisfaction with their own chain of command, as well as the fact that they had been brutally defeated.

We returned to our own house, which we had just paid for several days before the invasion, cleaned up what was a mess, and got ready for the arrival of our first guest to be billeted with us. After dark there was a knock at the door, and from the shadows appeared our guest, the padre from 45 Cdo, Reverend Wynne Jones. Whilst somewhat nervous that we might not conduct ourselves in a manner appropriate to our guest, the padre very soon put us at ease, and what a wonderful and pleasant man he was. The first time I had encountered a military padre and we chatted for hours whilst he was billeted with us.

****

Aftermath

Once the surrender had taken place and the fighting had ceased, all the parties had one overriding desire – to get home.

Thousands of dispirited yet mightily relieved Argentine POWs were transported home by the *Canberra* to Puerto Madryn. The reception most of them received from the Argentine Government and people was of disdain and they became persona non grata, not dissimilar to returning Vietnam veterans in the USA barely a decade before. The injured were not met by ambulances on the quayside or afforded the necessary medical treatment or support.

The Falkland Islanders returned to their homes to find many in a state of disrepair, either from military bombardment, or from disrespectful occupation and wilful vandalism from the Argentine soldiers. Huge amounts of military hardware were strewn across the island, with some of it booby trapped, all of which had to be cleared. Thousands of mines had been laid indiscriminately, requiring years of mine clearance activity by the British military. The last mines were cleared in 2018, still causing casualties to that date.

For those British service personnel on board ships, the long journey home commenced almost immediately. Others were flown home to the UK often via Ascension. On arrival at ports and airfields, they were greeted by thousands of flag waving triumphant and relieved families and friends. Great national celebration followed across the nation both with formal events at Westminster Abbey and grand parades as well as local or personal ones. For those injured servicemen, they began roads of varying lengths to recovery and rehabilitation. For some the scars, physical and mental, will last with them for ever. For others, lifelong friendships have endured.

Memorial services were held on the Falkland Islands to commemorate those who died from a large service in Stanley Cathedral, to numerous graveside services across the islands attended by senior officers and their men. The graves are still tended exquisitely by the Commonwealth War Graves Commission and are regularly visited by veterans today.

Politically, the popularity of the Thatcher government reached new heights and the PM was returned to power in the following year's general election with a landslide victory. Within a few days of the cessation of hostilities and the Argentine surrender, their president, General Leopoldo Galtieri, resigned to be replaced by retired army General Reynaldo Bignone.

Since the end of the war, the British Government has made huge investments in the defence of the Falklands to demonstrate their ongoing support for the Falkland Islanders and to act as a deterrent against any ill-judged future aggression. In 1985, RAF Mount Pleasant opened to handle all military flights on a longer runway. Some 50 service personnel have died whilst on duty in the Falklands since 1982, whether from a combination of accidents, land mines, other explosions and other causes, but none as a result of enemy action.

****

Neil Maher, Signaller, Army Air Corps
Courtesy of the Army Flying Museum

Proper Food and Promotion

Then eventually I moved over to Stanley, and I ended up in an old school which the Argentines had used as a hospital and went into what was a kitchen. We'd been living off rations basically, tin rations that had biscuits, no fresh food for a few weeks now, we went into this kitchen and we both spotted at the same time this piece of bread on the other side of the room, suddenly there was this big race to the other end of the room and I won. I got this piece of bread, and it went straight in my mouth, and it was gone. That's how it goes.

When we were in Stanley the OC came up to me and said, "*Right you are promoted now.*" He said, "*It's probably the first time since*

Korea that somebody has been promoted in the field, so we're promoting you to full corporal, Lance Corporal."

****

Andrew Lockett, HMS Endurance

Heading to Southern Thule

After the recovery of the Falkland Islands, Captain Barker, CO of HMS *Endurance* was then directed to carry out Operation Keyhole to remove Argentine personnel from a meteorological station on Southern Thule in the South Sandwich Islands just a few miles north of the Antarctic Treaty area. They had occupied the British Island from 1976. He chose to take HMS *Yarmouth,* RFA *Olmeda* and tug *Salvageman.*

During the stealth approach to Southern Thule on the 20th June 1982, I was able to inform the captain that the Argentine station had released its morning synop informing us of good conditions for our approach. It possibly suggested that we were not expected; however an inspection that followed the surrender indicated that the equipment at the station had been systematically destroyed.

HMS *Endurance* sailed from Southern Thule to South Georgia and then to the Falkland Islands where the ship took Governor Hunt on a tour of his islands. The photograph was taken during a ship's TV interview with the Governor at Fox Bay on the 22nd July 1982. The ship then made its way north to arrive at Chatham Dockyard on the 20th August where it received a tumultuous and emotional welcome from the Medway towns.

****

Alan Gratton, Steward, HMS Yarmouth

Prisoners on Board *Yarmouth*

My 21st birthday was spent on the way to Southern Thule where we took on board Argentine prisoners who had surrendered there. The prisoners were locked in the ship's company dining room so we had very little sight of them as they were guarded by the marines onboard.

****

Stuart McCulloch, Radio Operator HMS Fearless

Stanley lit up

Just before the final push on Stanley there was a bombardment of the airport which, again without permission, I stood on deck with some others and watched. It was a dark night but the whole of the horizon in the distance was lit up with this light from the bombardment. Years later I saw a firework display that ended with a full set of exploding fireworks that lit up the sky and it just took me straight back there.

****

Peter Galloway, Weapons Engineering Officer, HMS Glamorgan

The Rapier missile system on the hill

When we were hit by the Exocet, we retired to the Tug, Repair and Logistics Area (TRALA) well to the east of the islands. The staff on board the repair ship, *Stena Seaspread*, worked wonders repairing the damage to our various weapon systems until we were ready to re-join the Task Force, albeit with a slightly reduced capability. However, there was one major problem, which could not be readily solved on the open seas and that was the matter of welding massive steel plates on the main deck where the missile had struck. After several attempts, it became clear that we needed calmer waters if the welding was to be completed. As luck would have it, the Argentines surrendered on 14th June and on the 18th we were able to enter San Carlos Water and anchor to carry out the repair.

On that day, it was a remarkable feeling to leave the confines of the ship and walk around on the upper deck. For most of us, this was an occasion for many firsts. The first time we had breathed fresh air for many weeks. The first sight of the Falkland Islands. The first daylight we had witnessed. The ship had been 'closed up' for action since well before our first action 1st May and it was a relief after about nine weeks of 'confinement' to relax and stroll around in safety.

****

Alex Manning, Assistant Staff Minewarfare and Clearance Diving Officer (ASMCDO) HMS Fearless

Surrender - or is it?

Although the Argentines had surrendered, everyone was keeping their guard up, not just then but throughout the whole Task Force for a good while afterwards, for it was not at all clear whether the garrison on West Falkland would comply, although they were required to (and did, thankfully), whether the Junta on the mainland would continue the war or whether disaffected pilots would attempt to purge the humiliation of defeat with an unauthorized last-ditch strike. Happily, this didn't happen and we heard on 17th June that the Junta had collapsed.

****

Gerald Cheek, Falkland Islands Defence Force

After the Surrender

The helicopter had a machine gun mounted in the doorway and this was manned throughout the flight to Stanley. En route we flew over the harbour at Fitzroy, where the two landing ships had been bombed on 8th June. RFA *Sir Galahad* was still burning.

Our families were not expecting us and the surprise of being reunited made the homecoming that much better. However, it was soon apparent that the residents of Stanley had suffered a great deal more than we had at Fox Bay. Stanley and surrounding areas were subjected to shelling by the Royal Navy almost every night. It was extremely fortunate we only suffered three civilians killed during these bombardments.

The airport could be described as a right mess. Hundreds of Argentine prisoners were detained along the sides of the runway in makeshift shelters, while preparations were being made for their return to Argentina. Many damaged aircraft, mainly Pucaras, littered the airfield.

Stanley had suffered quite badly with three houses destroyed by shell fire and many badly damaged. Ammunition and weapons together with a host of Argentine equipment, clothing etc littered the streets.

One thing I remember when arriving back in Stanley was the absence of house sparrows. Not one could be seen anywhere and they only re-appeared some months after the surrender.

****

Brian Summers, Falkland Islands Defence Force

Audio transcript courtesy of the Falkland Islands Museum

Back to C&W - Telegrams to Process

I resumed work at C&W almost immediately with Royal Marines alongside us. It was back to normal operations, but incredibly busy with over 3,000 telegrams processed in two weeks. British Telecom waived all charges. However, each one was painfully slow as the system only ran at quarter speed and even a short telegram of 20-30 words would take several minutes to go through.

****

Chris Clarke, Master, Europic Ferry

Danger of Ice

Somewhere north of South Georgia an entry in my night order book read *"The danger of ice is now greater than that of enemy action"* which is self-explanatory. We met the two southbound ships as expected and were able to land one Chinook on our deck. Now the weather took a hand when several days of Force 11 gales with a very rough sea and heavy swell played a part in delaying the rest of the operation. We subsequently received a signal informing us that the Argentine command in the islands had surrendered – the war was over!

****

Nigel Turner, Leading Cook on HMS Hermes

Victory Cake

News bulletins came regularly as the battling ground forces made progress and when news of the Argentine surrender came, a huge relief and sense of how lucky I was. My thoughts turned to home and family. But work still to do. It was a comfort not to have to sleep fully booted and spurred and maybe to have a can of beer to celebrate.

When eventually news came of the Argentine surrender, a huge sense of relief that we had survived and that I would see my family again.

I put an idea to Captain Middleton and his staff that I could bake a cake and it could be presented to the Falkland Islanders. The 'go ahead' was given. Close liaison with the catering staff to see what ingredients were available. Luckily enough dried fruit etc. was on board and three 12" cakes were baked in the captain's galley. A piece of seven-ply was cut and prepared for me by the shipwright shop 'chippies' to place the cake on. The cakes were then marzipaned and iced.

The cake was further decorated with baskets of marzipan fruit, and a penguin and bulldog motif designed by a fellow cook was wet iced directly onto the cake. It was a hectic few days between normal duties to get the cake finished and not knowing how or when it would be delivered to the Islands.

On Saturday 3rd July HMS *Hermes* steamed toward the Falkland Islands. The cake was loaded onto a Lynx helicopter and I was kitted out in cold weather gear, survival suit and lifejacket. HMS *Hermes* anchored. The Lynx was piloted by Lt. Commander Sear. On board were myself, Captain Middleton, Reverend Devonshire, Leading Airman Brown and a ship's photographer.

We lifted off at about 0830 hours and headed for Goose Green where the Captain wanted to see and pay his respects at the grave of Lt. Nick Taylor, a Harrier pilot shot down and the first to be killed in the conflict.

As we flew along the coastline the barren and bleak snowy landscape made me realise what the ground forces had had to endure. Bits of twisted mental could clearly be seen and again a sense of how lucky I had been. More detritus of war and twisted metal as we came into land at Goose Green. The strange sound of bagpipes welcomed us as we disembarked from the Lynx and were met by the Gurkhas. The captain and Rev. Devonshire were met by a Major and escorted to the grave of Lt. Nick Taylor.

I was escorted into one of the huge sheds, taking care to stay on the marked path as uncleared mines were still in the ground around the settlement. I had a scalding cup of tea and chatted briefly to the

Gurkhas and watched them going about their business and trying to stay warm.

From Goose Green we flew back over the snow-capped hills towards Stanley, where once again we thoughts of what the ground forces fought for and the conditions that they had to endure to liberate the Islands.

We landed next to the Government House where with help the cake was taken into the sitting room of the residence. We briefly met Sir Rex Hunt at the door but he was on his way to a funeral. We were welcomed into the house by members of the Islands Administration staff.

The cake was presented and later given to the hospital for distribution. A cheque for £1,500 was also presented from HMS *Hermes* ship's company to help rebuild the Islands. Photographs were taken and a tot was offered and warmly received as we stood around the blazing fire in the hearth - home from home - a world apart from the recent weeks living aboard a warship.

A further tot was offered and again gratefully taken and further photographs taken. I think the second tot had gone straight to my head - as the squint in my eye shows standing next to the captain and sharing an aside. I had not had a "tinny' since sailing from Portsmouth as I wanted to be always 100% alert at all times in case of any action by the enemy. After a successful welcome, presentation and pleasing hospitality we boarded the Lynx and flew back to the *Hermes*. Noticing the Union Jack flying from the flagpole, a warm glow was within me along with the reality of going back to normal duties and wondering when we would be sailing for home.

****

Jack Ford, (aged 5) Falkland Islander

Extracts from: The Falkland Islands Journal 2005 Vol 8

The Jetty at Kingsford Valley Farm, San Carlos

A bomb hit the jetty in 1982. It was repaired by the Royal Engineers. The jetty was used to bring rations and ammunition ashore. When the Scots Guards came ashore their piper walked them up the jetty playing the bagpipes. It was a calm day. The bagpipes could be heard all over the settlement.

****

Gary Mcilvenna, Royal Marine on HMS Fearless

POWs

In the coming days, we moved troops, vehicles and stores whilst the land battle continued and to our great relief the Argentines surrendered on 14th June 1982. After the hostilities finished, our main task was to transport Argentine prisoners on our craft to the *Norland.* The Argentines looked dispirited, their faces and hands black with dirt and appeared to me to be a well beaten army.

****

Nicolas Bracegirdle, DWEO, HMS Antrim

Dinner with the Governor

This story is not about war but it is a consequence of the conflict and may be amusing to some. It concerns the Governor and his wife Sir Rex and Lady Marcia Hunt who were reinstated to their residence after the Argentines had left.

We were lucky to be invited to dinner in our last days in the Falklands as we were very late to go home. Captain Brian Young DSO and several officers including myself were invited into Stanley and I think that we took the captain's motorboat into the jetty and were met by an aged retainer in a battered London Taxi. Upon arrival, we were warmly greeted by our hosts and offered the largest gin I have ever seen - about three fingers! Dinner was very cordial and we remarked upon the strawberries as we had had no fresh food for three months perhaps more. *"Did you like those"* asked Lady Marcia who continued *"Oh we got three in the strawberry patch!"* We silently gulped about the efforts of the brave Royal Marine sentries who had defended Government House at the beginning.

Lady Marcia then gave us a tour which included several bullet holes and also the visitor's book which of course included everyone since the start of the conflict. We saw the entry for "*General Menendez Governor of the Malvinas*" but under his name was a neat ruled line and then an entry 'Major General *Jeremy Moore Commander British Forces Falklands Islands"*.

There was absolutely *NOTHING* to say what had happened between the two entries!

We laughed all the way back to *Antrim*. I flew home from Ascension Wideawake airport as the Senior Officer of the advance party.

I left the ship with some regrets in 1983 and after all those months spoke to the 100 or so of the Weapon Engineering department to say goodbye and thanks. As I walked to the flight deck where the whole department were assembled, I found out my nickname from a WE JR who was late. "*Where are you going Jones?'* I asked. *"To say goodbye to DINGBAT"*, he replied.

Ah as an Australian, I now understand! *"DINGBAT"* is someone who has kangaroos in the attic! Thanks WEM Jones.

****

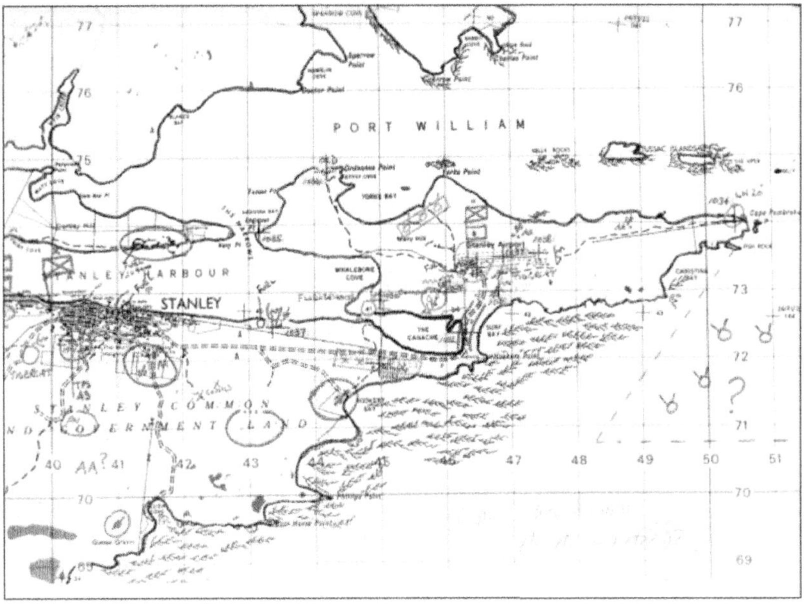

How Stanley looked as interpreted by our Int guys. Given to Lt Col Eve and me to make up a target list for the three NGS ships to bombard the airfield in daylight.

Intelligence map used by NGS to identify Argentine positions around Stanley.
Courtesy of Brum Richards

Rapier Missile launcher over San Carlos on 24 May.
Courtesy of Gerry Akhurst

After air raid at Ajax.
Courtesy of Ade Thorne

The Red and Green Life Machine.
Courtesy of Chris Nunn

Minesweeping – Armed Team Sweep.
Alex Manning archive

'Dawn of Victory' - I took from my action station on *Intrepid* just after dawn on 19th May as the Amphibious Task Group headed for its RV with the Carrier Battle Group later that day for a final cross-deck of troops and stores before commencing the run-in to San Carlos that night and over the next day, the 20th, the weather kindly helping us with low cloud and poor visibility (for Argentines). The night of the 20th/21st was crystal clear, however, as was the 21st itself - but we were in.

Alex Manning archive

Scout on the burnt-out deck of *Sir Tristram.*
Courtesy of Chris Nunn

The aftermath of Fitzroy. *Sir Tristram* beached and *Sir Galahad* still burning eight days later.
Alex Manning archive

Islanders in Captivity.
Courtesy of Neil Hewitt and the Falkland Islands Journal

Liberation: Neil Hewitt with the Paras.
Courtesy of Neil Hewitt and the Falkland Islands Journal

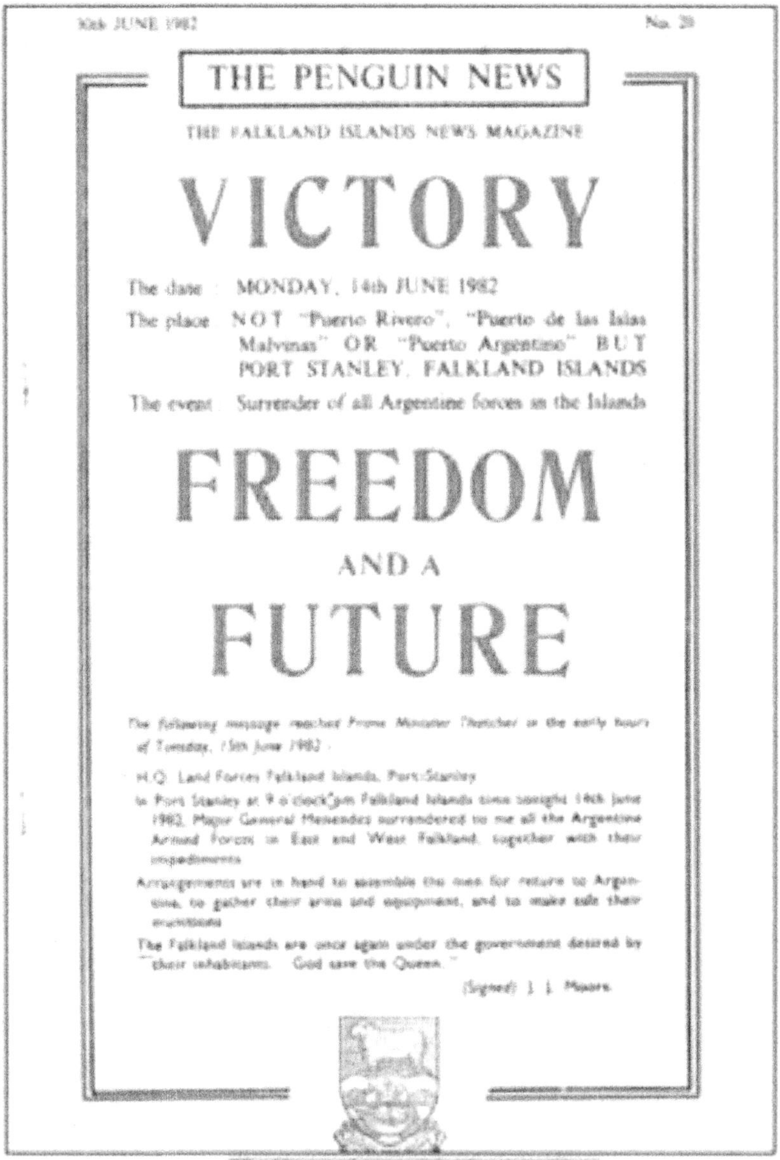

30th JUNE 1982

THE PENGUIN NEWS

THE FALKLAND ISLANDS NEWS MAGAZINE

VICTORY

The date : MONDAY, 14th JUNE 1982

The place : NOT "Puerto Rivero", "Puerto de las Islas Malvinas" OR "Puerto Argentino" BUT PORT STANLEY, FALKLAND ISLANDS

The event : Surrender of all Argentine forces in the Islands

FREEDOM

AND A

FUTURE

The following message reached Prime Minister Thatcher in the early hours of Tuesday, 15th June 1982 :

H.Q. Land Forces Falkland Islands, Port Stanley

In Port Stanley at 9 o'clock pm Falkland Islands time tonight 14th June 1982, Major General Menendez surrendered to me all the Argentine Armed Forces in East and West Falkland, together with their impedimenta.

Arrangements are in hand to assemble the men for return to Argentina, to gather their arms and equipment, and to make safe their munitions.

The Falkland Islands are once again under the government desired by their inhabitants. God save the Queen."

(Signed) J. J. Moore.

The Victory Issue of the Penguin News

The Penguin News was not published during the war as a lot of people went to camp. The Victory Issue came out on 30th June 1982 and had a cover designed by Joe King.

Courtesy of the Penguin News

The McLeod family with Capt Philip Piper and LCpl Les Berrisford at Goose Green.
Philip Piper archive

Some of the Argentine munitions strewn around after the surrender.
Courtesy of Ade Thorne

Mount Tumbledown overlooking Stanley.
Philip Piper archive

17th June - POWs waiting for ship transport. Discarded Argentine equipment. Globe Hotel Panhard, armoured vehicles outside. Smoke top left from overnight fire in Globe store.
Photo Eddie Bairstow

17th June - Argentine weapons pile, Mercedes 4x4, *Malvinas* sign, and POWs at Stanley Harbour. There was a similar pile next to it and lots of ammunition on the ground.

Photo Eddie Bairstow

Reverend Roger Devonshire; Captain Middleton; Sir Rex Hunt; unknown.

Courtesy of Nigel Turner

Leading Cook Nigel Turner and Captain Middleton showing the cheque for £1,500 raised by HMS *Hermes* crew in aid of the Falkland Islanders in front of cake.

Courtesy of Nigel Turner

FIQQ 1ZZ
May 2019

Dear Nicci

For years I have been going to write to you and thank you so very much for your book of years ago. I love the book and I have read it several times, as it relates to that August conflict. What you all did was wonderful, and I can't thank you enough. We, 22 of us were locked in one room for four days so we know what FREEDOM means.

The Invaders that locked us up cut the Telephone lines, took all our radio's and our 2 metre sets, so we had no way of knowing the Task Force had arrived and did not know ships were in San Carlos waters, and had no idea troops were ashore. Forty one Argentines ruled over us at Douglas Station.

If they needed me to go get them beer from the Farm Shop, I always had a Bayonet in my back.

When we saw the British walking over the Camp we thought it was more Argentines.

Its a long story. I don't think we have recovered.

Last week in a Cafe here, I saw a lady and gents at a table I guessed they were from M.P.A so I went over to them and said "I want to thank you for keeping us safe" They stood up, gave me a hug each, and said, "You have made our day" I said "You have made mine. I'm a Falkland Islander, born and bred, and I will be 96 in June."

We are all so very grateful to the Task Force. We love to see all who visit back here. More and more come, and we can't thank them enough.

I sincerely hope you will come to these Isles some day in a summer when you will be taken all round the Isles.

All sorts of free transport is layed on to take hundreds of Tourists to the Penguin Rookeries. Many cruise Ships come, spend all day. My address is No 20 Ross Road West, Stanley and you are always most welcome to my house.

I will close this scribble for now, and put it in Shirls Ockams envelope with the hope that Ossie Ockam can pass it on to you. All the 'Thanks in the World' for your part in 1982. God Bless.

Very best wishes always

from,

Clara. X

Letter from Falkland Islander Mrs Clara McKay to QAARNS Nurse Nicci Pugh.

Courtesy of Mrs Clara McKay and Nicci Pugh

HMS *Hydra* alongside SS *Canberra* on 25 May 1982. The sea proved too rough for a transfer of patients while alongside and the transfer was completed by ship's helicopter shortly afterwards with HMS *Hydra* underway.

Courtesy of Lester May

RAS (L) 2 Jun 1982 – HMS *Hydra*, RFA *Olmeda*, HMHS *Uganda* – the first underway replenishment for both hospital ships.

Courtesy of Lester May

Richard Nunn beside his helicopter on route south. It was in his camera and found after his death.

Courtesy of Chris Nunn

First Day Cover addressed to Lester May, signed by Commander R J Campbell RN, captain of HMS *Hydra*.

Courtesy of Lester May

Mass grave at Ajax Bay.
Courtesy of Chris Nunn

10th July - *Canberra*. Up Channel night. RM band who served in Falklands entertain embarked forces. A superb and very memorable occasion.

Photo Eddie Bairstow

11th July - Southampton. Part of the welcome boats (and blimp) for *Canberra's* return. Taken onboard *Canberra*. Embarked forces waving from the Starboard side.

Photo Eddie Bairstow

11th July - Southampton. *Canberra*. BBC's John Humphreys interviewing Brigadier Julian Thompson, Commander 3 Commando Brigade.

Photo Eddie Bairstow

11th July - Southampton. On board *Canberra*. Prince Charles meets Senior RM and Army Officers. Speaking with Major Rupert van der Horst 2i/c 45 Cdo Gp.

Photo Eddie Bairstow

Falklands Memorial wall, outside the Falklands Memorial chapel at Pangbourne College, Berkshire.

Courtesy of BMMHS

Clearing Up

Tony Pitt, Commander RFA Sir Percivale
Extracts from his personal diary

The Clear Up

Tuesday 15th June

RFA *Sir Percivale* anchored off Teal at 0600 hours. Received instructions to discharge maximum cargo, back load Amphibious Beach Unit (ABU) and Mexeflote and be in a position to sail overnight 15th/16th. We later received further information that we were to be used in Stanley as an R and R facility and this had to be achieved with only three days balanced diet remaining.

Wednesday 16th June

Cleared Port Salvador narrows at 0640 hours and proceeded to Stanley. We kept our fingers crossed that the stated minefield areas were correct and nothing had been laid in Port William (port on east coast of East Falkland). There was no sign of RFA *Sir Bedivere* in the area and at first light we turned into Port William on the final leg. The only vessel in sight was the Argentine Hospital Ship *Admiral Iridzar* which was at anchor to the west of Port William. We thought that RFA *Sir Bedivere* might already be lying alongside in Stanley but no, as we passed through the narrows at 1230 hours precisely, preceded by a V formation of helicopters, we realised we were the first to arrive and were very honoured to be doing so. We anchored off the public jetty and had our several blasts on the ship's whistle answered by the cathedral bells. This was a better day for the RFAs and the LSLs in particular.

Later in the day X, Y and Z Companies of 45 Cdo were embarked for R and R, all very dirty and tired. Relaxed water rationing for the first time since leaving UK and resolved to make them as comfortable as possible. We sailed from Stanley at 1930 hours bound for San Carlos Water and an important meeting for re-supply of provisions, both solid and liquid.

Saturday 19th June

It's not very easy to give R and R if there is no beer or minerals available. On completion of that task, at 1800 hours, we returned to Stanley and changed our R and R participants to personnel of 2 Para.

Monday 21st June

Retarded clocks three hours to agree with local time but also adjusted meal times to normal which meant an effective change of one hour.

Wednesday 23rd June

Emptied out Teal, recovered Mexeflote and sailed at 1230 hours. On arrival Port William secured alongside RFA *Stromness* at 1630 hours to finally top-up with provisions before transporting troops back to UK. On completion launched Mexe in Stanley and berthed on MV *Elk* to discharge remainder of cargo from Teal.

Thursday 24th June – Saturday 28th June

We sailed Stanley just after 0800 hours on Saturday morning for one last berthing on tanker *Fort Toronto* to finally top up. That was completed and we slipped at 1430 hours and set our sights for home. Officially hostilities were still not at an end, but we felt they were for us, although we continued to take sensible precautions to remain undetected keeping as far away from the Argentine coast as the weather would allow.

****

Brian Short – Royal Marines Bandsman

Extracts from Brian's book 'The Band that went to War'

Transporting POWs Home

With the war now won by the efforts of brave men at one end of a weapon, with the approaching southern hemisphere winter upon us, there was some concern about the welfare of the many thousands of Argentine POWs now held ashore. It took a few days for the Argentine government to eventually agree to accept their army home, but the details were agreed and *Canberra* loaded up over three thousand weary soldiers to take them back home. Some of them incredulous at being on *Canberra* as they had been told we had been sunk! The band took turns as armed guards for the prisoners, keeping order and helping secure the ship.

Flying under the Geneva Red Cross flag, it was with some trepidation that we were first met by an Argentine destroyer and then escorted into the industrial mining harbour of Puerto Madryn. Many hundreds of armed Argentine marines and soldiers lined the dockside as the gangway was lowered and the Red Cross officials began their administration. An Argentine general came aboard and asked our captain *"Where is the damage?"* another victim of his government's lies and propaganda. Having unloaded all the stretcher cases and walking wounded, one of the Argentines presented me with a signed *Canberra* menu card, thanking me [but of course us] for looking after them and taking them home safely. This was the feeling of most of them, but there was a plot to mutiny during their journey home, luckily reported by one of their sergeants and needless further bloodshed avoided.

****

Ade Thorne, RAF EOD
Extracts from my Falklands Diary

Searching for IEDs

15th June - POWs at Ajax Bay

Now back at Ajax. It still housed the hospital, but there were hundreds if not thousands of POWs. There were a load inside, and I can't remember if it was Dave or Tony who got the job of sitting in the doorway with a GPMG in case any of them moved. They all had P&O passenger level cards around their necks. A for officer, C for conscript etc.

18th June Arriving at Stanley

Stanley was a complete and utter mess. The Argies had totally trashed everything, and they had crapped everywhere too. The boss met us at the quayside, and he had managed to secure rooms in two houses for us to stay. The one I stayed in belonged to Romeu and Hilary Pauloni, whose son was in the RAF stationed at Kinloss. Our hosts obviously provided us with shelter but had no rations or running water.

So, our first job was to cordon off the Falkland Islands Company warehouses on the quayside to search for possible IEDs, whilst loading the landies with bags of flour, sugar, tea, spam and anything else we could blag. That, coupled with bags of peat to light the fires and get some hot water. They put an RFA on the dockside and we had to go down and remove all our clothes and jump into this big bath, basically a square of pallets draped in a tarpaulin filled with water, wash off, we all got issued a new set of DPMs. The old gear went for burning.

One thing I noticed was the amount of officer ration packs, with cigarettes, whisky etc, whilst the poor conscripts on the mountains got bugger all. Mind you, their boots were much better than ours. There were crude traps everywhere. The boss picked up a coke can and a grenade fell out of the bottom; luckily it was only a smoke grenade. Leaving Stanley to the Royal Engineers, our job now was to concentrate on the airfield. They needed the runway and operating surfaces clear to get the first Hercules in and establish an airbridge.

At first the airfield was full of POWs, but they quickly got moved on. The Vulcan might only have got one and a half bombs on the runway, but it made one hell of a mess everywhere else. There were about 20 aircraft of different types, some of which we needed to pull the ejection seats out of as they looked like they had been tampered with. The ground was littered with UXBs, fired shells and empty cases, rocket pods, missiles. You name it, it was there. There were British, American, French and Israeli made weapons. It took nearly four days of hard graft to clear the stuff away to the edges of the operating surfaces to allow them to bring in the Hercules.

****

Alex Manning, Assistant Staff Minewarfare and Clearance Diving Officer (ASMCDO) HMS Fearless

The Clear Up

The day after the surrender, work began in earnest for the combined mine countermeasures team. Chris was straight in to Stanley with the Commodore on 15th June requesting, and receiving, without demur from the Argentines, all their minefield charts and information about the mines themselves, which confirmed that there were only two fields, one off the eastern approach to Port William and one to the south-east of Cape Pembroke, involving contact mines only and, to our great professional satisfaction, within a cable of where we had reckoned they would be if it had been us laying them. Precise navigation warnings were flashed to all ships to replace the ones previously sent out that had been based on our own appreciation and we prepared to set up the sweeping task.

The biggest shock was seeing *Galahad,* only 400 yards away, still smouldering a full week after she'd been hit, with many bodies still aboard, a sobering sight.

Stanley

I can confirm that Stanley was indeed the mess at this time that most observers say it was. Not in terms of battle but of physical dirt and smell. It was a still, overcast day and the abiding smell hanging in the air, which I couldn't put my finger on at first (probably just as well, when I discovered what one of its main constituents was) was a combination of smoke (primarily peat but also charred wood smoke from a building torched by disgruntled Argentines), dirt and excrement. That the water supply had been affected by our shelling and the plumbing and sanitation were designed for a town of no more than 800-1,000 may have been one reason why there was shit everywhere (the Argentines numbered nearer 10,000) but ignorance, indiscipline and collapsed morale among the defeated enemy were almost certainly the bigger ones. I recall finding mounds of it inside the small perimeter wall of the memorial to the 1914 Falklands naval battle - deliberate desecration, possibly, but equally perhaps, a place where an ignorant peasant conscript caught short could crap in some degree of semi-privacy out of the wind. Many streets were littered with abandoned equipment and a major clean-up was already under way. The Argies were responsible for the mess, so supervised parties of them were being made to clean it up.

Another discovery was of a shipping container close to the road in the field beside Government House and of a warehouse near the Falkland Islands Company jetty that were both chock-full (and I mean chock-full) of food of every description from Argentina. A revealing discovery among it was the 2-tier ration packs they issued, a clearly substantial one for officers that even included a miniature bottle of whisky and an equally basic one for the rank and file. Unbelievable! No wonder they lost, despite the amount of kit they had (I saw 155mm and 105mm guns, AA cannon and missiles, armoured cars and Exocets) for it counted for nothing if they lacked what mattered: well-trained, well-motivated and well-led soldiers who knew their officers led by example and ate the same rations too.

The Falklanders themselves seemed to be keeping a low profile, coming to terms with all that had happened to them. Although maybe not outwardly demonstrative people, their gratitude was clear, with Union Flags and notices of thanks in many windows. One I remember was in the window of the LADE office (Lineas Aerolinas Del Estado, the Argentine airline that had provided the main air link to the rest of the world before the invasion). Underneath the company's name and logo set in the glass was a sign that simply said "Under New Management"!

A call into the small Kelvin Store brought an unsolicited and very welcome cup of tea and a chat with the owner and his wife. When I said that I hoped life hadn't been too difficult for them under the occupation they just said "*Oh, we just put up with it - because we knew you'd all come.*" It was a sobering experience, surreal almost, to be greeted and regarded as a liberator by my own kind, a source of pride too; and a determination surely, that we must never let such a thing happen to the Falklanders again.

****

Philip Piper, Gazelle Pilot, 656 Army Air Corps, aboard MV Nordic
Diary extracts: 'Musings from the Cockpit'

Transporting the General

14th June

At about 1100 hours today a white flag was seen flying over the capital of the F.I.s. The Argentine Army had eventually surrendered. Two hours previous to this the Argentine troops had been seen clearing away from their positions on Mount William and

Sapper Hill. The Argentine troops were cold, hungry and very dispirited.

We later learnt that there had been a mutiny in Stanley itself led by one of the Argentine Regiments. They had shot the officers and had gone on the rampage. I think this was a contributing factor to their surrender.

I was ferrying around Major General Moore, Commander of the Task Force, today and mine was the first British aircraft into Stanley; no big deal really. The locals were over the moon to see us and we seemed to spend the rest of the day shaking hands.

15th June

Again, I was taking the General around today. Spent the morning in Stanley looking around the capital. The town itself is in a real mess. Many of the houses have been ransacked and there is military hardware and trenches everywhere. We saw two dead bodies (Argentine soldiers) on the streets, which was not a pretty sight. It's going to be some time before they get this place back to some form of normality.

Took the General to the West Falklands in the afternoon, which was most interesting. The first port of call was Port Howard. There were over 1,000 Argentine troops having their weapons taken off them and then being herded off to the local wool shed. Within four days they will find themselves back in Argentina having been taken there by either the SS *Canberra* or the MV *Norland*. The Argentine troops can't wait.

The second port of call was Fox Bay in which the Argentine troops were even more organised. By the time the navy had arrived there first thing in the morning the Argentine troops had stored their weapons and were busy clearing minefields. They too want to get back home as soon as possible. They numbered about a 1,000 strong and were being administrated by a mere seven sailors, half of whom were sipping tea and quaffing shortbread in the homestead.

18th June

Took Deputy, Brig Walters to the Memorial Service at San Carlos this afternoon. The service was for all those men that had lost their lives in San Carlos. The Service, although short, was very moving. There was a solitary bagpiper playing at the end which certainly sent the shivers up my spine.

20th June

Attended a really good Memorial Service today here at Fitzroy. Sang some well-known hymns and had an oration from each of the Regiments that had lost men in this location. All in all, it was a very moving hour.

24th June

Eventually took the General back to Goose Green for a Memorial Service for 2 Para; again, it was a very moving service. The 1/7 Gurkhas were clearing up the trenches around Darwin today and one soldier tragically struck a grenade which exploded. It killed him and badly injured two others. What a tragedy after all they have been through.

25th June

Was supposed to be flying Brigadier Wilson, Comd 5 Inf Bde today. I took him down for a quick trip to Darwin for the memorial service for the Gurkha soldier who was killed yesterday. He was buried at Burnside graveyard next to the Harrier pilot that got shot down and killed. It was a very good service; had a trumpeter and a piper doing their stuff. It was good to see at least 20 of the locals present at the service as well.

The Squadron had another lucky escape today. Some of the boys were clearing out the Beaver hangar in Stanley in preparation for our move there. One bloke was busy shovelling rubbish onto a fire when he luckily saw a grenade on his spade! It could have been a very nasty incident.

All of the boys are well and looking forward to returning to England. Morale is high but I think the general tasking is eventually taking its toll and many of us are turning in much earlier now.

3rd July

The only good thing about today was that we managed to haul a piano out of the bowels of an Argentine freighter, the *Bahia Buen Suceso* that had been grounded at Fox Bay, having been shot up by Sea Harriers. We eventually got it up onto the deck and then Sgt Roy and his aircrewman L/Cpl Gammon flew it back to our Nissen hut underslung by the Scout helicopter. One of the technicians, Sgt Balchin, is now busily tuning the piano so I can now look forward to having some entertaining evenings!

By this time a lot of UK warships were moored up together in San Carlos Water and I remember very clearly it was a bit of a challenge to find which of these warships I was supposed to land on. All had removed their names which didn't help. I hovered behind a likely warship and asked over the radio whether she was HMS *Bristol* and after a slight chuckle was kindly told that she was two down from where we were! You live and learn!

****

Darren Yates, RAF 1(F) SQN ground crew

A Fortunate Scots Guard

It's a day or so after hostilities ended and I am with RAF 1(F) SQN ground crew main party aboard the MV *St Edmund* now anchored in Port William. Used for a sort of post operations clean-up and feed station to get troops out of freezing conditions. Anyhow my first buddy up was a Scots Guard and unknown to him he has had a fortunate outcome from the last battle on Tumbledown Mountain. A 7.62mm bullet head was lodged in his full magazine carried in the breast pocket of his hairy green shirt. I discovered this by my curiosity as there was a matching hole in same place in every garment he took off and I bagged for laundry. He didn't even know.

****

Post War Supply and Defence

David Drew, Senior Pilot, Hercules C-130

Hercules Airbridge to Stanley 1982 - 1984

July 1982. At that time, I was the Flight Commander Training and the senior pilot on the unit because the Boss and the other Flight Commanders were all navigators.

"*David, you know that four Hercules are being converted into tankers to assist with the effort of resupplying the Falkland Islands garrison and to provide air-to-air refuelling (AAR) to the Phantoms and Harriers to be based at Stanley for the air defence of the islands.*"

Operation Corporate had ended on 14th June and, like all Hercules (C-130) aircrew, I had spent long hours flying back and forth from UK to Ascension Island carrying supplies for the forces deployed on the operation since the beginning of April. Some Hercules, flown by crews mainly from 47 Squadron's Special Forces Flight, had operated south of Ascension and the "Airbridge", as it became known, had started on 24th June with the arrival at Stanley Airport of the first Hercules onto a short runway hastily repaired by the Royal Engineers after the Vulcan "Black Buck" bombing raids had caused a fair amount of damage.

The airbridge, flown entirely by Hercules as the only aircraft capable of using Stanley's runway, required at least two tanker rendezvous to refuel the transport aircraft for each daily flight against the wind to the Falklands. The trip back to Ascension could usually be managed without AAR. The only tanker available at the time was the venerable Victor, So, it was also decided to convert four C-130s to tankers to cover both the airbridge and the AAR requirement from Stanley; Nos 24 and 30 Squadrons would provide the operating crews.

"*I'd like you to lead 30's AAR effort*" the Boss continued. "*This does mean that you will spend much of the next two years based either in the Falklands or in Ascension. You can select your own crew but please don't take all the most experienced people."*

We knew that we would be among the first crews to deploy to the Falklands for four months, starting at the end of November.

Apart from refuelling the fast jets at Stanley, the C-130 had several other tasks to carry out around the Falklands. These included Maritime Surveillance – identifying and keeping an eye on all non-RN vessels in the 150-mile radius Protection Zone; delivering mail and supplies to the small garrison on South Georgia; other long-range surveillance and reconnaissance tasks around the southern part of the Atlantic Ocean and being available, if necessary, to refuel any inbound airbridge Hercules. So, our flying and training was intense, and also included practice in fighter evasion (we had no electronic warning or jamming aids so the idea was just to keep turning tightly so that any missiles would fly past!) and taking off from short strips at 20,000 lbs above our normal maximum weight. My logbook shows that I flew over 400 hours in the seven months since the start of Operation Corporate; we normally averaged only some 30 to 35 hours a month.

I set off for Ascension in late November. We then flew the airbridge aircraft down to Stanley, refuelling twice from Victor tankers. Luckily, the weather was kind and we had no difficulties with the AAR rendezvous or the arrival at Stanley on a gloriously sunny summer evening. Then reality set in.

With two tanker C-130s and three 5-man crews permanently based at Stanley, together with a dozen or so engineering staff, our detachment was small. The aircrew accommodation consisted of three 10-man tents, a small store tent and a large wooden crate, later christened "The Turdis", which housed an Elsan toilet. One tent was used as a crew room, one as the operations and planning room and the final one had ten beds in it; luckily, I don't remember anyone snoring! Heating was provided by an aircraft ground heater unit with its hoses running under the tent sides. Washing facilities were basic, to say the least, but the Mobile Catering Unit provided meals of a very reasonable standard and also provided our in-flight rations when we got airborne on the longer sorties [uh – pilchard sandwiches again!). However, after two nights sleeping in the tent, a crew got the opportunity to spend a night aboard MV *Rangatira,* a former ferry and sometime prison ship that had been requisitioned to act as an accommodation vessel in Stanley Harbour. Here we had individual cabins and a mess room and bar, so life every third night was relatively luxurious, even though we were 'hot-bedding' with our own sleeping bags.

My first trip to South Georgia took place on 21st December 1982. There was nowhere to land on the island, so the deliveries of mail and supplies had to be dropped into Cumberland Bay, to the south of the small military detachment at Grytviken. The packages were fitted with flotation devices and a small boat would then retrieve them from the water. Sadly, we were unable to reach Cumberland Bay which had become covered in a thick fog during our flight from Stanley. We returned the following day and managed to creep in under low cloud to carry out our drop. We normally carried a few passengers from across the detachment to give them the opportunity to get away from Stanley and to see South Georgia, and we usually took advantage of our visit to fly at low level to the glacier at the end of the bay to see some of the wildlife, mainly sea lions and penguins. On a later visit I also investigated the beaches along the northern shore of the island to identify a possible emergency landing strip.

Other highlights during my time in the Falklands included briefing press crews on our operations; leading a mixed formation of aircraft types for the BBC's *"Songs of Praise";* meeting Margaret Thatcher when she visited the island on 10th January 1983, making a two-minute phone call to my wife on Christmas Day and a mess dinner under canvas laid on for us by the caterers of the field kitchen. I have to say that my flying in that period was some of the most interesting and challenging of my career despite long periods of boredom and a lack of modern communications.

I completed my tour in March 1984 and headed off to the RAF Staff College.

Malcolm Smith, Commander on staff of Flag Officer Naval Air Command (FONAC) at Yeovilton.

First published in Jabberwock No. 104 August 2021

A Life on the Ocean Wave

When the Falklands war broke out in April 1982, I was minding my own business as a newly promoted Commander on the staff of Flag Officer Naval Air Command (FONAC) at Yeovilton.

In early June, after the successful amphibious landings on the Islands, it became known that Admiral Reffell would relieve Admiral Woodward in the South Atlantic as soon as hostilities were over. With this in mind, he ordered me and my colleague Geoff Cavalier, the Staff Aviation Officer, to go south to join HMS *Hermes* as an advance party of his staff. We travelled by RAF VC10 from Brize Norton on a lengthy flight to Wideawake Airfield on Ascension Island. The field was a dramatic sight, with VC10s, C130 Hercules and a Nimrod (all hastily modified with In Flight Refuelling probes) lined up on the dispersal. Also beside the dispersal was a mountain of boxed spares and equipment, optimistically addressed to the naval party there, to be picked up by deploying ships as they passed. Another old AEO friend of mine, Tony Woods, who had been sent there at the outbreak of war, pointed out to me in robust naval language that he had no way of knowing who the intended recipients of all this material were, while being bombarded with exasperated signals from home demanding to know why ships' demands were not being satisfied. He showed me one enormous package, which had split open and contained nothing but filing cabinets. Another smaller box was full of boots.

We had no time to sort out logistic problems because we were told to join HMS *Dumbarton Castle*, a smallish vessel normally used for fishery protection in the North Sea. She had a good-sized flight deck, on which was stored a huge quantity of equipment, spares and ammunition. There were thousands of rounds of ammunition, two crated Sea Skua missiles and a full Liquid Oxygen (LOX) bowser, intended for HMS *Invincible*, whose LOX plant was playing up. (LOX is used to provide breathing oxygen for Sea Harrier pilots.) Somewhat overcrowded and overloaded, *Dumbarton Castle* sailed south, occasionally exercising her main armament (a single Oerlikon on the foc'sle) on the way and breasting the enormous swells of the South Atlantic as easily as if she were off the Dogger Bank.

Eventually we sighted the grey silhouette of *Hermes* and a Sea King came to hover over *Dumbarton Castle's* flight deck and send down a strop to uplift Geoff and me one by one for a short trip to the carrier. Here we met the Admiral's staff, who, after months of high intensity effort in directing the naval war, looked tired and withdrawn. We were received politely but without warmth. I had a particular responsibility for engineering standards in the Wasp and Lynx flights in the accompanying frigates and destroyers, so started to find out how they had fared in the conflict. Over the following weeks, I was able to visit most of the deployed ships and discuss the recent conflict with their Flight Commanders and small maintenance teams, who were led in almost every case by experienced Chief Petty Officer Technicians. They had worked long hours in difficult wartime conditions and throughout the conflict had kept their aircraft at a high state of readiness and in commendable condition.

Meanwhile, back in *Hermes*, we learned that the old vessel was returning home almost immediately for a long overdue refit. Our Admiral would establish his staff in the Type 81 destroyer, HMS *Bristol.* Before *Hermes* departed, I spent some time watching aircraft operations from the Admiral's bridge, standing discreetly at the back, as Admiral Woodward was also present. We watched as a Sea Harrier made a decelerating approach to the port side of the flight deck, coming to the hover alongside. The pilot edged across to align with the landing spot, hovered briefly, then reduced thrust to land vertically with a thump. He taxied forward, obeying the signals from the aircraft handler. Admiral Woodward turned to me and said:

"Do you know anything about these aircraft?"

"Yes, sir, quite a bit," I replied.

"Humph", said the Admiral, *"I think they're bloody useless"* and he turned on his heel and left.

He was a submariner of course.

****

Tony Babb, Weapons Action Repair Team (WART), HMS Southampton

After Ceasefire

The ship held a farewell dinner dance at the Holiday Inn in Portsmouth. The cease-fire was announced at the dance and we were thrilled, although a few were gutted.

Summer is coming at home, and winter is already gracing the Falklands with the arrival of snow. No ships have arrived home yet, but we pass several battle-hardened veterans going the other way. Training for war continues as this last group journey southwards, calling in at the Ascension Islands. Now we qualify for Local Overseas Allowance, £1 per day for those on Operation Corporate.

Briefings told us that the threat was really from Argentine rogues who wanted to get their own back, and of course, the surrender was only on the Falklands. We still managed to hold a crossing the line ceremony, which was very well attended, and we had a couple of nice evenings with a sundowner's drink in hand.

As the islands drew closer, we changed into defence watches and prepared to do our bit. My job was in the Computer Room running the Weapons Action Repair Team (WART), and so started my first ever period of watch keeping.

Our first job was to patrol between the Falklands and Argentina, watching for them coming over the horizon. We were the first to do this and were selected because we had the best long-range radar. It was a huge improvement over the obsolete 965, and could differentiate between static and moving objects, which is very useful in the South Atlantic with its large flocks of seabirds and big waves. In the early days, the Task Force was suffering from many false alarms, which is why "Chaff" stocks were so critical, and this contributed in a small way to the loss of the *Sheffield*.

All the Rapier batteries around Stanley Airfield were out of action due to the winter weather, and we were needed back on duty to provide air defence. This was my only time off the ship from Portsmouth to Portsmouth, four months in all, probably similar for many in the RN.

The Argies never came back, but we kept looking. What did come back was all the foreign fishing vessels that had run away when the war started. Spotting an intruder was almost impossible; the helicopter (Monty) had to visually check each one, which made our job considerably harder. I now realise that fishing licences would be the saving of the island way of living.

The pattern of life was hard for me and especially getting some sleep. Our normal routine was to do system checks at midnight, which involved moving missiles etc. This pump was extremely noisy and woke me up every other night, right in the middle of a bit of shuteye.

On the other hand, we were at least dry, reasonably warm, could have a shower and were well fed, unlike the many others stuck on the Islands, in the middle of winter, with next to no facilities, so I think we were lucky, stuck in our tin can.

I did not even get to see the Islands during this visit; every time I went outside, it was dark.

Finally, we were given a date to return and HMS *Newcastle* relieved us. Their helicopter “Kev” after Kevin Keegan was unserviceable so they took ours and renamed it “Little Kev”.

****

Ordnance Clear-Up

At the end of the war, we went from hero to Zero as the ammunition left on board wasn't needed; however, the listed defence stores of pickets, barbed wire, body bags and formaldehyde were.

On the *Lycaon* we came under naval command, as such I was promoted in the field to 2nd Lieutenant RN. This allowed us to use the Officers Wardroom, and fine dining! At the end of the war, this caused a problem because Commander Stiles didn't want me to leave and as the ship's captain he had overall say.

4th August: I was summoned to the bridge with Capt Dick Gill on the other end of the ship's radio, as the war had ended: "*Why was I not ashore yet?*" – apparently there was a signal authorizing my release, Commander Stiles refused. Quote from D Gill "*We didn't bring you 4,000 miles to sit on that bloody ship*". Commander Stiles summoned ashore to explain. He came back smiling and said I'm to be released on completion of handover.

7th August: Went ashore. Was really the start of the clean-up of ammunition around the island. Majority of the work was Chinook orientated with underslung pallets. The clean-up was straightforward.

Cleaning up Port Stanley, there were numerous ISO Containers with all sorts of "goods" some from Argentina and some from the UK dumped ashore. One container contained knitted clothing and letters of support from Argentina.

I was 2417… Sgt Johnson, Ammunition Tech Class 1.
So I might have been the longest serving person to stay down there, in my Certificate of Service it noted: -

Op Corporate 4th May - 31st July,

Falkland Islands 1st August - 8th November 1982

Setting up Stanley Airfield Post War

Following the recapture of the Falkland Islands on 14th June 1982 a number of strategic requirements were identified. These included:

- The establishment and long-term support of a permanent defensive garrison
- Setting up an airbridge to resupply the garrison and to provide rapid reinforcements.
- The building of an airfield capable of handling long range transport aircraft and providing a base for Air Defence aircraft.
- The installation of an Early Warning Air Defence System to provide the Command and Control of the interceptor force.

Immediately after the recapture the Stanley airfield was restored to a useable state so that Hercules transports could fly in. The runway was extended using aluminium interlocking panels so that Phantom fighters could operate. Radio communications were installed and a satellite terminal was operated by Cable & Wireless. A long-range radar installed on Mount Kent provided cover for Stanley. East Falkland was then defendable. The Royal Navy retained a patrol off West Falkland to provide early warning.

The airfield at Stanley was too short to handle large aircraft so one of the first decisions, made by PM Thatcher in June 1982, was to authorise the construction of a strategic airbase. The location chosen was south of Mount Pleasant which gave its name to the base. This allowed a full military – army and air force – base to be established away from the centre of the civilian population at Stanley thus minimising the impact of the incomers on the traditional way of life of the Islanders.

Having selected the site, a ship was berthed south of Mount Pleasant to provide a deck across which other ships discharged their cargo. The process of planning the arrival of the enormous logistic delivery in the right order across the deck of a single ship was extremely complex. The first equipment went ashore in November 1983. This was for earth moving and a road was scraped across the peat to the airfield site. A vast convoy of equipment followed. Workers were brought to site by sea from South Africa and worked long shifts in an often unpleasant environment. A quarry was established to provide the required hard-core. Construction on site commenced on 31st December 1983. It took two years to erect the domestic camp, build the runway and a hangar and to install a complete set of airfield navigation aids, air traffic control [ATC] and the communications fit. A specially equipped Hercules was used to calibrate the ATC fit. A road was built to Stanley through the minefields.

We needed to provide radar cover looking towards Argentina. A long-range Plessey AR3-D radar was shipped to West Falkland and was unloaded by a Chinook helicopter and installed at Cape Orford. This allowed us to see out to 250 nautical miles, which part covered the whole distance to the Argentine coast.

It took two years to build the first phase of the Mount Pleasant Airfield [MPA]. On 12th May 1985 a TriStar brought Defence Secretary Michael Heseltine to land on the brand-new unmarked runway precisely where the automatic landing system had determined it should. This meant that we could now fly to the Falklands directly from Ascension Island without relying on air-to-air refuelling. A year later we had a fully operational airfield with all the military forces located at MPA except for the out stations.

Apart from the equipment of MPA with all its local electronic systems for air defence and air traffic control, I was engaged in establishing an integrated Air Defence System on West Falkland. Mt Byron and Mt Alice were selected as permanent radar sites. We had to build two complete radar stations which meant designing and building a full technical and domestic capability in ISO containers. The Royal Engineers built the sites and RAF signals staff, working with Plessey Radar, managed the procurement and equipment deployment.

For the concrete foundations we flew sand and gravel to the site in bags under a Chinook. It must have been the most expensive way of delivering basic materials ever invented. We needed water, sewage disposal, electrical power, a cookhouse, bedrooms, messing and workshops. Everything was fitted in 20-foot ISOs and the whole lot was taken by ship to the nearest coastal site from where it was lifted under a Chinook and flown in. If you ever want an exciting time try grabbing a rope hanging from a corner of a 10-ton ISO container as it swings in the downwash of the twin rotors of a Chinook. Why did we grab the ropes? So we could guide the container down precisely – within an inch – on to its supporting concrete base. The Chinook was operating right on the limits of its lifting capability. It could only carry 20 minutes of fuel so there was only one chance for the unload and if the aircraft was put at risk, the winch man would simply let go of the load and all our careful planning would be ruined as we had no replacements for most of the deliverables. We got Byron operating in 1984 and we then moved the radar from Cape Orford on to Mount Alice, which had also been prepared as a long-term base with a full set of life support facilities. Each site had a team of around 24 RAF personnel each serving four-month tours.

The Royal Signals established a line-of-sight telecommunications network across the islands. Relay stations on hilltops, manned continuously, initially required permanent manning and resupply from the regular helicopter shuttle service that serviced West Falkland sites. Life on the hilltops was grim in the winter. Progressively the comms network was fully automated.

Looking back 36 years later, all involved can take pride in the way in which a full military defence capability was installed on the other side of the world in a very difficult environment within three years. A clear political directive led to a well-coordinated civil – military partnership and a capability fully operational to this day.

****

Returning Home

Neil Maher, Signaller, Army Air Corps.

Courtesy of the Army Flying Museum

Return to Brize Norton

We were just counting down days to go home. Eventually it was our turn, so we all tipped up at what was left of Stanley airport, not a good description of it really but a building, in our battered combats and webbing, we were all wrapped up because it was the middle of winter. We got onto this Hercules that had been adapted with this great big fuel tank inside that would give it the range to fly. You could just smell fumes, but we were all just happy to be going, we were all wrapped up. We flew for, I don't know, 18 hours or something to get to Ascension Islands.

We landed there and it was quite amusing cos the tail of the Hercules went down, the ramp went down, we went to walk off, we were all lined up ready to get off as we'd been sat there for 18 hours in these bags and all this heat comes in, we'd gone from minus something silly to 100 degrees. We had all these squaddies coming off the aeroplane starting to strip off - what a funny sight that must have been. Then we waited for a [Vickers] VC10 to come and take us to Brize Norton.

It was a great surprise because no-one had told us but our family, including my new wife, was waiting there for us.

****

Alex Manning, Assistant Staff Minewarfare and Clearance Diving Officer (ASMCDO) HMS Fearless

Return to RAF Lyneham

I arrived at Lyneham around 0500 hours on 10th July, which I seem to remember was either the same day, or the day before, Canberra got home. I do remember watching that with great emotion so it may be clouding my memory by combining two close but different dates. Whatever, I was home, to a very happy and relieved wife and two happy but rather uncomprehending three year-old and one year-old daughters. If they are able to read this one day, Daddy's sometimes funny moods might make a bit more sense. A lot has been written since 1982 about lots of aspects of the Falklands War but very little about the naval minesweeping and clearance diving side. I hope that, in some small way, I have been able to put that right, for it is only right that the FCDTs and the little-known and unsung workhorses that were the MSAs and their crews are given their proper due. For my part I consider it an honour and a privilege to have worked with and been associated with them.

****

Ade Thorne, RAF EOD
Extracts from my Falklands Diary

Heading Home - Stanley to Swindon

We continued the clean-up for another ten days before finally leaving the Island on June 30th on the RFA *Sir Geraint*, straight into a Force 14 hurricane. It was four days before I even got out of my pit. Fourteen days sailing back to Ascension seemed a lifetime. One night, sat up on deck, I suddenly got hit on the head. Thinking it was one of them I turned around. Dave put his lighter on to reveal a flying fish flapping around on the deck. Suddenly another one, then another. In a flash the Chinese cooks were up and smacking the fish and putting them in a bucket.

All the way back from the Falklands there were daily tannoys about the spoils of war, and that an amnesty was in place. Loads of stuff was dumped overboard as a result, but not mine. I fully expected to catch the bus back to Wittering to collect my car and then drive home. A RAF policeman just said, *"Job well done boys. Enjoy your time off and go meet your families."* Little did we know, but Al, the Boss, had got everybody's families there. I had 28 family members in total. It was pretty emotional and overwhelming, for sure.

From there we went to my Auntie's house in Swindon for some good old bacon butties and a cup of tea. More importantly, a sit-down toilet with a flushing mechanism that doesn't rip your guts out if you don't move away quick enough, like there was on that bloody boat. At home, all the neighbours were out in force. The house was fully decorated with Union Jacks and RAF flags. It was really, really very humbling. Although to be honest I was knackered, and just wanted to go to sleep. Plus, all my good clothes were at Wittering. I was pretty grumpy.

Two days into my leave we were ordered back to camp so we could attend the memorial service at St Paul's Cathedral. Then in October we marched through London on the victory parade.

****

Mike Huitson, Portsmouth Dockyard

Aftermath

I witnessed most of the ships returning from the conflict. One of my strongest memories was when HMS *Glamorgan* berthed alongside North West Wall. Families were crowded on the dockside banners held high anxiously awaiting their loved ones.

With the crew stood 'to attention' on board and with the ship only 20 or 30 metres from the jetty one of the sailors broke ranks, removed his cap and hurled it like a frisbee towards the jetty. Within minutes there were sailors' caps everywhere including the water!

****

Simon Sugden, Weapons Engineering Mechanic Ordnance, HMS Coventry

The Queen Mother and Rule Britannia

As the day of our arrival was finally here, we couldn't believe the welcome that lay before us as small boats started to join us from a few miles out of port to escort us in. We all had to clear lower deck to take the salute from the Royal Yacht *Britannia* where Her Majesty the Queen Mother would receive the salute.

Then the moment we had been waiting for, we had our few belongings packed and we were ready to disembark. As a destroyer with a four-ring captain made us the senior ship which means we would be first off, with gangways attached and secured we finally were given the order to disembark. With the Royal Marine Band playing and the families singing *Rule Britannia* we were directed to the area where we would meet our families. As families hugged and kissed it was difficult to fight your way through the crowd *"Where were my Mum and Dad?"* Then suddenly I spotted my Dad then mum. We ran to each other, mum grabbed me so tight I thought she would crush my ribs. The sight of my Mum on that day troubled me for some time, in fact to be honest it still lives with me today, guilt is probably too strong a word but the image of this grey-haired woman before me was not the same woman I had left a few months before and I guess I felt I had caused these changes.

So home we went, the welcome home was fantastic although there was that uncomfortable label of "hero", I did a job I was being paid for I don't consider I did anything heroic. I saw people do heroic acts whilst we were down south, I did my duty but was no hero.

****

Howard Ormerod, Civilian previously on Atlantic Conveyor

Back in the UK - Was my offer of marriage still open?

Uganda's return to the UK was delayed a couple of times. When she finally left the South Atlantic, I received a telephone call from Liz – the first conversation we had managed for over three months. The question she posed was "*Was my offer of marriage still open?*" It was, and thus, with much help from families, I started making the necessary plans. But my interpretation of the question, as I later revealed on a BBC TV programme, was that it had thus been Liz who asked me to marry and not vice-versa. I'm still not sure that she has forgiven me; she certainly hasn't forgotten!

****

Jack Bedbrook RCNC, Managing Director HM Dockyard Devonport 1979-1984

Courtesy of his wife Sylvia Bedbrook

Return to Normal

On 14th June the Argentines surrendered, and on 24th June HMS *Alacrity*, the first warship back from the South Atlantic combat area, arrived at Devonport for repairs. She was followed by HMS *Arrow*, HMS *Argonaut*, *Atlantic Causeway* and the other ships which had acquitted themselves so well in the conflict. The merchant ships taken up from trade dispersed to their home ports while the RN ships were absorbed into the Dockyard programme for repairs and refit.

When HMS *Arrow* returned on 7th July, the Red Arrows flew overhead as a welcome gesture. This was a most moving sight.

The Dockyard, after its supreme effort, quickly returned to the state which existed prior to the Falklands Conflict.

It would be naive to contemplate that the exceptional spirit which prevailed in those three months could be maintained in peacetime. The war was over. The very clear and simple objectives had gone and had been replaced by less vivid and vital objectives.

The tremendous extra surge of goodwill and effort seen in Devonport dockyard during the Falklands campaign was spontaneous. With such a groundswell of enthusiasm, a clarion call for action by the Managing Director was not needed.

One may reasonably ask why the supreme effort evaporated as quickly after the conflict ended.

It would appear that freedom and principles need to be threatened before such an extraordinary response can be expected. It was comforting to know that in 1982 when the crisis arose, the Dockyard rose to the occasion and achieved exceptional results.

Epilogue

Great camaraderie has always existed between the Dockyard and its customers - the navy. This is especially so in time of war.

There was therefore a great sense of sadness that three of the ships we had prepared for war were sunk - HMS *Antelope,* HMS *Ardent* and *Atlantic Conveyor.*

****

RO(G) Anthony Lawrence, Radio Operator HMS Fearless

***Fearless* returns to Pompey**

We arrived back at Portsmouth on 14th July 1982, anchoring at Spithead at 0700 hours in the morning to ballast down and float the landing craft out of the dock. We could have gone alongside earlier but we'd had to wait overnight for HMS *Intrepid* to catch up as their captain was more senior to ours, (rank has its privileges!). Notwithstanding, the morning dawned a bit cloudy and misty, but nothing was going to dampen our spirits at coming home. Even at that time of the morning we could see lots of small boats and yachts gathering to escort us into the dockyard. We had a flying visit by the Commander-in-Chief Fleet, Admiral Sir John Fieldhouse, and the Secretary of State for Defence, John Nott, and then we were off, all crew that could be spared lining the ship's sides in best No.1 uniform.

As we got closer to the harbour entrance, the sun rose higher, clearing the mist and we could see the shoreline, from Southsea Pier to the Round Tower, crammed with people waving and cheering; and overhead a flypast by RAF Buccaneer aircraft and Fleet Air Arm helicopters, what an amazing spectacle!

As we passed Round Tower to turn into the dockyard proper, the cheering and waving reached fever-pitch. People filled every available space, even perched on roofs and cranes, all waving flags, banners and clapping and cheering. Boats were sounding hooters and sirens, the Royal Marines Band on the jetty struck up '*Rule Britannia*' followed by '*Land of Hope and Glory*' and the navy ships berthed in the harbour and the WRNS from the shore-base were all waving their caps in the air; even visiting American and Canadian warships joined in. I don't think any of us expected the scale of the overwhelming reception we received. It really did make you proud to be British.

As we got closer to the jetty everyone on the port side of the ship rushed over to the starboard side to try and spot their families amongst the hundreds of people on the jetty. Police and base staff had to hold the crowd back whilst the ship was moored up, with lots of frantic waving and shouting back and forth as sailors spotted loved ones and vice versa. Seeing my mum, dad, brothers and sister waving from the jetty amongst the crowd was a sight for sore eyes but none of us could hear what we were saying due to the noise; not that anyone cared – just seeing our families again was fantastic enough.

The gangways finally went down but before we could all go and greet our loved ones, a small quiet dignified party of relatives was escorted onboard by the captain's wife to meet the captain, commander and padre. These were the next-of-kin of the six crewmen killed in action on 8th June when the landing craft *Foxtrot 4* was bombed and eventually sank. A sad and long day for all of them and I don't think anyone who saw them was not touched by the poignancy of the moment as they disappeared inside the ship searching for answers as to why their loved ones didn't come home.

But for the rest of us it was a day of celebration and at last the permission was given for the crew to go ashore and meet the families and fighting my way through the throng I found my family. Hugs, greetings and tears all round. I could see they were all immensely proud of me and of the navy as a whole; but although I was glad to be back on dry land again, my euphoria was somewhat dampened with a feeling of extreme tiredness and overwhelming relief that at last it was all over.

****

Brian Short, Royal Marines Bandsman

Extracts from Brian's book The Band that went to War

Canberra is welcomed Home

Having dropped off the Argentines, *Canberra* was requested to pick up the many Royal Marine Commando units and head home as quickly as possible. It seemed the politicians were keen to make the most of the triumph, the public wanted to see us and as it happened, we were all very keen to get home! *Canberra* steamed as fast as she could and the atmosphere aboard was one of happiness, relief and tinged with sadness that not everyone was coming back with us. With military duties no longer needed, the band returned to their core role of musicians and entertainers. We played concerts, rock music, jazz and a young Royal Marine called 'Eric' accidentally invented rap music!

Our entry into Southampton was absolutely incredible, with tens of thousands of people lining the docks and thousands more the roads back to Plymouth. We played at several of the major thank-you parades and our unique role as medics, prisoner guards, and a dozen other jobs was recognised as being important. The troops also enjoyed our morale-boosting music and it cemented a bond between the marines and the musicians of that era.

****

Mark Willis, Captain (Adjutant of the 1st Bn) 7th Gurkha Rifles

Returning to the UK on *Uganda*

When the fighting was over, we all felt a big sense of anti-climax, but most of us also felt relief to be still alive and able to properly relax for the first time in several weeks. Our battalion spent about a month in Goose Green and in several of the settlements in West Falkland, helping to clear up the detritus of the war and return the local communities to normality.

Unfortunately, it was at this time that we lost our only fatal casualty of the campaign. A LCpl from our Signals platoon was killed by a previously undetonated rifle-grenade projectile while helping to fill in Argentine trenches near Darwin. Two of his colleagues were also wounded.

After a big farewell party at Goose Green, attended by Governor Rex Hunt and the British commander Major General Jeremy Moore (and which featured 1/7GR's Pipe and Drums beating Retreat in the snow!), we embarked on the SS *Uganda* (which had until recently been acting as a hospital ship), and made our way home to Southampton whence we had departed about three months earlier. Such was our short moment of fame. We didn't get a big part to play, but what we did was done with competence and done with pride. And we added a final Battle Honour to our Regiment's tally!

These days 7GR no longer exists. It was absorbed into the Royal Gurkha Rifles, which was an amalgamation of men from all the Gurkha regiments.

****

Aftermath and Home

There was rumour and counter rumour about how long we would remain on the Islands. Some said that we could remain for weeks or even months until a garrison force arrived. Without any warning, someone came into the shed and said that the FOO parties (Forward Observation Officers) would be leaving immediately on the MV *Norland* and sailing to Ascension Island from where we would fly back to the UK.

I made a miraculous recovery from my mystery illness. Brass artillery shells are normally a very tightly controlled commodity in the artillery since they were expensive and recyclable. Following days of bombardment, there were thousands of used cases on the gun position. After shoving a couple of shell cases into my bergan, we flew by helicopter into Stanley where we met up with some of our other FOO parties. All had shocking tales to tell of their own exploits with their respective infantry units.

We had a very boring voyage back to Ascension Island. Highlights were that the ship ran out of water when the desalination unit broke down, going to lifeboats stations in the middle of the night when the ship had a fire. The annual Airborne Forces night was celebrated with unlimited beer.

Many of us had weapons that we had *liberated* from the Argentines. There was an announcement on board to the effect that there would be an arms amnesty on board for 24 hours, we should label the Argentine weapons with our name, rank and number and hand them in. Once in Aldershot they would be kept in the armoury and could be used on the practice ranges. That night, when they had all been collected they were (wisely, in my opinion) tipped over the side into the South Atlantic.

I remember wondering how any of us would go back to a normal life after this experience. Sadly, to date more veterans have committed suicide than were killed during the conflict.

Home at Last

As soon as we arrived in Ascension Island, we boarded VC10 aircraft and landed back in Brize Norton on the 7th July and were met at the bottom of the stairs by Prince Charles. We were amongst the first troops home. I went home for two weeks' leave and was then called back to Aldershot to represent the Regiment in a West End show televised across the UK – the British Theatre Salute to the Task Force – an equally surreal but much less dangerous experience.

****

Brum Richards, 148 Commando Battery Naval Gunfire Support

***Canberra* back in the Solent**

On the morning of 11th July we came into the Solent to a sight never to be forgotten. There were hundreds of small boats to escort us home. At the dockside there were an estimated 30,000 people and my wife was amongst them. It was nice to be home. I later on discovered I was the only serviceman to have been involved in all three areas of operations namely: South Georgia, The Falklands and Southern Thule, not that anyone ever noticed. Well, why should they anyway?

****

Chris Clarke, Master, Europic Ferry

Return to Southampton of *Europic Ferry*

We departed from Stanley on 25th June *and* sailed for Southampton and arrived on 14th July to a tremendous welcome from our families, the company and our customers who lined the quay with their freight vehicles. We hadn't been forgotten! Our ship, which was normally at sea for voyages of nine hours, had been continuously at sea for three months in a hostile environment without a serious breakdown save nine days in Stanley.

****

Tony Babb, Weapons Action Repair Team (WART), HMS Southampton

Arriving Back in Portsmouth

After over 100 days in defence watches, we changed back to normal seagoing routine and the captain, God bless him, spliced the mainbrace, which is the picture. That was my first alcoholic drink since we had gone into a war state. This was just a part of my survival strategy which was to do my job to the best of my ability and try to influence my chances of survival.

We arrived back in Portsmouth, four months to the day after we left with a rusty ship, but who cares. Everybody wanted to be on the upper deck, including me and it was my first time on deck entering a harbour, that's in almost 18 years.

There were people on the Round Tower, just like when we left and our joyful families, waiting on the jetty in the dockyard. I only realised later how hard it was for them as well, the war, the worry and the helplessness they felt.

Arriving home without any port visits meant there was no way of acclimatising ourselves to civilian life. That was a real challenge, and my language was not what it should be for a few days. Fortunately, my wife understood and that's one advantage of being married to a WREN.

The flowers I had ordered for her had not arrived, I severely cursed the supplier in Jersey, and the perfume saved the day.

Captain Sam Salt of HMS *Sheffield* fame took over from Captain Argles for our next trip south, and some other *Sheffield* survivors joined as well.

You might think that this is the end of my Falklands War story, but in hindsight, my naval career was probably defined by the Falklands.

****

Stephen Potts, Military Police at Military Port Marchwood

Repatriation of Coffins

War ends! RFA *Sir Geraint* and RFA *Sir Percivale* arrive back at Marchwood on 23rd July. The band plays, the WRAC girls make a banner for the HK Chinese, and string it across the port headquarters building. It says "*Welcome Home*"in Cantonese. The ships are quickly off-loaded and an air of normality returns.

In the week RFA *Sir Lancelot* arrived back at Marchwood, one of the ship's officers invited me on board. He took me into the crew's mess deck and pointed out a welded temporary repair. He explained that a bomb had come through the side of the ship coming to rest in the crews' mess. *"It failed to explode, thank God"*. He also said that written on the side of the bomb was *"Made in the UK"*.

16th November 1982. 64 of the fallen repatriated to the port in a refrigerated container on board RF *Sir Bedivere* for reburial in the UK. The funeral directors worked from the customs sheds and a man from the Ministry inspected the engraving work ensuring it was perfect. Each coffin is draped with a Union Flag and has a single red rose on top. The hearses leave port one by one, including one carrying Sgt Ian McKay VC. The TV cameras are present. The soldiers on duty saluted as each of the hearses left the port. The effects of the war had come home to the port. I have never forgotten 1982.

****

Views from Across the Water

While events in the South Atlantic put the military and UK forces at war, those who were not involved or were only indirectly involved had a different perspective. Latin American countries generally favoured Argentine claims to the islands, while the USA gave indirect assistance to Britain but were always wary of alienating or diluting their influence in Latin America. The French were a major arms supplier to the Argentine military forces.

For people of British descent, in whole or part or indeed dual British–Argentine nationality, who lived or had family members living in Argentina around that time, there were mixed views as to the causes and the rights and wrongs of the Falklands War. The common theme suggests that whenever the Argentine economy was going through bad times, the Government or military Junta stoked up their claims on *Las Malvinas* to distract their population from the economic hardship as home. Such was the case leading up to 1982.

Forty years on, at time of writing, the Argentine Foreign Minister once more repeated Argentina's claim to *Las Malvinas*.

****

Gerald Seymour, Journalist and Author

<u>A Hack's Perspective - An Afghan diversion</u>

The British Embassy in Buenos Aires ('BA' to our diplomats) is a grand building sited on Dr Luis Agate, 2412, and is within a good whack of a polo ball from the Hurlingham Club, the prized watering hole of those with social aspirations. In the 'good old days', the Embassy was known for throwing most generous drinks parties. I was there in 1978 when Argentina hosted the soccer World Cup.

A First Secretary said to me, having just refilled my glass, *"You know, Gerry, Anglo-Argentine relations are bedevilled by the three 'F's."*

Gosh, I thought, this rather intelligent young man is going to launch into obscenities – wrong. "*You see, Gerry, the perennial problems are Football, and Foot and Mouth, and the Falklands.*" It did not seem too serious then and I, and probably many within earshot, regarded it as more an amusing quip than a serious warning of something desperately dangerous and life changing to so many.

For the football tournament – eventually won, of course, by the home country – the generals of the Junta strutted around, with chests carpeted by clanking medals, and accompanied by soldiers in uniforms that seemed left over gear from Ruritania. But there was, if you looked for it, a darker side to the military dictatorship, and a pervading atmosphere of fear and intimidation. I was then a TV reporter and seeing out my last days in that job and we were to film one afternoon a demonstration outside the Presidential Palace by the mothers of the Disappeared. Men and women who were thought to endanger the authority of the regime were scooped from their homes at night by the secret police, were tortured in secret gaols, were killed without judicial process, were dumped – many being chucked from helicopters far out over the deep wide waters of the Rio de la Plata: gone from sight.

They would be brave women who showed themselves on the pavements even when the regime was hosting a tournament attracting so many foreign visitors. We were watched from the big Falcon saloon cars by the hoods, contempt for us on their faces, but my BA based colleagues demanded one particular security precaution be taken for my safety and that of my European cameraman and sound recordist. The colleagues had slipped into a tall apartment building where they could film our every movement, watch us like hawks, so that if we had been lifted, had 'vanished', there would have been proof of what had happened ... that was Argentina, posturing and arrogant and sadistically cruel, in 1978,

Four years later, and I had swapped a microphone for a keyboard, and branded myself as an 'author'. When the Task Force sailed for the South Atlantic, I was in the Pakistan city of Peshawar, alongside the North West Frontier, the Khyber Pass. Up the road was a frontier and beyond it, the Russian army and airforce were engaged in a ferocious struggle to beat Afghan resistance into the dirt.

Some evenings I would slip out of the hotel and get a taxi ride to the villa occupied by a retired major from the Black Watch and would take a sip with him and try to catch up with events on and around those islands some 10,000 miles away. The major had a regularly refreshed crate of Johnny Walker, Black Label, and a massive radio with Short Wave access: from the radio came, hissing and coughing, the World Service of the BBC, and Radio Newsreel. The Argentine communiqués were released ahead of those from London, so the broadcasts told us only of fresh Argentine claims – gloomy stuff for me who had friends on the ships and knew some of those who would be yomping across country.

The Pakistani papers carried those BA reports with great prominence ... enough emphasis given to make me understand that much of the world would have a bit of a chuckle if the old British lion had his tail chopped or his nose bloodied. It was a time when you get to know your friends, the real ones.

So, while events unfolded on South Georgia and San Carlos and Mount Harriet, here on the other side of the world the Russians were sinking ever deeper into the Afghan quagmire. I fancy that our own politicians and generals, while rejoicing at the Falklands news, were tittering with laughter at the Kremlin's discomfort. It was going badly for the Russian military, and we were doing our damnedest to turn 'badly' into 'worse than badly'.

When not imbibing with the Black Watch veteran I used to go and take a beer with a Yank spook in his compound. He ran late night seminars for *mujahideen* commanders where he taught the tactics of evading, then destroying, the fearsome Mi-24 (Hind) gunships and handed out diagrams with shaded areas of the helicopter marked clearly and showing where they were vulnerable to machine gun fire, where they had no armour protection. The advice given was good.

One night, at a Brit hosted 'social evening', I met one of our people doing time here in the foothills of the Hindu Kush range. He told me that, a few weeks before, two Mi-24s had been patrolling over a rock-strewn valley. One had been hit by marksmen, disabled, and had fluttered down into a dried-out riverbed, and the crew were alive, and the tribesmen were creeping forward darting amongst the cover. The second helicopter for a short time hovered overhead and a decision was made by its commander. The full weight of their armament was turned on the crew of the downed machine. They were killed by their own people rather than have them captured – better, a sharp and brutal death.

1980 I had reported on the Moscow Olympics. Over a coffee, I'd talked with the KGB minder attached to the ITV crowd and we'd discussed his country's invasion of Afghanistan and I quoted Kipling to him: *When you're wounded and left on Afghan's plains, And the women come out to cut up what remains, Jest roll on your rifle and blow out your brains, An' go to your gawd like a soldier.* He promised he would immediately send those words to his intelligence chums posted there. While the Russians were learning the lessons of Afghan warfare, our marines were striding into Stanley. I was back home in time to see on TV the fleet's return to Portsmouth and the bunting was flying and the bands were playing.

I could not have believed then, in the elation of a surgical military success in the south Atlantic that less than two decades later our politicos and senior commanders would have failed to read the history books and would be returning to Kabul – had learned so little and ignored all the evidence stacked against a successful outcome.

In my office, I have a photo-gravure print of Lady Butler's picture, the Remnants of an army, showing the arrival of the army surgeon, Dr Bryden, at the fort at Jalalabad in late January 1842 - the only British survivor from the Retreat from Kabul not to have been killed or captured, the start of a long history of foreigners' failed involvement in Afghan affairs – the books were there and available, just were not read.

So, thank Heavens for the brilliance and courage of the Falklands campaign, a real jewel in the units' battle honours, a journey far away for us all to be so proud of.

Gerald Seymour was a reporter for ITN for fifteen years: he covered Bloody Sunday, the Munich Olympics, and worked all over the world, including Borneo, Vietnam, Aden, Israel, Russia and Northern Ireland. He is a full-time author and his work includes 'Harry's Game', set in Belfast.

****

Chris Nash, Anglo-Argentine born in Buenos Aires

An Anglo-Argentine Perspective

By many viewpoints the Falklands War was (as with many other military conflicts) the result of careless misunderstandings and political incompetence and miscalculation. It has been well-documented by many highly respected military historians, not least in Martin Middlebrook's excellent *Task Force* and *The Fight for the Malvinas* when he was granted full access to Argentine military resources and personnel.

However, there is one perspective on this conflict that has been overlooked and this relates to the impact of the conflict on the resident Anglo-Argentine community.

British interests in Argentina date back to the era of Spanish colonial rule when in the early 1800s South American liberals in London helped persuade Britain to try to wrest political influence and the associated trade monopoly in that region from Spanish control.

Two British military attempts were made between 1806-1807 to seize treasure and impose commercial authority on the Spanish colony. Thus conditions were set for a long period of strong Anglo-Argentine relations that reached a peak of commercial and social influence in the early 1900s. It is estimated that between 1900 and 1927 British investment accounted for between 70% and 90% of foreign investment and 80% of government loans. In addition to a massive expansion of the railway network there was British investment in new ports, water and sewage systems, power stations, tramways and food-processing facilities. Migration from Southern Europe (mainly Italy) provided the labour

Significant (and long-lasting) cultural influence of the British was achieved through the introduction of sports, mainly football but also rugby, hockey, tennis, polo, rowing - something that flourishes in the country today.

Although in 1914 the number of British residents in Argentina only numbered 30,000 out of a population of nearly 8 million (2.3m foreign born), their overall influence was disproportionate with British capital and investments dominating the economy. Pedigree livestock was imported from Britain with sheep and cattle farms established in all regions of Argentina. Falkland Islands sheep farmers were welcomed to settle in the bleak lands of Southern Patagonia and a flourishing British community developed exporting meat and wool to the UK. Production of meat on the vast *pampa* (the central region of fertile plain) was transported on railways, meat processing factories and shipping lines to Europe - all owned by British companies.

It is with this background that the author was born in the British community of Buenos Aires. Educated at St Alban's College in the southern suburbs where there remained a strong British ethos in the cobbled streets and Tudor-fronted houses in this part of the capital - a historic locality that exists to this day.

The College educational curriculum was set to Argentine standards in the morning and English Overseas Cambridge Certificate in the afternoon. This gave rise to some curious anomalies when Spanish was prohibited as a language in the afternoon and history with morning geography lessons describing the '*Islas Malvinas*' and in the afternoon as the 'Falkland Islands'!

The patriotic commitment of insisting that the Islands were the *Malvinas* and part of the territorial integrity of Argentina was a consistent theme during early school days.

Fast forward some twenty-five years and living in Boston, USA on a two-year work contract, the onset of the Falklands conflict appeared bizarre and unreal. The political posturing on both sides looked and sounded hollow on the international stage and showed a total disregard for the constructive and positive relationship between the two countries.

It looked like a sad and unnecessary argument about a remote island group where few Argentine citizens wanted to live and where the long-established British settlers lived in harmony with their nearest neighbour. In the early 1900s many Falkland Islanders moved to Patagonia in Argentina to establish large prosperous sheep farms. Many of the towns in this region had large British communities and commercial investments in wool and meat exports to Britain.

However political pressures on the Argentine government of the day encouraged a distraction from the constant economic upheavals and so patriotic propaganda was broadcast publicly to take possession of what had always been simply a historic territorial region of Argentina. The lure of rich fishing grounds and a possibility of finding oil in the surrounding seas may also have played a part.

This short account will offer small vignettes on the impact of this war on Anglo-Argentine families including one as a recruit into the Argentina military and another on the impact on a farming family in Patagonia.

Alan Craig was a pupil at St Alban's College and his recollections are quoted in Martin Middlebrook's book (p.52). Note that all those born in Argentina were liable for military service no matter what the nationality of the parent: *I was called back only one month after finishing my service. I wasn't going to go at first. I knew enough about the British forces to know what we would be up against; my father was a Mosquito pilot in the RAF in the Second World War, and my grandfather won the DSO with the Scots Guards in the First World War. My mother was Swiss so I was the first Argentine in our family. But my father insisted that I went and I reported for duty.*

Alan Craig became a conscript in the 7th Regiment on Mount Longdon and he provides a harrowing description of conditions in this bleak landscape comparing this to the trenches in WW1 He describes how many of the conscripts accustomed to the warmer climes of Buenos Aires, educated and from a good home suffered more than those from the slums who were used to rougher conditions.

After the surrender of Argentine troops, many were repatriated on the *Canberra.* The ship docked near the early Welsh settlement of Puerto Madryn and Craig then took a flight to his home town of La Plata. He was then released from military service.

Craig mentions another Argentine military recruit of British descent:

'El teniente Enrique Sylvester creo que es descendiente de Britanicos, piloto de Super Etendard durante la Guerra y entrenador mio de rugby'.

(Translated as 'Lieutenant Enrique Sylvester, I think, is a British descendant, he was a Super Etendard pilot during the war and my rugby coach when I was a boy')

Another Anglo-Argentine involvement in this conflict was the Blake family, long-established farming pioneers who managed a large sheep station near Rio Gallegos Patagonia opposite the Falklands which was the base for the Argentine Air Force 6th and 8th Fighter Groups.

Stuart Blake, now living in the UK and son of John Blake the founder of one of the many British sheep farms in that area, recalls the suspicions of the local Argentine authorities of the activities on their sheep farm. The tall radio aerial on the roof used for receiving the BBC Overseas Service was regarded as a means of passing on information to the British about the military activity on the mainland. It took a lot of persuasion and diplomacy to allay these fears.

Another story told to the author by a St Alban's College (SAC) school friend Michael Cassels is:

This supposedly true story involved an Argentine conscript by the name of Michael Savage (from the Buenos Aires, Temperley area and, I believe, an Old Philomathian (OP- old pupils of SAC).

Michael was returning to Argentina on the British Hospital ship *Canberra* (sic) and the Argentine prisoners were being processed. When Michael's turn came the British Officer asked him for his name to which he replied 'Michael Savage', a short exchange ensued, and then the British Officer gave a great shout that ran something like; '*Corporal Savage, come here a minute and meet another Savage, but one who speaks a damn sight better English than you do!!!*'

There is a further Anglo-Argentine connection: one contemporary OP from SAC now living in England is also called Allan Craig and has a distant connection with the Allan Craig mentioned above. This Allan Craig was born in England; his family were in shipping and he spent some time in Buenos Aires and studied at SAC. He was subsequently also involved with merchant shipping and sailed with the Task Force aboard the '*Atlantic Conveyor*' when it was sunk by an Exocet in mistaken belief that it was an aircraft carrier.

Then rather like the two Savages (!) above, the two Allan Craigs met each other on the *Canberra* on its way to Argentina!

One other OP of my acquaintance with a Falklands connection is Rory O'Regan who was temporarily based on the mid-Atlantic island of St Helena and worked on military broadcasting and intelligence gathering for the Task Force.

Hopefully these stories illustrate some aspects of our many communal interconnections and dependencies and maybe offer some guidance before generating antagonism over principles and alleged national 'possessions'.

Perhaps the last words should belong to Sub-Lieutenant Carlos Vasquez, 5th Marine Infantry Battalion:

'I have always admired the British, and it made me very sad that the only war I ever fought in was against the British'.

And also those of Second Lieutenant Augusto La Madrid, 6th Regiment:

'I think the British fought well; I had a sporting respect for them, just like opponents after a good rugger match, even if you have lost. But I have not lost hope that one day I might fight again in the Malvinas with better equipment, better training, and settle the debt for those of my men who died there'.

Sources: Martin Middlebrook, The Fight for the Malvinas; The Penguin Group, 1989

****

David Foot - Memories of the Falklands War

A Brit Living in Argentina

My first memories of the Falklands were from my primary school where I did all but one of the corresponding years at the Province of Buenos Aires.

Life in Argentina was not always easy for my British parents who registered my birth at the British Embassy, so that I have two nationalities. They kept this in this way: two sets of documents for us to decide, we learned English at home and Spanish at school, so we all spoke only English before we went to school. When I was very young my parents told me and my brother to shut up and not speak in the street *"because the mad dogs are out*" and that was it, '*shut up!'* That is one of my first memories of politics and the final times of Peron.

I remember it all changed one day and we were all happy and went to visit a fleet at the port and I was taken aboard an aircraft carrier. Peron had fallen.

At school, we had our subjects in Spanish in the mornings and in English in the afternoons. We would ask our English teachers what they made of what our Spanish teachers had told us earlier about the *Malvinas* claim and they would smile, but I think they never gave us an answer, we had to figure out that for ourselves.

I also remember one adult apologizing to me and saying that he didn't know that there was a dispute with "England" (i.e. UK). I believe I lived as the constant indoctrination worked its way through all the society of Argentina. Churchill once commented that "*They are telling them that the Falklands are Argentine*" but I think that few British politicians noticed this change.

When I was very young, this *Malvinas* poison had just only started to be put into the minds of the Argentines, and it wasn't so much of an issue when I was very young in the 1950s times of primary school. I noticed how it grew as I grew. In 1961 my family moved to Mendoza to the west of the country, close to the Chilean border.

My high school started in 1962 (Colegio Universitario Central) and the Falklands were taught, but I was respected and was never under attack nor forced to say what I didn't believe. The school started off originally taking Eton as a model, so as you can see England was admired in Argentina as well, but the poison of this invented dispute continued to grow with the bad governments.

When I was in my teens I wanted to join the Royal Navy but this was very difficult for me and my family was anything but rich, and at the time I would have needed a special ministerial dispensation and this regulation persisted until I stopped looking when I was about 20.

By 1982 I was studying electronic engineering, working at a private bank in a foreign department as Secretary to the Foreign Department Manager and would translate a lot of documents which reflected a lot of things including inflation of 100% and I could tell there were few countries or banks prepared to release funds for letters of credit to fund the collection and export of the Argentine crop by March 1982.

Close to the time when the war broke out, I distinctly remember friends from the University telling me that I should start calling the Falklands "*Falklinas*": there was aggression in the air towards

England to cover up what was going on inside Argentina, the assassinations, the economy: lots of things were all wrong.

A former high school mate who was an officer in the Argentine Armada (Navy) came to my place in about January/ February 1982 time to try and get me to join their navy because it was such a good future etc.! That really was a warning which I didn't understand: English speakers! To make matters worse I turned him down and I told him at that time that I would never do anything which could be construed as treason to my Queen.

The Falklands issue grows with the instability in Argentina: if things are wrong you can tell by the amount of times the Falklands are mentioned. In my view Galtieri, for that reason, confused internal politics with external politics and went into the Falklands at the worst possible time for the Argentine economy.

So, on April 2nd 1982 I couldn't believe my ears, I was terribly shocked and I told the Secretary to the Directory of the Bank (who was smiling at me that day) "*or you change Galtieri or we will do it for you*", this was another thing I later regretted saying. I used to go around with a British lapel flag on my coat all the time, and at the request of my mother. I took it off when the *General Belgrano* was sunk.

I was also Secretary to the British Society in Mendoza, at the time of the war. I was shocked to hear some in our community saying that they were with the Argentines, I estimated a 50:50 division but I never wanted to carry out a formal sounding. We were under an arbitrary dictatorship after all and they had no problem with assassinations in the illegal regime governing Argentina.

What I did decide to do was to go to Chile and offer my services at the British Embassy, but at the same time I wanted to tell them that the Royal Navy had to do its duty. Many in the Argentine's British Community were saying that there was much more than the Islanders and this should be taken into consideration before anybody entered into action.

I would have been so ashamed if the Royal Navy had returned without doing its duty.

After the war when I was in Mendoza I can remember Galtieri falling and talking to the Secretary of the Board of Directors who reminded me of what I had said to him, that the English would replace Galtieri. I was treated always well in Mendoza, but we had news in our community that in Buenos Aires it wasn't always like that towards the British.

Also, I remember on a day at work, a nationalist colleague shook my hands thanking me out of the blue about three weeks after the defeat. He told me that his young cousin told him that the British military had treated them so much better than their own officers, and at the time he had told him *"And we were fighting these people?"* I hope this is still remembered.

So there you are, that is me and the Falklands. This must be a truly different experience to that which most people have of the Falklands War, and I hope it helps build a larger picture of those times, I used to be a bit ashamed of part of our British community in Argentina and then I realised that most of what is reported by Argentina could have been deliberately distorted

My feelings towards Argentina have evolved after living in England such a long time. I returned to visit my family and friends in 1995 and 1998 but I was already feeling insecure and being a foreigner in those lands where I would once cycle, walk around and jump out of buses with confidence to go to school and work. On both occasions when I went there, I felt very bad crossing the border into Argentina and I have never returned.

****

Martin R, Argentine Serviceman

Rio Gallegos Military Base, 10th Air Brigade

During my stay in Rio Gallegos, during the conflict over the *Malvinas*/Falkland Islands and in my capacity as an Aerostar aircraft mechanic, I worked with the planes under my maintenance supervision and also flew with the pilots.

In the middle of the war, in June 1982, there was not a day when the aircraft were not brought together for different operations. While all six Aerostars and a C-130 Hercules were away on scheduled mission to the islands, and having waited for a period of time, we decided in the strictest secrecy to have a barbecue with supplies provided by pilot Vega, another "Volunteer".

As the family of this pilot had a general store in the city, he brought the provisions to be able to carry out the culinary mission. Guess how we lit a bonfire on the base and among the hangars? (Much as the Islands, Rio Gallegos is on barren land. No wood for fire): so we found models (mockups) of Mirage airplanes made of wood at the airport that were used as decoys. We got down to work, dragged one with a tractor, broke it down to bits and pieces and we had our fuel for our BBQ. Everything was OK!

Grill and salad also provided, we were on the final preparations ready to attack the meat when Comodoro Natalio Rodone, head of the base, appeared in an air force Jeep, who, alerted by the treacherous smoke, rebuked us to send us to the brink threastening to court martialed for "alerting the enemy"!!! (We estimate he was thinking local Indians!). The Islands are several hundred kilometers away.

However, before our court martial, we gave him a big apology, piece of meat in his hand, and once the fire was extinguished, he was invited to eat a sandwich (choripan). At first he strongly refused our offer, but food was scarce at the base and he ended up sharing the a*sado* (roast meat) with us. Several glasses of wine as well as whiskeys antifreeze was needed) later provided by pilot Carlos Prozeny, and under the condition of not committing such rebellious and treasonous acts again, he went away. The rebels in question were Ricardo C, Jorge R, Carlos P, Vega, Martin J, Lieutenant Alberto G and Jose Maria F. (See note below)

During that episode, the fat one (gordo) Rechea took ice off LV-MSN, since it was all frozen up, to add to his glass of whiskey.

Argentine Veteran Martin Sánchez J.

My dear friend Jose Martin (Pepe), who flew shotgun with me numerous times to the Falklands (including West Falkland), was a civilian aircraft mechanic, drafted in spite of being a Spanish national with a Spanish passport. He, as well as many other civilians, served with Fenix Squadron, a civilian "air force" flying civilian aircraft. After the war, Fenix Squadron has never been officially recognized.

Note: full names withheld at author's request

****

Thomas Wardle, An Anglo-Argentine Barrister living in Canada

An Anglo-Argentine View of the Falklands War

The British contribution to the development of Argentina, Chile and Uruguay was profound but mostly unknown.

After two unsuccessful invasions of Buenos Aires in 1806 and 1807 the British presence became pivotal in the development of commerce and trade. British capital developed Argentina. Widespread investment in starting businesses in the agricultural and commercial sectors flourished. The banking and insurance sectors were started by the British. The railways were built and maintained by the British until their nationalisation after World War II.

Along with this development came British settlers who worked in all these fields. The foundation of Anglican and later Presbyterian and Methodist churches followed. The staunchly Roman Catholic authorities, in appreciation, allowed Anglican services from 1824. St. John's Anglican Cathedral in Buenos Aires was consecrated on 6th March 1831.

Another important contribution was the founding of British schools mostly by the churches. These schools are still operating and provide the highest standard of education available in the country. Classes are now bilingual with classes for part of the day in English and the other half day in Spanish. Another major contribution from early days has been in medicine with the British Hospital in Buenos Aires and suburban clinics offering the highest standard of care. The British also developed sports clubs which remain popular in a wide field including football, cricket, rowing, tennis and sailing. On the retail commercial front there were many Anglo-Argentine and British owned stores with branches of Harrods and James Smart of Edinburgh. Harrods was well known for their afternoon teas, which has become an Argentine tradition.

Although a smaller minority in Argentina, the British community has remained together because they are overwhelmingly Protestant in a Roman Catholic country with English as their mother tongue. They have had their own schools, churches and clubs. However, they have mixed in the business and commercial world with their Spanish-speaking neighbours and are now bilingual themselves. Co-ordinating their activities has been The Argentine-British Community Council with an office in Buenos Aires, branches and a magazine.

The last thing which the Anglo-Argentines wanted was a war over the Falkland Islands. There had been British Government encouragement in the 1970s for closer ties between the Islanders and Argentina. Although reluctant and cautious about contact with Argentina, Islanders began being sent there to British schools and to the British Hospital for medical care in fields unavailable in the Islands. A new air service by the Argentine military operated between the Islands and the mainland. Before this time Islanders mostly went by ship to Uruguay. The Falklands issue was dormant until Juan Peron became President after the Second World War. His demagogic rhetoric stirred up the poor uneducated Argentines demanding sovereignty over the Falkland Islands. The Islanders wanted to remain British and the Anglo-Argentines wanted to be left alone to continue with their lives and their connections with the Commonwealth. Neither one wanted a conflict. It was a profound shock to Anglo-Argentines when the military government suddenly decided to become vociferous and make unrealistic demands of the British. Low level "negotiations" for years brought no changes.

I arrived in Buenos Aires in February 1982 to visit family members. The whole political climate had changed. The economy was very poor and the majority of the population wanted an end to military rule and free elections. The Falklands issue came to the forefront as a diversion. Hostile rhetoric mounted. Mass rallies were held in the main government square. Poor people were bused in to attend the rallies and many were paid to attend. Hateful and demagogic speeches by Government officials including the President Leopoldo Galtieri were broadcast. Demonstrations also took place by the British Embassy with the burning of Union Jacks an essential part of the rallies. Concerns grew that an invasion was imminent.

Fear spread amongst the Anglo-Argentines that they would be targets of unruly crowds and suffer personal problems. The daily English language "Buenos Aires Herald" gave all the reports and updated the readers about every event. Problems forced most of the Anglican churches and other "English language" churches to erect wrought iron security fences and gates to protect their properties. I was on a suburban train and was threatened by a fanatic who saw me reading The Herald. He shouted and told me to *"Go back to London"* and *"Live in England"*. Fortunately I left at the next station with assistance from a local young man. Other people suffered similar incidents. The Anglo-Argentines decided not to speak English in the streets and keep away from any controversy.

As tensions mounted the Anglican Bishop Richard Cutts, an Anglo-Argentine, held a special Lenten Evening Service at the Cathedral in late March. The largest congregation in many years attended. I was there along with other family members. People wanted to be together. Afterwards there was tea where the main topic of conversation was the threat of an imminent war. The irony of the attitude towards the Anglo-Argentines was that those causing the hated rhetoric mostly were post the two world wars. Italian and Spanish immigrants and their descendants whilst the British community had been settled there since the early 1800s and most of the current community members in 1982 had been Argentine born. They had as much right to be treated with respect as the later immigrant families.

I happened to be in south Argentina in late March as well at Rio Gallegos just across from the Islands. A large number of military aircraft were in the airport area and bustling activity. This must have been in preparation for conflict.

War was declared on 2nd April. Argentina had compulsory military service for young men. My family knew four young Anglo-Argentine men in the military reserves after their compulsory service. With family assistance they quickly fled across the River Plate to Uruguay to evade a call up for active war service. None wanted to be forced to fight against their "kith and kin". Several others also escaped service. Sadly a few of the Anglo-Argentine youth forced into combat died and their British names are engraved on the Argentine "Malvinas War Memorial" in Buenos Aires.

After the war declaration the military officials wanted Bishop Cutts to fly to the Islands and be the chairman of a town hall meeting in support of the Argentine takeover of the colony. He was also the bishop over the Islands. He did not want to go and had a telephone discussion with the Archbishop of Canterbury Robert Runcie who removed Cutts' jurisdiction over the Islands giving him a valid excuse not to travel to Stanley. Not satisfied the military demanded attendance from the Anglican, Presbyterian and Methodist churches at such a meeting with a prominent Anglican leading the delegation.

Our family friend the late Norman Mercer as the Chancellor of the Diocese was forced into the position as Chairman. The other churches were forced to send representatives. They were flown to Stanley where a public meeting was held in the Town Hall. It was a very raucous meeting with the Stanley public who attended. Norman and the others were forced to speak about their positive life in Argentina and the question and answer session after the speeches was tumultuous. The Stanley population made it clear that they wanted nothing to do with the invading Argentines. For Norman and all the delegation it was a traumatic and tearful experience. They rightly feared the consequences of the meeting and what next would be forced on Argentines. There were no further meetings.

Fortunately during the war most of the Anglo-Argentines carried on cautiously with their normal activities hoping that the conflict would end sooner rather than later. Many of their Spanish-speaking neighbours were sympathetic to their problems. There were indeed incidents against them but the Argentine middle-classes had little part in the problems created for their Anglo-Argentine fellow citizens. From Argentina's earliest days the British people were always highly regarded. A long-term expression amongst the population was "*la palabra de los ingleses*" which translated is "*the word of an Englishman*". The British community were trusted in commercial and personal matters. A Spanish-speaking friend whose son was a soldier and taken as a prisoner- of-war was so happy and relieved when news came that he was in British hands. Their family knew that he was being well treated by the British authorities and would be safely returning home.

There was great relief when hostilities ended. Two prominent Anglo-Argentines serving in the Argentine forces were Major Barry Melbourne Hussey and Commodore Carlos Bloomer Reeve. They were stationed in Stanley to assist the civil authorities and were very helpful to the population in protecting them from the more nationalistic and vengeful Argentine officials. They both helped to lessen tensions between the occupiers and the occupied. Neither one wanted the war. The most positive result of the conflict was the quick downfall of the military government who were completely disgraced. Many of their officials were later prosecuted for many crimes. Free elections were held and the country returned to a more normal life. Sadly the connections the Islanders had begun with the British schools and the British Hospital ceased after the war.

Most of the Anglo-Argentines with whom I speak still believe that it must be the decision of the Falklands people themselves as to their future and not a decision of either Argentina or the United Kingdom. Many Argentines have since visited the Islands and from personal reports all were welcomed and well treated by the Islanders.

****

Group Captain Patrick Tootal, OBE, DL

After a distinguished career in the RAF, Patrick Tootal became Defence Attaché in Buenos Aires in 1990 towards the end of his career.

Making Friends After The Conflict

At the end of March 1982, I was driving back from a West Country boarding school to High Wycombe with my eldest son, Stuart, for his Easter holiday.

On the journey the radio was full of reports about Argentine activities in South Georgia and speculation about a possible invasion of the Falkland Islands. On 2nd April the invasion became a reality and two weeks later I was on 12-hour shifts in Bomber Harris's old bunker, the UKRAOC, filling my war appointment. As Wing Commander Air Plans 4, my war role was as staff officer to the duty Air Officer on the bridge. I was able to observe the conflict at close hand. At times the outcome was a close-run thing. Little did I know then how Argentina would feature in my RAF career. Following the Argentine surrender on 14th June I was back at my desk in B Block as a planner and a few weeks later tasked to draw up plans for what was to become RAF Mount Pleasant.

I became the first Defence Attaché in Buenos Aires on the resumption of diplomatic relations with Argentina in 1990 towards the end of my career.

In August 1989, the director general of the Argentine Foreign Ministry, Lucio Garcia del Solar, and British Ambassador Sir Crispin Tickell announced in a joint communique that the two governments had agreed to hold talks in Madrid in October aimed at restoring diplomatic ties. These talks were to have a marked influence in what happened next to my career. A fallout from the talks was that there would be initially three key diplomats, the Ambassador, Deputy Head of Mission and the Defence Attaché. They wanted an experienced military attaché to be the DA so my Ambassador, Lord Nicky Gordon-Lennox, recommended me to Crispin Tickell for the post. After six months back in the UK for briefings and language update I was off to BA.

Before moving to BA, I visited the Falkland Islands for briefings and I was delighted to land at Mount Pleasant Airfield to see the fruits of my labours way back in 1982. I met members of the Legislative Assembly who, after questioning me as to why I wanted to live in Argentina, explained to me that despite the tragedy of the conflict, General Galtieri had done the Islands a great service. The Islands were now prospering with the fishing concessions and other developments having made the GDP per capita of the population the envy of many nations.

On arriving in Buenos Aires my first impression was, why did we ever go to war with Argentina? Everywhere there is evidence of the long historical association which our two countries had had. There is a British clock, the British schools are the best and the main railway station would not look out of place in London. The commuter railway stations are replicas of early Southern Railway stations.

When I in arrived in BA, it was agreed that we *"won't talk about the war"*. Alas even the taxi driver taking me to the British Embassy when he found out I was a new diplomat cursed the Junta. On my first day at the Embassy I settled into a newly decorated and carpeted office, but the cupboards had a mass of newspapers dating back to March and April 1982. In August my first caller was the chairman of the BA Branch of the Royal British Legion who asked me to approach the Argentine military to see if Remembrance Sunday services at St Andrew'athedral could be resumed. Many Anglo-Argentines served in World War Two and there are several ex-Service organisations including a large RAFA branch.

In the first week I called on the Argentine Chief of Defence staff. He made me feel most welcome. He readily agreed to my request for the RBL to resume Remembrance Sunday services and asked if the Argentine Armed Forces could be represented. On the day, the Cathedral was full, the St George's British School sang Amazing Grace and there was not a dry eye in the house.

My first Attaché visit in late August was to the Edeficio Liberatore then the Argentine Army HQ. When I arrived the attaché corps were lined up on one side of the huge foyer and Lt Gen Balaza, the vice chief of the Argentine Army, a Colonel who served with some distinction in the conflict, and his staff were in front of me. You could have cut the atmosphere with a knife. How was I going to be received? Gen Balaza came forward with his arms outstretched, gave me the Latin American bearhug, the *abrazo*, and said in a very loud voice, "*Whilst you are here, my house is your house*". This kind gesture by a very wise man resulted in my acceptance by the Argentine military and my fellow attachés.

From then on, I was fully integrated into the Attaché Corps and made to feel most welcome. I was even made treasurer of the attaché corps fund. Jokingly they assumed as a Brit I was honest!

Perhaps the most poignant moment of my time was early in the Gulf War. As the RAF Tornado losses were mounting, I received a call from the embassy reception to say the Chief of the Armada (navy) was in reception asking to see me. This is unheard of. Normally it is the Attaché who calls on the heads of the country's armed forces. I rushed down to meet him and brought him up for a coffee and alerted the Ambassador. The Admiral wished me to pass on his condolences to the Chief of the Royal Air Force on his losses. A very kind gesture.

As I have hinted the Falklands conflict was an unnecessary war. Had the wide-ranging recommendations of Lord Shackleton's report in 1975, which included the provision of a strategic airfield, been implemented in full the Islands would not have been easy to invade. The F&CO policy of "lease back" only encouraged the Junta, which was not helped by the chairman of the US Joint Chiefs of Staff allegedly saying the British military were only good at ceremonial. The projected withdrawal of HMS *Endurance* and the Nott defence cuts did not help either. The intelligence failings were significant. The proposed invasion was the talk at the restaurants on La Recoleta. These rumours were reported by the Embassy but discounted by King Charles Street (the F&CO). The greatest failure, of course, was that the Junta took no account of what action Margaret Thatcher would take. I had the opportunity to talk to a senior official from the Argentine Ministry of Foreign Affairs who said the Junta in 1982 needed a "*Golpe de Estado*" (a coup) to redress its poor popularity. A military takeover of disputed territory on the Chilean and Brazil borders was considered but in the end the Junta considered that the Falklands were the easy option. How wrong they were.

Before I close, I said I would revisit the Hurlingham Club some 45 years after my first visit. I was "volunteered" to be a member of the Ambassador's cricket team to play the Club's First XI. Alas we were heavily defeated. Once stumps were drawn, the party was great.

Glossary - UKRAOC United Kingdom Regional Air Operations Centre, F&CO the Foreign and Commonwealth Office, BAT British American Tobacco

****

Reflections 40 Years On

With the benefit of four decades passing since the Falklands War, those young men and women who participated in whatever capacity are now in or nearing retirement. Several have shared their thoughts looking back on the tumultuous events of those few weeks in 1982, which influenced and, in some cases, fundamentally changed their lives.

There is an overwhelming view from the Falkland Islanders and British service personnel that liberating the Falkland Islands was the right thing to do, but had British Governments been more forthright in their support of the Islands in the years leading up to 1982, the war could have been avoided.

The Falkland Islanders are truly grateful to the British forces that they sacrificed much to give them their freedom. Much sadness too that so many young lives were lost. For some who lived through those tumultuous days, there is a feeling of guilt, while a bitterness remains towards the Argentine Government of the day.

Minimal personal animosity exists between the military personnel on both sides with a respect particularly for the professionalism of the British forces and skills and tenacity of the Argentine Air Force. Over the years, friendships between some British and Argentine veterans have developed, while at the same time more nationalistic and radical factions still regard *Las Malvinas* as rightfully belonging to Argentina. Even in 2022, the Argentine Foreign Minister has reiterated this desire.

For many caught up in the war, however, there is sadness, that a war that cost nearly one thousand lives happened at all when it could have been avoided. For some, this book has given the opportunity to exorcise internal demons that have festered for over 40 years.

****

Geraldine Carty, QARNNS nurse on HMHS Uganda

In 1982, little did I know that I was going to be one of the "Famous Forty" naval nurses going to war on a schools' cruise ship, which was converted to a hospital ship in Gibraltar en-route to the Falkland Islands in the South Atlantic. I was a newly qualified nurse. Forty years on, I think of the members of the armed forces I looked after with my colleagues. I always watch the "Festival of Remembrance" as this reminds me of why I did my duty. You are always told, *"Never volunteer for anything."*

I dealt with lots of casualties and did the same in civvy street, ending up in a Mental Health Specialised Unit looking after casualties of war and members of the public. I did my Conversion Course and gained a DipHE Adult Nursing at the local college and UEA and felt that being in the forces gave me the confidence to do this.

The Falklands War, would I do it again? Yes, if I wasn't retired, after all, it was an experience I will never forget.

****

Dr John Burgess, Regimental Medical Officer 3 Para

In the Falklands War the soldiers in 3 Para understood why we were there and what we were required to do. We went, we achieved the aim and we left. We had faith and belief in our commanders and respected our politicians. Far too many died on both sides, but I personally feel we were justified in what we did. That feeling of justification makes the loss of friends, colleagues and all others feel bearable. The word honourable is often overused; in this context I feel it is justifiable.

****

George Birkett, Chief Engineering Mechanician, HMS Invincible

My wife was part of a group of wives who kept each other company during our time away. They did play a big part while we were away. To that end, we hold a reunion weekend each year which is a designated "Ladies weekend" at which we wine and dine our ladies as a thank you.

****

Chris Clarke, Master, Europic Ferry

If there is a lesson to be learnt, it must be the need for an island nation such as the UK to maintain a strong merchant fleet under its national flag ready to come to the support of the government in times of national crisis. Unfortunately, this lesson always seems to be forgotten as soon as the crisis is over.

****

Nicolas Bracegirdle, DWEO,* HMS *Antrim

We were a little ruffled but alive! We had one wounded and CPO Terry Bullingham had been blinded for life during an airstrike. His friendship is very precious to me after 40 years and we keep in touch. It is prophetic that his organisation (Blind Veterans) will receive a very substantial legacy from a late naval friend for whom I am executor but that may be fate!

There are many heroes involved especially 22 SAS who risked their lives on the Fortuna Glacier in South Georgia and who were rescued by the incredible flying skills of Lt Cdr Ian Stanley DSO and Lt Chris Parry. Some unsung ones were the crew of the *Stena Seaspread*, who patched up many holes whilst welding with their feet in sea water i.e. over the side. These included Chippy and the Buffer and Warrant Officer Mick Fellows DSC MBE.

One of my officers, Lt. Mike Bonney, was awarded a CINC commendation for amazing quick thinking as he and CPO Latham drained down the free surface in the Sea Slug traverser space after a 1000lb bomb destroyed all of the hydaulic pipes and fire main. Lucky it didn't explode otherwise all of us would have been dead. Many weeks later Mick and many others had the left-hand lanes of the Sea Slug working again and even the Vicar Revd Richard Sigrist was put to work cleaning microswitches - I am proud of all of them, especially the WE Junior Rates. I spent many nights in their mess deck ressassuring them - with the permission of the Leading Hand - of course.

****

Dougie Leask, LCA, Leading Caterer, HMS Exeter

The *Exeter* had an affiliation with the Falkland Islands as the cruiser HMS *Exeter* went into Stanley following the Battle of the River Plate in the Second World War to repair the ship and bury some of the dead. At the end of the conflict in 1982, the locals asked for *Exeter* to be the first ship into Stanley Harbour. We went in and went ashore where we held a memorial service for the Old Exeters from the Second World War.

****

HMS *Exeter* - Falklands Remembered

I've been asked to talk of the 82 crew,
And tell you of things that we went through.
A crew of young men, who became a team,
Whilst going through a time, you don't want to dream.

We were in the Caribbean having a ball,
When news came in, we'd got the call.
A ship's been hit, it's now a race,
You're needed now to take its place.

So off we sailed, suntanned and under prepared,
With trepidation, and a little bit scared.
Two weeks we had to get fighting fit,
And join with the Task Force to do our bit.

Her blue hull shining on the sea, *Exeter* stood out from the Fleet,
With battle honours that did her proud, she never knew defeat.
The River Plate crew from Thirty Nine
Had sailed this course… it was now our time.

Through troubled times she held us tight,
But we always knew… we'd be alright.
The aircraft came, they sent their best
But we chased some home and laid some to rest

They brought their Exocets out to play
But we stood our ground and won our day,
We lived to know the smell of fear and how it gets to you
We also learned that being a team works best to see it through
We'd played our part, the war was won,
The Falklands saved, that job was done.
But before we sailed we had one thing to do,
We were asked ashore, and Old Exeters, we remembered you!

Now through those days we made a bond, we'll never cast aside,
The old girl meant so much to all who walked her decks with pride.
She served us well, protecting all with honour and with valour,

To serve on board our blue hulled ship, it was our finest hour.

Semper Fidelis, *Always Faithful*, of that we still abide,
And when we meet, we raise a glass as we stand there, side by side.
We toast to all who sailed in her, and to all the *Exeter* crews,
But special thanks goes to the man, who saw that we got through,
The calmest man, you ever saw, who cared for all his men,
He'll always be our hero, Captain Hugh Balfour… (RIP Sir), Amen.

****

Clifford Ball, MOD, Royal Naval Supply

Following her epic achievement, I was privileged to be on board one of the leading tugs during her triumphant return to Portsmouth. The mass of boats, water jets, helicopters, crowds, sirens and flags thronging the Solent, Spithead and the whole of the waterfront had to be seen to be believed. It is a sight I shall never forget.

In total, 255 British souls lost their lives in the Falklands Conflict. That number included leading cook, Michael Foote, a family friend who lost his life at just twenty four years of age.

Michael was serving on HMS *Ardent* when she was hit amidships on 21st May 1982. Twenty-two of the ship's company lost their lives. The ship was captained by Commander Alan West who went on to become First Sea Lord.

Six hundred and forty-nine Argentines also fell in the conflict. I respect them all.

****

Neil Hewitt, 12 year old Falkland Islander in 1982

Over the last 40 years I have reflected a lot on the experience. I struggled to get the images out of my head and they drove me mad at times. The last 20 years have been easier and I feel very lucky to have survived when others died.

Andrew Cave, HMS Hermes

These are just a few of my memories from 1982 which are still difficult to think about, but I was one of the lucky ones, I came home. There were many of course who didn't. These are the real heroes who will never be forgotten. There were also of course many who made it home but had extensive physical or psychological injuries who are still suffering to his day.

****

Simon Sugden, Weapons Engineering Mechanic Ordnance, HMS Coventry

Fast forward 40 years and I find myself writing down some of my memories. I really can't believe 40 years have passed, some of the memories and images remain so vivid in my mind it could have been yesterday. I will be attending some of the planned commemorative events this year as I have always felt for me they have helped suppress any demons that may be bubbling below the surface. No amount of counselling could ever replace time spent with shipmates that shared the same experiences. I know for a lot of people attending these types of events is not for them and that is fine as long as they can handle their demons and they can be strong enough to keep them at bay.

****

Stuart McCulloch, Radio Operator HMS Fearless

I left the navy at the end of 1982 and, for many years, played down my going to war. Mentally I locked it up in a little box in my head and kept it there. A key factor in this was that I was being known initially as the Stuart who'd been to the Falklands as a kind of celebrity which was embarrassing. My brother survived on HMS *Arrow* and stayed in the navy, embracing it all and being a Falklands veteran kind of defined him and I didn't want to be like that.

I successfully kept it locked up for over 35 years until I started thinking about it more and more, resulting in a bit of a breakdown and recognition that I needed to process it. I was diagnosed with PTSD and have had counselling. However, I still get upset sometimes and cannot even explain why. My wife has been very supportive throughout and we are hoping that attending events in 2022 will help to process it all even more.

I am embarrassed that I didn't serve in the navy for very long after the war, so shouldn't qualify as a veteran when I compare my experiences against those that served in the two world wars or even the Gulf War and Afghanistan. I can still quote my service number without hesitation after all these years and even though I didn't serve for that long.

I recently attended a fireworks event at a neighbour's but the whole display was too much and it did take me back to those air raids with all the sounds and the explosions going off. I think I may avoid firework events for a while.

I do have a fear of confined spaces and open water, both of which I think are down to my experiences in the Falklands. The fear of the ship going down and being in the water in a vast ocean. Or being in enclosed spaces with no access to the outside I think as a result of a battle going on around me and not being able to see it.

My Parents' view

My brother did come back from the Falklands with issues, and I think this took my Mum's focus a lot. I have never really spoken to my parents about it all and how they felt. I just know they must have been worried out of their minds. My Dad died in 1996 and my Mum is still alive and in her mid-90s.

****

Colin Hamilton, Lieutenant Commander, HMS Leeds Castle

In retrospect, and to some extent in line with what is happening today, I look back today and reflect on how such horrible events have a habit of bringing together divided communities. It happened throughout UK and is doing so now across the divide in the States and indeed the world.

****

Major James Ryan, No. 2 Field Surgical Team, 'A Medic at War'

Reconciliation - A Poignant Visit to Argentina 2016

The Falklands War was a tragedy. At the end the UK reported 255 dead and 775 wounded. The Argentine casualties were 649 killed and 1687 wounded. Three Falkland civilians died. In the years following many Falklands war veterans felt that we should reach out to our Argentine opposite numbers. The late Surgeon Captain Rick Jolly OBE, who commanded '*The Red and Green Life Machine' Field Hospital*, recalled that the British surgical teams had taken care of many hundreds of Argentine wounded and he too was anxious to know how they fared following their return. At this time too the 1,000 strong SAMA 82, a UK veterans association led by Rick indicated their desire to make contact with Argentine veterans.

The opportunity to further this came with the visit of HRH Prince Charles to Argentina in 1999. He took Rick Jolly with him and saw to it that he met senior members of the Argentine Army, Navy and Air Force, many of whom took part in the war and they in turn introduced Rick to groups of wounded Argentine veterans. Enduring friendships were made and repeated visits followed. Rick was made an "*Officer of the Order of May, with Merit*" by the President of Argentina, the equivalent of a UK OBE. Reconciliation was well and truly under way.

By 2016 Rick Jolly was seriously ill and unable to travel and asked me to represent him. I was treated with great warmth and was given the opportunity to meet with many wounded veterans. My host, General Sergio Fernandez, was a war veteran himself. He was a junior officer in Argentine Special Forces in 1982 and was credited with shooting down a Royal Navy Sea Harrier. He then swam out to the wreck and rescued the pilot. They remain firm friends. I am now in regular contact with my Argentine military friends.

****

Marvin Clarke, Falkland Islander

After a period of reflection and when the cost of life had been made known, this was a particularly challenging time and for many a feeling of significant guilt at the cost of British lives to secure freedom, something that remains in the shadows on many to this day.

On a brighter note, in September 1982, we were proud to announce the arrival of our first son, and it did not take a lot to come up with what we considered to be a suitable name, Jeremy (after Major- General Jeremy Moore).

****

Chris Nunn, Captain, M Company 42 Commando

On 9th July 1982 M Company, 42 Commando Royal Marines sailed out of King Edward Cove in South Georgia. The Company had taken part in the operation to recapture the Island from Argentine forces on 25th April and then received orders to remain to defend King Edward Point [KEP] and Grytviken against any counter-attack. Elements of M Company Group also moved further south in June 1982 to recapture the 'icehole of the world', the volcanic island of Southern Thule in the South Sandwich Islands.

As their Company Commander, I knew that my thoughts then mirrored those of all the other 140 or so Royal Marines – we had no regrets at leaving the Island. For all of us, the time on the South Georgia was a test both physically and emotionally.

Little did I realise then that while you can leave South Georgia, South Georgia never quite leaves you! Proof of this is that for the intervening 30 years a large framed map of the Island has hung on the wall of every office I have occupied since.

In 1982, my first sight of the settlements in King Edward Cove was sitting in the door of a Royal Navy Lynx helicopter as it skimmed at wave height across West Cumberland Bay to land my group of black-faced commandos on the flat and boggy expanse of the Hestesletten. My most vivid memory then was of the bright red roofs of the KEP buildings, dominated by the large, long, green building that was Shackleton House nestling in the shadow of Duse Mountain and the shelter of Hope Point.

Our arrival this time was somewhat more stately! The white cross on Hope Point and the familiar outline of Brown Mountain conjured up still familiar feelings of anticipation; this time they were a little less fuelled by adrenaline, nevertheless, they were still pretty profound.

It was strangely relevant that this was to be where I should step ashore on South Georgia for the first time in 30 years. Only Siobhan (my wife) knew how poignant this place is to me: the cemetery also contains the grave of Chief Petty Officer Felix Artuso, a crewmember of the Argentine submarine Santa Fé, damaged and captured during the assault. Two days after the landings, one of my men shot and killed Artuso because of a catastrophic misunderstanding that happened while moving the submarine to another mooring. Quite correctly, the subsequent inquiry exonerated the Lance Corporal who killed him. The responsibility for this tragic incident lies with others who were not members of my Company; nevertheless, I will always regret Artuso's unnecessary death. Despite the passage of time, standing before his grave, it was easy to recall the cold, grey morning when he was buried with full military honours in the presence of his comrades. At the time, only I knew that there were Royal Marines snipers hidden in positions overlooking the cemetery fully prepared to forestall any last foolhardy act of Latin bravado.

Ernest Shackleton's grave itself has a special significance for me. It was to here that I walked through the snow after learning that my brother Richard had been killed during the battle for Goose Green on 28th May 1982

Somewhat shamefaced, at the museum I handed Sarah the original Argentine flag we captured on 25th April and which later covered Felix Artuso's coffin. After 30 years of travelling the attics of the world, it has at last returned to where it should be!

A couple of days later, looking out of the window of Carse House early in the morning, the spectacular view across to the Barff Peninsula was obscured by a similar katabatic mist. I was reminded immediately of another such misty morning when the Hope Point lookout reported two large, ghostly silhouettes gliding unheralded into Cumberland Bay. They were quickly identified as the *QE2* and the *Canberra*, tasked to use South Georgia as a safe haven in which to transfer the troops of 5 Brigade from one ship to the other. Amongst these troops were the Welsh Guards and associated sub-units. None of us could know then but many of them would be killed when the Landing Ships transporting them were attacked with devastating results at Fitzroy Creek a week or two later.

The most over-riding impression is of Grytviken, a testimony to a by-gone age of man, caught in a time capsule and surrounded by a savage landscape. A landscape that, on the one hand, is suffering from the effects of climate change; on the other it is clawing its way back to its natural state becoming once more a safe habitat for threatened species on land, in the air and under the sea.

For my part, I am proud that together, we, the members of M Company Group, 42 Commando Royal Marines, played a vital part in securing an enduring and positive future for the islands of South Georgia and Southern Thule.

****

Gerald Cheek, Falkland Islander

I still continue to wonder why the Argentine president thought he would get away with invading a British territory not expecting that Britain would respond in the way that they did. Sadly though the Foreign Office of the day were giving the wrong signals in their discussions with the Argentine government about the likely agreement of the British government to cede our sovereignty to them and I guess they, the Argentines, thought they would regain the islands as part of their territory.

Of course, as with any war, it is always extremely sad that so many lives were lost, even just as sad as I understand that more British veterans have taken their lives since the war than were actually killed at the time. I think I should also add how fortunate we the Islanders were in not losing any more lives than the three we did or indeed receiving any long-lasting injuries etc. Of course, I believe all of the residents here at the time will never forget the tremendous efforts together with no expense spared that the British government did in ensuring that we were liberated.

Like so many of these hostilities it is of course mismanagement of the politicians involved that created the situation.

****

Neil Wookey, 801 NAS Sea Harrier Squadron on HMS Invincible

I have to say on a personal note that at no time from the moment we left Portsmouth, until 14th June when the Argentine garrison surrendered, did I feel anything but absolute certainty that we would win. My faith in the Fleet and the ground forces was absolute. Our skipper Captain JJ Black engendered total belief.

****

Steve Walsh, Royal Artillery

Whilst I will never comprehend why governments repeatedly resort to pitching men against other men to fight to the death to resolve political issues, those few short weeks in the South Atlantic gave me a perspective of life that I value. It was cold, dirty and exhausting and has made me appreciate what the soldiers of the world wars went through for so many years. I have subsequently spent many years working in the humanitarian aid field to trying to help people who are driven from their homes and countries by war.

****

Alicia Shepherd, (aged 11) Falkland Islander

Extracts from the Falkland Islands Journal 2020 Vol 11

On the 29th of May every year, we all gather on top of the hill at Goose Green to remember those who fought and those who lost their lives for our freedom. I think that the monument is the most beautiful out of all the monuments because when the service is happening and the two minutes silence takes place, you can see the whole of Goose Green settlement in the background reminding us what those soldiers fought for and how lucky we really are. "*I would like to say THANK YOU to the soldiers of 2 Para for saving my family and our home.*"

A Para's Words and Scars

Me and my family have been so lucky to get to know some of the Paras who fought through the war. They are like a second family to us. I have shared with you some of their memories and stories they shared with us. Bless the Paras!

John Gatshore, 2 Para

Over the last Liberation days John shared these words. "*Thoughts are with all of our men which we lost*". They were *True Heroes* to me. I would like to say *Thank You* to all the ranks of 2 Para and state that we will never forget those that paid the ultimate sacrifice for me and my fellow members of 2 Para and the residents of Goose Green.

My mind still casts back to meeting young Wayne Clausen and Colin Shepherd…. I like many have aged with the years but it was my greatest privilege to have laid my life down for you…I salute each one of you…You are never far from my daily thoughts. I wish you all well and THANK YOU!

35 years ago 2 Para MMGS (medium machine guns) platoon moved up to their start position on a small peninsula to start the battle. A battle which would go down in history. To take Goose Green and Darwin settlement…My thoughts this day are with the men we lost in this battle and those also injured. And remember the families of our fallen. Class of 82."

"As daylight started to break at Goose Green A Company were pinned down at the bottom of Darwin Ridge. My Company was behind A Coy watching and waiting and spending a lot of time running up and down a small re-entrant trying to find cover from constant mortar and shell fire, and the overshoots from the Argentine Positions firing down and across on A company. This was the RAP with gorse line burning, Bill Bentley MM in centre. Fireworks just about to start for real 37 years ago at Goose Green, amazing sight at first watching all the Red, Green Trace, until you came face to face with it, and hearing the piercing screams of the wounded throughout the darkness."

****

Brian Short, Royal Marines Bandsman

Extracts from Brian's book The Band that went to War

Was it all worth it? Was the human cost one worth paying? You would think that given my own father was killed serving in the Royal Marines just before I was born, and my own experiences above then, my answer would be a resounding 'no'. However, having gone ashore and met the Falkland Islanders and seen what they were put through by the invaders, then I have to report the use of military force was necessary, even though the human cost was high.

The band's war was comparable to that of the troops ashore. We did not have to suffer the deprivations or rough living conditions of our soldiers and marines, and neither did we risk our necks fighting on those craggy hillsides. What we did do was our duty and a little more besides, oiling the war machine and making little differences here and there, but hopefully contributing in some small way to the successful outcome of the mission and the liberation of the Falkland Islanders.

We were the Band of Her Majesty's Royal Marines; We were the band that went to war!

Brian Short has published a full account of the Band's experience during the Falklands war. Published by Pen & Sword, 'The Band That Went To War' is available to order.

****

Steve Regolo, General Communications, HMS Hermes

I have been back to the Falklands on a number of occasions since the campaign but recently in 2018 I finally laid my ghost to rest as I paid my respects to the fallen and especially to the *Atlantic Conveyor* for if it hadn't been for her I possibly wouldn't be here now.

****

Tim McClement, 2i/c HMS Conqueror

Reflecting on events in the South Atlantic 40 years ago conjures up one single question: Was Margaret Thatcher, the UK Prime Minister in April 1982, right to have ordered the liberation of the Falkland Islands? The answer is still a resounding '*Yes*'.

The Islands, a British Overseas Territory whose inhabitants see themselves as British and wish to remain under British Sovereignty, had been invaded and occupied by Argentine Forces. It was imperative for the Islanders, the UK's international reputation and the rest of the world to understand that the use of armed force to take over another country is not acceptable and would not be allowed.

The Argentines had started the conflict. They had been told by the UK that they must leave, either voluntarily or they would be forced to do so by military action. They chose to fight, so the UK engaged. The sinking of the cruiser *General Belgrano* was the correct military action to save the UK Carrier Task Group, without which the UK could not have retaken the Islands.

In 1903 Admiral Lord Fisher stated, *"The essence of war is violence, moderation in war is imbecility."* He was right.

****

David Drew, RAF Hercules Senior Pilot

Reflecting on the Falklands War, I would say that there were three major reasons for the success of the UK forces.

The first was the fact that the MOD was able to call on UK industry to design and modify enabling systems (AAR equipment is an obvious example) at very short notice and to cut down the lengthy procurement and testing process that is normally required whenever new equipment is introduced.

The second was the sheer hard work put in by everyone involved, from the planning staff in MOD and Headquarters at Northwood to the dockyard staff who prepared the vessels for sailing and the logisticians who gathered together everything required.

The third was the little-known (at the time) assistance given by other nations, especially the USA. Finally, for most of the aircrew involved in the operation, the flying was the most interesting, demanding and exciting of their careers.

****

Larry Jeram-Croft, Lynx Pilot, HMS Andromeda

For me, like many others, the Falklands War didn't seem real at first. Yes it might turn into something but there again it probably wouldn't. Then HMS *Sheffield* was sunk. That concentrated the mind rather a lot. However, at no time was I particularly scared or frightened. This was probably because we were so well trained and flew in pretty difficult conditions at sea anyway.

As a 'Cold War Warrior' I had already understood and accepted the risks of my profession. My greatest concern was what effect it would have on my family if I didn't come back. And our training really paid off. We didn't throw the rule book away but we did bend it on numerous occasions and it was the depth of our training that allowed us to take the calculated risks necessary and get away with it. In fact, coming back to peacetime flying was a bit of a wrench.

There is always the question of whether it was worth it. A few days after the surrender I was at Pebble Island talking to a young boy of about twelve. I asked what the Argentines had done and he explained they had been locked up in the village hall for a fortnight. This was his home and they had no right to be there. We did the right thing.

Finally, I always think it rather ironic that the Argentine Junta invaded to prop up a shoddy regime and failed completely. However Maggie Thatcher profited enormously even though it was largely the failure of her government that encouraged the Junta in the first place. Funny thing that.

****

Commodore Michael C. Clapp CB RN, Commander of the Amphibious Task Group, C.T.G.317.0

Amphibious Task Group

On the 2nd April 1982, I cannot have been alone in being concerned as to how we were to manage going to war after years of cuts and peace.

The assets and command structure I was given showed the lack of understanding of amphibious operations in the Fleet Headquarters in Northwood, who would be in overall command. Until then, all we had been allowed to consider was a reinforcement landing in the NATO Area in a time of peace or early tension. We were repeatedly assured that we would never have to fight our way in, despite the possibility of being under threat.

This extraordinary attitude reminded me of a conversation I had many years before. In about 1970, I was serving in the Ministry of Defence's Directorate of Naval Air Warfare (DNAW). I was tasked with obtaining MoD agreement to create the aircrewman branch for ratings in Anti-Submarine and Support helicopters. Helicopter numbers were increasing rapidly. A separate career structure was essential.

I asked the Naval Manpower Division to help. They were in the Old Admiralty Building and luckily, I found, them hugely supportive. An elderly lady confided that she was worried how the navy would manage without the Admiralty Civil Service in which she had served so long. She feared that the new Ministry of Defence Civil Servants would not be so supportive. She felt that many would be looking to their own promotion, possibly in another Department, and they were unlikely to have as full an understanding of naval strategy and its needs, as well as the loyalty the Admiralty Civil Servants offered.

In 1982, I was lucky in that I had more experience, if still very limited, of personal risk than most other surface warfare officers of my age and younger.

Later, as a captain, I was appointed as Assistant Director of Naval Plans (Warfare and Strategy). The First Sea Lord wanted to train some Convoy Commodores, just in case. This required a small number of merchant ships. My Director ordered me to talk with the head of the Civilian Division that would pay to charter them. I phoned the head of that department and was astonished at the reply I received. He bluntly refused to help as "The First Sea Lord should know that the next war would be in the Central Front and only last a week. The first five days would be conventional and then it would end with a nuclear exchange. Why on earth was he thinking that a Convoy would be needed?" My attempts to question how we might defend a Colony or member of the Commonwealth were pushed aside as ridiculous speculation.

This civilian's narrow attitude seemed to me just what the lady Admiralty Civil Servant had warned me about. My Director simply rolled his eyes.

While in Naval Plans my assistant, Commander John Hall, an All-Weather Fighter Observer, and I argued the case for the Sea Harrier against a team of RAF officers led by an Air Vice Marshal. We won the case just in time!

In 1981, I was appointed to be the Commodore Amphibious Warfare (COMAW) on the staff of the Flag Officer Third Flotilla (FOF3), Rear Admiral John Cox, Flag Officer Carriers and Amphibious Ships (FOCAS), a much clearer role.

In late 1981, Rear Admiral Cox ordered me to move my staff from Fort Southwick near Portsmouth to the Royal Marine Barracks in Stonehouse, Plymouth, to be closer to the Royal Marines. These were the men I would work with and needed to know and be known by. The move helped a lot.

In the spring of 1982, Rear Admiral Derek Reffel took command from Rear Admiral Cox as Flag Officer Third Flotilla. He had been the first Commodore to resurrect my job after it had lapsed due to the refusal to accept an amphibious assault might one day be needed.

He was experienced in working with the Royal Marines and he had the staff to command carriers, amphibious ships, Royal Fleet Auxiliary (RFAs) and Merchant Ships. If he had come south with us as the In-Theatre Commander, it would have avoided a lot of confusion.

I found it hard to accept the Government's apparent attempt to give the Falkland Islands to Argentine control. The islands were first found by a Briton and had no indigenous residents. The Falklands are a strategic asset, providing a base from which to protect South Georgia and the islands further south where British Scientists worked. British settlers, many of whom descended from the early Royal Marine garrison, largely populated it.

All in all, I felt that I had as good experience as was practical in peacetime to command the amphibious task group. I hope it gave confidence to my staff, the masters of the Merchant Navy and Royal Fleet Auxiliary and captains of the Royal Navy ships. Together we suffered the greatest loss of life but most were extremely brave and loyal.

It was astonishing that, despite the tension over the talks with the Argentines, the Ministry of Defence had not made any Contingency Plans for the protection or liberation of the Islanders, if invaded.

Trying to support the SAS and 5 Infantry Brigade became a nightmare. Between them, they appeared to make little attempt to understand naval problems. They disobeyed sensible authoritative orders and as a result lost several vital support helicopters that were in very short supply, a ship and both soldiers' and sailors' lives. A second Royal Marine Brigade would have been hugely welcomed.

HMS *Fearless* and *Intrepid* were not built to command an amphibious task group. They lacked adequate operations rooms, accommodation, briefing and staff rooms. Much of the equipment was very out of date but a Defence Secure Satellite System (DSSS) was fitted on the way south awkwardly in an electrical work room rather far from the operations area. The present Command ships are much better as a result of our experience.

Despite the problems of a rushed start, lack of planning and muddled logistics, Operation Corporate was a success but I was appalled to be told on my return home that there would be no debrief so that misunderstandings might be resolved, lessons could be learnt and future plans would be based on experience. Apparently, it was not needed because "*We won*". There had been a great many misunderstandings due to a lack of joint training. The naval staff failed to support those who deserved awards or make a good public recognition of the success of the ships involved. Equipment needed to be discussed. It seemed far more likely that a cover up was happening.

In the operational area, I was intrigued to hear several senior Captains telling me how they looked back into naval history to try and see what earlier naval officers might have thought about our plans and actions. Two days before the landings I was sitting on the bridge wing of *Fearless* watching a Replenishment at Sea (RAS). Short of sleep, I found myself day-dreaming and saw numerous men in antique uniforms. All shouted their support for Brigadier Thompson's and my plan. They strongly warned against any late changes as chaos might result. It was a great encouragement. A study of naval history is vital to all naval officers. Losing the Old Admiralty and the Royal Naval College, Greenwich, made this all the more difficult.

The confusion between the Foreign and Commonwealth Office, Ministry of Defence, Treasury and Cabinet failed us. Their decisions were a major cause of our shambolic rush to plan, get trained and for the logistics to be properly loaded in the correct order. Losses of personnel, ships and aircraft would have been far less.

Deterrence was seen as expensive and unnecessary. If HMS *Ark Royal* with her long-range aircraft had not been scrapped, the possibility of it operating in the South Atlantic would probably have deterred Admiral Anaya and others.

We still have 53 members of the Commonwealth and 14 Overseas Territories who look to us for trade and defence. Most are proud to be part of the United Kingdom. With China pushing in the Indian Ocean and Pacific and Russia playing risky games, their defence is vital and should not be left to others. A strong navy with a capable amphibious force that can work with the US Navy and Marines would increase the deterrence markedly. Merchant ships need to be selected and provided with flight decks and defences.

I doubt if the lady in the Old Admiralty building would have been surprised to find her opinion would prove to be so accurate.

****

David Jackson, Commanding No.1 Field Surgical Team attached to 16 Field Ambulance deployed with 5 Infantry Brigade

I would dwell many times on these surgical cases throughout my life and even now, nearly 40 years later, the impact has not significantly diminished. Indeed, as I have grown older, the emotions are harder to contain, as my resistance to the awfulness of the human cost of this and other conflicts I have been involved in has been markedly degraded with the passage of time. Having now retired from a busy civilian surgical practice, which occupied me almost to the exclusion of what had gone before, I have had more time to think and reassess, sometimes relive a little of my past, and it is not a place that I am altogether happy about revisiting. These recollections and others have been compartmentalised for many years, but now that they have been reopened, I don't think I will ever be able to fully close them again. I have heard too many agonised screams and cries of despair and attended too many funerals, burials and remembrance services.

I have got on with my life, with my career, with my family because I have had to, but that is not to say that I have not been afflicted, like so many of my service colleagues, with that other described cause of mental anguish, 'survivor's guilt'. This is an insidious thought that resurfaces now and again, to punish me and others who came back, whole and healthy, though never the same.

Why did I survive when 255 servicemen didn't? What marked me as different? I have had 40 years more life than them, 40 years more experience of the ups and downs of this world, the good and the bad, the pleasures and the pain. I did not have to fight for my life (medics are non-combatant but will fight to protect their patients). I just had to rely on serendipity and in truth, the fighting skills of those that I was there for, to try and save.

'They shall grow not old, as we that are left grow old: Age shall not weary them, nor the years condemn. At the going down of the sun and in the morning, we will remember them'. I know that I will.

Note: Robert Laurence Binyon, CH (August 10, 1869 – March 10, 1943)

****

Philip Piper, Gazelle Pilot, 656 Army Air Corps

Reproducing this diary into a digital format has raised many emotions and rekindled many forgotten memories; the most tragic of which was the loss of S/Sgt Chris Griffen and L/Cpl Simon Cockton. I knew Chris better than Simon simply because he was the one who tried to keep me (and the rest of the aircrew) on the straight and narrow from a pilot's point of view and he was ***the*** guru (Qualified Helicopter Instructor) as far as aviation matters were concerned.

Not only was he highly professional, very well respected but highly approachable. He was a very good man. I remember he had an aircrew teach-in/quiz session with us whilst we were on board on the MV *Nordic*, the aim of which was to ensure we knew everything that we should have known. I remember it was a long hot session (we must have been somewhere near to the Equator at the time) so by the time we had finished we were mentally exhausted but hugely grateful that all the stuff that we had let slip to the back of our memories had been rigorously brought back into clear focus. They were both sorely missed.

Re-reading the diary has made me realise what good companionships were made not only on the way down with the ship's company but also with those that we had to work with (the Squadron as a whole) and those kind and generous Falkland Islanders that we had met on the way. It is with huge regret that I never made any attempt to maintain those contacts once I had left the Islands and subsequently the Squadron. The biggest of those regrets was not keeping in touch with L/Cpl Les Berrisford. We had spent many an hour in the cockpit together ensuring that we kept our passengers and ourselves safe and a very strong bond was established between ourselves. I was hugely proud that he had been selected for pilot training and then devastated that he had been killed in a Lynx accident in Germany a few years after that.

****

Steve Regolo, General Communications, HMS Hermes

40 years on and the memories of those days in the South Atlantic live with me as if they were yesterday. I keep very close contact with quite a few of my shipmates and each year apart from last COVID year we would always meet for a weekend and share out dits over a few beers...well actually quite a few beers indeed.

As I mentioned I already have been back to honour our fallen and always with tears in my eyes I recount the 108 days spent out there and just how proud I was to serve.

Next year I had applied to visit the Islands for the 40th Liberation celebration but due to the demand and the restrictions won't be able to travel. So, along with several of my shipmates we will be going to Portsmouth to celebrate instead.

****

Nathaniel Cockwell, (year 6) Falkland Islander
From: The Falkland Islands Journal 2021 Vol 11

I think it would have been a frightening experience but also quite exciting. My dad says that the conflict has helped shape his life and motivates him to do his best for the Falklands. I think it is important to remember the Falklands War because a lot of people died on both sides.

****

Taelah Henry, (year 6) Falkland Islander
Extracts from The Falkland Islands Journal 2021 Vol 11

The 1982 Memorial Wood

The 1982 Memorial Wood was opened on the 10th June 1992 to mark the Tenth anniversary of the Falklands War. Tim and Jan Miller wanted to create a living memorial to all 255 British servicemen who fought and died for the freedom of the Falkland Islands: a place where family and friends can go to remember their loved ones.

In the beginning they were baby trees and Tim and Jan Miller and the Stanley Nurseries gang dug all the holes. The Cub Scouts also helped plant the trees. One tree was planted for each serviceman who was killed and had a plaque that was donated by Cable & Wireless. These plaques had to be replaced because of the harsh weather on the Falkland Islands. The money was raised by Tim and Jan doing tour guiding for tourists; the Welsh Guards, HMS *Glamorgan* and HMS *Ardent* donated money to buy their comrades' plaques and SAMA82 also helped with a donation. The trees took nearly 10 years before they started to grow properly because of the weather, but now you can notice that they are growing a bit each year.

The wood is made up of different trees that include willow, white beam, rowan macrocarpa, lodge pole pine, spruce, mountain pine, evergreen, oak and Austrian pine. Birds like to make nests in the trees. They feed on the rowan and white beam berries in the autumn and if you take a walk in the wood they can be heard singing in the trees which is so beautiful. Every year the Cub Scouts plant lots of daffodil bulbs in the wood and if you visit the wood in springtime you will see lots of yellow and white daffodils. Small gardens are also planted within the wood to make it a very beautiful place.

The Cub Scouts helped members of HMS *Glamorgan* Association find their crew members' trees. It is very important that Scouts and young people get involved with the Memorial Wood so we will always remember these people.

The veterans (the servicemen who fought the 1982 war) who come back, visit the battle fields where they fought and lost their comrades. They go to San Carlos Cemetery to remember their family and friends who died, but for the men who died at sea and do not have a grave, the wood is a very special place where they can come to remember.

If you walk in the wood you may see pictures of the soldiers and their families, flowers tied to the trees, or flags and crosses, even some rum which has been left by their families and friends. There is a map in a shelter marking every tree in the 1982 Memorial Wood.

For the Millennium Year, 2000, a new section was opened in the wood called The Annexe to remember all those servicemen and women who have lost their lives whilst serving in the Falkland Islands since 1982. There are approximately 50 trees to remember servicemen who were killed either in road accidents, a Chinook crash, or a fighter-jet crash. There are also trees dedicated to veterans who served in the Falklands War and have since passed away, but families wanted them to be remembered in the wood.

There is a group of willow trees in special memory of the Welsh Guards and also three trees dedicated to families of Admiral Von Spee, Admiral Craddock RN and Admiral Sturdee who fought in the naval battles in 1914.

****

RO(G) Anthony Lawrence, Radio Operator HMS Fearless

Looking back almost 40 years later, in a world more acutely aware of combat stress and mental health, I think the crew, and all veterans of the war, should have at some point been allowed to speak to mental health specialists so as to come to terms with our experiences in the South Atlantic. Whilst we had the journey home to unwind and reflect to ourselves our experiences, I don't remember anyone actually talking about it with each other. Instead, we came back to Portsmouth after 100 days at sea and the next day I'm home out with my friends who are still in 6th Form at school.

Everyone is saying well done and how great it was that 'we' beat the Argies, but they only watched it on TV, and try as you can, you cannot really convey to them what it was really like; hearing but not seeing what was going on, waiting for the crash of a bomb coming through the bulkhead; watching HMS *Antelope* explode; wounded shipmates and seeing grown men cry at the loss of friends and colleagues. I'm looking round thinking: "*You have absolutely no idea what we have been through.*"

After about a week at home, Mum saw a request from the local newspaper, The Kentish Express, asking for stories from the South Atlantic; so, she gave them a call and the next day a reporter/photographer came round and listened to me spin a few dits! But even then, I'm not sure my heart was really in it. (That was the only time I ever achieved celebrity status!).

A couple of years later when I was stationed at Fleet Headquarters, Northwood, some of us went to the Royal Tournament at Earls Court in London. One of the displays involved a Sea Harrier being flown off a 'flight deck' accompanied by the 'Action Stations' alarm going off to initiate the display. This alarm went off without any warning and I found myself for no reason breaking out into a cold sweat. My friends asked if I was ok, which I was after a few minutes, but that is the only time I have ever suffered what is termed as a 'flashback' even after hearing that alarm a hundred times afterwards during the course of my naval career.

Overall, I think the experience encompassed all manner of feelings; comradeship, fear, excitement, boredom, and finally guilt at coming home when other shipmates didn't. At 17 years of age that's a lot to try and take in. I went on to serve 23 years on the Navy. My experience in the war as a boy helped to define the man I became, as a sailor, husband and father. It's something I shall never forget and not a day goes by that I don't reflect back on the events of those 10 weeks or so in 1982. Am I glad I went? Yes. Would I want to go through it again, being older and wiser? Not so sure!

After all the euphoria had died down and we had all finished our leave, the ship's company was set to task preparing the ship for its next peacetime deployment. The 'anti-climax' of being home and settling down to regular naval routine was emphasized when one of the Leading Radio Operators casually came down into the mess-deck one afternoon, and with a *"Here's your disco dancing medals boys"*, proceeded to hand out the little white boxes with our names on containing the Falklands Campaign medal.

After seeing the victory parade in London on television we felt a bit cheated missing out on the country's thanks for our efforts. Not for us on *Fearless* the pomp and ceremony of a parade, with band playing and the Admiral pinning the medal on our proud chests; not for us a mention in the London Gazette. Quoting the time-old saying used by the old salts of the Royal Navy, the LRO simply said: *"Well, that's life in a blue suit chum, now get turn to, that signal deck isn't going to scrub itself!"*

****

Gary Mcilvenna, Royal Marine on HMS Fearless

It had been an exciting, exhilarating, interesting but exhausting three months, inevitably saddened by the loss of our six esteemed colleagues. I am proud to have participated in this successful campaign, which could never have been waged if it had not been for the landing craft and their parent ships, *Fearless* and *Intrepid.*

Showing no interest in Argentine sovereignty, the people of the Falkland Islands were proud to remain as part of the British colony and showed eternal gratitude for the sacrifices the Task Force made (255 lost lives).

Before closing this personal account, I must mention the names of my fallen shipmates who are forever in my thoughts: - C/Sgt B. Johnston, Sgt R.J Rotheram, Mne A.J Runde, Mne RD Griffin, Mechanical Engineering Artificer AS James, Leading Marine Engineer D. Mille

****

Rob Shadbolt, CPO Lynx, HMS Antelope

It is strange to reflect on an undeclared war which was never anticipated and took place 40 years ago. The Argentines had invaded the Falkland Islands, a British sovereign territory, claiming they were just taking back land that was officially theirs.

My involvement was as the senior engineer in charge of the helicopter on board the Type 21 frigate HMS *Antelope* and we were one of the first ships to leave UK.

Our fate was decided one Sunday afternoon in late May when we were twice bombed leading to the ship blowing up and catching fire, desperate attempts were made to save her. However, the crew had no option but to abandon ship and she sadly sank the next day. These life changing events are still vivid memories, no matter how many years go by I still cannot tolerate loud noises and bangs which remind me of the explosions. The heroic actions of the crew, the bravery of those who came to our rescue and those who looked after us on our journey home will never be forgotten.

There were so many lessons learned, ranging from materials for clothing, the lack of an Airborne Early Warning capability so no over the horizon radar was available since the demise of the Gannet aircraft in 1978. There must never be room for complacency as Argentina still presses her claim to own the islands especially now with the lucrative exploration for oil. Could we do it all again? With the opening of the Mount Pleasant airbase near Stanley there is now a permanent and effective deterrent on site and with the demise in the number of ships/aircraft in the Royal Navy due to continual defence cuts the likelihood of forming such a Task Force such as that in 1982 is remote. The determination of the Islanders to remain under the UK Government remains as strong as ever as demonstrated by the result of the latest sovereignty referendum.

****

Andy Hopper, Sea Harrier 809 Sqn on HMS Illustrious

The whole experience of 1982 and memories of the conflict with Argentina remain vivid, despite the passing of 40 years. Initially, when the news broke, it all seemed surreal. A place none of us had heard of.

I was cynical about the whole thing, convinced that when the Task Force sailed three days later - they'd get as far as the Bay of Biscay, diplomacy would win the day and everyone would come home again. So I was quite happy to be staying behind - initially. The Task Force sailed on.

Whilst we were preparing the squadron, we were losing men, aircraft, and ships in the conflict. I vividly remember the loss of HMS *Sheffield* on the 4th May - which suddenly escalated the conflict into something very real and very frightening.

An advance party went ahead with four aircraft embarked in the container ship *Atlantic Conveyor*. They were flown off and split between the Task Force carriers HMS *Hermes* and HMS *Invincible*, just a day or so later the *Atlantic Conveyor* was sunk by an Exocet missile. Grim beyond the word.

In December 1982, after some welcome R&R in Puerto Rico, Fort Lauderdale and Philadelphia - the ship came home. It had been a hugely successful trip, though the tragic loss of one of the ship's company from the quarter-deck just a few days from home left us all with an all-embracing feeling of abject sadness.

None of us on 809 Squadron knew the lost man, there were 1,200 of us on the ship, and he was a stranger to all of us. But we felt his loss. After exhaustive searching, the ship's skipper, the peerless Captain Jock Slater, came on the ship's broadcast system and said it was his painful duty to write to the parents of Able Seaman 'Dodger' Deacon to say we'd lost him.

A tragic loss - truly, felt just as much after 40 years as it was back in mid-December 1982.

****

Ade Thorne, RAF EOD.

Extracts from My Falklands Diary

In the seven short weeks that we were on island, we were shot at, bombed and rocketed, but we all survived – well, apart from Doc who got frostbite in his big toe. We had cleared 900 UXBs/bomblets, hundreds of plastic mines, tens of thousands of rounds of ammunition and a few tons of napalm.

All eleven of us got some form of award, starting at the top with Al getting the Queen's Gallantry Medal, and myself and Ken getting the Queen's Commendation for Brave Conduct.

Postscript 2007

In 2007, as a Flight Sergeant I returned to the Falkland Islands as an FS Arms Engineer. I took time out to find Romeu and Hilary's daughter, and we arranged to meet her parents in the old house I stayed at in 1982. I presented them with a plaque on behalf of 5131 BD Sqn as a thank-you for looking after us back then. Once word got out who I was, I quickly became a tour guide showing people Ajax Bay, Goose Green and San Carlos.

****

Garry Hearn, Lance Corporal Royal Signals attached to the 1st Battalion Welsh Guards

Looking back, excellence of training, experience, and the instilling of internal competition is a force-multiplier, it creates self-belief and brings resilience and a willingness to just go with the flow. Humour will always play a vital part of soldiering. Acute experiences both heighten and deaden humanity, a biscuit followed by a blasé view of death; three weeks later I wondered about the parents, family, and friends of the gun crew.

Personally, the experience has led to some personality traits that are good in the work environment; just get on with it (no buses or taxis) and recognising the trivial. Conversely, they are less good in personal relationships when sometimes people do need to stop and take stock, and what may be trivial to me is genuinely important to them.

In respect of those that fought in 1982, for those who lost friends and family, and who have suffered since…on both sides.

****

Tony Babb, Weapons Action Repair Team (WART), HMS Southampton

Leaving the Royal Navy in November 1987, as planned, 22 man's years for pension, I was staggered to receive the British Empire Medal in the 1988 New Year's Honour List. You never know who recommends you for this honour, but I am convinced it was related to the war, possibly Sam Salt; he was a good captain.

In 2013 I was also awarded the South Atlantic Medal (without rosette). I never expected to get a medal for what we did. Luckily it did enable me to return to the Falklands in 2015 for two weeks. Now I have looked properly, seen the wildlife, met the people and love the place, and everybody should visit if they can. During this visit, I also met some real war veterans, a few still fighting the horrors that the war had embedded in their minds.

In 2020, I visited Argentina and had a look at their Falklands Museum in Buenos Aires. I photographed everything and then translated it on my return. Their museum is a monument to indoctrination, missing significant historical facts and littered with lies, which their corrupt government has peddled since before World War 2.

Thus, it has taken until now for me to realise that the 1982 Falklands Conflict still goes on, both in the minds of veterans and in Argentina.

****

Martin R, Argentine Serviceman

My late dad used to say that the British are to blame for Argentina's permanently bad situation: You had three good opportunities to properly invade us: 1806, again in 1807 and you passed the opportunity again in 1982… (I think there was a lot of truth in it).

The *Malvinas* issue is brought up every single time the country is in deep economic crisis (way too often) as a diversion. Back then the military were ruling after a coup d'état and the country was enduring another crisis. The military badly needed something to distract the populace. They decided to invade the Islands.

I very deeply regret that the same people that were demonstrating against the military government one day, then went to the Plaza de Mayo to cheer… the same guys. We can't think clearly. We do not have memory. They never thought on the day after the invasion. This war has been a shameful and coward act. How many soldiers were at the time in the FIDF? May be two dozen? And they landed a thousand troops to boot.

You said you didn't know that food was scarce in the country at the time. That is not correct, but our military were so bad in planning that they sent troops down south with their northern (warm) uniforms, the wrong munition and no food. Same thing happened on the Islands, where containers of supplies were stranded downtown Stanley while the troops were starving, cold and wet in the battlefields.

The military were looking for a fight: four years prior they almost engaged the Chileans over the islands in the Beagle channel. Like street boys, they were looking for a fight. They just picked the wrong guy to bully.

We all won something, but at a huge cost in human lives. The Falkland Islands are now a beaming country on the map. Argentina got rid of the de facto governments and came back to democracy…Not that we managed to learn from the past…

We only need our government to leave us common people alone to deal with each other across our pond and move on complementing each other.

I am terribly sorry for what these idiots did and I feel tremendously embarrassed of being an Argentine for that. And other things of the present. But that is another history.

****

Alex Manning, Assistant Staff Minewarfare and Clearance Diving Officer (ASMCDO) HMS Fearless

Was it worth it? Sorry Argentina, but if the Falklands were 100% British before you invaded them, continuously settled since 1833 by a sovereignty claim pre-dating yours by over 50 years, they're 1000% British now and your ongoing attitude is keeping it that way. After you surrendered in 1982, Major General Moore suggested that the difference between you and us was that, while you were fighting for the islands, we were fighting for the Islanders. Your current attitude and approach would seem to confirm this and that, perhaps, is why your all-or-nothing approach won't get you anywhere. You've only yourselves to blame, so wake up and smell the coffee, I would affirm that the sacrifices were definitely not in vain.

Let the last words belong to Margaret Thatcher therefore: "*They may be small in number, but they have the right to live in peace, to choose their own way of life and to determine their own allegiance."* Amen to that.

****

Garry Hearn, Lance Corporal Royal Signals attached to the 1st Battalion Welsh Guards

I shake the hand of the smiling Argentine Officer, he is open, witty, hugely respectful of the British Armed Forces, and disappointed we ever fought over the Falkland Islands. It is 2019, Fort Leavenworth Kansas, and I am the UK Staff College Colonel leading a group of British Army and Royal Marine Majors on an exchange exercise with our US counterparts.

It is the first time in nearly forty years that I had met a member of the Argentine forces, and poignantly, it appears that the father of Major Alfredo Serrano and I had been on opposite sides of Sapper Hill during the final advance on Port Stanley. Respect, mutual memories of cold, wet, dark, and that of doing a professional job all quickly come to the fore, he tells me the same thoughts come to his Dad when he discusses his experiences but are also tinged with sadness at poor leadership.

****

Eddie Bairstow, RN Education Officer, 45 Commando Group

Falklands 82 - A Schoolie's Snapshots

I was 45 Commando Group's RN Education Officer (Schoolie) in 1982 when Operation Corporate to recover the Falkland Islands took place. I left 45's base in Arbroath, Scotland at around midnight on Sunday 4th April. I returned to Southampton on *Canberra* on 11th July, before flying back to Condor the same day. Most of 45 Cdo sailed south on RFA *Stromness*. As part of 45's B Echelon I went south on the LSL RFA *Sir Percivale*. I took two cameras with me: a Nikon FE with one roll of slide film and a small 35mm Rollei compact camera. On Saturday 3rd April, I found time to nip into Arbroath and buy five 36 frame rolls of print film. I finished all six rolls of film during the time we were away. When we landed on the Islands on 21st May, I left the Nikon on board RFA *Percy* as it would be too heavy to carry round when we started moving.

Throughout the campaign I did not think ahead to our return, I just went day by day. I didn't keep a diary or make any notes of what was happening and I didn't make any notes about the photos I took or dates. I didn't even think to ask if I could get any more films.

45 Cdo Gp intelligence team produced a campaign map when we got back from which I got a lot of dates and information. I got more details from posting photos on various Facebook group pages relating to the Falklands and getting feedback. A lot of that information has come from Falkland Islanders who were on the Islands at the time.

My photos were not taken with the idea of documenting what was happening: they were just "moments" that interested me at the time. In essence, they just reflect where I was and some of what I saw. There are very few posed photographs. The photos are in date order. Fortunately, the films lasted until we docked back at Southampton on 11th July at 11am.

The photos in this book, *Glimpses of the Falklands War,* are just a selection of over 170 photos I took between 5th April and 11th July 1982. Most of them were the ones which came to mind without looking through all the photos. The assault landings on 21st May and the 11th June night move and attack on Two Sisters could not be taken because of operational and photographic conditions.

****

Chris Nunn, Captain, M Company 42 Commando

<u>My brother, Richard Nunn - Loss and Reconciliation</u>

This is the courageous but tragic story of events that took place on 28th May 1982 when my brother Lieutenant Richard Nunn DFC RM, was killed in action and Sergeant Bill Belcher RM was seriously wounded flying in support of 2nd Battalion Parachute Regiment, during the Battle for Goose Green.

Richard joined the Corps in 1974. Soon after he completed his training, he served in 40 Commando RM in Plymouth and Northern Ireland. Richard became the fifth member of the Nunn family in two generations awarded his 'Wings'. I received my Wings in 1977.

During the first week of Easter leave, we began to hear about Argentine illegal activity in South Georgia and threats to the Falkland Islands. That weekend, with Richard, we had Sunday lunch with our parents - Pampy and Granny Margaret. It was the last time we were together. Soon Richard was embarked on the RFA *Sir Tristram*; with him was his flight Commander, my good friend Jeff Niblett. Jeff was flying with Richard when they were attacked on that fateful day.

Meanwhile, I flew in secret with my Company to Ascension Island and headed south by sea to attack South Georgia. M Company landed and recaptured South Georgia on 25th April 1982, but that is another story. Our only means of communication was through HMS *Endurance*. For the next few weeks we received very little news of what was happening to our comrades in the main Task Force. These are extracts I wrote in 1983 for Nick Vaux's book 'March to the South Atlantic' taken from the Chapter 'The Forgotten Company':

'We managed to pick up the World Service that evening and I heard with awful dread that during a large land battle a Scout helicopter had been shot down and the pilot killed. Having previously served in the Squadron for 3 years, I knew all the pilots as friends, but with selfish callousness, I could only think: Please God I do not care who, but not Richard. The following day 31st

May was my mother's birthday. Later that day I flew by Wasp to HMS Endurance to express to the captain my concern at the effect that the lack of news of the land battle would have on my men. Those fighting were our friends and probably from our own Commando, and so we had a right to know what was going on...Endurance had gleaned more news during the night. The battle was for a place called Goose Green. After fierce fighting, it had been taken by 2nd Battalion, The Parachute Regiment, but casualties were unknown. David Constance, my sister's husband, was the only Royal Marine with 2 Para. My heart sank further. Yes, a Scout was shot down and the pilot killed. Captain Barker, as usual, fully understood my point of view and gave his assurance that he would endeavour to obtain more and regular news. From him that promise was good enough.'

Between the 31st May and 4th June the weather in South Georgia was horrendous with storms and blizzards bringing very high winds, extreme cold and large amounts of snow, but still no news from the Falklands.

On 4th June: *'At about 1030 hours I heard a Wasp, one of the two from Endurance, land and close down. It was snowing heavily. Two or three minutes later I saw Lieutenant Commander Tony Ellerbeck, who was the ship's Flight Commander and by then a friend, walking past my window, obviously coming to my office in the old Post Office. I stood up and gave him a mock salute. The outside door opened and I heard him talk briefly to Mr Juleff, the Sergeant Major. I opened my office door. My greetings were cut short by his words, "I am sorry, I have a letter for you from the Captain.' I looked back and said, 'It's Richard isn't it? 'Yes' he replied. I said 'He's dead?' 'Yes, I am sorry,' he responded. No more was said. I sat and despite my best efforts broke down...'*

Tony left, having done a most difficult duty. Paul Juleff came into my office with a cup of coffee laced with 'brown sugar', our shorthand for navy rum! I drank it and saw that the snow had stopped and the sun was shining. I told Paul that I wanted some time to myself. I walked along the track that runs from King Edward Point (KEP) to Grytviken and into the cemetery where Ernest Shackleton is buried. Somehow, it seemed the place to go. I do not know how long I was there, but in time, I gathered my thoughts and realised that there was still a job to do and I had better get on with it.

By the time I returned to KEP, the word had spread around the Company and I received some touching comments from the Marines in the Company.

Once the fighting at Goose Green was over, David had to come to terms not only with having lost a number of his friends in 2nd Battalion Parachute Regiment killed in action but the enormous blow of knowing that Richard had also been killed. David was present at Richard's burial with his comrades-in-arms in a temporary mass grave at Ajax Bay. Later David recalled:

"The person who delivered the sad news of Richard's death was Andrew Eames. He suddenly appeared in the middle of a mortar stomp when Rod Bell and I were sharing some fold in the ground. Luckily, the ground was soft so the effect of the mortars was greatly reduced. However, it is of some interest that I read of the Pucara pilot's fate. I and others emptied our SLR magazines at his aircraft at the time and perhaps in some small way contributed to his demise. I do hope so!"

Jeff Niblett: *"On the 29th May, I flew down to the crash site to recover Richard and return him to Ajax Bay for a post mortem by Rick Jolly. The next day was the interment in the mass grave. Squadron officers, including myself, laid Richard to rest"*.

Peter Cameron, Richard's Squadron Commander, also had the unenviable responsibility of writing to Granny and Pampy soon after Richard's death. During a visit to the Falklands in 2010, Peter told me that at the Ajax Bay graveside David said, "*Tell them I was here*". He wanted us all to know that he was there representing the family.

David: "*That I was able to be at San Carlos for the interim burial was very important to me and I am grateful to 2 Para for including me and indeed inviting me to go along. I had no idea it was happening, until one of the guys mentioned it. I was not certain my message, via Peter Cameron, got through! I am grateful to know, even after all this time, that it did.*

After the Ajax Bay burial, Jeff arranged for the recovery of Richard's Will and other effects, including his camera, from *Sir Tristram*. Like others, Richard wrote his Will on board heading south when the serious reality of the future dawned on everyone in the Task Force.

It was yet another twist of fate that Surgeon Lieutenant Commander Rick Jolly RN commanding the only Field Hospital at Ajax Bay was a friend of our family long before the Falklands conflict. Rick knew Richard as a schoolboy.

These extracts from his book say it all:

"28th May 1982 - Then I discover the name of Sergeant Belcher's pilot, and a chill feeling envelopes me. Lieutenant Richard Nunn is the brother of Captain Chris Nunn, my son's Godfather. But there is no time to mourn or even reflect, only more work coming through the door."

"29th May 1982 - The moment I am dreading finally comes. Scouse informs me that the body of the dead pilot has arrived. The team forms up again...They are all aware of my friendship with our latest customer...I walk to the side again, trying to steel myself. The sheet is lifted off, and from previous experience in Northern Ireland I know what to expect, but it is still a severe shock to see the injured body of someone you have known well. Somehow, I sense that I have to prove to myself that Richard died before the crash and not because of it. It takes a few minutes of gentle probing, but finally I find what in a way I am hoping to find. There is a hole in his left cheekbone, which just admits my little finger. A ricocheting bullet has penetrated my friend's face and, an instant later, his brain. This knowledge helps me to adjust – whatever happened after death, no matter how unpleasant, doesn't seem important now. I resolve at once to write to his parents, old friends who live not far

from my home in Cornwall. Another neat silver bag joins the line waiting for tomorrow's funeral."

It was great solace to Granny and Pampy to know that Rick had examined Richard and could tell them, first in writing, and later face-to-face that Richard died instantly and did not suffer pain from the crash or the resulting fire.

On 8th October 1982, the following citation appeared in The London Gazette:

"The Queen has been graciously pleased to approve the posthumous award of the Distinguished Flying Cross to Lieutenant Richard James NUNN, Royal Marines in recognition of gallant and distinguished service during the operations in the South Atlantic."

On Friday 28th May 1982, the 2nd Battalion of the Parachute Regiment was engaged in fierce fighting to take enemy positions in the area of Darwin and Goose Green. Two Gazelles and two Scout helicopters from 3 Commando Brigade Air Squadron Royal Marines were tasked to support the attack.

From dawn, heedless of enemy ground fire, the two Scouts from B Flight, led by the Flight Commander, Captain Jeff Niblett RM with his air gunner Sergeant John Glaze RM in 'Delta Tango' with 'Delta Romeo' flown by Lieutenant Richard Nunn RM with his air gunner Sergeant Bill Belcher RM, supported the Battalion by flying vital ammunition forward to the front line and then evacuating casualties to safety. The two Gazelles from M Flight were also committed throughout the battle.

After flying continuously for three and a half hours, it was learnt that the Commanding Officer and others in the battalion's forward Tactical Headquarters had been severely wounded. Both Scout aircraft were tasked to fly forward once more to evacuate the wounded, the plan was to collect the Battalion Second in Command en route. Five minutes after take-off from their forward operation base at Camilla Creek House, suddenly and without warning two Argentine Pucara ground attack aircraft attacked both Scouts with cannon and rocket fire. With great flying skill Lieutenant Nunn evaded the first attack but on the second his aircraft was hit and destroyed. Lieutenant Nunn was killed instantly. Sergeant Belcher was seriously wounded but thrown clear. He lost a leg. By employing a combination of exceptional flying skill and superb teamwork with his air gunner, Captain Niblett successfully evaded a further three cannon and rocket attacks, eventually completing the mission. The crew of 'Delta Tango' resolutely continued support and evacuation operations until well after dark. The support given by the aircraft of 3 Commando Brigade Air Squadron was vital to the conduct of the attack and was instrumental in the eventual victory. Captain Jeff Niblett RM was awarded the Distinguished Flying Cross. Lieutenant Richard Nunn was posthumously awarded the Distinguished Flying Cross.

On Saturday 9th October, Granny and Pampy arranged a memorial service for Richard. There was a very large turnout of friends of Richard and the family. It was not a sad occasion and various people talked about his character, especially his sharp sense of humour.

Pampy, my sister Sarah and I were there when the Queen presented the Distinguished Flying Cross to Granny Margaret at a private investiture at Buckingham Palace

The Falklands Campaign was the first in British military history that the families of those who were killed were offered the choice of having their loved ones buried where they fell, or to have them repatriated to the United Kingdom. Granny Margaret and Pampy made the decision that Richard should be buried in the British military cemetery at San Carlos, a beautiful spot alongside San Carlos Water where the landings took place.

When Pampy died in 1993, he left a letter for me with his Will. In it, he asked me to arrange for his ashes to be buried with Richard in the San Carlos cemetery. I realised then that he made his decision on that bright, sunny day when we were standing together at Richard's grave in 1983.

I returned to the Islands in 2008 and visited Richard's grave. I also went to the Argentine cemetery, where the 237 dead, refused repatriation by their own government, lie buried in a simple corral.

Many graves are unnamed, but, from time-to-time, Argentine next of kin can make brief visits. Many adopt a particular unnamed grave as the focus for their remembrance for the loss of a family member.

It came as a shock for me to find out that one of the few known graves is that of Lieutenant Miguel Gimenez, the Pucara pilot who shot Richard's helicopter down. A few minutes after the action, he too died when he flew into Blue Mountain in low cloud. His aircraft, with his body still strapped in the cockpit, was not located until 1986.

Standing in front of Gimenez's grave, I could not feel any animosity towards him. After all: They were two young men whom, had they met under different circumstances, may well have found that they had much more in common than their national differences.'

****

Jay Morgan Hyron 'The Falklands Widow'

Extracts are from Jay's book 'The Falklands Widow'

For thousands of years man has been at war with his fellow man in one way or another. It is just over 100 years since we had the 'War to end all Wars' but it is only in the last couple of years that a light has been shone on the women left behind as one Professor and his team executed the 'Knock on the Door' study.

Women who waved their men goodbye holding back their tears, trying to put on a brave face as a uniform encasing their love disappeared out of sight. Those women slowly closed the door, sobs threatening to escape from the deep chambers of their heart as the mask slipped away.

The Falklands War was to become the last analogue war to be fought before the days of mobile phones and the internet. Communication was slow as those at home waited for the 'Bluey' to land on the doormat. The days when the mail was brown or white would bring an involuntary sigh, all we could do was wait for the next post. On special days there might be two 'Blueys' land on the mat at once, those coveted letters would be later opened, each word savoured over a cup of tea in quiet moments.

We all dreaded that 'Knock on the Door' hoping with every fibre of our being that it would not come, that we would be the lucky ones, that our men would return with a bag of dirty laundry and with a smile on their weary faces, glad to be home to savour the delights of womanly comfort, home cooking and a hot luxurious bath.

'She Who Waits' has an often-overlooked thankless task as she supports her man to go to War. It is she who lives as a virtual single parent dealing with all the responsibilities of daily life whilst sometimes struggling to breathe as fear takes over from time to time. She prays that her man will return, though she would not wish that 'Knock on the Door' on anyone else, she prays hard that she will be one of the lucky ones, knowing there will be casualties because that is the nature of the beast.

In 1982 I had been married almost five years. The Falklands War was not the first time I had heard of death amongst Gary's comrades. There had been parachute accidents, and the infamous Warrenpoint where 2 Para took a huge hit. Gary's own company was the one that was devastated on that hot August day in 1979. This was different though, this was not Northern Ireland, this was no skirmish or the 'Troubles', this was a whole Task Force leaving our shores. Nobody knew how long it would last, nor how bloody it would get…

If someone had told me 40 years ago that I would have written a whole book about being 'The Falklands Widow' I surely would have laughed in their face. Yet that is exactly what I have done, written a whole book about my journey some of it to be shared here…

The book is 'A vulnerable, honest, and spiritual Journey through Grief' it is not an easy read, but I am told a powerful one. These words from the back cover are a snapshot of 'my story.'

"For centuries women have grown up to believe in their 'Prince', men to believe they must 'Man up' so they can be the King of their own Castle, be the Warrior, the provider. Fairy tales are full of happy endings where women are feminine and cute and where men live up to an often-unrealistic standard.

As a young girl, Jay met her 'Knight in Desert Boots', fell deeply in love and married her Prince, fully expecting a 'Happy Ever After'. Instead, she discovered that he was not only human but also mortal. War ripped her life apart when she was just 24 years old.

Many years went by before she discovered the path back to her authentic self, a self she had lost in a less than ideal childhood.

Despite being a Grief Counsellor and fully able to hold the hands of others as they either grieved or crossed the great divide, Jay was as expert as anyone else in avoiding the pain she buried deep inside...until one day she made friends with both her vulnerability and her past.

Grief is something that many people avoid with the same ferocity they would an ageing body. It is almost like a demon lurking in the shadows of time, yet it is the price we must all pay if we are to love.

Unresolved Grief has the ability to build up in us forming a 'Grief Layer' that if we are not careful may become impenetrable.

For sure until we reach Acceptance, we will be forever wearing black..."

In Victorian times people wore their Grief like a badge of honour. Women wore black clothing for a whole year; men wore black armbands. Each person therefore did not have to explain their sadness or silence, they did not need to put on a brave face for others, they could just let people know through a simple visual cue a loss had occurred.

These days we live in a very different visual age, one of filtered photos, distractions, and enhancement as if sadness or despair are akin to the leprosy of old. People ask, '*How are you?*' or something similar, not really wanting to hear a negative response as they carry on walking. We as a society spend huge amounts of time on social media interacting with others 'commenting' on their posts with words that would be far more meaningful if they were said over the phone or better still in person over a coffee.

When I worked with the terminally ill thirty years ago, the reaction from others to my job was to me quite bizarre. It was my choice to work with the dying, nevertheless people would utter, *'Oh, I couldn't do that job'* as if I was spending all day, waist high in excrement… It was in fact one of the best jobs I ever had, something that gave back as much as it took from you. An honour and a privilege, but for me it was also a huge distraction. You see by looking after others' pain, we can become adept at avoiding our own.

After Gary died, I continued to avoid that pain until, *"Driving into Merville Barracks that day it is extremely hard to put into words the raw emotion that flooded my body. I felt it in every single cell. I wanted to drink a bottle of wine and numb out but could not because I was driving. I wanted to run away but could not, physically I could have turned the car around but somewhere inside I knew it was time to face this demon that had been inside me for 29 years, the demon of Grief.*

It was seeing those men in their berets, young, fit, incredibly proud and walking around that army camp that flooded me with all the emotion of 1982. Their uniform may have been slightly different but the beret with the coveted cap badge was positioned just as proudly on their 'ally' heads as it had always been. Most were a similar age to the men of 1982, and I may as well have been driving into Browning Barracks in Aldershot."

Between the end of 1979 and the summer of 1984, the three most significant men in my life died. First my Grampy, then my husband and finally my father. There were many reasons why my Grief was buried so deep inside. Ultimately, I have come to accept that whether we wear it like a badge or bury it to the deepest most caverns that our minds will allow, there are no shortcuts to Grief. We can only thrive once we have processed all the layers, anything else is like living with a festering wound.

"Although I will always be 'The Falklands Widow' at my core I am Just Jay, she is a good person, a free spirit, she has a strong heart who knows how long it will continue to beat..."

The strange thing about the unlikely match between a Paratrooper and a Pacifist was their love of freedom of both choice and spirit. The Paratrooper got to be that free spirit a long time ago, he died as he lived, in glorious technicolour. The Pacifist also an adventurer began to find peace as she tabbed the last footsteps of her 'Knight in Desert Boots', as she connected to the energy of the remote Islands he gave his life for and as she wrote about the 'Class of 82', those we lost and those who came home...

'The Falklands Widow', a Journey through Grief is available in hardback.

****

Anonymous (name provided to BMMHS) sent in by Karen Clapp of the Falklands Islands Association

<u>Horatio's Story - 'Absolution'</u>

The weak winter sun scattered light across Wireless Ridge and warmed the dying Sergeant Horatio Benitez awake, his skull torn open by shrapnel during his futile but courageous counter-attack. 2 Para's savage night assault, constantly switching direction, had crushed the final Argentine lines of defence, and broken the enemy's will to fight. As the Paras streamed off the mountains into Stanley, the pity of a passing combat medic cradled the dying sergeant back to life.

Repaired and repatriated to their homeland by the Hull based North Sea ferry MV *Norland,* Horatio and his comrades slowly recovered from their battlefield trauma, regrettably without the support, care and comfort of the local civilian population, who having abandoned them, left the veterans homeless; a cruel reprisal for disgracing the Nation's honour by losing *'Las Malvinas'*.

Not relinquishing his own duty to his platoon, Horatio nurtured and sustained his little 'band of brothers'. A contract for bottling water was established to raise money, not only to maintain their marginalised living, but also to send Horatio to the United Kingdom on a special mission.

He arrived at the UK's Ministry of Defence in London seeking to speak with a particular senior British officer from his war-time adversary, the Second Battalion, The Parachute Regiment; 2 Para. An agreed meeting place was arranged, and the conversation begun, helped by a Spanish interpreter, with accounts of his battlefield wounding, the social humiliation in the Argentine, and the slow process of his comrades' healing.

Horatio then, hesitantly, explained the purpose of his mission. He said that he came as an unofficial emissary on behalf of his platoon, his army, and the Argentine, to ask for forgiveness.

The other officer responded to Horatio's plea with some sincere but banal responses, none of which satisfied Horatio's deep and intense feeling of guilt, very obvious PTSD, and his spiritual desolation. After an hour struggling with Horatio's anguish, and the other's moral anxieties about the political prosecution of the war, an unexpected inspiration arose out of their dialogue.

The other asked Horatio to describe what it would be like in the Argentine, had the Falklands War not occurred five years earlier. Horatio became troubled and explained that the Army Junta would still be in power, there would be no democracy, death-squads would still be operating in the cities, the numbers of the 'disappeared' would have increased, and the grieving widows of those lost, would still be wailing outside the Casa Rosada, in Buenos Aires.

The Para officer said gently: "*Horatio, we were both on the same side*".

In that moment, Horatio received his absolution and the other realised for the first time that the suffering and death of all the combatants served a moral good far higher than the pragmatic political purposes of the campaign; the Argentine's freedom, rather than just the Falkland Islands' liberty.

Christ's Will is indeed 'done on Earth as it is in Heaven'.
CPBK©2022

****

Lorena Triggs, Falkland Islander

My Tribute

Words may be spun into threads rich and fine,
To embroider in singular style
On the parchment of thought, where they gently entwine,
Ere the page welcomes them with a smile.

These that I choose for my tribute to you
Have a poignant and powerful role,
Although simple, compared with work great poets do,
They've been spun in the depth of my soul.

From first invasion to Victory in June,
True support for the Falklands burned high,
Dockers toiled, knowing well they could lose their jobs soon,
All who sailed, knew that many might die.

Memories of aid so unselfishly given
That aggression should win no acclaim,
Will bloom as a rose with its roots set in heaven,
Will burn like a perpetual flame.

Prayers were all heartfelt and truly sincere.
Grief was real when disaster occurred,
Like buds that unfold, springs that rise, crystal clear,
Was your country's great pride in you stirred.

Dear lads, sleeping now, on land and at sea,
For your loved ones I pray with each thought,
Of you who've been injured, I think constantly,
Twas my island home for which you fought.

God Bless you too with the scars that don't show,
May he guide and protect you wherever you go.

****

Hansard

3rd April 1982 vol 21

The Prime Minister (Mrs. Margaret Thatcher)

'The House meets this Saturday to respond to a situation of great gravity. We are here because, for the first time for many years, British sovereign territory has been invaded by a foreign power.

The people of the Falkland Islands, like the people of the United Kingdom, are an island race. Their way of life is British; their allegiance is to the Crown. They are few in number, but they have the right to live in peace, to choose their own way of life and to determine their own allegiance. Their way of life is British; their allegiance is to the Crown. It is the wish of the British people and the duty of Her Majesty's Government to do everything that we can to uphold that right. That will be our hope and our endeavour and, I believe, the resolve of every Member of the House.'

Mr. J. Enoch Powell

'The Prime Minister, shortly after she came into office, received a soubriquet as the "Iron Lady". In the next week or two this House, the nation and the right hon. Lady herself will learn of what metal she is made.'

****

15 June 1982 Hansard vol 25

The Prime Minister (Mrs. Margaret Thatcher)

'With permission, Mr. Speaker, I should like to make a statement on the Falkland Islands.

Early this morning in Port Stanley, 74 days after the Falkland Islands were invaded, Major General Moore accepted from General Menendez the surrender of all the Argentine forces in East and West Falkland together with their arms and equipment. In a message to the Commander-in-Chief Fleet, Major General Moore reported: The Falkland Islands are once more under the Government desired by their inhabitants. God Save the Queen.

The House will join me, Mr. Speaker, in expressing our deep sense of loss over those who have died, and our sorrow for their families. The final details will not become clear for a few days yet, but we know that some 250 British Service men and civilians have been killed. They died that others may live in freedom and justice.

The battle of the Falklands was a remarkable military operation, boldly planned, bravely executed, and brilliantly accomplished. We owe an enormous debt to the British forces and to the Merchant Marine. We honour them all. They have been supported by a people united in defence of our way of life and of our sovereign territory.'

The Prime Minister

'I agree with my hon. Friend that this was a great military victory that will go down in the history books. I believe that the brilliance with which it was planned and executed is unequalled.'

****

Argentine Newsletter for their *Malvinas* Personnel

Translation of extracts of original documents found after the surrender of Argentine forces. Kindly provided by Alan Leslie, Chairman of the HMS *Exeter* Association.

WORDS FROM THE MILITARY GOVENOR OF THE MALVINAS, SOUTH GEORGIA AND SOUTH SANDWICH ISLANDS

Sailors, Airmen and Soldiers, on this 25th May 1982, whereas yesterday 172 years ago we found ourselves fighting to build a proud and Sovereign Nation. Like our forefathers we have had to leave our families, our homes, our towns and cities to fight and defend our beloved land. To my men on this glorious 25 May, on which Argentina finds itself at war for a right and just cause, I exhort them to give everything in order to secure an honourable victory, praying to the Almighty for his protection for everyone on this day. LONG LIVE THE FATHERLAND

Puerto Argentino 1 Jun 1982 Year I No 9 (SPECIAL EDITION)

1. TO MY MEN

The hour of battle has definitely arrived. All our efforts, the hours of waiting, the cold, the tiredness, the watching has come to an end. The adversary is preparing to attack Puerto Argentino with the audacious and daring intention of conquering the capital of the Malvinas Islands.

Each man ought to understand with full consciousness what is his duty. The enemy will be defeated by the determined action of everyone doing his combat duty. If each man with his rifle, mortar, machine pistol or gun fights with the valour and heroism that has always been our tradition, success is certain.

The eyes of the Argentinian people are upon us, our parents, our wives, girlfriends and children, all our families have complete trust in us. In the supreme hour we have the duty not to let them down.

We have undertaken a sacred responsibility before our comrades who have fallen in action here, to convert their personal sacrifice into a glorious page of history for Argentina and we cannot allow this heroism to have been in vain.

Not only should we rout him, but also we ought to do it in a manner such that his defeat is so crushing that never again will he have the impudent idea to invade our land. TO ARMS! TO THE FIGHT!

SIGNED
MARIO BENJAMIN MENENDEZ
Brigadier General
MILITARY GOVERNOR

5. NOW, YES, I AM A FIRST CLASS CITIZEN AND NOT A SECOND OR THIRD CLASS KELPER

Derek William Rozee, 22 years, became on 28 May, the first Argentinian citizen born in the Malvinas, he received the documents which gave him that distinction from the Chief of Federal Police; the ceremony took place in the City of Buenos Aires. At the end of the ceremony Rozee admitted finding himself exceedingly happy for feeling himself to be more of an Argentinian citizen and not a second or third class kelper "as individuals hold us in England". The new citizen is World Runner up in sheepshearing, and is representing Argentina in the World Championship to be held next August in Great Britain.

EDITORIAL:

This week will be the first May week celebrated in these recovered islands. The memory of the heroic revolution of 1810 acquires a special dimension for two reasons.

Firstly because during the course of the liberating revolutions of America came unity to those who had never been conquered. When General San Martin, in 1817, crossed the Andes to liberate the sub-continent, he brought the idea of a united people, free and independent of the Spanish America of those times.

Secondly, because it can be repeated today, and also other aspects of those events. Argentina undertook the difficult task of recovery from the remains of colonialism in its land. Its heroic faith acquired it a natural leadership, which is recognised by the American nations, which, understanding its posture, acknowledge its position, and equally they applaud its energy in facing "modern monsters", the strength to unmask the great to sustain those lands which were usurped.

The cry of liberty and independence had been given everything by Argentina. We hope that the robustness of the brotherly bonds between Americans is also the robustness of the ties between brothers in the country

By history, we know who were the men of Buenos Aires in 1810, and this same history will judge the men who are in the Malvinas, in this May of 1982

MILITARY EVENTS 30 - 31 MAY

30 MAY

1000 One of our own PUMA helicopters was shot down by a missile from the enemy airforce, six men from a patrol of the National Guard were killed on impact

1100 An enemy Sea Harrier was shot down on Mount Wall

1430 Two Super Etendards from the Naval Air Arm and 4 A4-C aircraft from the Air Force attacked the English fleet scoring a direct hit with an EXOCET missile on the aircraft carrier INVINCIBLE, followed up by the A4's bombing the ship with 250Kg bombs scoring a direct hit on the flight deck. The ship was seen burning in high seas. In the action two A4-C were shot down by the enemy.

List of Contributors

S

T

W

Acknowledgements

In November 2021, when we had the eureka moment to add in a Glimpses book to mark the 40th anniversary of the Falklands War, only a few weeks after the launch of *Glimpses of War* Volume 2, and then to set ourselves a ridiculously short deadline for publication, little did we realise the scale of the project. Equally the level of interest from all quarters, particularly from British military personnel and Falkland Islanders, has been beyond expectation, and what followed was an avalanche of written and oral contributions, articles and photographs.

To each and every person who has sent in their memories, recollections and stories, we say a big thank you. For those who have found it tough to dredge up difficult memories of what they experienced a huge debt is owed as we appreciate it was not easy to dispel the demons of 40 years ago.

Many people and organisations have assisted in advertising our requests for articles and stories. In the Falkland Islands, Karen Clapp from the Falkland Islands Association, Andrea Barlow at the Falkland Islands Museum and Jim McAdam the editor of the Falkland Islands Journal. Support has been given by Angela Perry from the Falklands Chapel in Pangbourne, Chris Howe of SAMA82, Sarah Robinson of the Nautilus Telegraph, historian Lester May, Alan Leslie Chairman of the HMS *Exeter* Association, and Andrew Cave who has led the way for many years to ensure the dockworkers, who prepared the ships for war, are fully and deservedly recognised.

Kyle Thompson at the Army Flying Museum transcribed audio diaries, while Brian Summers and Gerald Cheek who both experienced the Argentine invasion as part of the Falkland Islands Defence Force sent across diaries, oral and written, for my use.

We saw great generosity from several people who gave permission to use book extracts, diary extracts and original documents, including Brum Richards, Brian Short, Philip Piper,

Neil Maher, Alex Manning, Tony Pitt, Tony Babb and Jay Morgan Hyrons whose husband was killed on the Falkland Islands to name but a few. Particular thanks go to Eddie Bairstow for his generosity in providing to us a selection from his superb photos he took while serving in 45 Commando.

The range and coverage of contributions is vast but sadly not every piece we received could be included, nor did many escape the dreaded editor's red pen or scalpel. With over 100 contributors, I cannot mention everyone, but a handful deserve particular mention namely Dair Farrar-Hockley, Bob Tuxford, Chris Nunn, Keith Mills, Ewen Southby-Tailyour and Tim McClement for describing particular events and actions with vivid clarity, and to Mike Willis and Gerry Akhurst, who both served in the Falklands, and told of the involvement of the Gurkhas and Royal Artillery respectively. The medics and padres who feature provide a different dimension treating friend and foe alike, while the troubling description of Falkland Islanders under occupation in fear and uncertainty for up to seven weeks is hard to comprehend.

We have received hundreds of photos and images, so we have had to made tough choices on what we could include, not least as it was nor always easy to determine the ownership or image rights on many. Our apologies if your picture favourite has been omitted.

And last but not least, our sincere thanks to all those behind the scenes who have helped make the book what it is. To Barbara Taylor for her expertise in preparing the maps for us to help clarify the geography of the military actions. To our posse of proofreaders – Chris, Alex, Charlie, David, John, Mike, Nick, Howard and Liz - who have waded through sections of the nearly 550 pages and for constructively pointing out errors, inconsistences and incomprehensible passages. Special thanks must go to David Vassallo, who stranded in Malta with COVID and with time on his hands, kindly proofread the entire book from cover to cover, correcting, questioning and improving all parts... A greatly appreciated and invaluable effort, David.

Our thanks again to Richard Macauley for his fine work in creating yet another superb book cover for us and of course to war artist David Rowlands, who allowed us to use his moving painting of the troops going ashore at San Carlos. Once again the support of our '*Miss Moneypenny*', Karen Wheeler, was enormous and indispensable, taking the rough document into the final product. And finally to Nick Brazil for his sound advice and input to steer us in the right direction as we headed *off-piste* from time to time. For those we have inadvertently omitted, we apologise and will correct at the earliest opportunity.

And special mention must be made to our two wives, Jane and Sue, for their forebearance over many months when faced with both of us spending hundreds of hours working on the book from start to finish. It will come as no great relief to the two ladies that there are most likely to be other volumes of *Glimpses of War* in the future.

Every one of the articles helps create a book deserving of those who were touched by the Falklands War in whatever capacity, and which we hope you will find worthy of the charity for whom we are raising funds, namely Blind Veterans UK.

Andy and Jerry Cockeram

About the Editors

BMMHS Executive Committee and Editorial Team

Andy Cockeram is chairman and a founding member of BMMHS, having spent most of his career in corporate life, in the motor industry. His love and interest in military history have been from a very young age, Andy has travelled widely and has visited numerous battlefield sites and memorials across the globe. His main areas of interest are the Second World War, especially life under occupation and resistance movements.

Andy has been the Editor-in-Chief of *Glimpses of War* volumes 1 and 2, has also started a new career as a writer of novels, very much with a military history flavour. He lives in East Devon with his wife, Jane.

Jerry Cockeram Always passionate about military history, whether it be through books or films, he has been fortunate to travel to a number of Europe's battlefields to further his understanding of some of those key events in our more recent past. Having spent a career in IT working across a range of industries including aerospace and F1, and by virtue of his being 'the least *Luddite*' of the founding group, Jerry is responsible for the bmmhs.org website and IT support infrastructure.

Dr Linda Parker is a former history teacher, now researcher and author. Her research areas and publications include the histories of forces' chaplains in the 20th Century, and polar explorers, although she is interested in most aspects of military history. She has published six books with Helion and Co, the most recent one being '*Nearer My God to Thee: Airborne Chaplains of the Second World War*' (Helion 2020). She enjoys speaking at conferences and giving talks to various societies. In addition to her involvement with BMMHS, she is a member of the Western Front Association, The Society of Military History and the United States Commission for Military History. She enjoys travelling to cold places and musical activities. She is married to Nigel Parker.

Nigel Parker has followed a career in engineering and for 23 years ran the Cryogenics Department at Oxford University. Having a lifelong interest in military aviation and being involved in the research and recovery of many crashed military aircraft, he was editor of the Bomber Command Association Newsletter for seven years. He chose to take early retirement and follow his passion; writing a twelve-volume series on the German Air Force losses over Great Britain in World War 2; '*Luftwaffe Crash Archive*', followed by a three-volume series entitled '*Gott Strafe*

England'; the German air assault against Great Britain 1914 – 1918. He is now writing a book on the V1 and V2 campaign and also a revised history of the Battle of Britain.

Glimpses of War Current and Future Volumes

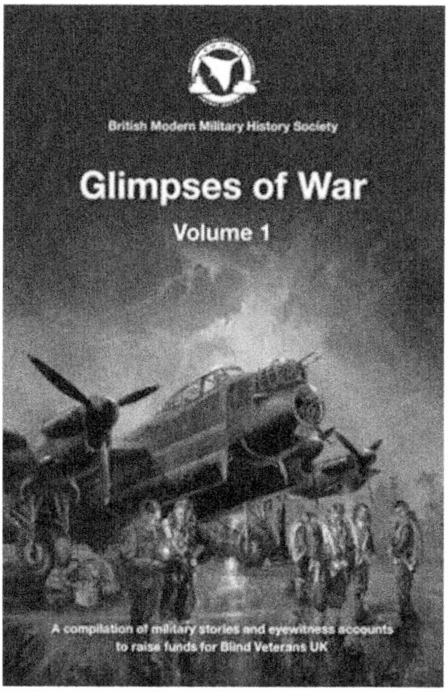

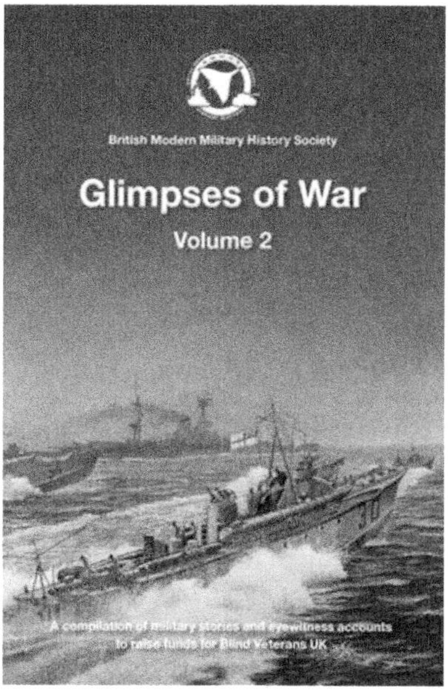

Following the success of the first two volumes of *Glimpses of War*, in collaboration with Blind Veterans UK, BMMHS will be publishing further volumes of *Glimpses of War*.

We have received some fantastic stories and historical articles already covering personal memories of the two world wars, the Cold War, and military actions into the 21st Century.

We are very happy to accept new articles or personal accounts for future volumes of *Glimpses of War*. If you have a personal or family story to tell or have an interesting article you would like to submit for consideration, get in touch.

Contributions can be any length but no more than 1500 words ideally. Diary extracts, copies of personal letters, some photographs and images can be included too, but you must have ownership/copyright to them. And remember, they do not have to be tales of great heroics or valour. Ordinary people's experiences in war time - any war, any role, civilian or military - are just as much interest to us. Articles from writers and historians are welcome too.

Do contact us on info@bmmhs.org if you have something you would like us to consider and include.

All volumes of *Glimpses of War* are available on Amazon

About the Cover

War artist David Rowlands kindly gave opermission to BMMHS to, use his stiring and emotional cover depicting British forces the landing on San Carlos Water.

'The Royal Marines landing at San Carlos'

In the early hours of darkness on 21st May, 1982 eleven ships, led by *Fearless* and *Intrepid*, sailed towards Falkland Sound, the channel between East and West Falklands, and into San Carlos Water. A Force 8 gale had been blowing for days; low cloud and heavy rain kept enemy aircraft at bay. But as the Task Force sailed into San Carlos Water and the landing craft put out from their mother ships, the sea was dead calm beneath a clear, cold sky twinkling with stars.

The Royal Navy's 4.5-inch guns opened up on the Argentine troops on Fanning Head. 40 Commando Royal Marines and 2 Para, heavy laden with equipment and weapons, clambered into the landing craft in the darkness. They were the first ashore, wading for the last few yards waist-deep towards Blue Beach. 3 Para's objective was Port San Carlos Settlement. By 0730 hours the landings by 40 Commando and 2 Para on Blue Beaches 1 and 2 were complete.

As the dawn rose, the next wave, 45 Commando, faces blackened, wearing a mixture of berets and helmets, splashed ashore at Red Beach in Ajax Bay, while 3 Para, followed by 42 Commando in reserve, came ashore at Green Beaches 1 and 2 close to San Carlos Settlement. The surrounding green hills were bathed in bright morning sunshine.

Once ashore, the units dug in, as helicopters ferried in guns, ammunition, stores and vehicles. In the darkness the Argentine defenders had withdrawn, and it was to be a few hours before their first response was to fire a machine-gun at two of the Gazelle helicopters, killing three men.

War Artist David Rowlands

David Rowlands is a professional war artist. David's paintings aim to present a realistic record of war. He has received many commissions from the army and RAF. He has had a passion for sketching soldiers since childhood.

In 1974, he joined the staff of the National Army Museum. He began as a full-time artist in 1977.

He was invited to accompany soldiers on exercises in Germany during the Cold War, and on operations in Northern Ireland. In 1991 he was the only professional artist in the Gulf at the invitation of the army, attached to a Warrior crew of 3rd RRF in the desert, sharing the experience of soldiers in the front line and sleeping in bivouac alongside armoured fighting vehicles.

In 1993 he was the first war artist to visit Bosnia and British troops in Operation Grapple. In 1995 he painted British, French and Dutch troops around Sarajevo. In 1999, he accompanied the army into Kosovo. In 2001, he was commissioned by Permanent Joint Headquarters (PJHQ) to record Exercise SAIF SAREEA in Oman.

David has accompanied the army on operations in Afghanistan (2003, 2007 & 2008). He was hosted by 7 Armoured Brigade in Iraq in 2003.

He has painted numerous pictures for the Special Forces.

Fuller details of David's work can be found on **www.davidrowlands.co.uk**

****

Blind Veterans UK Supported by BMMHS

Sight loss can take so much from our veterans.
Independence, confidence, purpose and self-belief - the very qualities that enabled them to face conflict.
Help rebuild lives.
Do you know a veteran who could benefit from our support?
Could you take on the challenge of fundraising?
Are you part of an organisation or group that would like the opportunity to partner with us to support blind veterans?
Rebuilding lives after sight loss
For more information
0300 111 2233
supporter.services@blindveterans.org.uk
blindveterans.org.uk/glimpsesofwar
Registered charity No. 216227 (England and Wales) and SC039411 (Scotland)

Friends of Millbank www.friendsofmillbank.org is a friendly and welcoming military medical history society, open to all. We celebrate the heritage and achievements of military medicine and promote its ongoing relevance. This is exemplified by our support for our Charity of the Year, the David Nott Foundation which provides war surgery training to Ukranian surgeons caring for the current victims of war, forty years after a similarly unprovoked war was unleashed on the Falkland Islands.

We hold monthly online Zoom talks, as well as in person at the former Royal Army Medical College (now Chelsea College of Arts) in Millbank, London, hence our name. The Royal Army Medical College was the British Army's centre of excellence for postgraduate military medicine and tropical health between 1907 and 1999, hence its motto and ours. We are affiliated with the British Society for the History of Medicine, and also support the Museum of Military Medicine.

You are most welcome to attend our talks and to explore our website which is rich in historical resources, including recordings of our previous talks. A number of personal accounts also feature here in *Glimpses of the Falklands War*.

In Arduis Fidelis

David Vassallo, Chairman
chairman@friendsofmillbank.org